THE ENGLISH CATHEDRAL

THROUGH THE CENTURIES

Mediaeval Chantries and Chantry Chapels
The English Mediaeval Parish Church
Old S. Paul's Cathedral
English Collegiate Churches

1. Liverpool cathedral from the south-east

THE
ENGLISH
CATHEDRAL

THROUGH THE CENTURIES

G. H. COOK

WITH 115 PLATES AND
63 PLANS

PHOENIX HOUSE LTD
LONDON

To my Friends J.B. and E.B.

Printed in Great Britain
in 11 point Monotype Baskerville by
The Bowering Press of Plymouth for
Phoenix House Ltd, 38 William IV Street,
Charing Cross, W.C.2.

First published 1957
Reprinted 1960

Contents

'As to these marvellous buildings, the half of their glories and wonder cannot be told. They are more than buildings, more than art, something intangible was built into them with their stones and burnt into their glass. The work of a man, a man may understand; but these are the work of ages, of nations. They are serene, masterly, nonpersonal, like works of nature—indeed they are such, natural manifestations of the minds of men working under the impulse of a noble idea.'

W. R. Lethaby

Illustrations

PLATES

1. Liverpool cathedral from the south-east, *Frontis*

Plans and Diagrams

A*

Acknowledgments

THE AUTHOR and publisher are indebted to the Provost of Blackburn for permission to reproduce Fig. 27b; to Sir Edward Maufe and the Provost of Bradford for Fig. 28a; to Sir Edward Maufe and the Cathedral Council of Guildford for Fig. 26b; to Sir Giles Gilbert Scott, O.M., R.A. for Fig. 26a; to the Provost of Sheffield for Fig. 27a; to the Society of Antiquaries of London for Fig. 3c; and to Mr Basil Spence, O.B.E. for Fig. 28b.

We also have to thank the undermentioned for providing photographs for reproduction in this work:

Archives Photographiques, 4
Provost of Blackburn, 111
Provost of Bradford, 109
C. J. P. Cave, 65, 66
Courtauld Institute of Art, 2
Fred H. Crossley, 13, 16, 18, 24, 26, 63, 68, 70, 71, 74, 80, 97
Elsan, Mann and Cooper, 1, 110
Herbert Felton, 88, 89
Hamilton Fisher and Co, 115
H. E. Illingworth, 12, 17
Albert W. Kerr, 11, 58, 90, 94
A. F. Kersting, 78, 99, 106, 113
F. C. Morgan, 6, 28, 29, 62, 93, 95
National Building Record, 5, 14, 15, 27, 31, 33, 40, 45, 47, 48, 55, 56, 59, 64, 75, 76, 79, 82, 91, 101, 102, 103, 105, 112
Sydney W. Newbery, 114
Rev. H. V. P. Nunn, 36
Photochrom Co Ltd, 23, 96
Phillips City Studios, Wells, 20
H. V. Richards and Son, 104
Walter Scott Ltd, 10, 34, 37, 39, 44, 60, 61, 72
Basil Spence, O.B.E, 107
John Stone, 3, 7, 30, 32, 35, 57, 83, 92
Rev. F. R. P. Sumner, 46, 50, 51, 54
Raphael Tuck and Sons Ltd, 22
Valentine and Sons Ltd, 9
Veale and Co, Bristol, 21, 73
Victoria and Albert Museum, 19, 25
Dr J. R. H. Weaver, 38
Marcus Whiffen, 108

Foreword

IN ITS MANY ASPECTS the story of the English cathedral throughout a period of more than thirteen centuries covers so wide a field that little more than a broad outline of the subject is possible in a work of this size.

To many people a great cathedral church is first and foremost an architectural monument of national importance, the main interest apart from its religious purpose being in the fabric; but a knowledge of the diocesan system, of the founding and history of the several bishoprics and of their capitular constitution is essential to an understanding of the cathedral as an institution, a consideration of which forms the subject-matter of the early chapters of this book. Of importance too is the influence of the religious cults of the mediaeval Church, notably on cathedral planning, the developing complexity of which culminated in a definitive lay-out perfectly suited to ritualistic requirements. The advances that were made to this end in the majority of our cathedrals are dealt with at some length in Chapter VII.

The interior of the English cathedral as we see it today presents a vastly different aspect from that of the Middle Ages. The purging zeal of the Reformer and the Puritan, and the vandalism of the Restoration enthusiast resulted in the wholesale destruction of shrines, images, altars, screens, glass and much else; nevertheless from what remains of the ornaments, fitments and furniture a fairly complete picture of the pre-Reformation interior can be visualized. A general survey of the changes wrought in the past four centuries will be found in Chapter XVII.

Necessarily the building and rebuilding of our ancient cathedrals and the character of their architecture figure largely in these pages; the chronological sequence of the works undertaken at various periods, as set forth in Chapters XII to XV, will enable the reader to trace the course of Gothic through four centuries. Alterations and restoration have however rendered the approximate dating of the various parts of every cathedral a far from easy task, and much must be left to conjecture. Unsatisfactory though it may be, Rickman's nomenclature has been adopted, the terms Early English, Decorated and Perpendicular now being generally accepted as a matter of convenience.

11

During the past century the number of cathedrals in this country has been nearly doubled by the creation of many Modern sees, which are deserving of more than the bare mention accorded them in most books on the subject. A short account of the founding of the new sees is given in Chapter VI, and the final chapter treats of their architecture.

1. The Constitution
of English Cathedrals

❡ FOREMOST AMONGST THE historic monuments of this country stand the mediaeval cathedral churches, symbols of the spiritual authority and the temporal jurisdiction of the bishops in their diocesan areas.[1] The cathedral, or more correctly speaking the cathedral church, was and is the mother church of the diocese, and in it was set up the 'bishop-stool' or 'cathedra'. From Saxon times it was the installation of the 'stool', now designated the 'throne', that constituted a cathedral church, whence also the seat of the episcopal power was called the see (*sedes*).

At the time of the Reformation there were nineteen cathedral churches in this country, and since then the number has been more than doubled by the creation of new sees in Henry VIII's reign and in the nineteenth and twentieth centuries.

As regards their capitular constitution they are classified as cathedrals of the Old, the New, and the Modern Foundation. Those of the Old Foundation were from the first served by colleges of seculars, i.e. priests who lived in the world and who owned property in their own right. The secular cathedrals remain more or less as they were originally constituted, and include Chichester, Exeter, Hereford, Lichfield, Lincoln, London (S. Paul's), Salisbury, Wells and York. The cathedrals of the New Foundation were

---

[1] The diocese was the bishop's parish. In this sense the term 'parish' was employed by the historian Bede in the eighth century.

churches that, prior to the Dissolution of the Monasteries, were served by monks, mainly of the Benedictine Order. Of these, Canterbury, Carlisle, Durham, Ely, Norwich, Rochester, Winchester and Worcester were cathedral-priories, i.e. bishops' seats to each of which was attached a monastic house or priory, an innovation of Anglo-Norman times.[1] These establishments were all served by monks of the Benedictine Order, except Carlisle which was a house of Augustinian canons. In such monastic cathedrals the bishop was the titular abbot, but the convent was ruled over by a prior. Of the New Foundations also are the cathedrals of Chester, Bristol, Gloucester, Oxford and Peterborough, all of which were monastic churches in the Middle Ages, but were refounded by Henry VIII as secular cathedrals; and as in the case of the cathedral-priories, the monks were replaced by a dean and prebendaries.

Within the past century the sub-division and re-arrangement of many dioceses has resulted in the creation of sees of the Modern Foundation, and the elevation of existing churches to cathedral status. Many of these, e.g. Newcastle and Chelmsford were originally parish churches; others, such as S. Albans and Southwark were monastic, and Ripon and Southwell were collegiate churches before the Reformation. The cathedrals of the Modern Foundation also include entirely new buildings, as for example Liverpool and Guildford, both of which are in course of erection at the present day.

The bishops of the mediaeval Church often combined the offices of diplomat and statesman with those of priest and administrator, and on occasion assumed the role of warrior. Holding their lands as tenants-in-chief of the Crown, they surrounded themselves with retinues of knights and men-at-arms; they built and fortified castles and sometimes went forth to battle and siege. In some respects they differed little from military barons, save in their spiritual jurisdiction and clerical immunities. Of Bishop Alexander of Lincoln, 1123–48, and of Nigel of Ely, a contemporary wrote: 'They were called bishops but they were men given up to pomp and display; they so devoted themselves to a military life and the world's pomp, that when they came to Court all men marvelled at them for the crowd of men-at-arms who attended them' (*Gesta Stephani*).

The authority of mediaeval prelates being of a temporal as well as a spiritual nature, the dignity of the see was sustained by large estates both within and beyond their dioceses. Early in the twelfth

---

[1] In the same category were Bath and Coventry, which were suppressed by Henry VIII but not refounded as secular cathedrals.

century security for their personal safety was ensured by some bishops by the erection of castles on their manorial estates. On the plea that such fortresses were essential for the protection of the see, Bishop Roger of Salisbury, 1102–39, built castles on his estates at Devizes and Sherborne, and his nephew Bishop Alexander of Lincoln erected castles at Newark, Sleaford and Bunbury. Such territorial magnates, possessed of almost regal powers within their dioceses, excited the envy of the Crown. The estates and revenues of the bishopric of Lincoln were commensurate with the magnitude of the diocese, for the property included forty manors and ten palaces. In addition to the palace at Lincoln, the bishop had a London house, Lincoln Place in Southampton Buildings, and palaces or mansions at Sidington in Rutland, Buckden in Hunts., Woburn in Beds., Bunbury castle, Oxon. and in other places. In perambulating their diocesan areas, bishops preferred to sojourn at one of their country houses than to accept the hospitality of a monastery, where they might or might not be welcome. The archbishops of York seldom resided in the palace at York, most of their time being spent at one or other of the seventeen manor houses scattered throughout the huge diocese. Bishopthorpe and Cawood were perhaps the most favoured. The London palace was York Place, later Whitehall Palace, which Archbishop Walter de Grey acquired in 1244 and settled upon his successors for their town residence. There, Cardinal-Archbishop Wolsey lived in regal state, modelling his establishment on that of the royal household; but on his fall, York Place was seized by Henry VIII and converted into the Palace of Whitehall. Later, the London mansion of the archbishop of the northern province was York House in the Strand.

There were many other episcopal residences in London, Exeter Street off the Strand is a reminder of the Palace of the see of Exeter that owned thirteen other mansions, nine of which were in the county of Devon. Adjoining the Priory of S. Mary Overie, Southwark was the princely mansion of the bishops of Winchester, and the see of Rochester also had a town house in Southwark, afterwards changed for one at Lambeth. Early in the thirteenth century, Lambeth was exchanged for property belonging to the arch-see of Canterbury, since when Lambeth Palace has been the official residence of the Primate. The town house of the see of Ely was Ely Place, Holborn, a double-courtyarded house, of which the large chapel dedicated to S. Etheldreda is still in use. The ancient palace of the bishop of London adjoined the nave of Old S. Paul's cathedral on the north side, but there were other palaces at Fulham and Stepney, at Bishop's Stortford in Herts., and at Witham and Chelmsford in Essex.

The bishop of Durham was a temporal prince, a Count of the Palace, in whom was vested almost sovereign power. By prescription he exercised complete jurisdiction over the Palatinate from the Tees to the Tyne, known in mediaeval days as 'the Bishopric' and not as the county of Durham. The diocese embraced the Palatinate and the county of Northumberland. In the Palatinate the bishop held his courts of Chancery, Exchequer and Admiralty; he appointed his own chancellor, justices, sheriffs and other officers; he served his own writs and indictments; he appointed commissioners to levy subsidies and raise forces; and he possessed the right to coin money in his own mint at Durham,[1] and to grant charters for free markets and fairs. He was also empowered to summon councils in the nature of parliaments and to create barons for the purpose. He could pardon felonies, infractions of the peace, treasons and murders. My lord bishop of Durham, as the holder of a fief, was under the feudal obligation of furnishing a contingent of men-at-arms for service with the Crown. Bishop Anthony Bek, 1283–1311, marching at the head of his force in peace and in war appeared as the military chief of a powerful independent franchise; and the warrior-bishop Thomas of Hatfield at the head of his retainers led his men into battle against the Scottish invader at Neville's Cross, 1346.

The see of Ely likewise possessed privileges and prerogatives of a County Palatine, embracing the whole of the Isle of Ely and known as the 'Liberty of the bishops of Ely'. In Henry VIII's reign the Palatine powers of Durham and Ely were curtailed and were finally vested in the Crown in the nineteenth century.

From the episcopate were recruited ministers of the Crown, and in the later Middle Ages, ecclesiastics who would be of service to the government were appointed to sees as vacancies occurred. Immersed in affairs of State and necessarily absentees from their dioceses, their relations with the sees were often purely nominal; their duties as 'Father in God' of the souls in their diocese were entrusted to vicars-general or suffragans. Trained in the law and official routine and experienced in worldly matters, mediaeval bishops were well equipped for administrative tasks entrusted to them in State affairs, and hence they occupied high offices such as Lord Chancellor, Treasurer to the Exchequer, Keeper of the Privy Seal, Master of the Rolls, and King's Secretary. Frequently bishops were dispatched on diplomatic missions abroad. William Longchamp, Bishop of Ely, 1189–97, combined the offices of Papal

---

[1] Other bishops enjoyed the regal privilege of coining. The Archbishop of York continued to mint money until Elizabeth I's reign. The coins minted by Cardinal-Archbishop Wolsey were marked with the Cardinal's hat.

Legate, Lord Chancellor and Chief Justiciary of England, and was appointed Regent of the kingdom during the absence of Richard I. He was one of eleven bishops of Ely who held the office of Chancellor. From the last quarter of the fourteenth century, the see of Salisbury was occupied by a succession of statesmen-bishops. So engrossed in the affairs of State was Bishop Courtenay of Norwich, Treasurer of the royal household, that he never visited his diocese, nor was he ever enthroned in his cathedral. He died at Harfleur in 1415, whilst on attendance to Henry V during the siege of the town.

Whether singled out for high office or not, bishops had a share in the government by their right to sit in the House of Lords. As a member of the House of Peers, Archbishop Stratford of Canterbury claimed privilege of Parliament when arraigned on a charge of treason by Edward III, and thus escaped a violent end. But bishops who engaged themselves in subversive activities were not outside the law. In 1405 Archbishop Scrope of York was executed at Bishopthorpe for the part he played in the northern rising against Henry IV. Thomas Merk, Bishop of Carlisle, who had conspired with the abbot of Westminster to restore the deposed Richard II, was treated with clemency by Henry IV.

> *'For though mine enemy thou hast ever been,*
> *High sparks of honour in thee have I seen.'*

Spiritual lords who meddled in politics that proved unpopular with the commoners did so at peril of their lives. Bishop Stapledon of Exeter, a loyal adherent of Edward II when the king's fortunes were at low ebb, was slain by a London mob in 1326, and Archbishop Sudbury of Canterbury, who proposed the poll tax that provoked Wat Tyler's rebellion in 1381, met with a similar fate; after his capture by the insurgents he was beheaded in the Tower of London.

Since the creation of Modern Foundation cathedrals, the number of bishops in the Upper Chamber has been restricted; today, both archbishops and twenty-four bishops have a seat in the Lords.

'There are three things that make a bishop in England; the will of the king, the will of the Pope or of the Court of Rome, and the money paid in large quantities to that Court. For thousands of pounds of English money are paid here in England to Lombards for exchange, to the impoverishment of the realm.' These were the words of an outspoken critic, Thomas Gascoigne, the distinguished Chancellor of Oxford University in the middle of the fifteenth century.[1]

[1] *Loci e Libro Veritatem* Ed. J. E. T. Rogers. 1881.

As patron of the English sees the reigning sovereign exercised the right to nominate candidates for vacant bishoprics, his choice being subject to confirmation by the Pope. The first *Statute of Provisors*, 1351, limited Papal encroachments with respect to 'providing' for the patronage of all the higher preferments and glittering prizes of the Church. The Statute deprived the Papal see of the right to present incumbents to any preferment and enacted that any person accepting a Papal 'provision' should be subject to fine and imprisonment; but in the case of the translation of a bishop from one see to another, the Pope retained the right of filling the see thus vacated. Occasionally the king would grant a licence to an individual to accept a Papal provision to a vacant bishopric, usually as a recognition of services rendered the Crown. Adrian de Costello an Italian was awarded the see of Hereford in 1503 and that of Wells the following year for conducting negotiations between Henry VII and the Pope. Neither of the sees was ever visited in person by the Italian.

The temporalities of a vacant see being held by the Crown, it followed that the sovereign should have some say in filling the vacancy. The *Constitutions of Clarendon*, 1160, laid it down that 'when an archbishopric or bishopric shall have become vacant . . . it ought to be in his hands, and he shall receive from it all the rents and outcomings, as though they were of his Lordship.' Such a provision was open to abuse, by affording an unscrupulous monarch a means of filling his pockets with the revenues of a bishopric for an indefinite period. When the see of Lincoln fell vacant in 1167, Henry II appropriated the temporalities, and by withholding the appointment of a bishop, continued to enjoy the revenues for nearly seventeen years. He then nominated his natural son Geoffrey, who was Archdeacon of Lincoln at the time; but realizing the anomalous position into which his father's greed had brought him, Bishop Geoffrey Plantagenet resigned the same year.

Papal assent to the appointment of the king's nominee for a see was not always a foregone conclusion, though in the later Middle Ages the filling of vacant sees became a matter of mutual agreement between the Crown and the Papacy (*A. H. Thompson*). The election of the king's nominee by the chapter, a time-honoured custom, was no more than a formal acquiescence, after which the election had to be confirmed by the archbishop of the province.

The career of William Warham, Archbishop of Canterbury, 1503–30, furnishes an instance of the rapid rise of a man of ability in the service of the Crown. Warham acted as ambassador for Henry VII to the Duke of Burgundy and on his return in 1493 he was appointed Chancellor of Wells cathedral. Shortly afterwards he became Master of the Rolls and subsequently was advanced to the dignity of Keeper of the Privy Seal, and then to the office of Lord Chancellor. In 1502 the bishopric of London was conferred upon him and the following year Warham was enthroned Archbishop of Canterbury.

In the earliest days of the English Church, bishops gathered about them a band of clergy who acted as a council of advisers, a primitive anticipation of the chapter of canons that formed part of every secular cathedral establishment after the Conquest.[1] The chapter became a corporation, vested with its own liberties and privileges, and the canonries were endowed with separate estates or prebends. Henceforth the chapter with a dean as their head exercised sole authority in all matters pertaining to the cathedral and the prebendal properties, with the result that in course of time the bishop's power became so limited that the chapter was virtually an independent corporation. In the administration of the cathedral establishment the prelate had little or no authority. Time and again chapters resisted a bishop's claim to conduct a Visitation, so independent were they of the spiritual father of the diocese.

The dean or president of the chapter was elected by the canons, and his appointment was confirmed by the bishop. He and the canons were responsible for the regular observance of the religious offices in the choir of the cathedral, for the decorum of all who recited the offices, for the discipline of the vicars choral, lay clerks and chantry priests, and for the control of other personnel attached to the cathedral. The chapter was also entrusted with the care of the cathedral fabric. When any part of the building was to be repaired or rebuilt, members of the chapter were appointed to negotiate with the masons and craftsmen and to supervise the fabric fund. The management of the prebendal estates and the preservation of the parish churches on the estates were the responsibility of the canons.

Once a week the dean and canons sat in the chapter house, and if he chose to be present, the bishop being in theory the head of the establishment, occupied the seat of honour at the east end, with the dean on his right. But he took no part in their deliberations, though he could summon a meeting of the chapter to discuss any matter concerning the administration of the diocese. In the chapter house the bishop and his clerks conducted Visitations, and here too he settled any disputes that might arise between a master-

---

[1] In the cathedral priories there were no secular canons; the whole body of the monks, exclusive of the novices, sat in chapter which was presided over by the prior. This proved to be a disadvantage that the monastic bishops sought to remedy by founding collegiate churches (p. 61).

ful dean and the chapter. On his translation to the see of Lincoln in 1436, Bishop Alnwick was involved in trouble with the arrogant and defiant dean, John Mackworth, who was perpetually in conflict with the canons. As arbitrator, the bishop issued a *laudum* or award to which both parties subscribed 'as far as in them lies', but the strife continued, Mackworth was suspended and excommunicated, and but for the death of the bishop would have been deposed.

The chapters and personnel of Henry VIII's newly constituted cathedrals were planned on a much simpler scale than the establishments of the Old Foundation, the numbers of canons or prebendaries being limited to a dozen or so, together with choristers, scholars, almsmen and others (Chapter 5).

In the cathedrals of the Modern Foundation the lack of endowments resulted in further reductions in the personnel; in addition to the dean, four residentiary canons and a body of vicars choral, it has become the usage to appoint a number of honorary canons who have no voice in the cathedral chapter.

2. The Mediaeval
Cathedral and its Purposes

❡ THE ANCIENT CATHEDRALS of this country, both secular and monastic, were the largest and most splendid churches reared in the Middle Ages, in the erection of which the art of architecture attained its noblest form of expression and fulfilment, and the ingenuity and resourcefulness of the most highly skilled masons and craftsmen were exercised to the full. The scale and magnificence of these great churches are a measure of the dignity and authority of the bishop and of the wealth of the see; their planning reflected the elaboration of the ritual and the growth of the religious cults that characterized mediaeval thought from the twelfth to the sixteenth century.

All our mediaeval cathedrals, with the exception of Llandaff in Wales, are cruciform on plan, the main axis running from east to west. From the Saxon period it was the established practice to orientate churches. The origin of the custom is obscure, but as early as the fourth century it was ordained that Christian churches should be built 'oblong', with the 'head', i.e. the sanctuary wherein stood the altar, at the east. 'We all look towards the east in our prayers,' wrote Basil, Bishop of Caesarea in A.D. 370. The method of fixing the axial line of a church has never been satisfactorily determined. According to the *History of Freemasonry and the Grand Lodge of Scotland*,[1] 'the patron, ecclesiastics and masons assembled on the site before the orientation and spent the time in devotional exercises; one being placed to watch the rising of the sun, gave notice when his rays appeared above the horizon. When fully in view, the master mason sent out a man with a rod, which he ranged in line between the [site of the] altar and the sun, and thus fixed the line of orientation.' Hence the theory that the axial line of a church was established by the point of sunrise on the day of the patron saint to whom the church was to be dedicated. This would account for the diversities in orientation, due to the varying position of sunrise from day to day.

There was no standard plan for the English mediaeval cathedral; no two are exactly alike. The exigencies of the site, the financial resources of the chapter, and the ever-increasing need for more space and light were factors that wrought the variations in planning and imparted to each cathedral its own individuality. Alterations and extensions that were made from time to time, notably in the thirteenth century, were to meet the ritualistic requirements, to provide more chapels, to increase the accommodation and to facilitate circulation in the eastern arm.

The very *raison d'être* of the cathedral was the High Altar, that stood in the sanctuary or presbytery at the east end of the choir, on either side of which aisles led to the retrochoir behind the High Altar. In pre-Reformation days the retrochoir usually consisted of a chapel in which was placed the shrine of a local saint, with an ambulatory to ensure free movement at that end, and at the extreme east a Lady Chapel for the adoration of the Virgin Mary. In some cathedrals, e.g. Lincoln and Salisbury, transepts were built flanking the choir, generally in proximity to the High Altar (Fig. 1). At the western end the choir was shut off from the rest of the cathedral by a screen or *pulpitum*. In the monastic cathedrals, the ritual choir, in which stood the monks' stalls, extended westwards into the nave.

Above the crossing rises the central tower, that is spoken of as a lantern, when as at York the windows light the area below. To the north and south of the crossing spread the lateral arms or

[1] W. A. Laurie. 1859.

transepts, generally aisled at the east so as to provide a number of chapels. The western limb of the cathedral is the nave, which is always flanked by north and south aisles; and attached to one of the aisles near the western end is often a porch. The perfect cathedral terminates at the west in an imposing façade with twin towers at the extremities.

In several cathedrals the eastern arm is not in exact alignment with the axis of the nave, but deviates slightly to the north or south, an irregularity that is imperceptible in most cases and is only revealed by accurate survey and measurement. The symbolists of the nineteenth century claimed that the deviation represented 'the attitude of the body [of Christ crucified] bent over from the upright tree of sacrifice. His outstretched arms are the two transepts; His pierced hands are the doors,' and another enthusiast declared that 'the choir-transepts above the great arms of the Cross represent the inscription above the head of the crucified Master'. Such fancies cannot be accepted today. The planning of our mediaeval cathedrals was dictated by the requirements of Christian worship; neither masons nor ecclesiastics concerned themselves with symbolic expression in the lay-out of a great church. Irregularities in planning were the result of faulty setting-out; the rough-and-ready methods employed by builders in the Middle Ages did not make for exactitude. Especially was this so when the choir arm of a cathedral was lengthened, for the extension was always commenced some distance east of the existing building, that remained in use until the new work was completed, so that the religious offices could continue without interruption. In 1337 the chapter of Lichfield solicited the advice and help of the King's master mason, William Ramsey, to solve the difficulty of linking up new work with old in the eastern arm of the cathedral (p. 293). Through no fault of this famous mason, the axis of the choir arm of Lichfield inclines about five feet to the north of the nave axis.

Gothic architecture developed more or less on parallel lines in England and France, but the insular quality of cathedral planning in this country is forcibly emphasized when we compare it with French methods. Hackneyed though the comparison of Salisbury with Amiens may be, these two cathedrals typify the differences in ideals as regards planning. These great churches were both begun in 1220, and save for the towers and sculptures of Amiens were completed within fifty years; and they are almost equal in length. The eastern limb of Amiens was laid out as a *chevet* with radiating chapels, the normal method of planning in the Gothic cathedrals of France; in England on the other hand, the squared

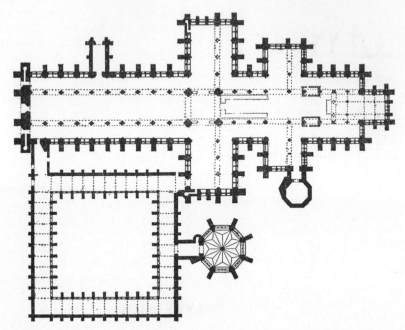

Fig 1. Comparative planning of English and French cathedrals;
Salisbury above and Amiens on right

choir arm in one form or another was the rule, so well exemplified
at Salisbury (Fig. 1) (Pl. 3, 4).[1]

In another important respect was there a difference in the ideals
of the English and French cathedral builders. Low and narrow,
the cathedrals of this country run to length, whereas the masons of
the colossal cathedrals in the Ile de France aimed at height. Old
S. Paul's, the largest in England, had an external length of 585
feet, but the high vault reached to a height of only 85 feet. Winchester cathedral, 526 feet in length, has an interior height of
78 feet. The loftiest mediaeval church in these islands is Westminster abbey, the high vault of which is 101 feet above the pavement. But the French masons, obsessed with the desire to roof
their cathedrals with higher and yet higher vaults, ventured beyond
the limitations imposed by the material. The race for height began
at Notre Dame, Paris, c. 1165, and thereafter each successive
cathedral, Chartres, Reims, Amiens, Le Mans and Bourges leapt
to greater height, until the vaulting ambition of the French masons

[1] Westminster abbey is a notable exception. Henry III's choir, begun in 1245 was
a reproduction on English soil of the French chevet.

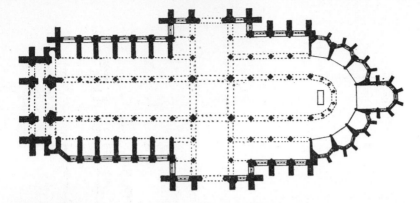

culminated in the mighty choir of Beauvais, 1247–71, where the high vault attains a height of 154 feet. From the diagram of comparative heights of English and French cathedrals (Fig. 2) it will be observed that the choir of Beauvais is more than twice the height of Exeter.

The structural unit of design in the interior of a cathedral is the bay, i.e. one compartment of the elevation of the nave, choir or transepts. Frequently the bays are defined by vaulting shafts that rise from the bases of the piers up to the springers of the high vault, as in the naves of Ely and Winchester. Elsewhere, as in Canterbury choir, the vaulting shafts rise from above the capitals of the piers, and from a point higher still in the naves of Wells and Salisbury.

The bays are generally designed in three horizontal stages, arcade, triforium and clerestory. The nave or the choir arcade consists of a series of arches springing from pier to pier; the triforium, usually a blind storey, has arched windows that open into the dark space between the vault and the lean-to roof of the aisle; the clerestory is the wall rising well above the aisle-roof, and is pierced with windows that provide top-lighting to the interior (Pl. 8). In most cathedrals the triforium chamber, reached by a narrow spiral stairway, serves no purpose at all. At Gloucester it is a wide and lofty ambulatory giving access to the apsidal chapels above those on the ground level. Some of these upper chapels retain their altar steps and piscinae. In many cathedrals the traceried openings of the triforium afford a feature of exquisite beauty. Set within the main arches are usually two or more subarches, whose forms are sharply defined against the dark background of the triforium chamber. To improve the interior lighting of a nave or choir, the outer wall of the triforium chamber was

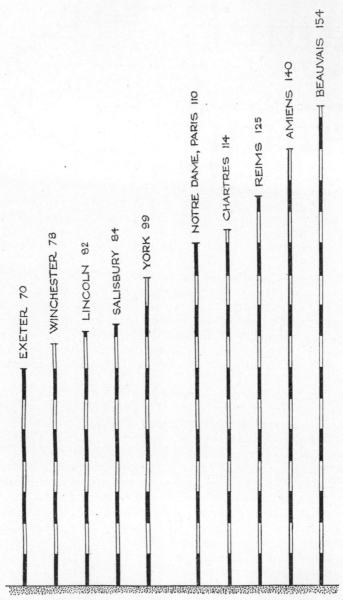

FIG 2. Heights of English and French cathedrals

often pierced with large windows. This was done at Norwich, Peterborough and in other churches in the fourteenth and fifteenth centuries. Often the outer wall of the aisle was carried up to a greater height and the roof raised, so as to provide headroom for large windows that would light the nave or the choir indirectly through the triforium chamber. In the Norman naves of Norwich and Southwell the triforium stage has a single broad arch with no sub-arches; the naves therefore received as much light as possible from the small windows in the outer walls. Unusual is the treatment of the triforium stage at Chester and Southwark cathedrals, where the arcading is backed by a wall that shuts off the chamber behind; there is however a passage between the arcade and the wall.

In the thickness of the clerestory wall is often a passage known as the clerestory way that runs beneath the sills of the windows. Its purpose was solely to afford masons, plumbers, glaziers and workmen access to the upper parts of the building whenever repairs were necessary.

After the Norman period the tendency was to reduce the dimensions of the triforium stage. In the nave of Ely cathedral it occupies about one-third of the elevation, but in the western bays of the north arcade of Ripon choir, c. 1180, the triforium is less than one-fifth of the total height. It loses its independence entirely in York nave, c. 1290, being incorporated in the windows of the clerestory. There, the five panels of the triforium being unglazed, appear to be merely blind lights at the base of the clerestory windows (Pl. 72).

The interior lighting of cathedrals and greater churches presented an ever-present problem to builders and ecclesiastics in the Middle Ages. Norman interiors were intolerably dark and gloomy, especially in the winter months, and except for the windows in the east and west walls, the choir and the nave were lighted only by windows in the aisle-walls and the clerestory. By suppressing the triforium stage the arcades of the nave and choir were pushed up to greater height, and lofty arcades meant more light from the aisle windows. At the same time the clerestory could be lengthened, with a gain to the top-lighting. Undoubtedly it was inadequate lighting that brought about the gradual suppression and finally the elimination of the useless triforium stage. In the last phase of Gothic the three-storeyed interior gave place to a two-storeyed elevation, as in the Perpendicular naves of Winchester and Canterbury cathedrals.

Architecturally, the crowning feature of the interior of a Gothic cathedral is the high vault, a canopy of stone carried by ribs, the construction of which demanded the utmost skill on the part of the masons. The erection of stone vaulting not only achieved a homogeneity of structure, so that walls and roofs were of one material throughout, but a great church was thereby rendered more or less fireproof. It was primarily to guard against destruction by fire that the builders of the Middle Ages abandoned timber roofing and evolved the stone vault as a covering for every part of a mediaeval cathedral.

In pre-Reformation days the English cathedral, whether secular or monastic, served different purposes from those of the present day. Primarily, the choir-arm was a chapel reserved exclusively for the canons in a secular cathedral, and for the convent in a cathedral priory, and as such was screened off at the west. The religious offices performed in the choir were confined to the ecclesiastics of the establishment; the laity had no part at all in the services. Standing in the nave lay-folk might hear the murmur of a mass being celebrated at the High Altar, but the very substantial screen or pulpitum at the entrance to the choir would preclude them from seeing anything.

The nave was a vast vestibule to the choir, and was used for processional purposes on Sundays and on Festivals such as Christmas, Easter, Ascension Day and Corpus Christi; however large it might be, it was not intended for lay worship, though in a few cathedrals part of the nave was used as a parish church. Until the close of the thirteenth century the parishioners of S. Mary Magdalen, Lincoln, whose church had been pulled down when the Norman cathedral was built, had their altar in the nave of the cathedral and on Sundays in Lent, one of the canons preached to the laity. Apparently the townspeople who attended the sermons were noisy and irreverent, for when Bishop Alnwick made a visitation of Lincoln cathedral in 1437, he complained that the vergers were unable to keep order and silence amongst the crowds who had assembled to hear the preaching. The main purpose of widespreading transepts was to afford room for additional altars, the eastern aisles being divided into a number of chapels which were fenced with screens of wood or stone. At Chester cathedral, the spacious south transept served as the parish church of S. Oswald until 1880. The right to worship at their own altar there was claimed by the parishioners after the convent had removed the church that occupied the site before the transept was erected in 1325–50. To appease the parish folk, a church was built for their use near by, but at the end of the fifteenth century the laity reasserted their right to worship in the transept which was accordingly partitioned off for their use. They retained possession until the church of S. Thomas was built in 1880.

From the fourteenth century onwards the English cathedral became an accumulation of chapels under one roof, a veritable storehouse of altars, at which an endless round of soul-masses was sung for ecclesiastical and lay benefactors, living and dead. In Old S. Paul's cathedral there were thirty or more altars, half of which were in the choir-arm, and in Salisbury cathedral the dedications and positions of at least twenty-four altars are known.

The canonical hours that were recited in the choir were virtually the same in both secular and monastic cathedrals, though the time table varied. The hours at which the offices were observed varied according to the season, the daylight hours being shorter in winter than in summer. Seven times in twenty-four hours, bells were rung to summon the community to the choir for the round of perpetual prayer and intercession which it was their bounden duty to observe. The offices began with matins, which was sung in the middle of the night and was followed by lauds at daybreak. At about six a.m. prime was said, and as the names imply, terce, sext and nones were recited at intervals of three hours. The chief service of the day was the celebration of High Mass, which took place between terce and sext. From an early hour every morning soul-masses were sung at minor altars in the cathedral by chantry priests; in many churches a 'morrow mass' was recited at dawn at an altar in the nave, on behalf of travellers who were about to face the perils of the road. After prime there was the daily Mass of the Virgin in the Lady Chapel, and in the late afternoon came vespers. The final office was compline, after which the doors of the cathedral were locked until prime.

The monotony of the daily routine was broken on Sundays and Festivals by special observances and ritual. Before High Mass a procession was formed of all available brethren for the purpose of sprinkling the altars in the cathedral with holy water. Anthems were sung during its progress, the procession being headed by the priest or monk who asperged the altars. Behind him were others bearing three crosses and two men carrying lighted candles. The great processional cross of Lincoln cathedral was 'of silver gilt, with a crucifix in the midst, Mary and John standing on two branches, and flower-de-luces in every of the four corners, with the four Evangelists graven, weighing 57 ounces; and one staff ornate with silver, having a bowl and a socket of silver'. The ceremony began with the hallowing of the water in the sanctuary, after which the officiating priest sprinkled the High Altar on all sides; and the procession having been formed, passed through the screen at the west into the north transept, and thence along the north aisle of the choir. The retrochoir was traversed by way of the ambu-

latory, stations being made in turn at all the altars in the eastern
chapels. Thence the procession wended its way along the south
choir-aisle to the south transept, and then passed along the south
aisle of the nave. Where there was a crypt the altars therein were
visited after the south transept; at Canterbury the route had to
be curtailed in January 1467 owing to the flooding of the crypt.
From the west end advance was made up the centre of the nave in
two files, and those in the procession took up stationary positions,
whilst the celebrant proceeded to sprinkle the altar beneath the
Great Rood, and to say the bidding prayer on behalf of the Church,
the royal family and all benefactors of the church. In several
cathedrals station-slabs were set in the pavement of the nave. The
plan of the old pavement of York cathedral published by Drake in
1736 shows two rows of circular stones, forty on each side, extending the full length of the nave, with a middle row of six larger
stones at the west end. Drake describes them thus: 'In the old
pavement . . . were a number of circles, which ranged from the
west end up the middle aisle, on each side and in the centre. There
were about forty-four on a side, about two feet distant from one
another and as much in diameter. Those in the midst were fewer
in number, larger, and exactly fronted the great west door. The
circle nearest the entrance in this row is the largest of all.' A precisely similar arrangement existed in the pavement of Lincoln
nave, where the stones were thirty-seven a side. An unpublished
plan of Wells cathedral by John Carter in 1799 shows two rows
of eleven circular stones on each side in three bays of the nave.[1] At
Old S. Paul's two parallel lines, seven feet apart, in the nave pavement marked the pathway of procession 'in keeping the distance
and directness of movement', and at Canterbury two lines incised
in the pavement about seven feet apart served the same purpose.
They were destroyed when the nave was restored in 1787–8.

After the bidding prayer, the procession entered the choir for
the celebration of High Mass. The order of the procession necessarily varied according to the disposition of the altars in the cathedral. A more elaborate ceremony characterized the proceedings on
the occasion of a great festival. The *Sarum Processionale* in the
library of Salisbury cathedral, compiled in 1445, sets forth in
detail the ritual to be observed on the major festivals, and other
ceremonies that were peculiar to Salisbury, e.g. the Blessing of the
Water, the Distribution of Ashes, and the Ejection of Penitents.

In cathedrals such as Salisbury and Wells where there were
cloisters, the procession usually passed from the south transept

---

[1] They are marked in the plan of Wells cathedral published by *The Builder* in 1892.
It has been estimated that there were in all fifty-eight of these roundels.

through the cloister door in the south aisle, into the east walk and thence along the south and west walks, re-entering the cathedral by the door at the west end of the aisle. In the naves of Wells and Exeter are minstrels' galleries, that may have been designed for use during the Palm Sunday procession, when the Sacrament was carried outside the church. The galleries accommodated a number of choristers who chanted responses to the procession as it entered the west door. The gallery at Exeter cathedral is inserted in the triforium on the north side of the nave, and the front is adorned with a row of twelve niches containing figures of musicians playing musical instruments (Pl. 5). The Wells gallery is in the clerestory stage on the south side of the nave and is faced with three quatrefoiled panels containing shields. At the west end of the north aisle of Winchester nave is a gallery carried by a four-centred arch, that may have served the same purpose.

Each festival was marked by a special ritual. For the Corpus Christi procession at Wells, a priest under a silken canopy borne by four clerks holding lighted candles, carried a tabernacle containing the Corpus Christi. After leaving the choir, the procession advanced down the nave and out of the west door to make a circuit of the exterior, via the north side, the east end and the cloisters. Thence the procession entered the nave at the west and made its way to the choir for High Mass.

Of all the ceremonies that graced the festivals of the Church in the Middle Ages, the most singular was the mummery of the boy-bishop, a custom that prevailed at Lincoln, Salisbury, Old S. Paul's and York, until it was suppressed by Henry VIII. On S. Nicholas day, 6 December, one of the choir boys was elected by his fellow choristers to assume the office and dignity of the bishop, and exercised a mock episcopal jurisdiction until Childermas day, 28 December. With a juvenile dean and canons he parodied the ceremonies and functions of the bishop. An account of the ceremonies enacted by the boy-bishop, a mimic transcript of the normal episcopal functions is given in the *Sarum Processionale*. During the three weeks of the buffooneries, the boy canons sat in the stalls for the services in the choir and the boy-bishop occupied the throne; and on the eve of Childermas, wearing copes and vestments, they recited all the offices of the day except Mass at the altar of the Holy Innocents. The ceremonies were repeated on the morrow in the choir, and the boy-bishop preached a sermon that had been prepared for the occasion. The pseudo-clergy went in procession outside the cathedral, the sightseers regarding the performance as a burlesque. A Statute of Sarum provided that 'no man whatever, under pain of anathema, should interrupt or press upon these children at the procession . . . or in anie other part of their service, but to suffer them quietly to perform and execute what it concerned them to do.' In the Register of Salisbury cathedral are entered the names of twenty-four boy-bishops.

Though the laity were excluded from the choir and sanctuary of cathedral churches, pilgrims were admitted to the aisles at stated times that they might visit the shrine in the saint's chapel beyond the High Altar, and there make their devotions and offerings. From the eleventh century, every church of any importance strove to acquire the relics of some wonder-working saint, and to erect a splendid shrine to contain them that would be an object of popular pilgrimage. The gifts and offerings of the faithful proved a profitable source of revenue in secular and monastic cathedrals alike. The offerings at the shrine of the very little saint, William of Perth, in Rochester cathedral provided the money for the completion of the choir begun in 1200; and at Salisbury the chapter obtained the canonization of S. Osmund in 1456 solely for the purpose of attracting pilgrims to the shrine, whose offerings were to be devoted to stabilizing the piers of the tower that were showing signs of collapse.

The foremost pilgrimage churches in this country were served by Benedictine monks. They include the following cathedral-priories:

Canterbury (S. Thomas the Martyr)
Durham (S. Cuthbert)
Ely (S. Etheldreda)
Rochester (S. William of Perth)
Winchester (S. Swithun)
Worcester (S. Wulfstan and S. Oswald)

At S. Albans, the premier Benedictine abbey in the Middle Ages and now the cathedral, were the shrines of S. Alban and S. Amphibalus. Benedictine Chester, one of Henry VIII's cathedrals, possessed the shrine of S. Werburgh, and in the Augustinian priory church of Oxford, also raised to cathedral rank by Henry VIII, was the shrine of S. Frideswide.

Though they never vied in popularity with the great Benedictine churches, the following secular cathedrals also made a bid for pilgrims by the acquisition of a shrine:

Chichester (S. Richard)
Hereford (S. Ethelbert and S. Thomas (Pl. 6))
Lichfield (S. Chad)
Lincoln (S. Hugh)

2. Chichester; Romanesque relief sculpture

3. Salisbury cathedral from the east

4. Amiens cathedral from the east

5. Exeter; minstrels' gallery in the nave

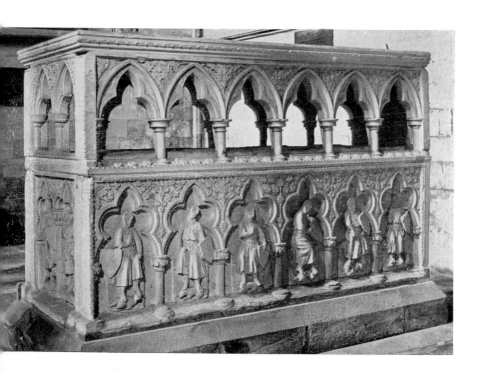

6. Hereford; pedestal of the shrine of S. Thomas Cantelupe

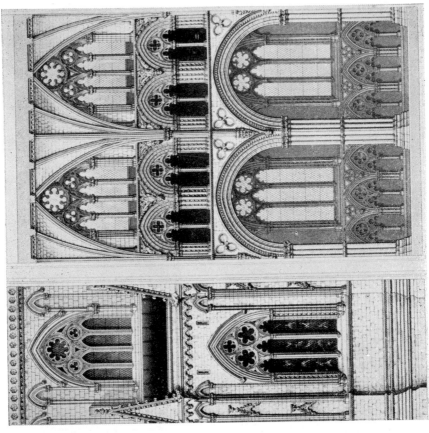

9. Lincoln: bay design of the Angel Choir

9. Canterbury; the Saint's chapel

10. Lichfield cathedral from the west

11. Canterbury cathedral from the north-west

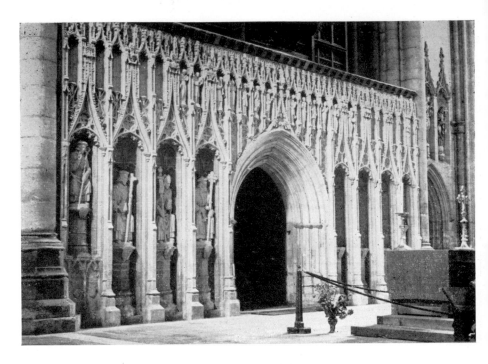

12. Ripon; the pulpitum

13. Exeter; the pulpitum

14. Misericords in the choir stalls at Worcester (*top*) and Chester

15. York cathedral from the south-west

16. Southwell: east front of the pulpitum

17. York; niched figures in the pulpitum

18. Southwell; detail of the pulpitum

19. Norwich; painted retable

21. Bristol; vestibule of the Norman chapter house

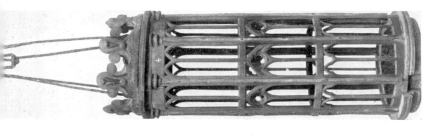

20. Wells; canopy of
the pyx

22. York; boss in the archway of the pulpitum

Old S. Paul's (S. Erkenwald)
S. David's (S. David)
Salisbury (S. Osmund)
York (S. William)

The craze for shrines that obsessed bishops and abbots led to many fruitless appeals to Rome for the canonization of some local worthy of saintly life. The chapter of Wells made unsuccessful attempts to secure the canonization of Bishop William de Marchia, d. 1302, and determined efforts were made by the canons of Lincoln to obtain the canonization of Bishop John de Dalderby, the ascetic, d. 1320. To this end letters from several English bishops were despatched to Rome; Edward III wrote to the Pope extolling the virtues of the Bishop. But the Pope was obdurate and Lincoln had to content itself with the shrine of the sainted Hugh of Avalon. From miracles purported to have taken place at his tomb, Dalderby was popularly acclaimed as a saint and his remains were enclosed in a massive silver casket enriched with diamonds and rubies. The pedestal on which it stood, made of rare marble, was surmounted by an elaborate canopy and was enclosed within a silver gilt grate. Part of the basement remains in the south transept of Lincoln cathedral. There were other unofficial 'saints' whose canonization was never ratified by the Papal Court. At Wells, the tomb of Bishop William Bitton, d. 1274, was popularly regarded as a shrine, to which crowds flocked with their offerings, especially those afflicted with toothache. In York cathedral was the unofficial shrine of Archbishop Richard Scrope, a favourite of Richard II, who conspired with nobles of the north against Henry IV. He was arraigned in his own hall at Bishopthorpe in 1405 and was condemned in the King's presence. After his execution the Archbishop's body was conveyed to York cathedral and buried on the north-east of the Lady Chapel; a shrine was erected over his grave and was visited by pilgrims in great numbers. Despite royal mandates, votive offerings poured in, and the veneration of the martyred Primate increased to such an extent that the convocation of York appealed to Rome for his canonization in 1462, though without success. Popular sympathy with the murdered Edward II exalted him to the rank of a saint and martyr, and a wondrous tomb, erected in 1329 in the choir of Gloucester abbey, now the cathedral, attracted throngs of pilgrims whose gifts amounted to vast sums and made possible the transformation of Gloucester choir, one of the marvels of mediaeval masoncraft. For persons of royal or noble lineage who met with a violent death in the Middle Ages, there seemed no bounds to

B

popular sympathy. Attached to a pier in the nave of Old S. Paul's
was a tablet portraying a figure of the unprincipled ruffian,
Thomas, Duke of Lancaster, who had been executed in 1322. It
was alleged to possess healing virtues and bade fair to outrival
the fame of S. Erkenwald's shrine. An appeal by the commoners
for the canonization of the Earl was rightly ignored by the Pope,
and the cult of *Saint* Thomas was short-lived, for in 1323 Edward
II ordered the Bishop of London to remove the offending tablet.

A shrine was a receptacle for the preservation and the exposition
of the bones of a saint (p. 127), and was set up in the Saint's chapel
that normally occupied the bay immediately behind the High
Altar, and was enclosed by screens usually of timber. One of the
main reasons that prompted the elongation of the choir-arm in
many cathedrals during the thirteenth century was the provision
of a Saint's chapel with an ambulatory for the easy circulation of
pilgrims. The new eastern arms of Canterbury, Winchester and
Lincoln, though differing from one another in many respects, were
perfectly suited to the purpose. Where space was restricted, it was
not always possible to have the chapel at the east of the High
Altar. At Oxford, due to the proximity of the city wall, the shrine
of S. Frideswide was placed on the north side of the choir; at
Rochester, the shrine of S. William stood in the north choir-transept, which was and is open to the choir, thus affording an unobstructed passage for pilgrims (Fig. 11). The Shrine of S. Thomas
Cantelupe in Hereford cathedral was erected in the middle of the
north transept, and the pedestal is now in the transept aisle.

The door by which pilgrims entered a church was generally at
the west end of the nave or in one of the transepts. Where there
were cloisters, the entrance was on the opposite side of the building. At Winchester the door, now built up, was in the west wall of
the north transept (Fig. 9); and at S. Albans the door is in the
end wall of the north transept. Pilgrims entered Canterbury cathedral by the south-west porch, and at Salisbury by the porch at the
north-west of the nave. They were met at the porch of Canterbury
by one of the monks, and having arranged themselves 'every man
after his own degree', they were sprinkled with holy water and led
through the nave into the north transept, where they knelt before
the altar of the Sword Point that marked the spot where Becket
fell. Thence they proceeded to the crypt, which was lighted by
lamps hanging from iron rings still to be seen in the vaulting, and
there they were shown relics associated with the martyrdom of
S. Thomas. Emerging from the crypt, the pilgrims ascended the
steps in the north choir-aisle and passed on to the Saint's chapel,
which was reached by another flight of steps, those who were fit

and able making the ascent on their knees. On entering the chapel they knelt before the shrine; the wooden canopy covering the feretrum or chest containing the Saint's remains was raised and the keeper (*Custos Feretri*) came forward and touched the jewels encrusting the chest with a wand, naming their respective donors. After the exposition, the pilgrims passed round the ambulatory and visited the Corona chapel to feast their eyes on more relics, including a mitred bust, known as *Caput Sancti Thome*, gilt and ornamented with many gems and enclosing Becket's scalp. Thence they returned to the nave by the south aisle of the choir. Much the same procedure was followed at other cathedrals on the occasion of pilgrim visitations, which were generally the only times that the ordinary laity passed through the iron gates that closed the choir-aisles at the west. The magnificent wrought-iron grille at the head of the steps from the south transept at Winchester cathedral, which was erected to exclude unauthorized persons from the choir is the earliest of its kind. It was made in 1093 and is composed of groups of C-shaped scrolls strapped together by iron ties. Unsurpassed for their sculptured detail are the stone archways enclosing iron gates at the entrance to the choir-aisles of Lincoln cathedral.

When the choir and transepts of a cathedral were furnished with their full complement of chapels, any other altars that were needed were set up against the piers of the nave, or alternatively, the aisles of the nave were divided into chapels by screens. At S. Albans several of the Norman piers of the nave retain their painted reredoses; at Canterbury from the eleventh century, a chapel of Our Lady occupied two bays on the north aisle of the nave, and at Durham cathedral two bays of the south aisle were appropriated by the Neville family for their chantry chapel.

In the Middle Ages, it was the custom for the naves of some of the secular cathedrals to be used by the townsfolk for purposes that would be deemed indecorous by churchmen of the twentieth century. At Wells, the laity were free to come and go at will, to loiter and to gossip, and buying and selling took place in the nave. Another custom foreign to modern ideas, was the performance of miracle plays in Wells nave, during the octave of Holy Innocents and other festivals. By 1300 the plays had degenerated into such unseemly exhibitions that the dean issued an edict forbidding play-acting in the cathedral, and half a century later a further prohibition was made and the sale of goods in the nave was proscribed. The pageantry that marked Corpus Christi Day at Hereford included miracle plays in the cathedral nave, which the City Gilds were under pain of performing by the articles of their incorporation.

From time to time Councils of Church and State, fraught with great consequence, were convened in the nave of Old S. Paul's. In 1232 at the invitation of Henry III, Cardinal Otho the White presided at a council and, from a throne raised on a platform in the nave, he expounded the Constitutions of the English Church to a great gathering of bishops and ecclesiastics. At a synod held in the nave in 1268, Cardinal-Legate Ottobuoni confirmed and amended the Constitutions, and the Code of English ecclesiastical law then formulated obtained until the Reformation.

From the fourteenth century, the nave of Old S. Paul's, popularly known as 'Paul's Walk' was the resort of idlers and gossips, a town promenade where people came to rest or walk about; it became the rendezvous of rogues and vagabonds, and people played ball within and outside the cathedral. Wares were exposed for sale in the nave as in a market hall. All efforts made by the dean to purge the building of profanities were futile. An Act passed by the City Fathers in 1554 shows the degradation into which Old S. Paul's had sunk; it was forbidden to lead horses or mules or to carry casks of beer or loads of fruit or fish through the cathedral. Doors in the aisles of the nave provided a short cut from the north to the south side of the building.

A privilege of ancient origin possessed by a number of English cathedrals in the Middle Ages was the right of sanctuary, by virtue of which, no legal processes could be executed upon 'any manner of man that had committed any great offence', if he sought refuge within the sacred precincts. The earliest mention of sanctuary in this country occurs in the code of laws drawn up by King Ethelbert of Kent in A.D. 600; the twenty or more chartered sanctuaries included the cathedrals of Durham, Norwich, Ripon, Wells, Winchester and York. The area of sanctuary, known as the *legua*, was defined by a series of upright stones, and felons who sought asylum were required to remain within the prescribed bounds for a specified period, e.g. thirty days at York and thirty-seven at Durham, during which attempts were made to reconcile the fugitive and his adversaries. Affixed to the timber door of the north portal of the nave of Durham is a large bronze knocker of the twelfth century, that may have been used by sanctuary-men to rouse 'serten men that dyd lie alwaies in two chambers over the said north church door, that when any offenders dyd come and knocke, straight waie they were letten in, at any houre of the nyght'. On admittance, a sanctuary-man had to take an oath of obedience to his protectors, and to wear a badge or cognizance on his upper garment; he was not to leave his lodging between dawn and sunset, nor was he to carry weapons.

Amongst the Harleian MSS. in the British Museum is a thin folio volume containing a list of people who were in sanctuary at York cathedral in the reigns of Edward IV, Richard III, Henry VII and Henry VIII, and in the Register are the instructions issued to the archbishop's bailiff for the administration of the oath of obedience. He was to inquire 'what man he [the fugitive] had killed, and wherewith, and both their names, and then bid him lay his hands upon the book saying "Sir, take heed on your oath. Ye shall be true and faithful to My Lord Archbishop of York, Lord of this town: to the provost of the same, to the canons of this church and all other ministers thereof. Also ye shall bear good heart to the bailiffs and governors of this town, to all burghers and commoners of the same. Also, ye shall bear no pointed weapon, dagger, knife, nor any other weapon against the King's peace. Also, ye shall be ready at all your power, if there be any debates or strife, or case of fire within the town, to help to success it. Also, ye shall be ready at the obits of King Athelstan, at the dirige and the mass at such time as it is done, at the warning of the bellman of the town, and do your duties in the ringing, and offering at the mass on the morn. So help you God and His holy evangelists!" And then bid him kiss the book.'

The fugitive could if he wished confess his crime to a coroner and take an oath of abjuration of the realm, whereby he undertook to leave the country and not return without the King's licence. Then, bearing a small cross in his hands, he made for the nearest port, keeping to the King's highway and not staying more than two nights in any one place. The crimes entered in the registers of the chartered sanctuaries include manslaughter, coining and horse-stealing, but the Church gave no protection to persons guilty of treason.

The Registers of Durham cathedral yield much information concerning persons who claimed sanctuary there from 1464 to 1524, in which period no less than three hundred and thirty-two are recorded, most of whom were guilty of homicide. The proceedings in the case of one named Colson are given at length and freely rendered from the Latin read as follows: 'Memorandum, that on 13 May 1467, one Colson, who had been detected in theft and lodged in gaol . . . fled to the cathedral church of Durham, on account of its immunity of [ar]rest. Whilst standing near the shrine of S. Cuthbert, he prayed that a coroner might be assigned to him. On the arrival of John Raket, coroner of Chester-le-Street, Colson confessed his felony and there took an oath of abjuring the realm of England and of never returning. This oath he took at the shrine of S. Cuthbert in the presence of George Cornforth, the sacristan of the cathedral, Ralph Bows, knight and sheriff of the County of Durham, Robert Thrylkett, the under-sheriff and many other witnesses. By reason of his renunciation and oath, all Colson's accoutrements were forfeit to the sacristan and he was ordered to remove his clothes to his shirt and deliver them to the sacristan, who freely restored them to the fugitive. Afterwards, Colson left the cathedral and was delivered by the sheriff to the local constables, and so on from constables to constables, holding a white cross made of wood . . . and was thus conducted to the nearest seaport to take ship and never to return.'

Severe penalties were imposed upon any who violated sanctuary. In 1378, Robert Hawle, a prisoner who had broken from the Tower of London, was pursued by soldiers into Westminster abbey and was slain in the choir during a celebration of mass. The offenders were excommunicated and subjected to a heavy fine, and were saved from a more dire penalty by the intervention of John of Gaunt. A Statute of 1529 provided that all sanctuary-men making abjuration should be branded on the thumb with the letter A, and later in Henry VIII's reign the right of sanctuary was curtailed and was finally abolished from the English Church in 1624.

From the early part of the fourteenth century down to the Reformation the foremost manifestation of religious belief in England was the chantry movement, that derived its impulse from the ancient doctrine of praying for the souls of the departed. In the middle of the thirteenth century the monks of Durham were under the obligation of celebrating more than seven thousand masses for the dead every year. The lovely little chantry chapels that grace many cathedrals today afford ample evidence of the patronage of the movement by kings, nobles and ecclesiastics in the fifteenth century.

A chantry was a mass that was recited at an altar for the well-being of the founder during his lifetime and for the repose of his soul after death. The endowment of a perpetual chantry provided a stipend for the priest whose office was the sing the mass, and usually took the form of lands, tenements, rents and other possessions. It was a costly business, the privilege only of the wealthy, and often included the erection, furnishing and maintenance of a special chapel that was reserved solely for the soul masses of the founder and his family. Persons not rich in this world's goods made bequests for chantries and obits at an existing altar in a church for a limited period. A great number of the chantry chapels that crowded the cathedrals and greater churches before the Reformation have long since disappeared. There were thirty-six chantries in York cathedral, the same number at Lincoln, and sixteen at Wells and at Exeter, yet these four secular cathedrals now have an aggregate of only nine chantry chapels; and at Chichester cathedral, where there were twenty chantry foundations, no evidence remains of any chapels, save the outer aisles of the nave. Notwithstanding, sufficient chapels remain in our cathedrals to indicate their general form and character.

Of upwards of seventy chantry chapels that are fairly intact in the greater churches, twenty-three are in cathedrals that were monastic, and fifteen are in the secular cathedrals. Four were founded for members of the royal family[1] and twenty-five by bishops of their respective dioceses.

In no church is so magnificent a series of chantry chapels to be seen as in Winchester cathedral; all but one of the nine there were founded by bishops.

The most attractive form of chapel is that which can best be described as a stone cage, a miniature building, usually rectangular on plan, erected between adjoining piers of the choir or nave, and consisting of a stone screened enclosure some eight feet or more in height. The stately chapel of Prince Arthur at Worcester cathedral presents a perfect example of the type. Within the chapel at the east end stood the altar, and, space permitting, the tomb of the founder was placed in the middle, enough room being left for the chantry priest to recite the mass. Unusual is the Hungerford chapel on the south side of Salisbury choir, which is a grilled enclosure of wrought iron standing on plinth walls.

In those cathedrals where a saint's shrine stood in the retrochoir, a site near the shrine was greatly favoured for chantry chapels. At Winchester, the chapels of four bishops (Fox, Gardiner, Waynflete, and Cardinal Beaufort) were erected within a few feet of S. Swithun's shrine (Fig. 9). At S. Albans, Abbot Ramryge's noble chapel stands on the north side of the sanctuary, adjoining the High Altar, the sites flanking the shrine of S. Alban being already occupied. At Wells cathedral, two almost perfect stone-cage chapels, viz. those of Bishop Bubwith and Dr. Sugar, are situated in the north and south arcades of the nave respectively (Fig. 17).

A less costly form of chantry chapel was made by utilizing the space between two projecting buttresses of a choir-aisle. The construction merely involved the removal of the walling between the buttresses up to a height of about eight feet, the building of an outer wall at the ends of the buttresses and then roofing the space

---

[1] Henry IV and Edward the Black Prince, at Canterbury; Henry VII's eldest son Arthur, at Worcester; and Humphrey, Duke of Gloucester, at S. Albans.

thus enclosed. Flanking the Angel Choir at Lincoln are three episcopal chapels of this kind, all of them near the shrine of S. Hugh (Fig. 20). An even simpler arrangement was to enclose the easternmost bay of an aisle of the choir with stone or timber screens, a method that was adopted at Winchester, where the Langton chapel occupies the eastern bay of the south aisle of the retrochoir. At Ely cathedral the bays at the extremities of both aisles of the choir were appropriated for chantry chapels, that on the north by Bishop Alcock and the southern by Bishop West (Fig. 19). The tabernacled screens and the elaborate vaulting of both chapels must have exceeded the cost of many a stone-cage chapel.

Elsewhere a bay in an eastern aisle of a transept was fenced with screens to serve the same purpose, as at York, where Archbishop Walter de Gray used a bay in the south transept, which he had been instrumental in building (Fig. 23). Nor was it a difficult matter to enclose part of an aisle of the nave with screens, an expedient adopted at Norwich cathedral by Bishop Nyx, and by Ralph, Lord Neville at Durham. Occasionally a chapel was constructed in the thickness of a wall, or in some obscure corner of a cathedral. Archbishop Warham's chapel at Canterbury was a narrow chamber between the north transept and the chapter house; at Exeter, Bishop Grandisson made use of the cavernous space between the west wall of the nave and the external screen, and in the angle of the north transept of the same cathedral is the small Sylke chapel enclosed by stone screens. On the south side of the choir of Durham cathedral is the striking monument erected by Bishop Thomas Hatfield, c. 1362, comprising a chantry chapel and the episcopal throne in one. It is thus described in the *Rites of Durham*: 'Thomas Hatfield, Bishop of Durham, lyeth buried over against the revestorye doore in the south allye of the quire, betwixt two pillars, under the bishopp's seate which hee did make before hee died, his tombe being all of alabaster, whereunto was adjoyned a little altar which hee prepared for a monke to say masse for his soule after his death, the altar being invironed with an iron grate' (Fig. 11).

The two chantry chapels remaining at S. David's cathedral are unique both as regards their position and character. When Bishop Henry de Gower, 1328–47, erected the great rood screen at the east end of the nave, he constructed his chapel in the southern half of the screen, which was deep enough to accommodate an altar and his tomb. More ingenuity was displayed by Bishop Edward Vaughan, c. 1520, who converted the open court between the presbytery and the Lady Chapel into a chantry chapel by the simple expedient of roofing it with a stone vault.

It was not unusual for a wealthy benefactor to found two or more chantries in different churches, but less common was the duplication of chapels for the purpose. Nevertheless one or two instances occurred. During his occupancy of the see of Hereford, Bishop Edmund Audley erected the splendid polygonal chapel that projects from the south side of the Lady Chapel of the cathedral (Fig. 15), and after his translation to Salisbury in 1502 he built the stone-cage chapel on the north side of Salisbury choir (Fig. 1). Both chapels are yet *in situ*; that at Hereford is two-storeyed, the upper floor being reached by a turretted stairway at the west end. Again, Bishop Nicholas West of Ely, in addition to his chapel in the cathedral, where he was buried in 1534, built a chapel attached to the parish church of Putney, the place of his birth. When the church was rebuilt in 1836, the West chantry chapel was transferred from the south to the north side of the chancel.[1]

The form that a chantry chapel assumed was subject to considerations of cost, site and goodwill. Cost alone precluded the erection of many, and the next best thing was a chantry tomb, that occupied less space but could be so designed that its chantry purpose could be fulfilled. If there was no room for a fixed altar, a small portable one was used, but there was always a space at the western end of the tomb for the priest to stand as he recited the mass. Many chantry tombs with ornate canopies remain in our cathedrals and other churches, notably that of Bishop Redman on the north side of Ely choir.

Whether or not he founded a chantry chapel, a bishop who took more than a passing interest in his see might wish to find a last resting place within the walls of his cathedral, and by the erection of a stately tomb would his memory be passed on to posterity. Not that a cathedral was regarded as a mausoleum. Until the early thirteenth century, intra-mural burial was not common, the privilege being reserved for the remains of founders. Even at Canterbury the archbishops of the seventh century were not permitted burial in the cathedral, the Roman custom being observed of burying the dead outside the city walls. Augustine was granted land beyond the walls of Canterbury by King Ethelbert for the site of a monastery that was to be the mausoleum for the kings of Kent and for archbishops; and in the abbey church of S. Augustine accordingly were laid the remains of the Saint and of seven kings and ten archbishops. In the year 740 the Papal Court decreed that archbishops should be buried in their own church 'to the intent that they might have their own resting place where, living

---

[1] Appendix B gives a list of all the chantry chapels now existing in English cathedrals
B*

they had ruled in honour'. Thereafter twenty pre-Conquest arch-bishops were buried in the Saxon cathedral of Canterbury.[1]

During the later Middle Ages, bishops and ecclesiastics, members of the royal family and of the nobility were laid to rest in cathedral and monastic churches, the fame of which was thereby enhanced. When the choir-arm of Old S. Paul's was rebuilt in the thirteenth century, tomb-chests containing the bones of the Saxon kings, Sebba and Ethelred were placed in wall-recesses in the aisles and tablets with Latin inscriptions were hung over them. Rather than leave it to their executors, many bishops made provision for the erection of their tombs during their lifetime.

A considerable number of mediaeval tombs, many surmounted by ornate canopies, remain in a good state of preservation in English cathedrals, the designs displaying features that characterize the Gothic style then prevailing (Appendix C). The tomb of Bishop Aquablanca at Hereford, with its gabled canopy supported by slender Purbeck shafts, is a graceful example of Geometric Gothic. Edward II's tomb at Gloucester, crowned with a mass of complex tabernacling, is a sumptuous product of the Decorated period (Pl. 7); and the monument of Archbishop Chicheley at Canterbury affords a notable specimen of Perpendicular mason-craft. Of no less interest are the recumbent effigies, wrought in freestone, wood, Purbeck marble, and alabaster that grace many mediaeval monuments in our cathedrals.[2]

Shorn of the polychromatic decoration and gilding that was lavished without stint upon them, the tombs and effigies present little of their pristine splendour to the modern eye.

[1] In his *Architectural History of Canterbury Cathedral*, Willis gives a list of the burial places, in most cases at or before an altar in the Saxon cathedral.

[2] On the tomb of Edward the Black Prince at Canterbury is the only mediaeval bronze effigy in any English cathedral. In Westminster abbey there are no less than eight, all of royal personages.

3. The Saxon
Bishoprics and Cathedrals

Pope Gregory's Scheme of Twelve English Bishoprics · The Sees of Canterbury, York and London · Northumbria and the Celtic Church · Wilfrid of York · Ripon · The Synod of Whitby, 664 · Unification of the English Church by Archbishop Theodore of Canterbury · The Early Dioceses of Saxon England, co-extensive with the Kingdoms · Obscurity of Sees in Remote Villages · The Short-lived Arch-See of Lichfield · Extermination of the Sees in Northumbria and East Anglia after the Danish Invasions · Lindisfarne and S. Cuthbert · The Founding of Durham Cathedral · Tenth-Century Changes in the Dioceses of Wessex · See of Crediton transferred to Exeter, 1050 · Saxon Bishoprics at the time of the Conquest · The Constitution of the Saxon Cathedrals · The Bishop's Familia · Use of the term Minster · The Office of Provost and the Introduction of the Canonical System · Descriptions of Saxon Cathedeals by the Chroniclers · Edmer's Account of Canterbury · Its Plan and Internal Arrangement · Wolstan's Eulogistic Poem of the Twelfth Century on Winchester Cathedral · The Foundations of S. Andrew, Rochester · Archbishop Albert's Basilica at York · The Tenth-Century Cathedral of Wells · Wilfrid's Crypt at Ripon · The Saxon Cathedral of Elmham, Norfolk · The Incorporation of Saxon Features in Post-Conquest Cathedrals · The Sculptured Panels at Chichester

❦ THE ROMAN MISSION of Augustine to Kent in 597 was the earnest of a plan devised by Pope Gregory the Great to convert this island to the Christian faith, and by parcelling out the whole of Britain into dioceses, to establish a complete ecclesiastical administration under the control of Rome.

In the year 601 Gregory conferred the pall, an emblem of ecclesiastical sovereignty upon Augustine, with injunctions that he should consecrate twelve bishops in England, of whom one was to occupy the see of London; and another, the bishop of York, was to enjoy the dignity of metropolitan. 'If that city [York] with its neighbourhood receives the word of God, he shall ordain twelve bishops.' After the death of Augustine, York was to be 'in no way subject to the jurisdiction of London, but priority shall belong to the one who has been consecrated first'. Gregory's intention therefore was that Augustine should exercise jurisdiction over the English Church as a whole, and on his death the metropolitan sees of London and York should rule in their respective provinces. But Augustine died before the Papal scheme reached fulfilment.

The see of London was founded in 604 and Mellitus, a monk who had been sent to England to assist Augustine, was consecrated bishop. Fifteen years later he was translated to Canterbury. But for the relapse of the East Saxons into heathenism, London would have been the seat of the primate; by the time it was finally Christianized, however, the arch-see was too firmly established at Canterbury to admit of its removal to London.[1]

The founding of the see of York followed the mission to Northumbria undertaken by Paulinus in 625, after his twenty years at Canterbury in the service of Augustine and his successors. The fervour and sincerity of his preaching were such that Edwin, King of Northumbria embraced the Christian faith, and in 627 reared a small church on the site of the present cathedral at York. Before embarking on his mission, Paulinus had been consecrated Bishop of Northumbria by Archbishop Justin of Canterbury, and York became the seat of the bishop in 627. In a letter to Edwin, the Pope wrote: 'We have ordered two palls, one for each of the metropolitans, that is, for Honorius and Paulinus, so that if one is called from this life, the other may in virtue of this, our authority, appoint a bishop in his place' (*Bede*). When Edwin was slain in battle in 633, Paulinus fled southwards and the greater part of northern England lapsed into paganism and anarchy. A century passed before the pall was again conferred upon a bishop of York, viz. Egbert, in 734, although bishoprics had been established in the north by the rival Celtic Church.

At the invitation of the Christian king, Oswald of Northumbria, Aidan the monk of Iona, who set himself the task of Christianizing the wild north, assumed the bishopric of Lindisfarne in 635; and in 669 the famous Wilfrid exercised the authority of a metropolitan bishop with his see at York, though he never received the pall. Wilfrid was bent on establishing the supremacy of Rome in the Northumbrian Church. At the Synod of Whitby, 664, in which he appeared as the leader of the pro-Roman party, the English Church became united in the usages of Latin Christianity. Until 678 Wilfrid was bishop of all Northumbria and of Lindsey, the north riding of Lincolnshire. Under his rule the church of York prospered and when he consecrated the basilica of Ripon in

---

[1] Five centuries later Richard de Belmeis, Bishop of London, petitioned the Pope to transfer the primatial see to London, an appeal that met with strong protests from Archbishop Anselm.

678, which he raised to cathedral dignity, 'the kings came with all their thanes and abbots of the north to a great dedication and a great feast'. But the see of Ripon came to an end in 686.

Wilfrid was tenacious of his rights as bishop of York, and in 678, when Archbishop Theodore of Canterbury proposed dividing his diocese into four sees, York, Lindisfarne, Hexham, and Witherne in Galloway, Wilfrid appealed to Rome and not without success.

Theodore of Tarsus, an Asiatic Greek appointed by Pope Vitalian to the see of Canterbury in 668, was the first to obtain recognition of the authority of Canterbury over all the bishoprics of England. Before his time the organization of the English Church consisted of a few bishops who presided over wide dioceses, the boundaries of which were ill-defined; but Theodore's unceasing labours welded them into one, owing obedience to the arch-see. To him may be attributed the formal organization of the diocesan system. The Celtic 'province' in the north was merged into the national Church, with its administrative centre at Canterbury, although Theodore failed to establish the northern province of twelve bishoprics subject to York, as planned by Pope Gregory.

Originally, the territory subjected to the bishop's authority was called his 'parish', which in early times implied the same as diocese. The diocesan areas of the Early Saxon period were more or less co-extensive with the kingdoms of the so-called Heptarchy. Thus, the diocese of Lichfield embraced the kingdom of Mercia, and Wessex formed the diocese of Winchester. Of the eight sees that were in existence when Theodore arrived in 668, those of Canterbury, Rochester, London, York and Lichfield were sited in populous centres, but Dorchester in Oxfordshire, Dunwich in Suffolk, and Lindisfarne were in relatively unimportant places. Before the end of the seventh century, Elmham in Norfolk, Hereford, Lindsey, Hexham, Ripon, Worcester, Leicester and Selsey had been added to the sees of Saxon England, all within a period of eight years, 673–80. The dioceses of Hereford, Lindsey, Worcester and Leicester were carved out of the wide-spreading diocese of Lichfield. Selsey in Sussex was founded by Wilfrid of Northumbria after his banishment from the see of York by King Egfrid. Of a number of these early sees only the names have come down to us, not a trace of the cathedral churches having survived; and in one or two instances, e.g. Lindsey and Leicester, their sites have not been identified. In others such as Dorchester and Sherborne the sees were subsequently transferred elsewhere. The churches of the bishops were henceforth distinguished by the name 'cathedral', deriving from the *cathedra* or episcopal chair that was installed in those churches.

In 785 Offa, King of Mercia, prevailed upon Pope Adrian I to exalt the wealthy see of Lichfield to the dignity of an archbishopric, with jurisdiction over the dioceses of Winchester, Hereford, Leicester, Elmham and Dunwich, but on the death of Offa in 795, Pope Leo III issued an edict reducing Lichfield to its former status.

In the second half of the ninth century, the devastation wrought by the Danish invaders, whose aim was to uproot the Christian faith and establish a pagan empire in northern Europe, was not conducive to the stabilization of the diocesan system in this country. By 875 Christianity was well-nigh extinct in Northumbria, East Anglia and the Midlands. York had been captured by the Danes in 867; the bishoprics of Lindisfarne, Dunwich, Lindsey, Elmham and Leicester were wiped out, though Lindsey and Elmham were revived in the tenth century. When the Vikings sacked Holy Isle in 875, the monks fled to the mainland, carrying with them the remains of S. Cuthbert, Bishop of Lindisfarne 685–7. After much wandering they settled at Chester-le-Street, which became the see of Lindisfarne until 995, when it was transferred to Durham, where a cathedral in honour of S. Cuthbert was erected on the site now occupied by the greatest of our Norman churches.

Wessex and western Mercia were saved from the Danes by Alfred the Great, and after the Peace of Wedmore 878, all fears of a permanent Viking conquest were at an end.

In 909 the diocese of Sherborne, Dorset, that extended over the west country embracing the present dioceses of Salisbury, Wells and Exeter, was divided into three bishoprics, Wilton or Ramsbury in east Wilts., Wells for the diocese of Somerset, and Crediton, the see of the county of Devon. Very soon afterwards a bishopric of Cornwall was founded with its seat at S. Germans, but in 1032 it was absorbed into the diocese of Devon. Cornwall was again constituted independent in 1046, but was re-united with Devon in 1050, when Edward Confessor removed the episcopal chair to the monastic church of S. Peter, Exeter. Leofric, the ninth and last bishop of Crediton, was appointed to the new see in these words: 'I will therefore the see to be there, that Cornwall with its churches and Devonshire with its, be together in one episcopate, and be governed by one bishop. So do I, Edward, place this privilege with my own hand upon the altar of S. Peter, and leading the prelate Leofric by the right arm, and my Queen, Editha, leading him by the left, do place him in the episcopal chair, my dukes and noble cousins being present' (*Dugdale's Monasticon*). The Benedictine church of S. Peter, founded by Athelstan in 932 was thus erected into a cathedral. In 1056 Ramsbury was once more united to Sherborne and at the same time the see was removed to Old Sarum.

The Norman ecclesiastics who swarmed across the Channel in the train of the Conqueror found fifteen sees in existence, of which all but four remain today. Though they retain nothing of their pre-Conquest fabric, the cathedrals of Canterbury, Durham, Exeter, Hereford, Lichfield, London, Rochester, Wells, Winchester, Worcester and York remain in the diocesan centres ordained by the Saxon hierarchy. More suitable centres were found for the sees of Dorchester-on-Thames, Elmham and Selsey.

Of the constitution and personnel of the cathedral establishments of the seventh century little is known. The seat of a bishopric was a central station for missionary activities, and the community ruled over by the bishop comprised a number of monks whose work was to evangelize the diocesan territory, and a body of clergy, the bishop's *familia*, who assisted him in the religious offices in the cathedral, and who in course of time acted as an advisory council. They were maintained from a common fund that issued from the fruits and profits of lands given or bequeathed to the see. From early days the chief member of the familia was the archdeacon, the bishop's right-hand man, who with other deacons supervised the churches in the diocese. From this primitive organization rose the regularly constituted dean-and-chapter of post-Conquest times. Though the familia observed no monastic rule, the cathedrals came to be identified in the popular mind with monastic establishments, and the term '*monasterium*' (i.e. minster) was applied to several cathedral churches, and still is the common designation of York, Lincoln and Southwell, none of which were ever served by monks.

In the ninth century a new office was created in the cathedrals of Worcester and Lichfield, where a vice-regent of the bishop was appointed under the title of 'provost'. At Worcester in 872 there were a provost and fourteen priests, and a century later, a provost and twenty-six seculars. Shortly before the Conquest a few Saxon cathedrals adopted the canonical system that obtained in the cathedrals of Lorraine, by virtue of which the seculars attached to the establishments followed a way of life not far removed from the monastic rule. They were known as 'canons', the term being derived from the canon or list of names entered in the register of the church. On his appointment to the see of Wells in 1060, Giso of Lorraine introduced a canonical system modelled on that of the cathedral establishments of Lorraine. He imposed a rule upon the canons, and built a cloister, a dormitory and a refectory, thereby forcing them to live a common life, and he appointed a provost to be the chief officer. His successor, John de Villula, 1082–1122, a native of Tours abolished the rule, tore down the cloister and other buildings and erected a palace for himself on the site. 'The canons whom Giso had taught to live by rule and religiously, were turned out of doors and driven to live a common life with the people' (*Historiale de primordiis Episcopatus Somersetensis*).

Of the cathedral churches of pre-Conquest England only a few scattered fragments remain. Contemptuous of their Saxon predecessors, whom they spoke of as 'boors and blockheads' (rudes et idiotás), the Norman prelates and ecclesiastics ruthlessly swept away the cathedrals that were described in such glowing terms by the chroniclers. The sum of our knowledge is therefore based on contemporary records and on excavations that have been made at various times. Allowance must be made for the exaggerations of the chroniclers in their extravagant and somewhat vague descriptions of the size and magnificence of Saxon cathedrals.

There is ample evidence that many of the pre-Conquest cathedrals were constructed of stone, though in scale and splendour they were in no way comparable with the mighty Norman churches that superseded them. It was natural that the Saxon historians, never having set their eyes on cathedrals of greater magnificence, should consider those of their own time to be the finest achievements in church-building; they praised them as immeasurably lofty and spacious. Wilfrid's church at Ripon, built in the late seventh century, was described by Eddius, one of Wilfrid's chaplains, as 'a basilica of polished stone from the foundations in the earth to the top, supported on high by various columns and porticoes'. It was the work of craftsmen from Italy who built 'in the Roman manner'.

The earliest cathedral of which any account is extant is Canterbury, reduced to ruins by the fire of 1067. From the writings of Edmer the precentor, who in his boyhood witnessed the demolition of the burnt-out cathedral, Prof. Willis gathered material that enabled him to determine the plan of Saxon Canterbury, the date of which it is impossible to establish.[1] The cathedral was subjected to a considerable restoration by Archbishop Odo, 940–60, who raised the walls to a greater height and re-roofed the building. Edmer's account is therefore that of the cathedral which in form and arrangement was substantially of the tenth century. He specifically states that it was to some extent built in imitation of the great basilica of S. Peter at Rome, and as he had accompanied Archbishop Anselm to Rome, Edmer was qualified to judge of the resemblance. His description makes it quite clear that the

[1] *The Architectural History of Canterbury Cathedral.* R. Willis. 1845.

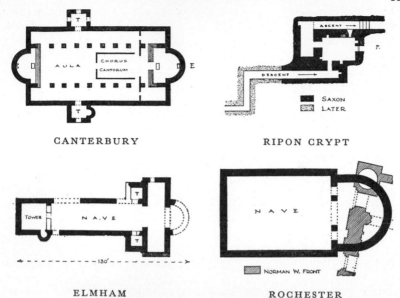

CANTERBURY   RIPON CRYPT

ELMHAM   ROCHESTER

FIG 3. Saxon cathedrals

cathedral was rectangular on plan, the central *aula* (the nave) being flanked by aisles (**Fig. 3**).

The presbytery, which was raised several steps above the nave, terminated at the east in an apsidal projection, and against the wall of the apse stood the High Altar, dedicated to Christ; beneath was a crypt or confessio, which is described as *curvatura* (apsidal), and was entered by a flight of steps constructed in the middle of the steps up to the presbytery. A second altar for matins stood at the west end of the presbytery. Extending nearly half the length of the nave from the choir steps was the *chorus cantorum*, an enclosure with low screens at the sides and the west, for the accommodation of the choir of singers. A flight of steps at the west end of the nave led up to another apse, on the chord of which stood the altar of S. Mary. Within the western apse was the bishop's throne. Probably the High Altar originally occupied this position, so that the bishop or officiating priest standing before it faced the east, an arrangement that was customary in the early churches of Italy. On either side of the church about midway up the length of the nave was a tower raised over a porch. The southern tower housed an altar. To the east of the cathedral and in close proximity was a detached baptistery, erected by Archbishop Cuthbert, 741–58.

A Latin poem of more than three hundred lines, written by Wolstan and addressed to Bishop Alphege of Winchester, 984–1005, describes in florid and glowing terms the cathedral and monastery at Winchester that was commenced by 'the holy Athelwold, a great builder of churches' who occupied the see from 963 to 984. 'He laid a foundation eastward so that an apse might be there built to the Deity and . . . he erected a new temple, but being removed from this world was unable to complete it. . . . He built all the dwelling places (of the monastery) with strong walls; he covered them with roofs and clothed them with beauty; he brought hither sweet floods of water abounding with fish; the runnings off of the pond penetrate all the recesses of the buildings and gently murmuring cleanse the whole cenobium. He repaired the court of that old temple with lofty walls and new roofs and strengthened it on the north and south sides with solid aisles (covered ways) and various arches.[1] He added also many chapels with sacred altars, that distract attention from the threshold of the church, so that a stranger . . . is at a loss where to turn, seeing on all side doors open to him without any certain path. He stands with wondering eyes, fascinated with the fine roofs of the intricate structures. Marvelling, he crosses himself, so dazzling is the construction and so brilliant the variety of the fabric that sustains this ancient church. . . . And', he continues, 'you, Alphege his successor, have diligently carried on the work begun. Above all you have taken care to add the secret crypts, which subtle ingenuity had so contrived that whoever entered them for the first time would be at a loss which way to turn. Their structure supports the High Altar and the venerable relics of the saints. . . . Moreover, you have here constructed such organs that the like were never seen. You have added a lofty temple, to wit, a sparkling tower that reflects the first rays of the rising sun. It has five compartments pierced by open windows; the lofty peaks of the tower are capped with pointed roofs, and are adorned with various and sinuous vaults, curved with well-skilled contrivances. Above there stands a rod with golden balls, and at the top a mighty golden cock which boldly turns its face to every wind that blows.' In October 980 that part of Winchester cathedral that had been completed was dedicated by Archbishop Dunstan of Canterbury and eight other bishops in the presence of King Ethelred. Though Wolstan's eulogy may be a poetic extravaganza, the cathedral thus described ap-

[1] A regular feature of Early Christian churches in Italy was the atrium or courtyard at the west end of the nave with arcaded walks on three sides, and a lofty enclosing wall. The atrium was the meeting place of converts and catachumens who were not privileged to enjoy the rights of the baptized. The church of S. Ambrogio, Milan retains its splendid atrium of the late eleventh century.

pears to have been a large and imposing structure. It was planned with a nave and aisles, an eastern apse and a crypt beneath the apse.

During the underpinning of the west front of Rochester cathedral preparatory to its restoration in 1889, the foundations of the seventh-century cathedral of S. Andrew were in part brought to light below the northern end of the façade and extending westwards.[1] The foundations of hard concrete were four or five feet wide, and examination proved them to be the remains of an eastern apse. Beneath the roadway outside, the foundations of the north-eastern corner of the nave were revealed, and subsequent probings show that the church, consisting of an apse and an unaisled nave, was of modest dimensions, being only 52 feet long and 28 feet wide (Fig. 3). The sleeper wall between the apse and the nave probably carried triple chancel arches, characteristic of seventh-century churches of south-eastern England, and the foundations of a straight wall at the west do not rule out the probability of an apse at that end of the church. The problem remains to be solved as to whether this was the Saxon cathedral of Rochester begun by King Ethelbert in 604.

Excavations undertaken in the crypt of York cathedral in 1930 revealed the foundations of a pre-Conquest church that in the opinion of Sir Charles Peers may be those of the basilica erected by Archbishop Albert, 766–82. The church extended westwards as far as the present crossing if not beyond, and was a rectangular building with an eastern apse and flanking aisles. It is impossible to say whether it was standing at the time of the Conquest; if it survived the onslaughts of the Danes, it must have been in a ruinous condition for in 1070 Archbishop Thomas of Bayeux started to rebuild the cathedral anew from its foundations.

The earliest mention of the Saxon cathedral at Wells occurs in the *Historiale de primordiis Episcopatus Somersetensis* (reprinted by the Camden Society), in which Bishop Giso, 1061–88 speaks of the church as 'but a middling one'. Beneath the cloister garth at Wells lie the foundations, discovered in 1894, of a basilican church that ran obliquely in a north-eastern direction and overlapped the east walk. The plan resembles that of the famous Saxon church at Brixworth, Northants, and the foundations may be those of the cathedral that was built soon after the see of Wells was erected in 909.[2]

So scanty are the actual remains of Saxon cathedrals that the

---

[1] A detailed account of the discovery, by G. M. Livett is given in *Archaeologia Cantiana*. Vol. XVIII.

[2] *Archaeological Journal*. Vol. LXVII.

crypt at Ripon and the low walls at North Elmham, Norfolk are all the more valuable. The former was originally beneath the church built by Bishop Wilfrid 671–8 (p. 98), and the walls at North Elmham have been identified as part of the early eleventh-century cathedral of Elmham[1] (Fig. 3).

On plan it consisted of an unaisled nave, eastern transepts from which projected an apse, a square tower at the west and smaller towers in the angles of the transepts and nave. It was of small scale, the total internal length being only 123 feet. The see of Elmham was removed to Thetford in 1075, i.e. only fifty or sixty years after the cathedral was built, and possibly it was then abandoned and gradually fell into ruins. The see was transferred to Norwich twenty years later.

Here and there fragments of Saxon work are to be seen that were incorporated in the post-Conquest cathedrals, and more may yet be discovered. In the triforium of the south transept of S. Albans are a number of baluster-shafts of Saxon craftsmanship that were re-used by the Norman masons who rebuilt the abbey church in 1077–88. The masons made use of any building material at hand; the sub-arches of the triforium spring from baluster-shafts that came from the pre-Conquest church. They were turned in a lathe and are marked with rings at intervals, a characteristic of Saxon architecture (Pl. 31).

In the south choir aisles of Chichester cathedral are two sculptured panels of rare interest that are believed to have been removed from the Saxon cathedral of Selsey. The reliefs are not carved on a monolith slab but on stone built up in courses and they portray The Raising of Lazarus and Christ about to enter the House of Martha (Pl. 2). Closely grouped about the Master are several attendant figures, all on a smaller scale than Christ, and the eyes are drilled with small holes, apparently intended to take crystals or coloured stones. 'In style they do not fit into any later period, and certain early features seem to justify us in assigning them to a date, c. 1000 or soon after.[2] In the *Archaeological Journal*, Vol. CX, 1953, Dr. G. Zarnecki ascribes them 'with some degree of certainty' to a date in the second quarter of the twelfth century.

[1] 'The Saxon Cathedral of Elmham. A. W. Clapham and W. H. Godfrey. *Antiquaries Journal*. VI.
[2] *English Mediaeval Sculpture*. A. Gardner. 1935.

4. The Post-Conquest Development of the Diocesan System

❡ THE LAST THIRTY YEARS of the eleventh century proved a marked epoch in the history of the English Church. The reorganization undertaken by the first Norman archbishop, Lanfranc, 1070–89 and completed by the end of the century, wrought several changes in the sites of the sees and defined more clearly the limits of the diocesan areas. In accordance with a decree promulgated at a synod convened in London in 1075, Lanfranc wisely transferred a number of the Saxon sees that were then in rural villages and towns, to more populous centres. The see of Dorchester, a little village in Oxford, was removed to 'the most illustrious city' of Lincoln, a busy trading place with a population of six thousand, where the royal castle afforded some protection in the unsettled times. As the administrative centre of the vast diocese that extended from the Humber to the Thames, Lincoln was far more suitable than Dorchester. Elmham, that had been the seat of the East Anglian bishop since 673, was removed to Thetford, which within twenty years was abandoned for Norwich.

borne gave place to Old Sarum, and Selsey, the see of the South Saxon bishopric was changed for Chichester.

At the same time the see of Lichfield was transplanted to Chester, where the collegiate church of S. John, a tenth-century foundation was made the cathedral, but in 1095 the see was removed to Coventry. In 1092 the episcopal chair at Wells was transferred to the priory church of Bath by John de Villula, whose wealth acquired as a physician there, had enabled him to purchase the bishopric of Wells. His attachment to Bath led him to fix his pontifical seat there. Dissensions arose between the canons of Wells and the monks of Bath as to precedence, and there were disputes respecting the rights of election to the bishopric. The differences were settled in the twelfth century by Bishop Robert of Lewes, who decreed that the bishops should be elected by an equal number of canons of Wells and monks of Bath, and the double title 'Bath and Wells' was conferred on the bishop of the diocese. A throne for the bishop was installed in both churches.[1] A parallel case was that of 'Lichfield and Coventry', a title that was assumed by the bishops of the diocese from 1129 when the see was removed to Lichfield. Here again there was continuous strife between the canons of Lichfield and the monks of Coventry, mainly concerning the election of the bishop.

Lanfranc's scheme of reorganization favoured the conversion of several of the secular cathedrals into cathedral-priories, an arrangement that had been adopted in Celtic foundations of Saxon England but was unusual on the Continent. The establishment of monastic cathedrals arose from the popularity of Benedictine monasticism in Western Europe in the tenth and eleventh centuries. Lanfranc himself had been a monk of Bec and abbot of S. Etienne, Caen, both Benedictine houses, and when he came to Canterbury in 1070 he planned a cathedral-priory to house a hundred and fifty monks of the same Order.

The union of cathedral and monastery obtained in eight Benedictine establishments in the second half of the eleventh century, viz. Canterbury, Bath, Coventry, Durham, Norwich, Rochester, Winchester and Worcester. In the two last named no radical

---

[1] That was not the end of disputes between seculars and monks in the diocese. In 1192 Savaric, a kinsman of Emperor Henry VI of Germany, became bishop of Wells. The Emperor held Richard I in ransom and to gratify Savaric he made it a condition of release that the wealthy abbey of Glastonbury should be annexed to the see of Bath and Wells. The monks of Glastonbury offered resistance and Savaric stormed the abbey, punished the inmates, and having advanced the abbot to the bishopric of Worcester, removed his seat to Glastonbury. In 1218 during the episcopate of Jocelyn, the convent of Glastonbury obtained a dissolution of their union with the bishopric, and Jocelyn resumed the title of Bath and Wells, which has been borne ever since by his successors.

change occurred in the constitution, for both had been monastic for nearly a century before the Conquest. On the other hand, at Durham, which had been served by seculars before William de S. Carileph was made bishop in 1080, all but one of the clergy in possession were driven to seek a new home in one or other of the colleges of secular canons at Norton, Auckland, and Darlington, and in their place monks were imported from Jarrow and Wearmouth.

In 1109 the renowned Benedictine abbey at Ely became a bishop's see, and the house of Augustinian canons at Carlisle followed suit in 1133. The creation of the see of Ely was probably occasioned by the constant disputes between the convent and the bishop of Lincoln, in whose diocese Ely lay. With the exception of a few parishes the county of Cambridge was transferred from Lincoln to the new diocese of Ely.

About the middle of the twelfth century Henry de Blois, Bishop of Winchester, is said to have obtained Papal consent to elevate his see to an archbishopric. Whether this was so or not, Winchester was never advanced to primatial rank.

Although the bishop was titular abbot in the monastic cathedrals, the prior as head of the convent was all-powerful and presided in chapter. The bishop stood at a disadvantage, having no prebends in the monastic chapter that he could distribute to clerks of his own choosing. So jealous of their rights were the monks of Durham, that a state of enmity long existed between them and the bishops throughout the thirteenth century. At one time the bone of contention was the custody of the priory during a vacancy of the see; at another, the appointment of a prior, and again a bitter quarrel would arise concerning the bishop's right of visitation. It is fairly evident that the convent aimed at a complete independence of the see, to which they were not entitled. When Philip of Poitou succeeded to the bishopric in 1197, his titular rights were contested by the prior and convent, and to enforce his claim he obtained letters from the Pope. The prior protested and aggravated the dispute by appealing to the King, who decided in his favour. Thereupon the bishop resorted to forcible measures; he excommunicated the prior and cut off the supplies of food and water from the monastery. When the prior was about to celebrate Mass on the Feast of S. Cuthbert, the bishop's men broke into the cathedral and seized the altar linen, and an unseemly struggle ensued. At length the dispute was settled and 'there was a great calm'. But not for long, for trouble again broke out during the episcopate of Bishop Richard de Marisco, 1217–26, who demanded to see the monks' charters. The prior refusing to produce them, a deadly feud arose between the two parties, followed by tedious and costly litigation. The disdainful remark uttered by Bishop Lewes de Beaumont, 1318–33, is a measure of the unfriendly relations that existed between the brethren and their spiritual father. 'Pray for my death, for while I live I will show you no favour.'

Towards the end of the eleventh century the secular chapters of York, Lincoln and Old Sarum, hitherto somewhat loosely constituted were recast on lines that subsequently influenced the internal organization of all other secular cathedrals in England. Henceforward the governing body was officially known as 'the Dean and Chapter'. The dean was the permanent head of the chapter and three other canons were vested with the offices of Precentor, Chancellor and Treasurer. Together with the archdeacons they were the chief dignitaries of the cathedral and were under the obligation of permanent residence.

The dean exercised complete authority over the canons, vicars and subordinate officers and ministers; he presided in chapter, heard all causes relating to the establishment, installed the canons after their nomination by the bishop and punished all those guilty of misdemeanours. The precentor[1] was the director of the music and the ceremonial observances in the cathedral; he controlled the recitation of the canonical hours, arranged the chants and processions and provided the books for use in the choir. The chancellor or *magister scholarum* presided over the department of theology and learning, and issued licences to schoolmasters in the diocese as well as appointing lecturers. He also prepared deeds and letters for the chapter and drew up the rota of duty for the canons or their deputies. To the treasurer were entrusted the furniture, sacred vessels, relics, crosses, plate, vestments, altar-cloths, bells and lights.[2] The care of all the cathedral treasures and the duties associated with the office being an onerous task, a Sacrist was appointed as the treasurer's assistant.

Next in dignity to the dean was the archdeacon, an office of old standing. As early as 798 there was an archdeacon at Canterbury.

---

[1] Precentor or *Primacerius*, i.e. the first tabled on the waxen tablets or roll of singers.

[2] The importance of lights and candles in mediaeval churches is evident from the account of the treasurer's duties at Hereford cathedral. He was required to provide '3 lights burning day and night before the High Altar; 2 burning there at matins daily and at Mass, and at the chief hours on festivals; 3 burning perpetually in the chapter house, before S. Mary's altar and before the Crucifix in the rood-loft; 5 tapers (candles) in basons . . . at Mass, prime and second vespers, 4 tapers before the High Altar, 5 in basons, 13 on the (rood) beam and 7 in the candelabra; and portable tapers for processions.' He was to find three clerks to light the candles, ring the bells and hang the palls and curtains on solemn days; and he supplied hay at Christmas to strew the floor of the choir and the chapter house.

The supervision of all the churches in a large diocese could not be exercised with thoroughness by one person, and often two or more were necessary. In the vast diocese of Lincoln there were eight archdeacons. Late in the thirteenth century it became usual for archdeaconries to be subdivided into a number of small areas, each of which was assigned to an arch-priest or rural dean.

The dean-and-chapter system was normal in the secular cathedrals of Normandy and its introduction on this side of the Channel is ascribed to Archbishop Thomas of York, one-time treasurer of Bayeux cathedral, and to Bishop Remigius of Lincoln. The reconstitution of the chapters of York and Lincoln may be dated c. 1090; amongst the witnesses' names to the charter of Bishop Osmund of Old Sarum appear those of Thomas of York and Remigius of Lincoln. Another innovation in the secular chapters was the allocation of separate prebendal estates to individual canons, thus providing them with regular and fixed stipends. There is no evidence that such a system existed in the pre-Conquest cathedrals, the canons and clergy of which received their emoluments from a common fund. Exeter cathedral alone retained the Saxon practice, each canon receiving an annual payment of 6 marks whether he resided or not.

During the archiepiscopate of Thomas of York began the struggle on the part of York for a position of equality with Canterbury. When Pope Honorius I sent the pall to Paulinus of York he decreed that in future one archbishop should be consecrated by the other. At the consecration of Thomas of Bayeux in 1070, Lanfranc demanded an acknowledgement of the supremacy of Canterbury. On the refusal of Archbishop Thomas to profess obedience to Lanfranc, an appeal was made to the Pope and the matter was referred back to William I, who decreed that Thomas should submit to Lanfranc but not to his successors. In 1093 when Anselm presented himself to Archbishop Thomas for consecration, he claimed the title of Primate of All Britain, an assumption promptly refuted by York. Successive archbishops of the northern province were equally zealous in refusing to profess obedience to Canterbury, and Rome withheld any pronouncement on the subject. Pope Honorius II, 1124–30, who absolved York from allegiance to Canterbury, empowered the suffragans of York and even the Pope himself to consecrate archbishops-designate of York should Canterbury refuse.[1]

The rivalry between the two archbishoprics resulted in an undignified incident that occurred at a council summoned by the Papal

[1] In 1114 Thurstan, who had the support of the Papal See, had been consecrated at Rheims by Calixtus II.

legate, Cardinal Huguzon, in 1176, in the infirmary chapel at Westminster abbey. When Archbishop Roger of York arrived, he found Canterbury already seated on the right hand of the legate, and 'disdaining to sit on the left, where he might seem to give pre-eminence to the Archbishop of Canterbury', with no more ado he thrust himself between them; whereupon the bishops and chaplains began to lay on him with bats and fists, and flung him to the ground. The assembly broke up in confusion and the humiliated Roger hastened to the king with his story which was greeted with royal laughter. The long-standing dispute was settled about the middle of the fourteenth century, when the Archbishop of York assumed the title 'Primate of England' and Canterbury 'Primate of all England', a peace-making expedient that apparently satisfied both parties. Each was granted the privilege of carrying his primatial cross erect when in progress through the other province, but as a symbol of the supremacy of Canterbury, the Primate of England was to present Canterbury with a golden image of an archbishop bearing a cross, within two months of his entering the southern province.

The jurisdiction of the Archbishop of York was over a small area compared with that of Canterbury; until the see of Carlisle was founded in 1133, Durham was the only diocese in the northern province other than York itself. The northern archbishops asserted their supremacy over the Scottish sees, a claim that was based on Edwin's conquest in the seventh century, when Scotland was absorbed into the kingdom of Northumbria. In 1101 Pope Paschal II ordered the Scottish bishops to profess obedience to the northern primate and to submit to consecration at his hands. Glasgow refused to acknowledge York and following disputes that spread over many years, the Scottish Church was declared independent by Pope Clement III in 1188 and was placed under the direct control of Rome. The diocese of Whithorn in Galloway, however, remained in the province of York until the fourteenth century; and Orkney, together with Man, continued subject to the archsee of Trondhjem in Norway.

In the reign of Henry I the metropolitan see of S. David's and the three other bishoprics of Wales, viz. S. Asaph, Llandaff and Bangor, were absorbed into the English Church and annexed to the province of Canterbury. They all claimed to have been founded in the sixth century, and until the time of Bishop Bernard, 1115–47, chancellor to Henry I's Queen, the Welsh bishops received their consecration from the bishop of St. David's. After the annexation they took the oath of canonical obedience to Canterbury.

After the creation of the see of Carlisle, no further bishoprics were founded in England until the reign of Henry VIII, nor were any see removed to new sites, with the exception of Old Sarum. The transfer of the see of Sherborne to the garrison town of Old Sarum in 1075 proved in course of time to be unpropitious for ecclesiastics and laity, and soon after his accession to the see in 1217 Bishop Richard Poore, who had been the dean for seventeen years, obtained a mandate from Pope Honorius III for the removal of the see to a more convenient site. The document leaves no doubt as to the desirability of the change. 'Forasmuch as your church is built within the compass of the fortifications of Sarum, it is subject to so many inconveniences and oppressions, that you cannot reside in the same without corporal peril; for being situated on a lofty place, it is continually shaken by the collision of the winds, so that while you are celebrating the divine offices you cannot hear one another, the place is so noisy; and besides, the persons resident there . . . are hardly able to keep in repair the roof of the church, which is constantly torn by tempestuous winds. Nor is there any access to the same without the licence of the castellan, so that the faithful being willing to visit the said church, entrance is denied them by the keeper of the castle, and on account of these and other inconveniences many absent themselves from the service of the said church.' On a new site about a mile distant from Old Sarum stands the cathedral of Salisbury, a monument to the lasting fame of Bishop Richard Poore.

The post-Conquest chapter of the English secular cathedral bore little resemblance to the 'familia' of the Saxon bishoprics, though the individual members of both bodies were appointed by the bishop. Under the dean-and-chapter system it was to the advantage of the bishop for some of the canonries to be held by clerks of his household, men of administrative ability and versed in the law. In course of time the Crown and the Papacy cast envious eyes on the remunerative prebends of such chapters as York and Lincoln, and put forward their own nominees whenever vacancies occurred, as a reward for services rendered.

The four dignitaries of the chapter, the dean, precentor, chancellor and treasurer, were required to be permanently resident within the cathedral precincts, but the obligation of canons to reside was not rigidly enforced. At Salisbury, the Constitutions of S. Osmund, 1096, ruled that no canons were to be excused residence, unless to teach a school, for service in the King's chapel or for the advantage of the Church. The rule was relaxed in 1319 and residence was not obligatory, provided that the dean and a muster of twelve canons with other officers were 'on the spot' to 'bear the heat and burden of the day and to conduct the affairs of the chapter'. In many cathedrals the majority of canons were absentees. Frequent and prolonged were the disputes concerning the residence of the canons at Old S. Paul's cathedral, many of whom were virtually civil servants whose duties kept them at Westminster. Only by fulfilling the conditions of residence was a canon entitled to a voice in chapter. The period of residence was from six to eight months during the first two or three years of a canonry, and about three months in each subsequent year. Whether residentiary or not, each canon had to maintain a priest-vicar or vicar-choral, who would deputize for him in the choir. In 1340 the canons of Wells were paying 'stall wages' of two marks each to their vicars-choral. The earliest mention of vicars-choral occurs in the second half of the twelfth century, when the famous Bishop Hugh of Lincoln enjoined his resident canons to provide temporary substitutes for the recitation of the offices in the choir. Non-residence became general in the thirteenth century; houses that were built for the canons in the cathedral precincts were rarely if ever occupied, and the canons spent their revenues how and when they pleased. 'Seeing their cathedrals perhaps once in their lives, many of them left their houses and their duties to their vicars' (*Cathedralia*).

On appointment, a vicar was instituted by the dean and chapter to 'the vicarial stall of the prebend of ——'. Often a numerous body, the vicars needed some form of control, as is evident from the measures adopted by Bishop Jocelyn of Wells, 1206–42. The conduct of the vicars-choral attached to the cathedral brought the chapter into disrepute and called for disciplinary action. It was therefore ordained that they were to be suspended for two months 'if they were slovenly in their office or talkative in choir; if they were hawkers, hunters or anglers, or idled about the streets or indulged in noisy loud singing abroad; if they were tavern-haunters, secular traders or public players with dice or at games of hazard', and a century later the vicars who carried arms or committed robbery in the church or cemetery of Wells, were to be 'deprived' (*Cathedralia*).

In several cathedrals the vicars-choral secured a degree of independence when they were incorporated as colleges, living in their own dwellings within the precincts of the cathedral and having their own hall and chapel. The Vicars' Close at Wells is a reminder of the importance of such colleges in cathedrals of the Old Foundation. The College of Vicars at York, founded in 1252, had a residence called the Bedern with its own hall and chapel. The discipline of the Bedern was under the control of the sub-chanter and a council of six vicars, who ruled with a firm hand.

For insubordination or unseemly behaviour, a fine of 3s. 4d. or more was imposed. The enormous number of sub-chanters' account rolls and other documents shed abundant light on the way of life and the various activities of the vicars-choral of York, who numbered thirty-six at the Reformation. Hereford cathedral still retains the cloister walk of the College of Vicars-choral that was incorporated in 1396; it led from the south choir-transept to the quadrangle round which were ranged the vicars' dwellings and 'a fayre hall wherein they constantly diet together and have their cook, butler and other officers, with a fayre library' (Pl. 94).

In the cathedral-priories there were no canonries in the gift of the bishops, for conventual chapters were wholly monastic. From the end of the twelfth century bishops of the monastic cathedrals often sought to remedy this state of affairs by founding colleges of secular canons in their diocese, the prebends being held mainly by clerks in the bishop's service or household. Episcopal intentions to set up such rival chapters of seculars were not always acceptable to the monks of a cathedral-priory. A notable instance is that at Canterbury. When Archbishop Baldwin, 1185–90, proposed to found a college of secular canons at Hackington near the city, the project was strongly opposed by the monks of Christ Church. He obtained a licence from Pope Lucius III to found a college of sixty canons, to be dedicated to S. Stephen and S. Thomas of Canterbury. The scheme was regarded by the monks as the transfer of the archiepiscopal chair to Hackington, and they feared that their rights in matters concerning archiepiscopal elections would be usurped by the college. On an appeal being made to Rome by the monks, Baldwin seized their possessions, and when the Papal licence was revoked by Urban III, the archbishop chose another site for his college outside the West Gate of Canterbury. In 1187 Henry II visited Christ Church to act as arbitrator, but royal intervention proved futile, and the dispute dragged on with increasing bitterness. Protests made by the convent to Rome resulted in another decree suppressing the college, but the Pope died before it could be put into effect. The climax of the quarrel was reached when Baldwin despatched a body of armed men to blockade the cathedral-priory; and but for the food that was smuggled in by the people of Canterbury during the eighty-four weeks' siege in 1188, the brethren would have died of starvation. Loth to abandon his scheme, the archbishop obtained the manor of Lambeth from the see of Rochester in exchange for lands belonging to the see of Canterbury. He built a mansion and a church at Lambeth and commenced a collegiate chapel and dwellings for the canons, for which purpose materials from the demolished college at Hackington were conveyed to London by water. Baldwin died in 1193 when the college was far from complete, but his successor, Hubert Walter pushed on with the building. Resistance by the Canterbury monks, however, led Pope Innocent III to order the chapel to be taken down and the canons already invested were deprived. A century was to pass before a college of secular canons was established by an Archbishop of Canterbury in his own diocese. In 1273 Archbishop Kilwardy converted the parish church of Wingham, Kent into a collegiate foundation. More notable was the college of All Saints, Maidstone, founded by Archbishop Courtenay in 1395; considerable remains of the collegiate buildings at Maidstone remain *in situ*.

The wealthy and ambitious Anthony Bek, Bishop of Durham, 1283–1310, who was constantly at variance with the monks of the cathedral-priory, raised the parish churches of Chester-le-Street and Lanchester in his diocese to collegiate rank, each served by a dean and seven or more canons. In the diocese of Worcester, Bishop Geoffrey Giffard, 1286–1301, made persistent but futile attempts to convert the collegiate church of Westbury-on-Trym into a cathedral, 'amongst whose canons he would feel more master in his own house than at Worcester'.[1] His plan was to augment the college at Westbury by nine canons, who were to hold as prebends certain parish churches belonging to the see of Worcester. The cathedral-priory put up a determined opposition and the dispute was brought before Edward I who pronounced in favour of the monks.[2]

With the rise of the chantry movement (p. 38) a goodly number of mass-priests became attached to the secular cathedrals, and it was deemed advisable by the chapters that such bodies should be incorporated into colleges and live communally in their own buildings rather than dwell in lodgings in various parts of the town. A

[1] *Cathedral Churches of England.* A. H. Thompson.
[2] Collegiate churches were also founded by bishops of the secular cathedrals. In 1267 Archbishop of York obtained leave of the prior and convent of Durham to elevate to collegiate status the parish church of Howden in the East Riding, that had belonged to Durham since the time of Bishop Carileph the Norman. The patronage of Howden was vested in the priory and to safeguard their rights, no dean or head of the college was instituted. In the diocese of Exeter was the famous College of Ottery S. Mary, Devon, erected by Bishop Grandisson in 1338. An appropriate gesture was it for a prelate to found a college of secular canons in the place of his birth; thus, Archbishop Kempe of York founded Wye College, Kent, in 1432. The most important collegiate churches in episcopal patronage were Beverley, Ripon and Southwell, which were in fact pro-cathedrals in the extensive diocese of York. Southwell was the ecclesiastical capital of the southern part of the diocese, as Ripon was of the north-west and Beverley of the East Riding. All these were of Saxon origin and their early constitution was maintained more or less after the Conquest. Although they owed nominal obedience to the Archbishop of York, who had the right to a stall in the churches, the canons brooked no interference in the internal affairs of these great foundations.

college of fourteen chantry priests was founded at Wells cathedral by Bishop Erghum, 1388–1400, the memory of which survives in the little thoroughfare known as College Lane. On a more magnificent scale is S. William's College, York, one of the historic monuments of the city. In 1461 licence was granted Bishop Neville of Exeter and his brother Richard, Earl of Warwick, to found the college for a community of twenty-four chantry priests attached to the cathedral. By the end of the century thirty-six priests as a corporate body were resident in S. William's College.

From an early period song and grammar schools formed part of the establishment of both secular and monastic cathedrals. National education really had its beginnings in the cathedrals of this country. In 627 a song school, probably associated with a grammar school, was founded at York by Archbishop Paulinus, who appointed 'James the deacon' as master. The establishment flourished under Archbishop Albert, 735–66, and was subsequently divided into grammar, song, and writing schools. Alcuin, a pupil and later a master of S. Peter's school has left some account of the curriculum in Albert's time. 'There [Albert] moistened thirsty hearts with divers streams of teaching and varied dews of study; busily imparting to some the arts of the science of grammar, pouring into others the stream of the tongues of orators. These he polished on the whetstone of law, those he taught to sing in Aeonian chant, making others play on the flute . . . others the said master made to know the harmony of Heaven and the sun, the labours of the moon, the earth's quake, the nature of men, cattle, birds and beasts; the different kinds of numbers, and the various figures of geometry . . . but above all, revealing the mysteries of holy writ, he opened the abysses of old and rude law.' The physical side of education was not neglected, for the boys of S. Peter's school were taught to ride, to fence and to shoot. After thirteen centuries the 'Grammar School of the Cathedral of S. Peter in the City of York' survives as one of the public schools of this country.

A Lateran Council of the twelfth century decreed that every cathedral should maintain a master who should teach the clerks of the church and poor scholars freely.[1]

In the accounts of the cathedral priory of Durham are items of expenditure for the maintenance of a school that was under the control of the almoner. It was quite separate and distinct from the school in the cloisters where monk-novices were taught. The 'children of the Almery' received their instruction from a chaplain who was paid a stipend by the priory. The Rolls for 1369–70 show that Nicholas the chaplain received 56s. 8d. a year *pro eruditione*

[1] *Educational Charters.* A. F. Leach.

puerorum, and in 1430 John Garner, master of the grammar school enjoyed a stipend of 53s. 4d. payable at Pentecost and Martinmas. The sacrist's Roll for 1536 records the cost of repairing the school-room, and the payment of 40s. to the bursar for the purchase of a table for the schoolmaster's use.

Three or four years after S. Peter's school, York, was founded, an archbishop's school came into being at Canterbury and was revived by Theodore; but it was situated in the parish of S. Alphege and was in no way connected with the cathedral. At the Reformation it was reconstituted as the King's school. Within the precincts of Christ Church Priory was the Almonry school for poor boys, that came to an end when the monastery was dissolved in 1540.

At Old S. Paul's was the famous school founded by Dean Colet in 1509, who expended a sum equal to £100,000 present value on the buildings. It stood against the eastern wall of the Close and was built to accommodate 153 boys who were to be taught 'good literature, both laten and greke'. The school which included a chapel and two houses for the masters was destroyed in the Great Fire of 1666. There is evidence of the existence of pre-Reformation schools at the cathedrals of Wells, Lincoln, Norwich and Winchester, and undoubtedly grammar as well as choristers' schools were attached to other cathedrals, both monastic and secular. In the New Foundation cathedrals of Henry VIII's reign, schools for the teaching of grammar and logic invariably formed part of the proposed constitution.

5. Henry VIII's
Sees of the New Foundation

The Re-constitution of the Cathedral Priories by Henry VIII · The Suppression of the Monastic Establishments · Creation of Secular Colleges · Provision for Education · The Appointment of Dean and Prebendaries · The Capitular Bodies of the New Foundation · Henry VIII's Scheme for Twenty-one New Bishoprics · The Proposed Personnel · The Six New Sees and Cathedral Churches · Westminster Abbey a Cathedral in the Diocese of London · The Collegiate Foundation at Gloucester and its subsequent elevation to Cathedral Rank · Katherine of Aragon and Peterborough · Chester Abbey raised to Cathedral Status · Its Connection with Coventry and Lichfield · The See of Bristol · Oseney Priory and Oxford Cathedral · The Redistribution of the Diocesan Areas

FROM THE EARLY HALF of the twelfth century until the Dissolution of the monasteries by Henry VIII, a period of four centuries or more, no additions were made to the seventeen dioceses of this country. Although the cathedral priories escaped the Suppression Act of 1536, four years later they fell within the category of the 'solemn monasteries of this realm', that furnished more profitable plunder under the second Act of Suppression. All the cathedral priories were then swept into the King's net of confiscation, and the monastic establishments attached to them were dissolved. The cathedral-priory of Bath survived as a parish church, but Coventry was swept away. Thus the great cathedrals of Canterbury, Durham, Ely, Norwich, Rochester, Winchester and Worcester ceased to be served by Benedictine monks, and the Augustinian canons of Carlisle gave place to a chapter of secular canons.

The King had assured Parliament that the sees should not be abolished but the monastic cathedrals should be refounded as collegiate establishments. In each case a chapter of seculars, invariably designated prebendaries and not canons, was installed, modelled on far more modest lines than the chapters of the Old Foundation. The late Prof. A. H. Thompson pointed out the big difference between the large chapters of Lincoln and Salisbury with their fifty prebends, and the thirteen or so members of the New Foundation chapters. A notable feature of the new establishments was the emphasis laid on education. There were to be ex-

c

hibitions at Oxford and Cambridge for students of divinity, and grammar schools were to be instituted as part of the foundation. On the average bursaries were to be provided for a dozen divinity students; at Durham for twenty, and at Rochester for four. In the schools for the teaching of grammar and logic, the number of boys varied from twenty to sixty. Much was professed by Henry VIII, but little was effected until the reign of Edward VI.

With the exception of Canterbury, the out-going prior of every monastic cathedral was made the dean of the new secular chapter, and the Crown was thereby relieved of the expense of providing large pensions for the dispossessed priors. At Canterbury, Prior Goldwell was passed over by Archbishop Cranmer in favour of Dr. Nicholas Wotton, an eminent ecclesiastical lawyer. Many of the former monks accepting the new dispensation, reappeared as prebendaries or minor canons. At Norwich Cathedral, which was 'secularized' in 1538, the last prior, William Castleton became the dean, five of the monks were made prebendaries, and several others became minor canons or officers such as precentor, sacrist or sub-sacrist. The new chapter at Canterbury, founded by royal charter in April 1541, consisted of a dean, twelve prebendaries, twelve minor canons, six preachers, and a host of other officers and servants, numbering one hundred and thirty-four in all. Peculiar to Canterbury were the six preachers, who were required to deliver sermons in the cathedral on Saints' days and in parish churches that stood on lands owned by the chapter. They dwelt in the cathedral precincts and were provided with horses for their journeys to the outlying parishes.

The newly constituted chapter at Durham was composed of a dean and twelve prebendaries; the former prior, Hugh Whitehead, assumed the office of dean and the prebendaries were chosen from the senior monks. When the cathedral priory of Winchester was dissolved in 1540, a secular chapter 'of the Holy Trinity' was created, with a dean and twelve prebendaries. The last prior, Basing, became the dean under the name of Kingsmill.

By letters patent dated 10 September 1541, Henry VIII 'did grant his royal charter for erecting the cathedral church of the late monastery of S. Peter and S. Etheldreda at Ely into a cathedral church by the name of the *Cathedral Church of the Holy and Undivided Trinity of Ely*, to consist of one dean, a priest, and eight prebendaries, priests, with other ministers necessary for the celebrating of Divine Service therein . . . and did ordain that the said dean and prebendaries be one body corporate, have perpetual succession, one common seal, be the chapter of the then Bishop of Ely and his successors.' The King granted the chapter the whole site of the monastery and most of the revenues thereof. Robert Wells, alias Steward, who had been prior from 1522 was made the dean. Again at Winchester, the former prior, Henry Holbech, was awarded the deanery. In the royal draft for the new establishment the head of the 'Colledge' is spoken of as the Provost; there were ten prebendaries, eight petty canons, ten students of divinity, ten choristers, and forty scholars who were to be taught grammar and logic in Greek and Latin. The cathedral-priory of Worcester was converted into a secular body by charter dated 23 January 1541; to be composed of a dean, ten prebendaries, ten petty canons, ten singing men, a master and usher of the grammar school and forty scholars, ten bedesmen, a master of the choristers, two vergers, two porters, two cooks, and a manciple, totalling in all a hundred and three persons. Of similar personnel was the capitular body of Rochester cathedral, which was incorporated by letters patent dated 20 June 1542, and which made provisions for a dean, six prebendaries, six minor canons, a deacon and sub-deacon, six lay clerks, a master for eight choristers, four students of divinity, twenty-three grammar scholars, six poor men, a porter who was also the barber, and a butler and cooks.

The New Foundation at Carlisle was served by a dean, four prebendaries, eight minor canons, four divinity students, four lay clerks, six choristers; and there were to be twenty scholars and a master of grammar.

To supplement the re-constituted cathedral priories Henry VIII devised an ambitious scheme for the formation of no less than twenty-one new sees from the proceeds of the Suppression.[1] Amongst the Cottonian MSS. in the British Museum is the proposed Bill to this end, in the King's own handwriting. The preamble of the document runs:

'For as muche as it is nott unknowne the slowghful and ungodly lyff whyche hath bene usid amonst all thos sort whyche have borne the name off religius folke, and to the intente that hensforthe many off them myght be tornyd to better use as heraffter shall [follow] werby God's worde myght the better be sett forthe, cyldren broght up in lernyng, clerces nuryshyd in the universities, olde s'vantes decayd to have lyfyng, allmes housys for pour folke to be sustaynd in, Reders of grece ebrew and latyne to have good stypende, dayly almes to be mynystrate, mendyng off hyght wayes, exhybission for mynysters off

---

[1] It is not without interest that shortly before his fall in 1529, Cardinal Wolsey procured a Papal bull authorizing him to 'inquire into the expediency' of suppressing certain monastic houses and elevating the conventual churches to cathedrals, but the Cardinal's fall put an end to his intentions. (*English Monks and the Suppression of the Monasteries.* G. Baskerville.)

the chyrche. It is thowght therfore unto the kyng's hyghtnes most expedient and necessary that mo byssopprycys, colegyall' and cathedralle chyrchys shalbe establyshyd insted of thes foresayd relygyus housys, w'tin the fondasion wereoff thes other tytylles affore rehersyd shalbe stablysyd.'

A further document in the King's hand and headed 'Byshopprychys to be made' names the diocesan areas and the seats of the bishops. In the list below the spelling of the names is modernized:

Essex	Waltham
Hertford	S. Albans
Bedfordshire & Bucks	Dunstable, Newenham, Elnestowe
Oxford & Berks	Oseney & Thame
Northants & Hunts	Peterborough
Middlesex	Westminster
Leicester & Rutland	Leicester
Gloucestershire	S. Peter's, Gloucester
Lancashire	Fountains & Richmond
Suffolk	Bury S. Edmunds
Staffordshire & Salop	Shrewsbury
Notts & Derby	Welbeck, Worksop & Thurgarten
Cornwall	Launceston, Bodmin with another

A roll of the personnel of each of the proposed foundations was prepared, stating in detail the emoluments of the dean, prebendaries, officers and servants, as well as other items of expenditure. That of the see of Fountains may be quoted as typical. The dean was to receive £27 a year, and the stipends of the six prebendaries, the gospeller and the epistoler were fixed at £7 16s. 8d. each. The six peticanons who 'kept the choir' were to have £10 a year each; six laymen to sing in the choir, £6 13s. 4d. each; a master to teach the children of the choir, £10; and six choristers £3 6s. 8d. per head. Two servants of the church were to receive £10 a year; other servants included the 'steward of the landes', £5 a year; the auditor, £5; the porter, butler and chief cook, £5 each; and the undercook, £4. The kitchen steward, who held an important office was to be paid £6 13s. 4d. a year, and the 'cater', who had to find his own horse, was to receive the same. Four poor men or 'King's servants decayd' were to be given £5 a year each, and £20 was to be distributed as alms. £20 was to be set aside for making and repairing highways; for reparations, the large sum of £66 13s. 4d., and a sum of £5 was to be expended on bread, wine, 'candells' and oil for the church.

Had the King's scheme been adopted in its entirety, Fountains abbey would not be the ruin it presents today, nor would the churches of Waltham, Dunstable and Shrewsbury be but mutilated fragments of their original glory.

Owing to the need for money to strengthen national defences, only six new sees were created, bishops' chairs being installed in the former monastic churches of Westminster, Gloucester, Peterborough, Chester, Bristol and Oseney.

The elevation of the royal abbey church of Westminster to cathedral status is of particular interest. The monastery was suppressed on 16 January 1539–40, and in December of the same year the church was made a cathedral in the diocese of London. There seems to have been no particular reason for the creation of a see of Westminster; but the abbey was a royal foundation, the church had been largely built by Henry III, kings and queens had been laid to rest within its walls, and in size and importance it ranked with the greatest cathedrals in the land. The first and only Bishop of Westminster was Thomas Thirlby, who was given the abbot's house, Cheyney Gates, as his residence. The last abbot, Boston, was made dean, under the name of Benson, and of the monks who had signed the deed of surrender, the prior and five others became prebendaries, and four others minor canons. The abbey church remained a cathedral for only ten years, the bishopric being surrendered in 1550. The estates of Paddington and Westbourne were then transferred from the see of Westminster to Old S. Paul's, whence arose the proverb 'robbing Peter to pay Paul'.[1]

Only a few days before Westminster was suppressed in January 1539, the abbey church of S. Peter, Gloucester was surrendered to the Crown, and shortly afterwards was converted into a collegiate church, served by a warden, a sub-warden, senior and junior clerks, and four Oxford scholars, all of whom but one had been monks of S. Peter's abbey. The collegiate body however, was of brief duration for in the following year the see of Gloucester was founded. The royal charter states that 'considering the site of the late monastery in which many famous monuments of our renowned ancestors, kings of England, are erected, is a very fit and proper place . . . we have decreed that the site of the said monastery be an Episcopal See. We also will and ordain that the said

---

[1] The chapter survived for another six years under the jurisdiction of the bishop of London, but in Mary's reign the abbey was re-endowed as a Benedictine monastery. It was finally suppressed in July 1559, and one of the first acts of Elizabeth I's reign was to refound Westminster as a collegiate church, served by a dean and twelve canons. Today the Collegiate Church of S. Peter is a royal peculiar, a distinction it shares with S. George's Chapel, Windsor. The dean is completely independent, subject to no episcopal authority or jurisdiction, and has no superior except the reigning sovereign.

dean and prebendaries, and their successors, shall for ever here-after be called the dean and chapter of the Holy and Individed Trinity of Gloucester.' John Wakeman, the last abbot of Tewkes-bury and one of Henry VIII's chaplains was made the first bishop of Gloucester, and the deanery was bestowed on prior Jenyns, formerly of S. Oswald's priory, Gloucester.

Like Gloucester, the abbey church of Peterborough may owe its cathedral status to the burial of royalty within its walls. There is a tradition that after Henry's divorced Queen, Katherine of Aragon, had been interred in the choir of Peterborough abbey, it was suggested to the King that it would become his greatness to erect a splendid monument over her grave, whereupon Henry declared that she should have 'one of the goodliest monuments in Christendom'. He therefore ordained that the church should be made the cathedral of a new see, and as such would be a worthy memorial of the late Queen. By letters patent issued on 4 September 1541, it was converted into the cathedral of the newly created diocese of Peterborough. The last abbot, John Chambers, who had voluntarily surrendered the house to the King's commissioners, was duly rewarded with the bishopric, and a dean and six prebendaries constituted the chapter.

In the King's draft of 'Bishoprics to be made', there was no mention of Chester. Undoubtedly it was the vast extent of the diocese of Coventry and Lichfield which covered a great part of the north and west of England, that led Henry to form a separate diocese of Chester.[1] By a charter of 4 August 1541, the Benedictine abbey of S. Werburgh was made a cathedral, dedicated to Christ and the Blessed Virgin Mary, to be served by a dean, six prebendaries, six minor canons, six singing men, six choristers, two masters of a grammar school, twenty-four scholars, almsmen, vergers and others. The chapter was vested 'with the same powers annexed to the diocese of Coventry and Lichfield . . . and a body corporate, with all privilege of suing, etc., and shall have a common seal'. The first bishop of Chester was John Bird, translated from Bangor, and Thomas Clerk, the abbot of S. Werburgh's became the first dean.

The see of Bristol was founded on 4 June 1542, and the Augustinian abbey church, dating from 1142 and dedicated to S. Augustine was made the seat of the bishop. The charter explains that 'having corrected the enormities into which the life and profession of the monks in the long course of time had most deplorably

<hr>

[1] The Norman bishop of Coventry and Lichfield had removed his seat to Chester in 1075. He converted the collegiate church of S. John, Chester, part of which is still standing, into a cathedral, but his successor preferred Coventry as his seat, and S. John's reverted to its collegiate status, although it continued as a pro-cathedral until the independent see of Chester was created by Henry VIII.

fallen, we have endeavoured . . . that in future in this same place, instructions out of the holy oracles and sacraments of our saving redemption may be purely administered, the discipline of good manners be sincerely kept, youth be liberally instructed in learning, old age failing in strength be cherished with things necessary for their support, that alms to the poor may abound, and the repairs of highways and bridges may hence be supported, etc., we have therefore established this bishopric.' The last abbot of S. Augustine's was awarded a pension of £80, and Paul Bush, master of the Bons-hommes of Edington, Wilts., was appointed to the bishopric.

On the formation of the diocese of Oxford in 1542, the King assigned the church of Oseney priory, formerly a house of Augustinian canons in the western suburbs of Oxford, to the bishopric. Four years later the see was translated to the church of the suppressed priory of S. Frideswide, also an Augustinian establishment. Cardinal Wolsey had obtained the surrender of S. Frideswide's from the King in 1525, for the purpose of converting it into a college of secular priests and two hundred students. In 1532, three years after the fall of Wolsey, Cardinal College as it was called, was refounded as 'Henry VIII's College', and in 1546 the chapel was made Christ Church cathedral, Oxford. The establishment was ordained to consist of a dean, eight canons, eight chaplains, eight clerks, eight choristers and a hundred and one students. The last prior of Oseney was the first to occupy the bishop's chair in Christ Church cathedral. The church is also the chapel of the college, of which the principal is the dean.

The areas of the newly formed dioceses were territories transferred from the older dioceses. The county of Middlesex was assigned to the see of Westminster; Gloucester was given an archdeaconry from Worcester, of which diocese it had always been a part. In the King's original scheme for twenty-one dioceses, that of Peterborough was to have embraced the counties of Northants and Hunts., but ultimately it was limited to Northants and Rutland, formerly within the diocese of Lincoln. The new see of Chester was saddled with archdeaconries in the dioceses of Lichfield and York, comprising an area of unmanageable size that included the counties of Cheshire and Lancashire together with parts of Westmorland, Cumberland and Yorkshire. The diocese of Bristol was taken out of that of Salisbury and consisted of the county of Dorset and a small part of Gloucestershire. The diocese of Oxford was an archdeaconry of Lincoln covering the small county of Oxford.

6. Sees
of the Modern Foundation

*The Ecclesiastical Commissioners and the Re-adjustment of Dioceses ·
The Constitution of Modern Foundation Cathedrals · Ripon · The
Collegiate Church of Manchester · Elevation of S. Albans in 1877 · The
See of Truro · The Diocese of Liverpool · S. Nicholas, Newcastle ·
Southwell Collegiate Church · Wakefield · The Founding of Southwark
Cathedral · Parish Churches raised to Cathedral Rank in the Present
Century · The Dioceses and Sees of Birmingham, Sheffield, Bury S.
Edmunds, Chelmsford, Coventry, Bradford, Leicester, Portsmouth,
Guildford, Blackburn, and Derby*

❡ EXCEPT FOR THE suppression of the see of Westminster in 1550,
Henry VIII's re-arrangement of the diocesan areas lasted until
the eve of Queen Victoria's accession. The enormous growth of
population in this country in the nineteenth century, especially in
the industrial areas, rendered imperative the sub-division of certain dioceses and the revision of the boundaries of others. In 1837
by Act of Parliament, a permanent body of Ecclesiastical Commissioners was established, vested with the power to lay before
the Crown schemes for the readjustment of the dioceses. Within
a few years the vast see of Lincoln stretching from the Humber
to the Thames was reduced by more than one-half by transferring
the counties of Beds. and Hunts. to the diocese of Ely; of Bucks.
to Oxford; of Leics. to Peterborough; and of Herts. to London
and Rochester. Further, the Commissioners put forward certain
recommendations that 'tended to reduce the time-honoured
Council of the Diocesan to a little body of four or five residentiary
canons', by this means attaining a uniformity in existing cathedral
establishments, that owes little to tradition.

Since 1836, twenty new sees have been founded, for which Parliamentary sanction has had to be obtained. Wherever practicable,
the largest church in the new diocese has been elevated to cathedral status, as at S. Albans, but not infrequently the bishop of a
newly constituted see has had to content himself with a less
stately parish church in which to set up his throne. A parish church
however, lacks the amenities that are essential in the mother

church of a diocese. Accordingly, to fit them for their new purpose and to meet the requirements of a cathedral establishment, several of the elevated parish churches have been or are being enlarged. When completed the cathedrals of Bradford and Blackburn, in each of which is incorporated a former parish church, will be worthy symbols of the work of their respective dioceses. Where the necessary funds have been forthcoming, an entirely modern cathedral church on a new site is being erected, as at Liverpool and Guildford.

The earliest cathedral of the Modern Foundation is Ripon. By the Act of 6 & 7 William IV, the Ecclesiastical Commissioners were empowered to create the diocese of Ripon by transferring thence the areas of the Chester diocese that lay in Yorkshire, and the ancient collegiate church of S. Peter and S. Wilfrid at Ripon was made the cathedral. The original church at Ripon was a Saxon foundation dating from the seventh century, and was subjected to many changes through its long history. It was successively a bishop's stool, a church of portioners,[1] a parish church, and a collegiate establishment. The famous Wilfrid reared the first church at Ripon c. 664, and fourteen years later it was raised to the dignity of a cathedral, although the see was suppressed in 688. Until the tenth century its subsequent history is obscure, but it survived as a church of portioners up to the thirteenth century, when Archbishop Walter de Gray of York, 1216–55, reconstituted Ripon as a college of secular canons. Thenceforth it served as a pro-cathedral in the north-western district of the diocese of York. After the suppression of the college under the Chantries Act of 1547, the minster was used as a parish church until 1604 when James I refounded the college with a dean and chapter. It was again suppressed during the Commonwealth, but was once more revived in Charles II's reign. Finally in 1836 the minster became the cathedral of the new diocese of Ripon, served by a dean and four residentiary canons.

In 1847 the diocese of Chester was subjected to further limitation, a measure that was rendered imperative on account of the rapid expansion of Manchester within the diocese of Chester. Accordingly, Manchester was taken out of the diocese and was made the seat of a bishop, and the church of S. Mary, formerly collegiate, assumed cathedral rank; a dean and four canons were installed. Originally parochial, S. Mary's was refounded as a

---

[1] Churches of portioners were quasi-collegiate. The priests or portioners, whose stipends issued from the tithes and fruits of the church they served and not from prebendal estates, were not regularly constituted as a corporate body. The system was general in the so-called collegiate churches of Saxon England.

C*

college of secular priests in 1421 and the church was then entirely rebuilt. The college came to an end in 1547, but was re-established in Elizabeth I's reign under the name of Christ's college. To the beneficence of Humphrey Chetham, a merchant of Manchester is due the preservation of the college buildings, now the famous school known as Chetham's Hospital, formally dedicated in 1658, a few years after Chetham's death.

In pursuance of Act of Parliament, 1877, the new diocese of S. Albans was carved out of that of Rochester, and the church of the premier Benedictine abbey of mediaeval England came into its own and was made the seat of the bishop of S. Albans. The abbey church might well have been raised to a cathedral at the time of the Monastic Suppression; it was one of the largest and most hallowed of monastic churches, and S. Albans was on Henry VIII's list of proposed bishoprics. The church was, however, held by the Crown until 1553, in which year Edward VI conferred a charter on the town and the burgesses purchased the vast church for £400 and used it henceforward as their parish church. The cloisters and monastic buildings with the exception of the gatehouse were granted by Henry VIII to Sir Richard Lee who promptly cleared the site. Today the cathedral is also a parish church, the dean being the rector. There are no resident canons, nor minor canons, the clergy under the dean being designated 'curates'.

In 1877 the County of Cornwall, which had hitherto formed part of the extensive diocese of Exeter, was constituted an independent diocese with the bishop's seat at Truro. There had been a see of Cornwall some time before the Norman Conquest, the cathedral being at S. Germans, but in 1043 the see was united with that of Crediton, Devon. The chapter at Truro consists of a dean, four canons in residence, a chancellor and lesser officers. The cathedral, in which is incorporated the south aisle of S. Mary's church that stood on the site was the first to be built in the Gothic style since the Middle Ages.

By the Bishoprics Act of 1878 the diocese of Liverpool was formed in 1880, thus securing its independence of the see of Chester. For many years the church of S. Peter, Liverpool, a poor Renaissance building dating from 1699, was pressed into service as the 'provisional cathedral', hardly a worthy symbol of the ecclesiastical activities of the see. But in 1904 King Edward VII laid the foundation of the monumental cathedral designed by Giles Gilbert Scott. More than half of this colossal church has now been erected, and when completed the new Liverpool cathedral will be the greatest achievement in the religious architecture of England since the building of S. Paul's by Wren.

In the reign of Edward VI a Bill was put before Parliament for suppressing the ancient bishopric of Durham, and for erecting two new sees, one at Durham and the other at Newcastle-upon-Tyne. The preamble of the Bill set forth the vast extent of the diocese of Durham and the barbarity of the people proceeding from their ignorance of the Christian faith. Nothing came of the Bill, and the diocese of Durham remained intact until 1882, when the see of Newcastle was created, and the County of Northumberland was transferred to the new diocese. Upon the parish church of S. Nicholas, Newcastle, was conferred the dignity of a cathedral church.

A new Bishopric for Notts. and Derby came into being in 1884, Southwell being chosen for the seat of the bishop on account of its magnificent collegiate church and its time-honoured ecclesiastical associations. Architecturally, Southwell is the finest of all mediaeval churches that serve as cathedrals of the Modern Foundation. Prior to the Suppression, it was the church of a collegiate estab-lishment, whose origin dates from the Saxon period. Throughout the Middle Ages Southwell was an ecclesiastical capital in the southern part of the huge diocese of York and the collegiate church was to all intents and purposes a cathedral for the archdeaconry of Notts., its constitution and charter being modelled on those of York. Henry VIII toyed with the idea of erecting a see at South-well and endowments were earmarked for the purpose. The col-lege was suppressed under the Chantries Act of 1547 but was reconstituted ten years later. The chapter was finally dissolved in 1840, its property was seized by the Ecclesiastical Commissioners for the endowment of the bishoprics of Ripon and Manchester, and the minster was reduced to the status of a parish church. When the see of Southwell was constituted in 1884, the endowment was derived mainly from subscriptions.

In 1888 the see of Wakefield came into existence and the large parish church of All Saints, Wakefield, was made the cathedral of the new diocese that was taken out of York.

To keep pace with the increasing population in the industrial districts of this country, further subdivisions of diocesan areas have resulted in the creation of twelve new sees in the first half of the twentieth century. In most cases a parish church has been ad-vanced to cathedral rank; with the exception of Southwark which was a pre-Reformation church of Augustinian canons, and Guild-ford, now in course of erection, these more recent Foundations cannot compare in size or architectural distinction with the cathedrals of the Old and New Foundation. Due to the lack of prebendal estates and endowments the governing bodies of the parish-church cathedrals are not modelled on the mediaeval pattern with a dean and a chapter of residentiary canons. The simpler modern plan is for the 'chapter' to consist of a sub-dean who is also vicar of the parish, and a number of honorary non-resident canons, who are selected by the bishop from the parish clergy of his diocese.

A Bishopric Act of 1904 authorized the formation of the see of Southwark out of the diocese of Rochester, and the church of S. Saviour, that belonged to the priory of S. Mary Overie before the Dissolution, was constituted the cathedral of Southwark. Since 1540 the conventual church had served the united parishes of S. Magdalen and S. Mary in Southwark, and was held in lease from the Crown until 1614, when it was purchased by the parishioners for £800. Formerly Southwark was in the diocese of Winchester, one of the largest in England, whereas the neighbouring diocese of Rochester covered but a small part of Kent. In 1877, in order to equalize the diocesan areas, the borough of Southwark was transferred to the diocese of Rochester and remained so until the separate see was founded in 1904. In anticipation of the elevation of S. Saviour's church, the nave was entirely rebuilt and other parts were subjected to a thorough restoration by Sir Arthur Blomfield from 1890 to 1897.

In 1905 when the diocese of Birmingham was carved out of Worcester and Lichfield, the chair of the bishop was placed in the parish church of S. Philip, a Renaissance building of the early eighteenth century, that has since served as the cathedral.

The diocese of Sheffield was created in 1914 and the parish church of Sheffield was made the cathedral church of S. Peter and S. Paul. In pursuance of cathedral measures of 1931 and 1934, the constitution and statutes of the cathedral were prepared, by virtue of which a chapter was established consisting of a provost, four residentiary canons, two archdeacons, a precentor, and twelve honorary canons appointed to stalls in the cathedral by the bishop. The constitution made provision for a cathedral 'council' of which the bishop is chairman, the chapter, the parishioners, and the laity of the diocese having duly appointed representatives thereon. The diocese of Sheffield embraces the city and several rural deaneries formerly in the diocese of Southwell.

The Modern see of S. Edmundsbury and Ipswich was formed in 1914, the diocese being taken out of those of Ely and Norwich. The parish church of S. James that stood within the precincts of the famous abbey at Bury S. Edmunds is the seat of the bishop.

A new diocese co-extensive with the county of Essex was taken out of S. Albans in 1914, and the county town of Chelmsford was chosen as the see. The old parish church of S. Mary the Virgin, a late Gothic building, enlarged since its elevation to a cathedral, has been re-dedicated to S. Mary the Virgin, S. Peter and S. Cedd.

In 1918 the see of Coventry was re-established. For six centuries from 1095 Coventry formed a joint diocese with Lichfield, though the designation was changed to Lichfield and Coventry *c.* 1700. In 1830 the see of Coventry was merged into that of Worcester, but an independent diocese was constituted in 1918, and the noble church of S. Michael, that was ruined by German bombs in November 1940, became the cathedral. By an Order in Council of 1936 the cathedral body of a provost and chapter was instituted.

Largely due to the munificence of the 'woolmen' of Bradford, who raised the sum of £50,000 towards the creation of a diocese independent of Ripon, the parish church of S. Peter, Bradford, dating from the fifteenth century was elevated to a cathedral in 1919.

Very fitting was it that Leicester, which had been the see-town of the Mercian kingdom from 680 to 869, should again be made the seat of a bishop in 1926. The diocese was taken out of that of Peterborough, and in 1927 the ancient church of S. Martin, Leicester, was hallowed as a cathedral.

In 1927 the diocese of Winchester was sub-divided and the dioceses of Portsmouth and Guildford were then formed. At Portsmouth the bishop's throne was installed in the old parish church of S. Thomas of Canterbury, and at Guildford the red-brick church of the Holy Trinity at the upper end of the town served for a time as the pro-cathedral. A site on Stag Hill having been given by Lord Onslow, the foundation stone of the new cathedral church was laid in July 1936.

The year 1927 also witnessed the establishment of the sees of Blackburn and Derby. The diocese of Blackburn was carved out of that of Manchester, and the parish church of S. Mary was raised to cathedral dignity. For more than twelve centuries the county of Derby had been within the jurisdiction of the Bishop of Coventry and Lichfield, but was transferred to the diocese of Southwell in 1884. When it became a separate diocese, the church of All Saints, Derby, a pre-Reformation collegiate foundation was made the seat of the bishop.

7. The Origin and Development
of the Cathedral Plan

The Post-Conquest Rebuilding of the Saxon Cathedrals on the Normandy Model · Benedictine Influence · The Cruciform Plan · Great Length of Norman Naves · Methods of Planning the Choir Arm · Parallel Apses and their Drawback · The Peri-apsidal Choirs of Gloucester and Norwich · The Apse-and-Ambulatory in Secular Cathedrals · Modified Form at Winchester · Conrad's Glorious Choir at Canterbury and the Influence of Cluny · Norman Transepts and West Fronts · The Importance of Cistercian Ideals · The Characteristic Square-ended Choir of English Gothic Cathedrals · The Twelfth-Century Eastern Arms of Old Sarum and York · Development of the Retrochoir at Southwark and Glasgow · William de Sens' Plan of Canterbury, 1175–84 · Bishop Hugh's Remodelling of Lincoln Choir · Reconstruction at Chichester and Wells late in the Twelfth Century · The Great Eastern Extensions of the Thirteenth Century · The Importance of the Saint's Chapel · The Cult of the Virgin Mary · Varying Positions of the Lady Chapel in Cathedral Churches · The Choir Extension at Hereford · The Eastern Arm of Lichfield, 1291–1337 · Remodellings at Chester, Winchester and Rochester · The Perfect Plan of Salisbury, Unhampered by Existing Remains · Durham Cathedral and its Eastern Transepts, 1242–80 · The Ingenious Lay-out of the Retrochoir of S. David's · The Two Types of Internal Arrangement of Choir Extensions · The Aisled-Rectangle Plan at Ely, Old S. Paul's and York · Late Remodelling at Peterborough · Squared English Extensions Diverging from the Continental Model · The French Plan of Westminster · The Addition of Outer Aisles at Chichester · Western Transepts at Lincoln · The Galilees of Durham and Ely · Western Towers built beyond the Aisles at Wells

❡ THE PERIOD OF sixty years that followed the Norman victory at Hastings was one of amazing building activity in England. Within a few years of the Conquest all the Saxon prelates in this country save one were deposed, and were replaced by Norman ecclesiastics who brought with them the ritual and the building traditions of their own land. They had no scruples in tearing down the unstately churches and minsters of the Saxons, which gave place to lordly and imposing churches on a gigantic scale. Lamenting the destruction of the pre-Conquest cathedral at Worcester in 1084, Bishop Wulstan tearfully exclaimed: 'We poor wretches

78

destroy the works of our forefathers that we may get praise for our-
selves. That happy age of holy men knew not how to build stately
churches; under any roof they offered up themselves living temples
unto God, and by their example excited those under their care to
do the same; but we alas! strive that we may pile up stones,
neglecting the while the cure of souls' (*Gesta Pontificum*).

It was part of William I's policy to overawe the conquered race
by planting what were virtually ecclesiastical garrisons throughout
the land; the cathedrals were rebuilt and a great number of religious houses were founded or refounded. Under the feudal system, the estates of the Saxon landowners were granted to the
military and ecclesiastics of the new régime, and the resources
thus acquired together with generous benefactions from the Norman nobles made possible the enormous schemes of building and
rebuilding then undertaken. In the fifty years following the Norman occupation were rebuilt the cathedrals of Canterbury,
Chichester, Durham, Exeter, Hereford, Lincoln, London (Old
S. Paul's), Norwich, Rochester, Winchester, Worcester and York,
and in addition many great monastic churches such as S. Albans,
Ely, Gloucester, Peterborough and Tewkesbury.

In their general lay-out and architectural character these great
churches were modelled on the contemporary churches of Normandy, though in scale and dimensions they surpassed the Continental churches. When Archbishop Lanfranc rebuilt Canterbury
cathedral in 1070–7 in form and arrangement it was a copy of
S. Etienne, Caen, a monastic church that Duke William had
founded in 1064.

The Anglo-Norman cathedral was planned to meet the needs
of the ritual observed by the Norman churchmen in their own
country. It was a cruciform building with a short choir terminating
in an apsidal east end, deep transepts and a long aisled nave. At
the crossing rose a low tower and often there were twin towers at
the west, as at Canterbury and Durham. A characteristic feature
of the cathedrals and greater churches of the Norman period was
the inordinate length of the nave. S. Albans and Ely were built
with naves of thirteen bays (Figs. 13, 19); that of Norwich was
fourteen bays long (Fig. 12), and at Winchester, the nave that is
now of twelve bays, was laid out by the Norman Walkelyn in
fourteen bays. The comparatively short nave of eight bays at
Durham was due to the cramped space at the west. Lanfranc's
nave at Canterbury was some 185 feet long, whereas that at Winchester reached about 318 feet from east to west.

The west front was usually treated as an important feature in
Norman cathedrals. The most grandiose design, following the

façades of the Conqueror's two churches at Caen, embraced twin towers, but less ambitious was the single-towered front. In the latter, the westernmost bay of the nave formed an internal narthex, above which rose the square tower, and breadth was added to the front by building lateral transepts or chapels. Such was the arrangement at Norman Winchester, the square flanking transepts giving a breadth of 128 feet to the western façade. At Ely the single tower at the west and the south-west transept with an eastern apse remain *in situ*, but the north-western transept collapsed in the fourteenth century.

Two distinct methods of planning the choir arm were introduced by the Normans to this country. In the first, that is generally spoken of as the parallel-apsed plan, the choir and its aisles were made to terminate at the east in apses. The central and larger apse, on the chord of which stood the High Altar, projected farther eastwards than the flanking apses. This was the form adopted for the choirs of the Conqueror's churches of S. Etienne and La Trinité at Caen, and made its first appearance in England in the Confessor's abbey church of Westminster. There, and in most other English churches of this type, the flanking apses were squared externally. No unaltered example remains in this country of a parallel-apsed choir. The cathedrals of the Old and New Foundation, whose Norman choir arms are known to have been planned in this manner include Canterbury (Fig. 4), Bath, Durham, Ely, Exeter (Fig. 4), Lincoln, Old Sarum (Fig. 4), and Peterborough. In the last named the central apse remains, though it was opened up with arches when a squared retrochoir was built in the fifteenth century. S. Albans and Southwell, cathedrals of the Modern Foundation, afforded variants of the parallel-apsed plan. The great abbey church of S. Albans, begun in 1077, had an arrangement of seven apses in echelon, for in addition to the three apses of the choir, two were thrown out to the east of each transept (Fig. 4). As at Lincoln the choir was divided from its aisles by solid walls, but elsewhere there were open arcades. At Southwell the sanctuary was square-ended but the aisles terminated in apses.

The parallel-apsed plan had one disadvantage; it was most inconvenient for processional purposes and for the circulation of pilgrims who might flock to the sanctuary to visit saintly relics on or beyond the High Altar. The difficulty was overcome at Hereford cathedral by making the three apses project from the eastern wall of the square-ended choir (Fig. 4). Here, the High Altar was set up between the easternmost piers of the choir, the bay beyond serving as an ambulatory that afforded access to the central apse. Each of the lateral apses was entered through a tower at the east end of the choir aisle.

The second and more complex type of choir-plan employed by the Normans in the greater English churches was the apse-and-ambulatory, or the peri-apsidal plan. In this form of lay-out the sanctuary terminated in an eastern apse, around which the aisles were continued as an ambulatory or procession path. The apse itself was pierced with a series of arches, and radiating from the ambulatory at the north-east, east and south-east were low apsidal chapels. By passing round the ambulatory, processions could visit the chapels without having to retrace their steps and the piloting of pilgrims was made easy.

The cathedrals of Gloucester and Norwich present outstanding examples of peri-apsidal planning. The choir of Gloucester is fairly intact (Fig. 4), despite the removal of the apse piers and the eastern chapel when the eastern arm was remodelled in the fourteenth century. At Norwich, begun in 1096, practically the whole of the Norman choir and ambulatory survive today, although the easternmost chapel was removed late in the twelfth century to make way for a large Lady Chapel. The two radiating chapels that remain are double-segments on plan (Fig. 12).

Of the twenty or more Norman churches that were built with apse-and-ambulatory choirs, the majority were monastic and include Worcester, Winchester, Chester and Conrad's Choir at Canterbury (Fig. 4). Old S. Paul's, Chichester (Fig. 4), and Lichfield were the only secular cathedrals whose eastern arms were peri-apsidal; the plan appeared in a modified form at Winchester cathedral, where a long apsidal chapel projected eastwards from the ambulatory, but the aisles were square at the east (Fig. 6). The choir arm of Chester was similar, the aisles of which ended in apsidal chapels.

Without equal amongst Anglo-Norman churches as regards the complexity of its plan was Conrad's 'Glorious Choir' at Canterbury, 1096–1126. The parallel apses of Lanfranc's church had stood for less than twenty years, when the rebuilding of a new eastern arm was embarked upon, that doubled the length of the cathedral. It was indeed a complete church added on to the Norman nave and transepts, comprising an aisled nave, a presbytery, transepts with paired apsidal chapels and a peri-apsidal sanctuary. The choir transepts were copied from the famous abbey church of Cluny in Burgundy, c. 1090. From the ambulatory radiated three chapels, the easternmost rectangular and the others apsidal; and in the angle of each transept stood a small square tower (Fig. 4). The new choir, completed by Prior Conrad was

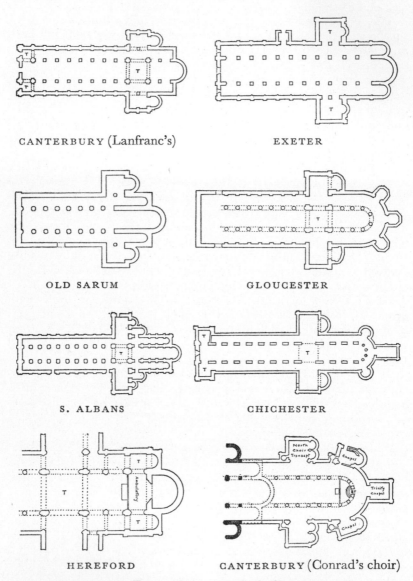

FIG 4. Norman cathedrals

consecrated in 1130, was certainly the latest word in choir planning.

Strange is it that the apse-and-ambulatory plan, so favoured in this country, was rare in Normandy, the preference there being for parallel apses. It was common enough in Burgundy, Auvergne and Poitou and seems to have been borrowed from these districts by the planners and builders who came to England and who were not necessarily *all* Normans. The abbey of Fécamp in Normandy, begun in 1082, was however planned with a peri-apsidal choir, and when Herbert de Losinga, the prior, was translated to the see of Norwich in 1096, the new cathedral he erected there was modelled on Fécamp. Significant is it that Bishop Herbert was not a Norman but a Lorrainer.

Until about 1130, when Benedictine monasticism was losing its pre-eminence and was being superseded by the austere Cistercian Order, the apsidal methods of planning held the field in the monastic and secular cathedrals of England. Peterborough abbey was the last great example of parallel apses, begun *c.* 1117; and Conrad's choir at Canterbury was the last of the peri-apsidal type.

There was considerable variation in the planning of the transepts of Anglo-Norman cathedrals. In their simplest form they were unaisled, but invariably had an apsidal chapel projecting from the east, as at Canterbury (Fig. 4), Old Sarum (Fig. 4) and Norwich (Fig. 12). The transepts at Durham cathedral were planned with eastern aisles to furnish room for additional altars (Fig. 11). At Ely and in the Norman cathedral of Old S. Paul's each transept had eastern and western aisles; at Winchester there were also return aisles across the transept ends (Fig. 9).

Subsequent development of cathedral planning in the Middle Ages was marked by two features that became characteristically English. The first was the substitution in one form or another of a square-ended choir in place of the apsidal; and secondly a general elongation of the eastern arm of our greater churches.

By the end of the twelfth century, the squaring of the choir became the normal English practice, the result of the Cistercian importation deriving from Burgundy. From the time of their first establishment at Waverley in Surrey, in 1128, the Cistercian Order employed the square east end almost without exception in planning their churches. By the year 1150, fifty Cistercian monasteries had been founded in England and Wales, and from the simplicity of their church planning, there gradually evolved a lay-out that was destined to influence the planning of the cathedrals and greater churches. Especially was this so in the Cistercian churches of Yorkshire, such as Byland and Jervaulx, whose choirs were virtually squared versions of the apse-and-ambulatory plan. In these churches the choir was square and the aisles were carried beyond as an ambulatory. The earliest secular cathedral to adopt the square presbytery was Old Sarum. Excavations undertaken early in the present century show that *c.* 1150 the apses of Bishop Osmund's church were taken down and a new choir four bays in length was built with a squared ambulatory and a row of three eastern chapels (Fig. 5). Ten or fifteen years later Archbishop Roger Pont d'Eveque replaced the Norman apses of York choir by a wider and longer choir rectangular on plan, with a squared procession path at the east. From the north and south aisles of Roger's choir projected small transeptal chapels. Nothing remains of this late Norman work save part of the crypt on which it was raised. In the Cistercian church of Abbey Dore, Hereford, dating *c.* 1190, the low ambulatory beyond the squared sanctuary was and is double-aisled, the outer aisle being divided into five chapels. This plan was further developed at Southwark cathedral (formerly the church of an Augustinian priory), *c.* 1230 (Fig. 18). There, the triple aisles east of the sanctuary, provided a spacious ambulatory or retrochoir, with four chapels at the east, and originally the second bay from the south was prolonged eastwards to provide a Lady Chapel that stood until 1830. With the choir of Southwark may be coupled that of Glasgow cathedral, *c.* 1235 in respect of its planning (Fig. 5) (Appendix A).

But despite Cistercian innovations Benedictine conservatism died hard, notably at Canterbury. In 1174 Conrad's 'Glorious Choir' was destroyed by fire, and the monks immediately set about a reconstruction that was to be a replica of the burnt-out building. The master mason, William de Sens, however, expanded the original plan by the addition of a peri-apsidal extension (Pl. 9) and a circular chapel at the extreme east (Fig. 16). The extension was an afterthought, apparently inspired by the cult of S. Thomas the Martyr, and the result was the most complex plan that had ever been conceived in church-building in this country. At the junction of the choir and the Saints chapel, a curious irregularity occurs, the arcade of the latter being out of alignment with that of the choir. As the convent wished to retain the chapels flanking Conrad's ambulatory, William de Sens had to constrict the choir at that point, but beyond he expanded the Saint's chapel in horse-shoe fashion (Fig. 16).

Cistercian methods of choir-planning were alike disregarded by the great Bishop Hugh of Avalon when he embarked on the complete remodelling of the Norman choir of Lincoln cathedral in 1192. His reconstruction, a great part of which is still standing,

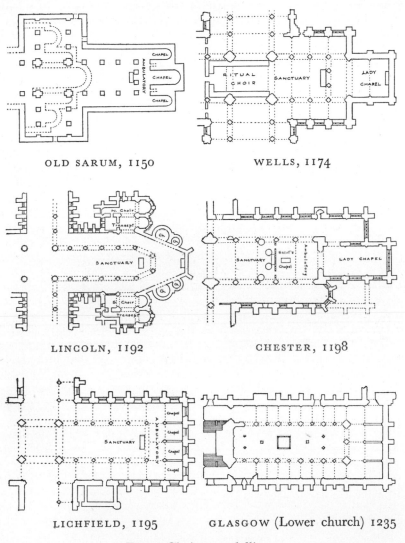

FIG 5. Choir remodelling

comprised an aisled choir of five bays terminating at the east in a three-sided apse, encircled by an ambulatory, from which opened four apsidal chapels. The choir is flanked on the north and south by transepts, each having coupled apsidal chapels at the east, a feature that was undoubtedly borrowed from the choir of Canterbury (Fig. 5).

The extensive reconstruction of the eastern arm of Chichester cathedral necessitated by the disastrous fire of 1186 resolved itself into a scheme for squaring and elongating the whole of the choir. The Norman apse and ambulatory together with the radiating chapels were swept away and replaced by a squared retrochoir, embracing an ambulatory of two bays with a rectangular Lady Chapel as an eastern annexe (Fig. 10). The work was completed by 1210 and in 1276 the bay behind the High Altar was enclosed with screens and made the Saint's chapel, wherein was placed the shrine of S. Richard, formerly Bishop Richard of Wych, d. 1253 and canonized 1261. Towards the close of the thirteenth century the Lady Chapel was lengthened by two bays.

Only a few years after the new choir of Chichester was begun, an entire rebuilding of Wells cathedral was undertaken by Bishop Reginald de Bohun, 1174–91. Here again the eastern limb was laid out in the new fashion, consisting of a short presbytery of three bays with aisles, an ambulatory or return aisle across the east end and a square Lady Chapel beyond (Fig. 5). A century later Reginald's choir was replaced by the present eastern arm (p. 94).

The momentous remodelling of Canterbury choir, 1175–84, heralded the great eastern extensions that characterized cathedral-building in the thirteenth century. The whole lay-out at Canterbury had been prompted by the desire of the convent to make their church worthy of the shrine of S. Thomas and to promote pilgrimages thereto. No longer were the relics of the murdered archbishop to be immured in the gloom of the Norman crypt; they must be translated to a gorgeous shrine that was to be set up, above ground in the Saint's chapel to the east of the High Altar; and in the circular chapel or Corona at the extreme east was to be a casket for relics of S. Thomas. Further the choir was planned to permit easy access to the Saint's chapel and to provide space for the shepherding of throngs of pilgrims. Canterbury set the fashion; one of the chief reasons for the elongation of the choirs in other great cathedrals, despite differences in the method employed, was the provision of a saint's chapel.

Of importance also, in the influence on choir-extensions, was the increased veneration that was paid to the Virgin Mary, in whose honour a chapel dedicated to Our Lady was regarded as a necessity in every church of any size, whether secular or monastic, from the thirteenth century onwards. From the early centuries of the Christian faith the saints and martyrs had been regarded as intercessors for the living, and in course of time the Virgin Mary as the 'Queen of Heaven' took precedence amongst the host of saints. The cult of Mary-veneration was fostered by the Church; Pope Innocent III, 1160–1216, under whose rule Papal power reached its zenith, did much to further the movement, and early in the thirteenth century the teaching of the Franciscan and Dominican friars popularized Virgin-adoration in this country as never before. 'The importance given to the chapel of Our Lady is the ritual development that stamps our thirteenth century cathedrals. . . . The bishops were zealous to make Our Lady the popular deity in England, and her worship thus had the chief place in their secular building.'[1]

In general the Lady Chapel is an unaisled hall, rectangular on plan, and was usually built as an eastern annexe of the retrochoir as at Salisbury, Exeter and Chichester; but the exigencies of the site did not always permit of this. Hence the varying positions of the Lady Chapel in the cathedrals and greater churches. At Durham the late Norman Lady Chapel stands at the west end of the nave. In 1175 Bishop Pudsey started to build a chapel of Our Lady at the east end of the cathedral, just beyond the shrine of S. Cuthbert. Cracks and settlements began to appear in the walls, which the monks attributed to S. Cuthbert's dislike of anything feminine; and the chapel was accordingly transferred to the other end of the cathedral, in the cramped space between the west front and the steep cliff above the Wear. 'Pudsey's Galilee' as it is called is a rectangular building divided into five aisles, all of equal width (Fig. 11).

There were no less than three chapels dedicated to the Virgin Mary in Canterbury cathedral. In the Norman church the two eastern bays of the north aisle of the nave were enclosed with screens to serve as a Lady Chapel, an arrangement that continued when the nave was rebuilt late in the fourteenth century. The whole of the crypt of Conrad's choir, completed c. 1105, was dedicated to Our Lady, and at a later period the two eastern bays of the central area were fenced with stone screens, still *in situ*, to form the Chapel of Our Lady of the Undercroft (Fig. 6). In the centre stood a silver image of the Virgin Mary, and silver lamps hung from the vault which was coloured a deep blue and studded with tiny mirrors to represent the ethereal vault itself. But the

---

[1] *The Cathedral Builders in England.* E. S. Prior. 1905.

crypt was cold and draughty in winter, and in 1448–55 a third Lady Chapel was built to the east of the north transept on the site of the small Norman apse (Fig. 16).

Bristol was remarkable in having two Lady Chapels. The Elder to the east of the north transept was commenced c. 1220, and less than a century later, another Chapel of Our Lady was erected in the normal position, east of the ambulatory (Fig. 21). Contemporary with the Elder Chapel of Bristol is the Lady Chapel of Oxford cathedral. The proximity of the city wall made it impossible to erect a chapel as an eastern annexe, and the problem was solved by adding an outer aisle to the north aisle of the choir (Fig. 14). A similar expedient was resorted to at Ripon, where, in the fourteenth century the 'Lady Loft' as it was called was built above the Norman sacristy that flanks the south wall of the choir (Fig. 23). In addition to the eastern Lady Chapel at Wells cathedral, another of the same dedication was erected in the last quarter of the fifteenth century, off the east walk of the cloisters (Fig. 17). The 'goodly Lady Chapel in the Cloysters' that occupied the site of an earlier chapel was a cruciform building, destroyed in 1552.

Early in the fourteenth century the convent at Rochester converted the south transept of the cathedral into a Lady Chapel, and in 1512 it was enlarged by adding a nave of three bays at the west (Fig. 11). At Ely, the Chapel of Our Lady, 1321–41, stands outside the choir on the north side (Fig. 19), and in the same relative position was the Lady Chapel, now destroyed, at Peterborough (Fig. 13).

In the eastern arms of Old S. Paul's, Lincoln and York, all of which were planned as aisled rectangles, no special chapel was erected for Virgin adoration, the altars dedicated to Our Lady being placed beneath the great east window of the choir.

Hereford cathedral presents an early example of choir-extension, 1186–1200. With the object of providing a square retrochoir with ambulatory and Lady Chapel, the three Norman apses were taken down, but little progress seems to have been made until well into the thirteenth century. The Lady Chapel at the extreme east, raised on a lofty crypt, was not begun until c. 1222. Later in the thirteenth century, the scheme of remodelling was elaborated by expanding the retrochoir laterally; low eastern transepts were added, each of which provided two chapels with western aisles to afford free passage thereto (Fig. 15).

At Lichfield cathedral, extension followed extension. Towards the close of the twelfth century a clean sweep was made of the Norman cathedral; the peri-apsidal choir and its chapels were replaced by a square east end, laid out with a low double-aisled retrochoir on the model of Abbey Dore (Fig. 5); but this new east-arm, finished *c.* 1210 lacked a Lady Chapel and a Saint's chapel for the shrine of S. Chad. For more than a century, whilst the transepts, the nave, the central tower and the chapter house were in course of construction, Lichfield was without these almost indispensable adjuncts. However, under the rule of Bishop Walter Langton, 1291–1321, a large and lofty Lady Chapel with a three-sided apse was commenced some distance east of the existing choir. By 1337 the old east end was taken down and the Lady Chapel was joined up to the choir by the insertion of an additional bay, in which was installed the shrine of S. Chad. The bay to the west of the High Altar, the normal position of the Saint's chapel, served as the ambulatory (Fig. 19).

The closing years of the twelfth century witnessed the initiation of a scheme for extending the choir-arm of the abbey church of S. Werburgh, now Chester cathedral. The peri-apsidal choir was demolished to give place to one on a much larger scale with a retrochoir and Lady Chapel, a project that was not completed until 1315. The new choir-arm was five bays in length, its eastern wall being pierced with one arch that opens directly into the Lady Chapel. The aisles terminated in three-sided apses (Fig. 5). The High Altar now stands in front of the arch, a most inconvenient arrangement for a pilgrimage church in the Middle Ages, for beyond the Altar space had to be provided for the shrine of S. Werburgh as well as an ambulatory linking up the north and south aisles of the choir, and an entry into the Lady Chapel. In pre-Reformation days the High Altar undoubtedly stood against a screen at a point one or two bays west of the Lady Chapel; thereby the ritual choir would not have been unduly short, as it extended westwards into the crossing. In the fifteenth century the aisles of the choir were lengthened and doorways made in the walls of the Lady Chapel. The pedestal of S. Werburgh's shrine is now placed at the west end of the chapel.

A big eastern extension was undertaken about 1200 at Winchester cathedral. The Norman apse of the sanctuary was allowed to remain undisturbed but to the east was planned a spacious squared retrochoir of three bays, with a Lady Chapel at the east flanked by chapels (Fig. 9). The central body of the retrochoir was made the Saint's chapel for the shrine of S. Swithun; the surrounding aisles gave ample space for processions and pilgrim-visitations. The reconstruction occupied about thirty-five years, and almost a century elapsed before the Norman apse was removed to permit of the rebuilding of the presbytery, which was finished by about 1360. The Lady Chapel was lengthened in 1494–1500.

Of the same period as the Winchester extension was the remodelling of the choir-arm of Rochester cathedral, 1200–27. Envious of the fame of S. Thomas of Canterbury and of the splendid chapel that contained his shrine, the convent at Rochester must needs have their local saint, William of Perth, who had been murdered near by in 1201, though official canonization was not obtained until 1256. The reconstruction at Rochester comprised an unaisled presbytery of three bays with north and south choir transepts each having an eastern aisle that furnished space for two chapels (Fig. 11). As the presbytery was without aisles, the shrine of S. William was set up in the north choir transept instead of behind the High Altar.

The removal of the see of Old Sarum to Salisbury in 1219 afforded a rare opportunity of erecting a great cathedral on a virgin site, unhampered by the remains or even the foundations of pre-existing buildings. Perfectly suited to the ritualistic requirements of the time, the regular and symmetrical plan of Salisbury cathedral may be regarded as the English ideal of the early thirteenth century. Begun in 1220 and completed within fifty years, Salisbury consists of an aisled nave of ten bays, a north-west porch, transepts of three bays with eastern aisles, an aisled choir seven bays in length, choir transepts two bays in depth, a retrochoir and an eastern Lady Chapel (Fig. 1). The choir transepts have eastern aisles, the only instance in England; and the choir, ambulatory and Lady Chapel are all square-ended. All Norman tradition was here cast aside and the plan is essentially English, uninfluenced by the complexities of contemporary cathedral planning in the Ile de France.

Similar to the lay-out of the new choir of Rochester is that of Worcester, dating c. 1224, and here again the shrine of the local saint was the *raison d'être*, and the offerings of the pilgrims furnished the means. The Norman apse and ambulatory were taken down and the eastern limb of the cathedral was entirely rebuilt and doubled in length in the process. The presbytery was planned in five bays with aisles and was flanked by eastern transepts; the bay behind the High Altar served as an ambulatory and beyond was the Lady Chapel, three bays in length, the two western bays being aisled. The shrine of S. Wulstan occupied a position to the north of the High Altar (Fig. 22).

Of the same general type was the planning of the new choir-arm of Southwell minster, Notts., 1230–50. The old and short Norman choir was replaced by a presbytery, retrochoir, choir transepts and two aisleless bays at the east that may have housed the altar of Our Lady (Fig. 10). There was no shrine at South-well, so no provision was made for a saint's chapel.

Amongst the schemes of choir-extension and re-modelling at this period, those of Durham and S. David's, Pembroke, are unique in cathedral planning. The inadequacy of Carileph's Nor-man choir at Durham, where the shrine of S. Cuthbert stood in the central apse behind the High Altar, and the shortage of altars at the east were all too apparent; and in 1242–80 the spreading Transept of the Nine Altars, modelled on that at Fountains abbey, was built athwart the east end of the cathedral (Fig. 11). The altars were set up against the east wall of the transept, the middle one being dedicated to S. Cuthbert and S. Baeda, the others 'equally devided of either hand, as on the south foure, and on the north foure, and betwixt everye altar a very faire and large parti-tion of wainscott all varnished over'. The shrine of S. Cuthbert was placed on an elevated platform of masonry that projected into the eastern transept from behind the High Altar. Much ingenuity was displayed in the arrangement of the new retrochoir of S. David's, as undertaken in the middle of the thirteenth century. The aisles of the choir were prolonged two bays eastwards and were connected by a north-to-south ambulatory. These three 'walks' enclosed a small oblong court, open to the sky and bounded on the west by the east wall of the sanctuary, which remained un-touched (Fig. 21). The purpose of the open court was to ensure adequate lighting of the sanctuary by the two tiers of lancet win-dows in the east wall. At the north-east and south-east angles of the ambulatory projected a small chapel, and about 1280 a rec-tangular Lady Chapel was built in the normal position at the east. Early in the sixteenth century the open court was converted into a chantry chapel by Bishop Vaughan who roofed it with a fan vault.

During the sixty years commencing *c.* 1270 the eastern limb of Exeter cathedral was completely transformed. The scheme was initiated by Bishop Walter Bronscombe, 1257–80; and embraced the building of a new choir, little less than the nave in length, a square retrochoir, a spacious Lady Chapel at the extreme east with a small chapel on either side, and small choir transepts (Fig. 22). Bronscombe's successor put the scheme into operation and the work of reconstruction proceeded for half a century, followed by the rebuilding of the nave. In the course of a century or more the Norman cathedral of Exeter was transmuted into a great Gothic structure.

With the exception of Canterbury, Lincoln and Durham, the

remodellings of the thirteenth century dealt with above fall into two distinct classes.

1. Those in which the sanctuary terminates in a wall pierced by one or more arches that open into the low retrochoir and ambulatory beyond.

2. Those in which there is no architectural division of choir and retrochoir, the arcades being continuous from west to east, and the High Altar being placed against a screen, usually of stone.

Of the first type are Hereford (one arch), Southwark (two arches, blocked by a lofty reredos), Exeter (two arches), and Salisbury (three arches). On the other hand, choirs with continuous arcades occur at Chichester, Lichfield, Rochester, Worcester and Southwell, in which the eastern arm terminates in an unaisled sanctuary or a Lady Chapel.

From the latter type was evolved the final and definitive method of planning the choir-arm of the English cathedral, which for want of a better term can best be described as the aisled rectangle. The choir and its aisles stop dead at the lofty eastern wall, with no Lady Chapel as an eastern annexe nor any other extension. Unlike the Salisbury type, which clearly defines the sanctuary, the retrochoir, and the Lady Chapel, the aisled rectangle maintains its full height from west to east (p. 94). The disposition of the various parts, of the indispensable Saint's chapel, of the ambulatory and the Lady Chapel, and of other altars was merely a matter of internal partitioning. The High Altar was placed against a screen three or four bays west of the eastern wall; behind the High Altar and fenced with screening was the Saint's chapel; the next bay to the east was the ambulatory, and the altar of Our Lady stood beneath the great east window. Other altars were placed at the ends of the choir aisles and against the piers of the retrochoir. Eastern transepts could be dispensed with. Simple in the extreme, the aisled-rectangle plan was adopted for the choirs of some of the greatest cathedrals in the country, notably at Ely, Old S. Paul's and Lincoln in the thirteenth century. The advantage of such a plan lay in the improvement of interior lighting. Further, the actual construction was simplified and involved far less labour than the building of the complex lay-out of the Salisbury type.

The choir of Ely cathedral, 1235–52, furnishes the earliest existing example of the aisled rectangle in a church of the first rank.[1] The parallel apses of the Norman cathedral were torn down

[1] It made its appearance as early as 1160 at S. Cross church, Winchester; and when Archbishop Roger Pont d'Eveque rebuilt Ripon minster c. 1180, he planned an aisled choir six bays long and square-ended at the east. It was co-extensive with the present choir; though largely rebuilt in 1288, after the collapse of the eastern bays, it has not been materially lengthened since (Fig. 23).

and the eastern arm was lengthened by six bays, the ritual divisions being demarcated by screens (Fig. 19). The High Altar was placed, in its present position, two bays distant from the east wall; the shrine of S. Etheldreda stood beyond the High Altar, and the easternmost bay of the choir-arm served as an ambulatory. Apparently there was no altar to the Virgin Mary in the retro-choir, and when in 1321, a Lady Chapel was needed, it was erected *outside* the choir on the north. The collapse of the central tower of Ely in 1322 necessitated the reconstruction of the Norman bays at the west end of the choir. Thus completed the plan of Ely choir is an aisled rectangle nine bays in length.

Eastern extensions on the same lines followed hard upon that of Ely. In 1256 the choir of Old S. Paul's cathedral was transformed; it was lengthened by eight bays, after which the Norman bays at the western end were recast to bring them into harmony with the new work. Twelve bays long, the Gothic choir of London's vast cathedral was the longest and the greatest in the land, imparting a total length of 586 feet to this famous church (Fig. 19). Beyond the High Altar that occupied the fifth bay from the east were the Saint's chapel, containing the shrine of S. Erkenwald, the ambulatory, and a Lady Chapel in the two eastern bays fenced with screens.

The elongation of the noble cathedral at Lincoln, by the addition of the Angel Choir, begun in 1256, was the outcome of a Papal injunction that the remains of S. Hugh should be translated to a more honourable place in the cathedral than the chapel in the north choir transept where they had long rested. The three-sided apse and ambulatory of Bishop Hugh's choir was removed and the choir was lengthened by five bays, modelled on the new choir at Ely (Fig. 20). The High Altar was set up in the fourth bay from the east; behind the Altar screen was the Saint's chapel for the shrine; the next bay to the east was the ambulatory and the most easterly bay was the Lady Chapel. By 1280 the Angel Choir was sufficiently advanced for the translation of S. Hugh to the new shrine that had been made, although the building was not completed until early in the fourteenth century.

After a great fire in 1292, the choir-arm of Carlisle cathedral was entirely rebuilt on the aisled rectangle plan, eight bays in length, an additional bay having been added to provide an ambulatory behind the High Altar (Fig. 14).

Pre-eminent amongst the eastern arms that were planned on this principle in the fourteenth century was that of York, 1361–1405. The twelfth-century choir being quite out of scale with the new nave then all but complete, was extended by four bays by

1373, after which the five western bays were rebuilt (Fig. 23). Approximately the same length as the nave, the new choir-arm of York furnished ample room for the canons' stalls, the sanctuary, an ambulatory, the shrine of S. William of York, and an altar to the Virgin Mary.

In point of time there was no period in which either method of planning held the field against the other. The magnificent aisled choirs of Old S. Paul's, Ely and Lincoln undoubtedly dictated the lay-out of the choir of York, but in the south-west Bristol and Wells followed the Salisbury plan. The monks of S. Albans modelled their eastern extension, 1257–1320, on that of Winchester (Fig. 13). The choir-arm of Wells, c. 1295–1340, is perhaps the finest of its kind in England, the culmination of the Salisbury type. The arrangement of the retrochoir, Lady Chapel and of the projecting chapels on either side, affords cross vistas that are unsurpassed for sheer loveliness in any other English cathedral. The Lady Chapel, the first part to be erected, is an irregular octagon on plan, the three western sides consisting of arches that open into the ambulatory (Fig. 17). Obviously its plan was influenced by that of the chapter house. Most remarkable is the two-bayed retrochoir, in the middle of which are four additional piers enclosing a square space that may have been intended for the shrine of Bishop William de Marchia, had his canonization been procured from Rome. The choir and sanctuary were then undertaken, the work on the six bays proceeding from east to west. As at Salisbury, the sanctuary terminates in a lofty wall carried by three arches that afford glimpses of the retrochoir and Lady Chapel.

The two methods of choir-planning exemplified at Salisbury and Ely were each distinguished by a particular form of elevation that is at once apparent when the cathedral is viewed from the exterior.

In the Salisbury type, the retrochoir and Lady Chapel are roofed at descending levels, in order that the sanctuary should be adequately lighted by the window in the upper part of the east wall. Externally, the east end presents a step-like arrangement of its parts, a grouping that demands 'a lofty central tower to which the eye is carried up, a climax to the pyramidal outline' (*Bond*). At Salisbury the tower and spire were an afterthought, the masons of the fourteenth century realizing the necessity of a crowning centrepiece.

The aisled-rectangle plan of Ely or York is devoid of the complexity of varying roof levels; the whole of the eastern limb continues at its full height from the crossing to the lofty east wall and the roof is therefore level along its entire length.

Peterborough was far behind the times as regards choir-remodelling. Until the last decade of the fifteenth century the parallel apses of the early twelfth century remained unchanged and even then the elongation was of modest dimensions. The lateral apses were removed and beyond the central apse was built a low square-ended annexe of the same width as the choir and deep enough to provide an ambulatory and space for three or more altars against the east wall (Fig. 13).

Both the Salisbury and Ely methods of east-end planning were peculiarly English. The cathedral builders adopted and adapted the squared choir, a Burgundian importation of the twelfth century, and subsequently evolved plans that utterly diverged from the Continental model. Henceforward the apse was cast aside; its re-appearance at Canterbury in 1175, and in Gothic form at Westminster abbey in 1245 was in each case due to French influence. The square choir-arm is extremely rare in France. The only cathedral of the first rank there with a squared choir is Laon; the mighty cathedrals of Notre Dame (Paris), Chartres, Amiens, Le Mans, Reims and Beauvais, to name a few that were reared in the Ile de France during the great outburst of cathedral building, 1160–1240, adopted an almost standard type of plan, generally termed the chevet, and from then onwards there was hardly any alteration in the planning of the Gothic cathedrals of Northern France. The chevet was the Gothic version of the peri-apsidal plan of Auvergne and Burgundy; the radiating chapels were increased in number and became polygonal on plan, and sometimes the ambulatory was double-aisled.[1]

Although the eastern arm of the English cathedral had been subjected to drastic changes in the thirteenth century, few changes were wrought in the planning of transepts and nave. The great Norman cathedrals usually had deep transepts often with eastern chapels or aisles. In the rebuildings of the thirteenth and fourteenth centuries aisled transepts were invariably the rule. At Salisbury the main transepts provided six chapels in all (Fig. 1), and at Wells and York the transepts were furnished with eastern and western aisles.

Few variations occurred in the planning of the cathedral nave in the Gothic centuries. In the second half of the thirteenth century the character of the nave of Chichester was altered by the addition of lateral chapels that form outer aisles on either side

---

[1] The choir-arm of Westminster abbey is a perfect example of the French chevet. The rebuilding, 1245–69, was a royal undertaking and Henry III sought inspiration for the planning of the abbey church in the cathedrals of Reims and Amiens. But the chevet was foreign to English ideals and the choir at Westminster had no influence as regards its lay-out upon the English cathedral plan of the Middle Ages.

(Fig. 10). The chapels of S. George and S. Cuthbert on the south side were each two bays in length, as were also two of the three chapels on the north, and they were all separated by walls or reredoses. Their construction entailed the piercing of the aisle walls with arches, and the erection of outer walls and vaulting. Chichester is the only cathedral that has chapels flanking the aisles of the nave, though they are fairly common in France, e.g. at Notre Dame (Paris) and Bourges.

Exceptional are western transepts, the purpose of which was to provide room for more altars. Towards the end of the twelfth century transepts with apses were thrown out at the west end of Ely nave, and when the nave of Peterborough was completed c. 1195, shallow transepts were built flanking the twin towers at the west (Fig. 13). Altars so far distant from the choir were found to be inconvenient, and western transepts were never in general favour, though they appeared at Lincoln cathedral c. 1240.

Where there were twin towers at the west, it was the normal practice to build them above the extremities of the aisles of the nave. A notable exception was at Wells cathedral, where the towers were erected outside the aisles, by which means greater width was given to the west front, c. 1320, a vast screen designed for the display of imagery (Fig. 17). The towers were incorporated in the façade, the tiers of statues being carried round the sides. A few years earlier, the monks of S. Albans had undertaken the lengthening of their church, and their intention was to build western towers that should flank the aisles. From its inception the work was grossly mismanaged and the building of the towers had to be abandoned. At the end of the south aisle of the nave is to be seen the lofty arch that would have opened into the south-west tower.

The cathedrals of Durham and Ely are peculiar in the annexes that were tacked on to the west front and were known in the Middle Ages as *Galilees*.[1] That at Durham was the Lady Chapel built by Bishop Pudsey, 1175–85 (p. 171); at Ely the Galilee took the form of a magnificent porch, architecturally one of the finest in Europe, dating 1198–1215. It has an upper chamber or gallery that once commanded a view of the nave and may have been used for the Palm Sunday procession.

---

[1] The name Galilee was given to the last place in the church visited by the Sunday procession, and was so called from the disciples being told that the Master 'would go before them into Galilee'. There is a noble Galilee porch attached to the south transept of Lincoln cathedral.

23. Winchester; choir stalls

24. Chester; the sedilia

25. Canterbury; mural painting of S. Paul

27. Ely; pedestal of S. Etheldreda's shrine

26. Chester: choir stalls

28 & 29. Hereford; reliquary of S. Thomas of Canterbury

31. S. Albans; Norman triforium in the south transept

30. Salisbury; chapter house

33. Rochester; portal of the west front

32. Lincoln; Norman recesses in the west front

Where was the Norman crypt

36. Oxford; north choir arcade

35. Gloucester; north nave arcade

37. Winchester; the Norman crypt

38. Ely; view from the north aisle of the nave

39. Durham; the nave from the west

40. Southwell; the nave looking east

43. Worcester; Transitional and Perpendicular bays of the nave

44. Norwich; east wall of the north transept

45. Exeter; north transeptal tower

8. The Crypt
in the English Cathedral

Early Christian Tradition in Italy · The Cubicula in the Catacombs outside Rome · Confessios beneath the High Altar of Basilican Churches · The Crypt of the Saxon Cathedral of Canterbury · The Seventh-Century Crypt at Ripon Cathedral · Anglo-Norman Crypts in the Monastic Cathedrals · The Apse-and-Ambulatory Plan · Aisling of the Central Area · The Double Crypt at Canterbury · The Late Norman Example at York · Abandonment of Crypt Building after the Eastern Extension at Canterbury · The Gothic Crypts of Rochester, Hereford, and Old S. Paul's

❬ A NOTEWORTHY FEATURE of several English cathedrals that were built or rebuilt in the eleventh and twelfth centuries is the crypt beneath the choir-arm, a survival of the tradition of the Early Christian Church in Italy. Before the Christian faith was legalized by the Emperor Constantine in A.D. 323 it had been the custom to bury the bodies of the saints and martyrs in the Catacombs outside Rome, and in course of time the chambers or *cubicula* containing the relics became objects of pilgrimage. Pope Damasus I, 366–84, affixed inscriptions in the Catacombs of S. Callixtus to direct pilgrims to the sacred burial places. When Christianity emerged from the gloom of the Catacombs, churches were erected over the graves of the saints. The vast basilican church of S. Peter's, Rome and the church of S. Sebastian on the Appian Way owe their foundation to the martyrs' graves on the sites. As time went on, the remains of the more notable saints were translated to basilican churches in Rome, and the practice was adopted of constructing a small undercroft or *confessio* beneath the High Altar to contain them. This was the prototype of the crypt; it was an Italian usage, a memory of the sacred burial places of the age of persecution. Outside Italy crypts were not necessarily the resting places or repositories of the sanctified dead, but were in the tradition and sentiment of the Early Church. The line of development was from the tomb under the altar to the undercroft beneath the sanctuary.

The crypt made its appearance in England in pre-Conquest

D

days. In the Saxon cathedral of Canterbury, a crypt extended beneath the apsidal sanctuary at the east 'fabricated in the likeness of the confessionary of S. Peter [at Rome] the vault of which was raised so high that the part above could only be reached by many steps. Within, this crypt had at the east an altar.'[1]

The most ancient crypt in this country is that of Ripon cathedral, dating 671–8. It is all that remains of the basilican church founded by Bishop Wilfrid of Northumbria, who imported craftsmen from Italy to build it 'in the Roman manner'. This is confirmed by the character of the masonry and the vault, which is far in advance of any Saxon building of the period. Originally the crypt lay immediately below the High Altar of Wilfrid's church, but is now beneath the crossing of the cathedral (Fig. 3).

It is a rectangular chamber approximately 11 feet by 8 feet and is roofed with a Roman barrel vault. On the north, west and south are narrow passages, the southern of which has been extended westwards to provide access from the nave. In accordance with Italian custom an altar was placed at the west end, and in the east wall is a window that commanded a view of the interior and of the relics deposited therein.

In our Norman cathedrals is a remarkable series of crypts, five of which are in what were monastic churches of the Benedictine Order, and were built within a space of twenty years in the late eleventh century. In chronological sequence they are: Rochester (1077), Winchester (1079), Worcester (1084), Gloucester (1089), and Canterbury (1095). Lanfranc's cathedral at Canterbury begun in 1070 was raised on a crypt, but the reconstruction of the choir in 1096 involved a clearance of the site and the planning of a new crypt by Prior Ernulf. The only secular cathedral of the same period that was built with a crypt was Old S. Paul's, London (1087). For other reasons than the date the late Norman crypt of York cathedral (1160–70) cannot be included in the monastic group.

The marshy nature of the soil precluded the construction of crypts in the cathedrals of Ely, Norwich and Peterborough.

With the exception of the crypt of Lanfranc's cathedral at Canterbury and probably that of Rochester, the Benedictine crypts were planned with an eastern apse and an encircling ambulatory, a determining feature of the superstructure. At Winchester and Worcester the crypts indicate the lay-out of the choirs of those cathedrals prior to their remodelling in the thirteenth century.

---

[1] The quotation is from the writings of Edmer, the precentor of Canterbury, who was a boy in the school of Christ Church priory when Lanfranc rebuilt the cathedral, 1070–7.

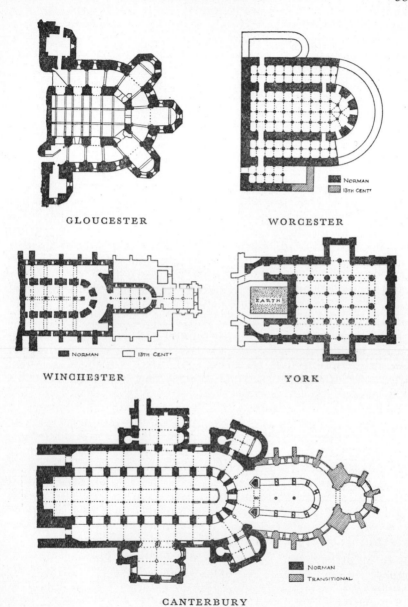

FIG 6. Norman cathedral crypts

The Benedictine crypts are planned with a wide central area or nave, flanked by aisles, the dividing arcades being carried by huge masses of masonry on which were erected the piers of the choir above. They are all roofed with groined vaults which support the pavement of the choir. To simplify the construction of the vaulting over so wide a span, the central area is subdivided into two or more aisles by circular columns that carry the vaulting. In the crypt of Winchester cathedral the nave has two internal aisles (Fig. 6); the flanking aisles are squared at the east end and from the centre of the ambulatory projects a long apsidal chapel, divided into two aisles by a central arcade of four bays.

The Norman crypt at Gloucester is an almost perfect example of the peri-apsidal type and forms a complete church below ground level. The nave which is 30 feet wide is triple-aisled and the three radiating chapels are apsidal within but polygonal externally. Here the crypt extends beneath the eastern chapels of the transepts (Fig. 6). At Worcester the central area is divided into four aisles by no less than thirty columns, and the aisles that flank the nave are double and are separated from the nave by solid walls instead of by arcades (Fig. 6). The ambulatory of the crypt was filled in and blocked up when the choir was re-modelled in 1224.

The crypt at Canterbury is the largest in any mediaeval church in England. In fact it comprises two crypts; a western that lies beneath Ernulf's choir begun in 1095, and an eastern on which was reared the Saint's chapel and Corona, c. 1180–1 (Fig. 6). The nave of the earlier crypt is divided into three aisles, and has north and south transepts each with two apsidal chapels; and as in the superstructure, there are chapels off the ambulatory. The crypt beneath the Saint's chapel has a central arcade of three bays, and the piers dividing it from the ambulatory are double, the more effectively to carry the double columns above (Pl. 49).

Of the eleventh-century crypt at Rochester only two bays at the west survived the rebuilding of the choir in 1200–20; and at Old S. Paul's the crypt of 1087 was walled up and used as a bone hole when the much larger crypt was built at the east in the great reconstruction of the choir-arm that was begun in 1256.

The last Norman crypt to be built beneath an English cathedral was that of York, c. 1160, when Archbishop Roger extended the choir. It was rectangular on plan with north and south aisles four bays in length, and with a square ambulatory. The central area was divided into three aisles (Fig. 6). Little of Roger's crypt remained after the remodelling of the choir, but six of the main columns were used to provide a vaulted platform for the High Altar.

Long before the end of the twelfth century, the crypt had fallen out of fashion as a repository of a saint's remains in the cathedrals and greater churches. The momentous eastern extension at Canterbury after the fire of 1174 established the Saint's chapel above ground as an integral part of the choir-arm of the English cathedral. The crowds of pilgrims that surged into Canterbury cathedral after the shrine of S. Thomas had been installed were easily controlled in passing round the ambulatory.[1] Small wonder that other cathedrals followed the lead of Canterbury. As a result, the only cathedral crypts built in the Gothic period were those at Rochester, Hereford and Old S. Paul's, all of the thirteenth century. The Gothic crypts were roofed with quadripartite vaulting.

When the building of the new eastern arm of Rochester cathedral was undertaken in 1200, the greater part of the Norman crypt was removed and the present one erected. The main portions of the Gothic crypt are the presbytery and a long rectangular compartment extending from the north to the south wall of the choir transept, forming as it were a wide vestibule at the west. Both the presbytery and the western area are subdivided into three aisles, that run east to west in the former and north to south in the vestibule (Fig. 7). Corresponding to the church above are two eastern chapels in each of the crypt transepts.

Dating from c. 1220 the crypt at Hereford cathedral was built as a charnel house, and extending only under the Lady Chapel, is planned with a nave and aisles. In the epitaph on the tomb of Andrew Jones, a merchant of Hereford who repaired the crypt in 1497, it is styled 'domus carnaria'.

The largest and finest Gothic crypt in any English cathedral was that of the choir of Old S. Paul's, commenced in 1256. It was eight bays in length and, being 100 feet wide, was divided into four aisles, all of approximately equal width, the arcades being carried by stout clustered piers (Fig. 7). Stretching from north to south, a timber screen divided the crypt into two equal portions; the eastern half was the Jesus chapel, and the western part was allotted to the parishioners of S. Faith whose church had been demolished to make room for the new choir extension. It is of interest that Wren's cathedral is reared on a crypt that extends beneath the whole of the church from east to west.

[1] For the same reason the relics of S. Eleutherus and S. Rusticus in the Abbey of S. Denis, near Paris, were translated from the crypt to the choir in 1144.

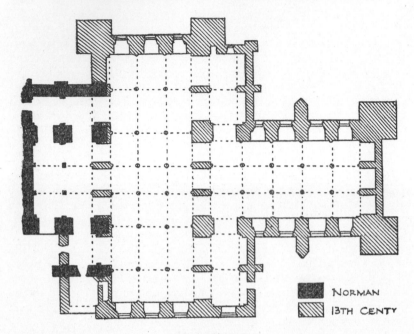

NORMAN

I3TH CENTY

ROCHESTER

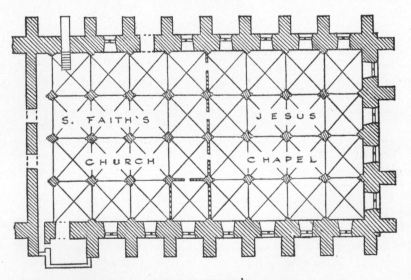

S. FAITH'S

JESUS

CHURCH

CHAPEL

OLD S. PAUL'S

FIG 7. Gothic cathedral crypts

9. Towers and West Fronts

❡ SEEN FROM AFAR the one arresting feature of the English medi-aeval cathedral is the central tower, rising above the roofs of the building of which it forms an integral part. The cruciform plan demands a tower at the crossing, for the lower parts of the tower walls provide the roofs of the nave, transepts and choir with something solid to abut against. With the notable exception of Exeter, all our mediaeval cathedrals have a tower at the crossing, frequently in conjunction with two at the west. The Norman ideal of three towers for the design of their greater churches was not departed from in the succeeding centuries, and thus it is that the cathedrals of Canterbury, Chichester, Durham, Lichfield, Lincoln, Peterborough, Ripon, Southwell, Wells and York have a central and twin western towers (Pl. 11).

The abbey church, now the cathedral of Gloucester was originally built with three towers, but the pair at the west were taken down when that end of the nave was rebuilt in the fifteenth century. S. Albans, the largest Anglo-Norman church of the eleventh century, was planned with a central tower only, but when the nave was lengthened in the thirteenth century, towers were designed to flank the new west front, although they were never raised above the ground level. When the triple-arched western façade of Peterborough was erected *c.* 1200, flanking towers were built to withstand the thrust of the lateral arches, and thus, of the five towers at Peterborough, four are at the western end of the cathedral

(Fig. 13). The third pair of piers from the west end of the nave, which are more massively built than the others, were probably intended as supports for western towers before the nave was prolonged by two bays. Of the three towers of Bristol cathedral, the western pair are modern.

Peculiar to Exeter cathedral are the mighty transeptal towers that are all that remain of the Norman church begun in 1111. In 1285–6 the towers were incorporated into the Gothic cathedral then in process of erection, and were converted into transepts by opening up the inner walls with lofty arches (Fig. 22). In the original disposition of its three towers, Hereford cathedral was even more exceptional; for in addition to the one at the crossing smaller towers were raised over the eastern bays of the choir aisles, an arrangement that was copied from the Romanesque churches of the Rhine valley (Fig. 4).

The cathedrals of Winchester and Ely both had a single tower at the west as well as one at the crossing. Ely retains its western tower but the Norman central tower was replaced by the famous Octagon in the fourteenth century. At Winchester the western tower has gone. Had the original scheme there reached fulfilment, the Norman cathedral would have had no less than six towers, for there is evidence that the intention was to rear towers at the outer angles of each of the transepts.

The only cathedral that retains its complement of three Norman towers is Southwell, Notts. At Durham the squat Norman tower at the crossing was struck by lightning in 1429 and became so ruinous as to necessitate an entire rebuilding, but the twin towers at the west end of the cathedral remain.

The central tower of S. Albans, built mainly of Roman brick, has no peer amongst those of the eleventh century, and that at Norwich is a more slender example of the twelfth century crowned by a later stone spire. Other English cathedrals that have central towers only are Rochester, Gloucester, Hereford, Worcester and above all Salisbury, the spired tower of which has no rival for sheer architectural grace.

Externally, a central tower forms a dominating feature about which the lesser masses of the cathedral, the choir, nave and transepts are grouped and are thereby merged into one architectural ensemble. The pyramidal massing of the various parts of the eastern arm of Salisbury, culminating in the tower and spire, emphasizes the expression of stability that is an essential of all architecture.

Internally a central tower may serve two divergent purposes, viz. as a lantern and as a stabilizer. Where the lower stage is not sealed with a vault or roof, the windows in the tower walls to a limited extent light the area at the crossing, though this is rarely effective, on account of the height of the tower and the smallness of the windows. York and Ely provide outstanding examples of central towers that have a lantern value; in general, the tower at the crossing is roofed with vaulting as at Wells cathedral. Structurally the enormous weight of a tower at the crossing enables the four piers that carry it to resist the gathered thrusts of the arcades of the nave, choir, and transepts.

Not the least remarkable feature of the central tower of the English cathedral is the treatment of the internal walling of the lower stage. From the Norman to the Perpendicular period the walls were often lavishly adorned with arcading or panelling, not always easily visible from below. At Norwich, the walls above the tower arches are faced with three tiers of Norman arcading, the topmost pierced with windows; and at Durham the internal walls of the fifteenth-century tower are overlaid with panelling surmounted by ornate crocketed gables.

Throughout the Middle Ages, central towers were a constant source of anxiety to those responsible for the safety of the fabric. Owing to unsound methods employed in their construction, towers were proverbially unsafe and frequently collapsed without any warning. Particularly was this the case with Norman towers. In 1107 within twenty-five years of its erection, the central tower of Winchester cathedral crashed, its fall being attributed by the monkish chroniclers to the burial of William Rufus beneath it 'who, all his life had been profane and sensual, and had expired without the Christian viaticum'. The circumspect William of Malmesbury was nearer the truth in declaring that the tower would have fallen in any case, from the unsoundness of its workmanship, whether the body of Rufus had been buried there or not. The tower was immediately rebuilt, on more massive piers that were erected at the crossing, the cost being met by funds left to the cathedral by Bishop Walkelyn.

It was only by trial and experiment that mediaeval masons mastered the principles governing stability. 'They began by making their structures as strong as they could; if from bad workmanship and original settlements, the building fell, they made it much bigger next time. Finding it then too large they reduced the next building of the kind, and so by gradual experience were brought to proportions at once safe and beautiful. All their works show that they had no just conception of statical principles, and were guided by natural ingenuity alone, assisted by the numerous opportunities which the Middle Ages afforded for the erection of

D*

churches' (*Willis*). How imperfectly the 'statical principles' that govern the construction of towers on four isolated piers were understood is again evidenced by the catastrophe that befell Lincoln cathedral in 1239. One of the canons was preaching a sermon denouncing the masterful Bishop Grosseteste, who was then at loggerheads with the chapter. 'Were we silent the very stones would cry out for us,' exclaimed the preacher, whereupon the masonry of the central tower fell with a crash, killing three people and causing such damage to the adjoining bays of the choir and transepts that immediate restoration was necessary. The piers at the crossing were reinforced and new arches and stouter walls were put up to carry the present tower which was completed by *c.* 1310.

Ely cathedral owes its particularly glory, the magnificent Octagon, to the collapse of the Norman tower in 1322. The vast lantern flooding the area at the crossing with light is a triumph of ingenuity and mediaeval engineering (p. 248).

Less than a century ago, the insecurity of the central towers at Chichester and Peterborough rendered imperative their entire reconstruction. In 1861 whilst the former was in the process of being underpinned, the spire sank vertically into the tower and both were rebuilt in 1866. At Peterborough, the tower showed signs of breaking up in 1882 and the following year it was pronounced to be in a state of movement. The south-eastern pier at the crossing had been strengthened with iron bands as long ago as 1593, in which year the sum of £47 4s. 9d. was spent on 'the great column near the choir, repaired with iron and timber'. In 1884–6 the tower and the piers that carried it were taken down and rebuilt, more or less on the model of the mediaeval work.

Grave cause for alarm was manifest at S. Albans cathedral in 1870 during the restoration undertaken by Gilbert Scott. The Norman tower at the crossing having betrayed ominous signs of weakness was shored up with timber and walling, but examination revealed that the rubble core of the two eastern piers had decrepitated under the enormous weight of the fabric, and in the south-eastern pier a huge cavity was discovered filled with decaying timber. The piers were reinforced with brickwork and cement and the tower was clamped by iron rods.

The structural expedients resorted to by mediaeval masons when faced with the problem of stabilizing central towers are instanced at Wells, Salisbury and Canterbury. In each case strainer arches were inserted between the piers supporting the tower. The trouble at Wells dated from 1321, when the addition of an upper stage increased the weight of the tower. The extra load

imposed on the four piers at the crossing caused alarming settlements, for the sinking piers tore away the masonry of the adjoining
arcades and produced gaps between the tower arches and the
main walls. The collapse of the tower was arrested in 1338 by the
construction of the inverted or scissor-like arches beneath the
north, west and south arches of the crossing. These somewhat ungainly insertions belittle the architectural character of the nave
and transepts (p. 246).[1] Less dramatic was the method employed
at Salisbury; until 1330 the crossing was roofed with a squat tower
like that at Westminster abbey today. The rearing of a spired tower
was certainly not contemplated by the builders of the thirteenth
century, or the piers that support it would have been more massively built. When the new tower was erected, the walls were constructed of thin shells of masonry with a passage between and were
braced together with iron bars; flying buttresses were put up at the
external angles and others in the triforium and clerestory of the
nave, transepts and choir immediately adjoining the crossing. To
load the four piers with the enormous weight of six thousand tons
was certain to cause displacements and settlements, which in fact
occurred during the building operations. When further signs of
instability became apparent in the fifteenth century girder-arches
of masonry were thrown across the north and south arches at the
crossing at the triforium level. This may appear illogical, inasmuch
as the tendency was for the tower piers to be pushed outwards; the
adjacent piers of the choir and transepts all have an outward
inclination. The tower was strengthened in the seventeenth century by Sir Christopher Wren, and both Gilbert Scott and Arthur
Blomfield in turn did much to render the structure sound in the
nineteenth century. Notwithstanding, as recently as 1945 its condition was stated to be far from reliable; it is indeed little short of
a miracle that the tower and spire of Salisbury cathedral have
stood so long.

Early in the sixteenth century the piers that carry the central
tower of Canterbury cathedral, commonly known as the Angel
Steeple, were showing signs of weakness although they had been
recased and strengthened before the tower was commenced in
1433. Girder arches of stone were therefore inserted between the
southern and western piers at the crossing, and four minor ones
between the western piers and the transept walls. These strainer-
arches are four-centred and carry girder walls pierced with tracery.

---

[1] Early in the sixteenth century similar scissor-arches rather less obtrusive were
erected beneath the north and south arches of the crossing at Glastonbury abbey,
where the piers were bulging under the weight of the tower. The spandrels were
pierced with rectilinear panelling.

As adjuncts to Christian churches towers first appeared in Italy in the fifth century, their primary function being to house bells. In general the central tower of a cathedral church was unsuitable for bell-ringing; a mass of swaying bells could imperil the safety of a tower standing on four legs. In the interests of safety therefore, it was not unusual for a detached bell-tower to be built hard by.[1] At Rochester the shell of Gundulf's Norman tower stands to the east of the north transept (Fig. 11). There is documentary evidence that it was being used as a bell-tower in the twelfth century. Long before the tower and spire of Salisbury were raised a detached tower had been built at the north-west corner of the cathedral close, but it was demolished by Wyatt in 1789. Until 1647 a 'clocherium' stood to the north-east of the choir of Worcester cathedral. It was an octagonal building surmounted by a timber spire and probably dated from the thirteenth century. In the eastern part of Old S. Paul's churchyard was a bell tower that belonged to Jesus chapel in the crypt of the cathedral. Formerly the common-bell of the City of London hung in the tower and was rung to summon the citizens to the folk-motes in the churchyard. In the sixteenth century there were four Jesus bells in the tower.

The sole remaining detached bell tower of an English cathedral is that at Chichester, situated at the north-west of the nave and dating from 1411–36 (Fig. 10).

Of the six mediaeval cathedrals whose towers are surmounted by stone spires, Lichfield is the only one with three spires (Pl. 10). In other cathedrals the more perishable timber spire was by no means uncommon in the Middle Ages. Originally the central towers of Hereford, Rochester, Lincoln and Old S. Paul's were crowned with timber spires, as also were the western towers of Canterbury, Durham, Ely, Lincoln and Ripon. Those at Durham were taken down in 1657 and a few years later Ripon cathedral lost its timber spires. The steeply pitched pyramidal roofs of the western towers of Southwell cathedral are a modern version of the Norman roofs, a form that was gradually elongated into the octagonal spire of wood or stone. The timber spire of Old S. Paul's, destroyed by fire in 1561, rose to a height of 450 feet, and that of the central tower of Lincoln, wrecked by a storm in 1540, was some 50 feet loftier. The western spires of Lincoln remained until 1807; a proposal to remove them some years before almost provoked a riot amongst the townsfolk.

The erection of a stone spire above a central tower placed an

---

[1] Detached towers are often called campaniles, a term that strictly speaking should be applied to unbuttressed towers.

additional load on the piers at the crossing, and to minimize the weight, the sides were constructed of comparatively thin masonry. The bottom courses of Salisbury spire, more than 404 feet high, are only 2 feet thick, and those at the top are 9 inches; the timber scaffolding inside the spire was allowed to remain after completion, to give greater rigidity. The capstone of a spire and the stonework a few feet below it were always built solid.

The difficulty of raising an octagonal spire above a square tower was solved by throwing squinch arches across the internal angles of the tower, to carry the canted sides of the spire. To effect a unity of design, so that the spire should seem to grow out of the tower and not appear as a superimposed afterthought, the mediaeval masons masked the transition from square to octagon by placing pinnacles at the tower angles. The pinnacles were also of structural value, for the angles thus weighted resisted any tendency to be thrust outwards by the load of the spire. At Oxford cathedral, which has the earliest large stone spire in the country, dating from the first half of the thirteenth century, a perfect homogeneity of design was achieved by the use of angle pinnacles and by the lofty dormer windows at the base of the spire, which associate themselves with the coupled windows of the tower beneath. The same unity characterizes the tower and spire of Salisbury, begun *c.* 1340; in addition to pinnacles at the angles others are grouped about the base of the spire, and three belts of tracery are carried round it similar to the bands that define the two stages of the tower.

A most effective means of unifying tower and spire was to make the latter spring from within the parapet of the tower, as in the Lichfield spires of the mid-fourteenth century. In the western pair angle pinnacles are attached to the base of the spire in the nature of buttresses, but in the central spire *c.* 1380, they stand free. All the Lichfield spires are hexagonal and are divided into stages by moulded bands. The tall spire of the Norman tower of Norwich cathedral, 315 feet high, was built to replace the wooden spire that was struck by lightning in 1463. The lower part is strengthened by slight buttresses with off-sets attached to the arrises or edges.

WEST FRONTS

In the secular cathedrals of the Middle Ages the west front was the main façade of the building, but the design was in general arbitrary and not based on any accepted principle. In France it was otherwise. From the twin-towered façades of the Romanesque period the Gothic builders of the Ile de France developed an almost standard design for the west fronts of their mighty cathedrals in the twelfth and thirteenth centuries. The two towers, the deep projecting portals, three or more in number and enriched with magnificent sculpture, and the great rose window high up above the central porch, render the French façade an architectural composition with which its English counterpart compares but ill. For the Frenchman the west front was to be a splendid entrance to God's house, the very gate of heaven, about which were clouds of witnesses to remind those who entered of the foundations of their faith. The difference between the ideals of the two countries was one of social conditions and environment. It was the age of the Communes in France, when the cities and towns were increasing in importance, and the influence of monasticism was weakening. The bishop was accepted as the spiritual father of the people and it was fitting that his cathedral church should stand in the midst of crowded streets, at the best on one side of the Grande Place. In contrast the English cathedral was usually ensconced within walled precincts and was never to a like extent a church for the people. Hence the west front of no English cathedral can compare with those of Notre Dame (Paris), Reims and Amiens. The twin-towered façades of York (Pl. 15) and Ripon (Pl. 63) are the nearest approaches to the French design, although they lack huge portals glorified with 'dedicated shapes of saints and kings' and the rose window. With the exception of Peterborough, the west fronts of the monastic cathedrals, where the laity other than pilgrims were regarded as intruders, are usually nondescript in character and of little architectural significance, e.g. Winchester, Norwich and Gloucester. In some secular cathedrals of England the western façade was conceived as a screen to be peopled with statues, and as such fails to indicate the internal *ordonnance* of the building behind it. Foremost amongst the screen-façades is the west front of Wells cathedral, begun *c.* 1225, though fifty years passed before it was filled with its full complement of statues. In order to secure a greater width for the façade, the two western towers were embraced in the scheme, being built outside the aisles of the nave. The figures and the relief sculptures are disposed in seven tiers; the choice of saints and kings to be sculptured was not the whim of the master who designed the façade. 'The best theologian available at Wells set out the story that the sculpture has to tell, named the saints represented and ordered their position.'[1] The tall free-standing figures that occupy the niches are in perfect keeping with the architecture of which they are a part; the six deep buttresses, affording light and shade to the façade, divide it into compartments corresponding with the nave, aisles and towers; neither windows nor doorways conflict with the main purpose. The

[1] *The Cathedral Builders in England.* E. S. Prior.

insignificant portals of the nave and aisles have been likened to mouseholes in the wainscot, but it must be borne in mind that the main entrance for the canons and clergy was the north-west porch, and the open space to the west of the cathedral was a lay cemetery.

The west front of Salisbury cathedral, which was but a few years later than Wells, fulfils a dual purpose, for it is at one and the same time a screen for the display of imagery and a buttressed façade expressing the *ordonnance* of the cathedral interior. The result is somewhat of a jumble, a confused arrangement of windows, arcadings, niches and belts of traceried stonework. There are in all one hundred and twenty niches for statues, few of which now remain, and it is doubtful whether all the niches were occupied in the Middle Ages (p. 213).

Contemporary with Salisbury is the gigantic screen that constitutes the west front of Lincoln cathedral. The addition of western transepts resulted in a lateral expansion of the Norman three-arched front, which served as a nucleus about which tier upon tier of Early English arcading was ranged, extending beyond the towers and embracing the western transepts. The angles of the Lincoln façade are emphasized by octagonal turrets capped with spirelets. Owing to the widening of the front, the fine towers behind it appear too close together.

Dating *c.* 1275 the west front of Lichfield cathedral is a combination of a twin-towered façade and a screen with rows of statues standing in brackets set within wall arcading, a less satisfactory arrangement than niches (Pl 10).

Of an entirely different character is the screen façade of Exeter cathedral *c.* 1370, which was purposely kept low so as not to block up the great west window. The three tiers of niches are packed with a mass of statuary representing saints, angels, kings and warriors (Pl. 96).

The superb and imposing west front of Peterborough cathedral, a triple-arched Gothic portico of colossal dimensions, is without an equal in any mediaeval church in Europe. The problems of equilibrium involved in its construction (p. 204) justify the description 'the architecture of adventure' that is often applied to Gothic.

10. Interior Arrangement, Fittings, Furniture and Decoration

❦ THE CATHEDRAL CHURCHES of the Middle Ages were built primarily for the religious offices that it was the bounden duty of the capitular body of clergy or monks to observe. The choir was their private chapel, and the supreme act of worship was the celebration of the Eucharist at the High Altar that stood in the sanctuary or presbytery at the east end of the choir. The western part, known as the ritual choir, was occupied by the stalls for the accommodation of the canons or the monks.

In the secular cathedrals, the choir was shut off from the rest of the church by a screen, usually of stone, called the *pulpitum*, that stood beneath the eastern arch of the crossing, as at Exeter, Lincoln and York (Fig. 23). The simplest form of pulpitum was a solid wall with a central portal closed by a stout wooden door or a gate; but it often consisted of two parallel walls roofed over to make a deep screen with an open arcaded front. Within the thickness of the pulpitum were stone stairways that led to a platform or loft above. The eastern or inner face was backed by the return stalls of the choir.

The arrangement in the monastic cathedrals was somewhat different, for in addition to the pulpitum was a rood-screen situated some distance to the west. Centrally placed against the front of the rood-screen was an altar for the laity, on either side of which was a processional doorway through which the two files of monks re-entered the choir on Sundays and festivals.

At Durham and Canterbury the pulpitum stood between the eastern piers at the crossing, and the rood-screen at the east end of the nave. Frequently the ritual choir extended into the area at the crossing, or further west into the nave. Thus, at Norwich the stalls of the monks intruded into the two eastern bays of the nave; the pulpitum occupied the third bay and one bay to the west was the rood-screen, in front of which was set up the nave altar. The choir and sanctuary together occupied nearly one-half of the interior length of Norwich cathedral. At Winchester the pulpitum was situated in the second bay of the nave from the east, and the rood-screen in the next bay to the west. In Worcester cathedral the monks' choir occupied the crossing and one bay of the nave; in the second bay was the pulpitum, and between the third pair of piers was the rood-screen.[1]

In both secular and monastic cathedrals the purpose of the screens was to ensure privacy for the performance of the religious offices in the choir. The rood-screen that spanned the nave west of the pulpitum in monastic churches isolated the ritual choir and the transepts; it was generally carried across the aisles as well, or failing that, iron gates were put up. In either case the purpose was to preclude access by unauthorized persons to the cloister doorway at the eastern end of the aisle. The cloisters and the conventual

[1] Westminster abbey furnishes a perfect example of the arrangement of the ritual choir in a Benedictine church. To this day the stalls are all to the west of the crossing; in the fourth bay of the nave is the modern pulpitum, beyond which was originally the rood screen.

buildings were not, in modern parlance, open to the general public.

In the secular cathedrals the ritual choir rarely intruded into the nave, though there were two notable exceptions. When the eastern arm of Wells was completed *c.* 1180, the presbytery of three bays being unduly short, the ritual choir was extended westwards and the pulpitum was erected between the first pair of piers beyond the crossing (Fig. 5). The subsequent reconstruction of the choir-arm early in the fourteenth century provided ample room for the canons' stalls, and the pulpitum was then set up beneath the eastern arch of the crossing (Fig. 17).

At Chichester cathedral the ritual choir embraced four bays of the nave, but in the fifteenth century a new pulpitum was built at the western crossing, and the stalls were then moved into the eastern arm. Despite choir-extensions, the monks of Ely and Worcester clung to the old arrangement, and in both cathedrals the pulpitum and the ritual choir occupied the east end of the nave until the Suppression.

In no English cathedral that was formerly monastic have both pulpitum and rood-screen survived. The Suppression accounts for the absence of a single complete example of the pre-Reformation arrangement in a monastic cathedral, for when the cathedral priories were reconstituted as secular establishments, though the canons often retained the pulpitum, the rood-screen was superfluous and in most cases was taken down. At S. Albans only is the mediaeval rood-screen intact. Standing three bays west of the crossing, it was erected by Abbot Thomas de la Mare *c.* 1363, and is 43 feet long and 22 feet high. In front of the screen stood an altar dedicated to Our Lady, on either side of which is a processional doorway. The face is adorned with canopied niches and panelling, and though the screen has lost its statuary and colouring, it is an invaluable relic of pre-Reformation times.

At Canterbury, the rood-screen which differed entirely from other known examples, remained in position beneath the western arch of the crossing until *c.* 1750.[1] It consisted of a lofty open grate of ironwork with gates for processional purposes on each side of the nave altar, and dated from the closing years of the fifteenth century.

The pulpitum was invariably a substantial structure with a central portal, and presented a solid front to the nave. All the pulpita now remaining in English cathedrals are of stone, with the sole exception of that at Carlisle which is built of timber. A diversity of opinion exists as to the use of the loft of the pulpitum in the

---

[1] *Greater English Church Screens.* Aymer Vallance. 1947.

Middle Ages. The fourteenth-century *Customary* of Salisbury cathedral makes it clear that on Sundays and festival days, the Epistle and the Gospel were read from the loft; on the Rule of Sarum were based the ceremonials observed in other secular cathedrals, e.g. Lincoln; but in the monastic cathedrals the pulpitum was not put to such use.

In many a cathedral the pulpitum was deemed a suitable support for a huge organ in the eighteenth and nineteenth centuries, an unlikely position for the small 'pair of organs' that piped out a few feeble notes in pre-Reformation churches. In the twelfth century a pair of organs was in use at Ely cathedral. Bishop Nigellus, 1133–74, surrendered part of the tithes of a farm at Littlebury 'for the repair of the organs' in the choir. Two centuries later the accounts of the precentor of Ely, 1396, give in detail the cost of making a new pair, amounting in all to £4 8s. 5d. For making the twelve pipes, 20 stones of lead were bought for 16s. 9d.; 4 horsehides for four pairs of bellows cost 7s. 8d.; ashen hoops for the bellows, 4d.; 12 springs, 3d.; 12 sheepskins, 2s. 4d.; 6 calf skins, 2s. 6d.; and sundry other items including glue, quicksilver, wire, nails, cloth, and hooks. A carpenter was paid 2s. 8d. for eight days' work in making the bellows, and 40s. was spent in fetching the organ-builder and providing his keep. This pair of organs was without a keyboard and had a compass of only twelve notes, sufficient for plain-song accompaniment. At the Suppression, Ely cathedral possessed 'two pair of organs in the quyer and a pair of organs in the Ladye Chaple'. These instruments were furnished with keyboards and with several sets of pipes extending over a compass of four octaves. In the sixteenth century there were three organs at Durham cathedral, one of which stood 'over the quire door and was opened and played upon only at principal feasts, the pipes being all of most fine wood and workmanship very fair. . . . Also there was a lettern of wood, like unto a pulpit, standing and adjoining to the wood organ over the quire door, where they had wont to sing the nine lessons in the old time on principal days, standing with their faces towards the High Altar' (*Rites of Durham*).

Many mediaeval pulpita have long since disappeared. Of those with open arcaded fronts, Exeter and Southwell furnish outstanding examples of the early fourteenth century and both are situated at the eastern crossing. The Exeter screen, described as *La Pulpytte* in the Fabric Rolls, 1317–26, has three wide depressed arches, above which is a parapet faced with thirteen panels, for which a London image-maker carved some sixty-eight small figures (Pl. 13). The images have gone and the panels are now filled with paintings of the seventeenth century. Within the lateral arches altars were set up against the wall at the back, at a cost of £1 6s. 8d. The northern was dedicated to S. Nicholas and that on the south to S. Mary. The western face of the screen at Southwell, dating *c.* 1330, is opened up with three cinquefoiled arches, flanked on either side by a small blind arch, and is crowned with a cornice of pierced undulating tracery. The eastern face is designed in two tiers, and the three recesses on each side of the doorway served for the return stalls of the choir (Pl. 16). The exuberant carved ornament of extreme delicacy that is lavished upon the eastern side of the screen presents Curvilinear Gothic in its maturity (Pl. 18).

Prior to the collapse of the central tower of Chichester cathedral in 1861, a pulpitum of the arcaded type erected by Bishop Arundel, *c.* 1470, stood beneath the western arch of the crossing. It was a triple-arched structure, the lateral bays being occupied by the altars of S. Augustine and S. Mary at Stok. The screen was taken down in 1859 and replaced by the present oaken one, but the masonry was preserved and in 1904 a great part of the pulpitum including the ribbed vaulting was re-erected in the detached tower at the north-west of the cathedral.

Of an entirely different design are the pulpita at Canterbury, York, Lincoln and Ripon, which are quite frankly solid screens faced with a tier of tall niches for figures of saints, apostles or kings. In the Lincoln screen, erected *c.* 1360 and 17 feet high, the wide portal in the centre is flanked on each side by four tabernacled niches with ogee arches and divided by buttressed shafts. The portal passage has a flat vault supported by skeleton ribs, a *tour-de-force* in vault construction that occurs also at S. David's cathedral; and the masonry above the doorway and niches is encrusted with carved leafage. Hardly a stone is not sculptured, and traces remain of the colours and gilding that were originally applied to the ornament. Within the thickness of the screen (13 feet) are stairways to the loft. Owing to the elevation of the choir above the crypt, the pulpitum at Canterbury, built by Prior Chillenden, 1391–1411, is approached by a flight of steps in the area of the crossing, an arrangement that is peculiar to Canterbury. The earlier screen, *c.* 1304, was encased in the new pulpitum and is to be seen from the choir side. The western face is adorned with three canopied niches on either side of the doorway, tenanted by statues of crowned but unidentified kings of England, and in the arch orders of the portal are twelve canopied niches that once housed figures of the Apostles. Above the inner door was Christ in Majesty. The front of the loft is divided into panels and niches, the latter formerly occupied by statuettes of saints. Of this imagery only the kings have survived.

The pulpitum at York presents an array of regal statuary. In niches on either side of the choir door are figures of fifteen English kings from William I to Henry VI, above which is a double tier of intricate tabernacling (Pl. 17). 'To William Hyndeley the minster of York is indebted for its splendid screen, and the presence of a hind lodged among the carving would seem to show that Hyndeley had a hand in designing it, as well as executing the work' (*Fabric Rolls of York*). Hyndeley and his family were brought to York from Norwich at the expense of the chapter, and for twenty years he and a dozen or more assistants were engaged on the work. The screen was not completed until *c.* 1515, ten years after the master's death. The names of the kings in the niches are inscribed in Latin on the pedestals beneath them; the figure of Henry VI is a modern replica of the original that was removed by order of Edward IV. In the vault of the choir entrance are several carved bosses, the central one representing the Assumption of the Virgin, supported by angels and cherubs (Pl. 22). In the loft of the pulpitum was an altar dedicated to the Name of Jesus; mention is made in a Return of 1543 of several ornaments, including a 'hanging of silk with lions of gold before the altar'.

Contemporary with the screen at York, but on a smaller scale, is that at Ripon, that measures 36 feet in length as against the 51 feet of York. The choir doorway is flanked by four tall niches on each side, now tenanted by modern figures, and above the gabled canopies is a range of twenty-four smaller niches, each with a bracket for a statue (Pl. 12).

Of singular design is the pulpitum at S. David's cathedral, the asymmetry of which is due to the incorporation of portions of the earlier screen in the reconstruction undertaken by Bishop Henry Gower, 1328–47. It stands beneath the western arch of the crossing and projects considerably into the eastern bay of the nave (Fig. 21).

The northern half of the screen has a shallow arcade of three arches that formed part of the thirteenth century pulpitum and served as a reredos for the altar of the Holy Cross; and south of the choir doorway are two small chambers, the southern of which was the chantry chapel of Bishop Gower, whose tomb and effigy are within. The chapel is opened up with richly cusped arches on the south and west sides. The choir entrance is vaulted with skeleton ribs; the oak cornice of the screen is a restoration of the nineteenth century.

In the secular cathedrals, iron gates were erected at the entrances to the aisles of the choir to exclude the laity during the canons' services. At Lincoln the gates are framed within stone archways of the late thirteenth century, with Purbeck shafts and exquisitely sculptured capitals and arch orders.

Through the aisle gates were admitted the pilgrims who came to visit the shrine of the local saint. To safeguard the sanctuary against intrusion by any aimless wanderers amongst the pilgrims, screens, usually of stone were erected between the piers on each side of the choir, and for the convenience of the clergy, doors in the screening, known as *ostia presbyterii*, opened into the aisles. At Rochester and S. Albans the choir is divided from its aisles by solid walling, though the easternmost bay at S. Albans is filled with a chantry chapel on either side.

Behind the choir stalls at Lincoln, a low wall extends from the choir transepts to the crossing, enriched on the aisle-sides with fine wall arcading of the thirteenth century; and the bays opposite the choir transepts are fitted with iron grilles, 8 feet high, dating from 1297 and the finest of their kind in England. At Canterbury the choir stalls are backed by lofty stone screens of the fourteenth century standing on low walls that were built when the big reconstruction of the eastern arm was undertaken in 1175. The screens which consist of ranges of two-light Gothic openings were erected by Prior Eastry, 1284–1331, at the same time as the pulpitum, though only the inner part of the latter is *in situ*. A late example of aisle-screening occurs at Winchester, put up when the choir aisles were rebuilt by Bishop Fox *c.* 1525. The design is that of a range of Perpendicular four-light windows, the frieze above being carved with antique ornament in relief. Of elaborate design and carved with a plenitude of classic ornament is the timber Renaissance screen on the north side of the presbytery of Carlisle cathedral. It was installed by Lancelot Salkeld, the last prior, and the first dean of the New Foundation. Not a vestige of Gothic is to be seen in this early example of Renaissance woodwork, dating *c.* 1545.

In the choir arcades of many cathedrals tombs and chantry chapels of bishops, ecclesiastics or nobles were erected beneath the arches. Thus at Ely, the arches on the north side of the sanctuary are occupied from west to east by the tombs of Bishop Redman, 1505, and Bishop William of Kilkenny, 1256, the pedestal of S. Etheldreda's shrine and the monument of Bishop Northwold, 1254; and in the south arcade, from east to west stand the tomb of Bishop Hotham, 1337, the cenotaph of Lord Tiptoft, who was beheaded on Tower Hill in 1470, and the tombs of Bishop Barnett, 1374, and of Bishop William de Luda, 1298.

Of first importance in the sanctuary was the High Altar, a long stone slab resting on a mass of solid masonry that was raised on a pace above the pavement of the choir. Pope Innocent III, 1198–

1216, decreed that the stone slab or *mensa* should be a monolith, as symbolical of the unity of the Church. At each angle and in the centre of the mensa was incised a cross, to mark the spots touched by the bishop with holy oil when the altar was consecrated.

In the Early Christian basilican churches of Italy the High Altar was placed on the chord of the apse at the western end of the building. The seat of the bishop or officiating priest was in the apse, so that at High Mass he faced the east, with the Altar between himself and the worshippers. This was the arrangement in the Saxon cathedral of Canterbury and was the common usage in pre-Conquest churches. After the Conquest the apse and the High Altar were transferred to the east end of cathedral churches, but the episcopal chair retained its traditional position behind the High Altar. At Norwich the ancient throne of the bishop, approached by wooden steps, stands between the piers of the Norman apse; and in Conrad's Glorious Choir at Canterbury, dedicated in 1130, the archbishop's throne occupied a similar position behind the High Altar.

The choir extensions that became the fashion in the thirteenth century put an end to the ancient tradition, and the bishop's cathedra was translated to the south side of the sanctuary. The addition of a saint's chapel brought about an entire rearrangement of the eastern arm of the greater churches behind the High Altar (Chapter 7). At Salisbury cathedral (Fig. 1), the original site of the High Altar was not as at present, at the extreme east end of the choir, but in the bay farther west that is flanked by the choir transepts. At the base of the piers of this bay are the remains of two or three steps on which the High Altar originally stood and which extended right across the sanctuary. Further evidence of the paramount importance of this bay is confirmed by the Majestas painting with roundels of the Evangelists on the surface of the high vault immediately above (p. 138). The High Altar was undoubtedly shut off from the bays beyond by a screen wall with traceried openings or niched figures that stretched across the sanctuary as in the aisled-rectangle choirs of Lincoln and York (p. 92), where the chapel of the local saint lay east of the Altar. The stone altar-screen at Durham is typical, though now shorn of the images that formerly peopled the niches. It was the gift of John, Lord Neville of Raby in 1372, and was made in London by masons well skilled in Perpendicular Gothic. The chiselled stones were transported by sea to Newcastle and thence in wagons to Durham. The tabernacled niches, divided by slender coupled buttresses once held a hundred and seven images, all lavishly coloured and the product of the alabaster workers of Nottingham. 'Right over the High

Altar was artificially placed, in very fine alabaster, the picture [figure] of Our Lady standing in the midst, and the picture of S. Cuthbert on the one side, and the picture of S. Oswald on the other, all being richly gilded' (*Rites of Durham*). On either side of the Altar are doors in the screen by which the monks could enter the chapel of S. Cuthbert from the sanctuary.

Most of the altar-screens now in our cathedrals are modern. That at Lincoln, re-erected in 1769 incorporates portions of the mediaeval screen and at York is a reproduction of the Perpendicular screen that was destroyed by the fire of 1829. Beverley minster, Yorks., furnishes an admirable example dating *c.* 1330, of the type of altar-screen that was in use in the greater churches in pre-Reformation days. The Fabric Rolls of Exeter cathedral shed much light on the altar-screen and reredos, no longer extant, that were in course of erection from 1317 to 1322. The main feature was a silver retable above the altar, with figures of the Virgin Mary and Child wearing silver-gilt crowns, and statues of S. Peter and S. Paul. The group probably represented the Coronation of the Virgin and was the work of John, a London goldsmith. The same Roll (1321–2) mentions sheets of metal for making the lilies in the Virgin's hand, and six thousand leaves of gold, in addition to forty-eight images (for the altar-screen?) at 1s. 2d. each. There is also reference to a large altar canopy, the shafts, capitals and brackets of which cost 108s. 4d. It was adorned with bosses on the underside.

At Winchester 'the nether part of the High Altar [was] of plate of gold, garnished with stones; the front above being of broidery work and pearls, and above that a table of images of silver and gilt garnished with stones' (*Dugdale's Monasticon*).

Of painted reredoses, the retable at Norwich, dating *c.* 1380, is the finest now preserved in any English cathedral. Measuring about 9 feet by 3 feet, it is painted on oak boards in a moulded frame and is divided into panels depicting the Scourging of Our Lord, Christ bearing the Cross, the Crucifixion, Resurrection and Ascension. The figures are painted on a gilt gesso field with floriated designs in relief (Pl. 19).

In a class apart are the reredoses of the High Altars at S. Albans, Winchester and Southwark, which occupy the whole of the eastern wall of the sanctuary and block out everything beyond; on either side of the Altar are doors opening into the retrochoir. No more appropriate setting was ever devised for the Divine mysteries celebrated at the High Altar. They are designed in three tiers of tabernacled niches, which were tenanted by a glorious array of saints and kings resplendent in colour and gold, with the Crucifix

as the centre-piece. The reredos at S. Albans was installed by
Abbot Wallingford *c.* 1484; those at Winchester and Southwark
were erected by Bishop Fox in the early years of the sixteenth
century. The present statuary of all three is mainly modern. An
earlier reredos of this type was set up in Lichfield cathedral in the
middle of the fifteenth century, and when it was dismantled six
of the canopies were used for making the sedilia on the south side
of the sanctuary.

The High Altar was always covered with a cloth and draped
with a frontal, the colour of which varied with the seasons and
festivals of the Church; and on either side were curtains or 'ridels'
that were suspended by rings from metal rods projecting from the
altar-screen. At the ends of the rods were prickets for candles.
The mensa was primarily a table on which the consecrated ele-
ments were placed during the celebration of Mass, but in course of
time it became the custom to display reliquaries on the Altar. In
1483 the High Altar at York was laden with silver-gilt images of
the twelve Apostles in addition to several reliquaries.

Above the Altar was a wooden tester or canopy from which was
suspended the Pyx, a vessel of silver or of ivory containing the
Reserved Sacrament. It was generally cylindrical in shape and was
draped with a silken veil. A drawing in the Islip Roll of Westminster abbey, 1532, shows a flat tester projecting over the High Altar
with the pyx hanging from the front. At Wells cathedral is preserved an oaken canopy of the thirteenth century that is believed
to have been a pyx-container (Pl. 20). Cylindrical in form, it measures 4 feet in height and has a diameter of about 15 inches; it is
divided into three stages of pierced tracery surmounted by trefoiled cresting, and was originally coloured and gilded. The container was suspended from the high vault or from a tester by iron
rods.

The sanctuary normally occupied three or four bays to the west
of the High Altar, and was kept clear in order to leave ample room
for the ritualistic observances. Generally it was raised a step (the
gradus presbyterii) above the choir level and below the step was
placed the matins altar, which was known as the *minus altare* at
Worcester cathedral, and as the *altare in choro* at Ely. A little to the
north was the lectern, from which the lessons were read at matins.
On the south side of the sanctuary within a few feet of the High
Altar were the sedilia for the seating of the celebrant, the deacon,
and the sub-deacon during the singing of certain portions of the
High Mass. They were permanent fixtures of stone, the seats
usually three in number being surmounted by lofty canopies or
tabernacling. At Chester (Pl. 24) and Gloucester the sedilia have

four seats, those at Southwell five, and at Durham there are four on each side of the sanctuary. The sedilia of Exeter cathedral dating *c.* 1317 are truly marvels of stone-cutting, and the open tabernacling is a translation in stone of that surmounting the episcopal throne of oak that had been made for Bishop Stapledon. Also of the fourteenth century are the sedilia at Southwell and Durham. The former are of a more solid Decorated design, with which is incorporated a piscina or drain at which the sacred vessels were rinsed after the celebration of Mass. The sedilia at Durham are of the same style as the Neville altar-screen. At S. David's cathedral the Perpendicular sedilia are built of oak and are crowned with a coved cornice.

In the massive piers to the west of the sedilia on both sides of Durham choir are small recesses that served as cupboards or aumbries 'to set the chalices, the basins and the cruets in, that they did minister withal at the High Altar, with locks and keys for the said almeryes' (*Rites of Durham*).

In pre-Reformation days the season of Lent was marked by a custom that was universally observed in English churches of all kinds. On the eve of the first Sunday in Lent, a great curtain, known as the Lenten veil was hung between the sanctuary and the western part of the choir, being suspended from a beam or rope that stretched across the choir, and there it remained until the Wednesday of Holy Week. At Durham cathedral a beam was fixed to the walls above the second pair of piers from the east for the Lenten veil; and at the base of the piers that formerly flanked the High Altar at Salisbury is a small winch, a wooden roller with an iron handle that was used for drawing the veil across the sanctuary.

The Lenten observances culminated in the ceremony of the Easter Sepulchre, that symbolized the Entombment and Resurrection of Our Lord. On Good Friday after the Passion was sung, a receptacle containing the Blessed Sacrament was solemnly laid in the Easter Sepulchre, that took the form of a tomb-like structure erected on the north side of the sanctuary. Generally it consisted of a timber framework, draped with palls or hangings, or faced with carved panels depicting the Burial and the Resurrection of Our Lord. A few examples are extant of permanent Sepulchres of stone, notably the one in Lincoln cathedral that occupies three of a range of six gabled niches north of the High Altar. The sculptured panels at the base represent the sleeping soldiers. The Easter Sepulchre was watched day and night and the 'Pascall' or Pascal candle was kept burning before it until Easter Day. At Canterbury a 'grete paschall maste' was erected to support an enormous candle for which 815 lb. of wax were purchased in 1541 at a cost of £19 19s. 6d., probably equal to £500 of our money. The huge candelabra of the Pascal at Durham was made of 'latten metal glistering as gold' and rose almost up to the high vault. It had six branching candlesticks, and at each of its four corners was a winged dragon; there were also figures of the four Evangelists and 'antick work [such] as beasts, and men uppon horsebacks'. In 1545 the chapter of Rochester granted Nichols Arnold, a priest, certain lodgings by Gundulf's tower at a rent of 'one pound of wax to be offered on Good Friday to the Sepulchre of Our Lord' in the choir. On Easter morn the Blessed Sacrament was transferred amid much pomp from the Sepulchre to the High Altar. At Durham cathedral on Good Friday a golden crucifix on a velvet cushion was deposited in the Sepulchre 'nigh to the High Altar; and there it lay with another picture [image] of Our Saviour Christ, in whose breast they did enclose with great reverence the most Holy and Blessed Sacrament of the Altar, censing it and praying unto it upon their knees a great space, setting two lighted tapers before it, which did burn unto Easter Day in the morning' (*Rites*). Between three and four a.m. on Easter Day two of the senior monks at Durham brought 'the Image of Our Saviour, in the breast whereof was enclosed in bright crystal, the Holy Sacrament' to the High Altar, and after the singing of the anthem, *Christus Resurgus*, it was carried in procession beneath a canopy of purple velvet round the church and then placed on the High Altar until Ascension Day. According to Inventories compiled in 1536 and 1548, the receptacle used for the Sepulchre ceremony at Lincoln cathedral was a silver-gilt image of Christ with a void in the breast to contain the Sacrament.

The western part of the choir in the English cathedral was and is occupied by rows of wooden stalls. Usually there are two rows on either side, the upper or back row for the canons or their vicars and the lower row for the choristers. Against the pupitum, on each side of the choir entrance are two or three return stalls; the seat to the south of the doorway was reserved for the dean in the secular cathedrals and for the prior in the monastic churches. The number of stalls depended upon the strength of the chapter. In the two upper rows at Lincoln are sixty-eight seats, of which six are modern, and fixed to the backs are tablets bearing the names of the prebends, a practice that was adopted in other secular cathedrals. The *Consuetudinary* of Lincoln, c. 1383, records: 'It is the ancient usage of the choir to say one mass and the whole psalter daily, on behalf of the living and deceased benefactors of the church.' Each canon or his deputy was required to read the portion of the psalms as set forth in the tablet on his stall. The same custom of reciting the whole psalter every day obtained at Wells. In some cathedrals the canons had to contribute towards the cost of making and erecting their stalls. Each canon at Wells paid 30 solidi when the stalls were set up in 1325, but as the cost was far in excess of that charge, the non-residentiary canons were called upon in 1337 to contribute the sum of £200.

Each stall was furnished with a tip-up seat or *misericord* and a broad arm-rest; on the underside of the seat was a projecting ledge, so that when the seat was turned up, the occupant could assume a half-sitting position, the arm-rests ensuring greater ease. These misericords or indulgence-seats enabled the clergy to comply with ancient discipline that enjoined standing during the Divine offices in the choir. The ledges on the underside were invariably carved with clumps of foliage or sacred subjects, with grotesque or comic figures, animals or representations of the countless occupations of everyday existence. Taken as a whole they constitute a history of life and thought in the Middle Ages, portraying agricultural activities such as ploughing, sowing and reaping; sports and pastimes, the hunt and the chase; fabulous creatures from the mediaeval bestiary, myths and fables, incidents from the Old and New Testaments, domestic scenes pleasant and unpleasant. Knowing that his work would be seen by only a privileged few, the woodcarver indulged in the humorous, the satirical and whimsical to his heart's content. In the normal design of the misericord, the carved clump was flanked by foliage or figures cut in low relief (Pl. 14).

Of the two thousand misericords in English churches, more than one-third are to be found in the cathedrals. Upwards of sixty examples occur in each of the cathedrals of Lincoln, Norwich, Winchester, Hereford and Gloucester. The earliest are those at Exeter, some of which date from the late thirteenth century.

Of equal interest as examples of mediaeval wood carving are the finials or poppy-heads that cap the stall-ends, variously carved with a figure, a human head, an animal, a grotesque beast or a clump of foliage.

Choir stalls as permanent features did not come into general use until the fourteenth century. The magnificent stalls at Winchester, the earliest of their kind, date from *c.* 1308, and thenceforth tabernacled canopies in some form or other became an essential part of stall-design in the cathedrals and greater churches. The gabled canopies of the Winchester stalls are lithic in design, a transcription in oak of the Gothic forms evolved by the mason (Pl. 23). Here are crocketed gables with traceried arches and circles of Geometric design, which are repeated as blind decoration on the backs of the stalls. Towards the close of the fourteenth century the fashion set in for two-staged tabernacling. At Ely, the stalls of which date from *c.* 1338, the arcading above the seats is surmounted by a range of panels for relief carving, above which rises crocketed tabernacling. Thirty years later are the stalls of Lincoln cathedral, the two ranges of complex tabernacling piling up to a height of 25 feet. The ogee arches, gables, pinnacles and profuse ornament are wrought with superb skill; the upper tier consisting of open niches is now filled with modern figures. Of the same general design are the tabernacled stalls at Chester, *c.* 1380 (Pl. 26), and at Ripon, *c.* 1500; and those at York that were destroyed by fire in 1819 also followed the Lincoln type. The post-Reformation stalls at Durham, erected by Bishop Cosin *c.* 1665 serve to remind us that Gothic tradition had not been utterly stamped out by the Renaissance.

The choir-arm remodelling that characterized English cathedral building in the thirteenth century resulted in the removal of the bishop's throne from its age-long position behind the High Altar to the south side of the choir, at the eastern end of the stalls, where it will always be found today.

The most ancient bishop's 'stool' now remaining is the seventh-century *frithstool* at Hexham, Northumberland, which was probably the throne of the Saxon cathedral and was used as such by Bishop Wilfrid of Hexham. It is hewn out of a block of gritstone, but the original base having long disappeared, the chair measures only 1 ft. 10 in. in height, about the same in width and 2 ft. 8 in. in depth. The arms are decorated with interlacing scrolls, and other ornament consists of incised mouldings of simple form.

In his description of the Saxon cathedral of Canterbury, Edmer the cantor writes of 'the pontifical chair, constructed with handsome workmanship and of large stones and cement' that stood in the western apse behind the altar of S. Mary. It perished in the fire of 1067 and the one that replaced it, 'formed out of a single stone', suffered a like fate when Conrad's choir was destroyed in 1174. The ancient patriarchal throne of Purbeck marble now in the Corona at Canterbury is not earlier than the end of the twelfth century and may have been made for the Translation of the Shrine of S. Thomas in 1220. On the south side of the choir in the normal position is the archiepiscopal throne that was erected in 1844 and is notable for its lofty stone tabernacling.

The most splendid of all episcopal thrones and the earliest now existing of the Gothic period is that at Exeter, erected by Bishop Stapledon, 1308–26. The Fabric Rolls of Exeter record the payment of £6 12s. 8½d. for 'timber for the Bishop's seat' in 1312. The oak from Stapledon's woods at Newton and Chudleigh was kept for four years after felling, and in 1316 £4 was paid to Robert of Galmeton for making the throne by task work. The wood-carver received 32s. for six images for the tabernacling, and there is an entry of £1 10s. for painting. The throne is 57 feet high and the carved foliage and animals' heads present choice examples of the art of the mediaeval woodworker.

Of exceptional interest is the throne at Durham, built by Bishop Thomas of Hatfield, 1345–81. It is constructed in two stages; the lower is a small chantry chapel containing the tomb of the bishop, and above is a gallery for the episcopal throne. On the tomb rests an alabaster effigy clad in pontifical robes, at the foot of which was once an altar for the soul masses. The gallery is supported by a ribbed vault enriched with carved bosses, and the throne with two seats on either side for chaplains is surmounted by tabernacling.

Dating from the end of the fifteenth century is the throne at S. David's cathedral, flanked by a chaplain's seat. In design it is an inferior version of the Exeter type, the crocketed tabernacling terminating in a pierced spire reaching to a height of 30 feet.

In the cathedrals and greater churches the shrine of the Saint was invariably raised on a lofty pedestal behind the High Altar, and was therefore visible above the altar-screen, unless the latter was unusually high, as at S. Albans and Winchester. Occasionally restricted space necessitated the placing of the shrine in some other part of the cathedral, as at Hereford, Rochester and Oxford (p. 34).

At Westminster abbey 'the shrine of the most illustrious King Edward the Confessor was placed on high like a candle so that all who enter the House of the Lord may behold its light' (*Liber Trinitas*). Normally the shrine was erected in the bay behind the High Altar, which was enclosed with screens of timber or stone, or it might be effectually guarded by surrounding tombs. On the verge of the stone platform at Durham cathedral that was specially built for the shrine of S. Cuthbert, was an iron grate on which candlesticks were disposed at intervals. After the Suppression the grate was replaced by a Renaissance screen of oak and there remained until 1844. It has now been re-erected. The costly shrine of S. Erkenwald in Old S. Paul's stood within an iron grille, coloured and gilded and 6 feet high. It cost £64 2s., and 3,428 lb. of iron were used in its construction. To keep it in good condition Dean Thomas de Evere bequeathed a sum of £100 in 1407 for the building of houses in the city, the rents of which were to be assigned to the preservation of the grate and for the provision of lights about the shrine.

The Saint's chapel at Canterbury where the remains of S. Thomas were enshrined set the fashion; the idea may have had its origin in the arrangement of Conrad's Glorious Choir of the early twelfth century that was destroyed in the fire of 1174. 'Behind the High Altar', wrote the monkish chronicler Gervase, 'were two wooden columns, gracefully ornamented with gold and silver and sustaining a great beam, the ends of which rested upon the capitals of two pillars [at the curve of the apse?]. On the beam was a representation of Our Lord in Majesty and images of S. Dunstan and S. Alphege, together with seven shrines (*scrinia*) covered with gold and silver and filled with the relics of divers saints.' It was then but one step from reliquaries displayed on a beam beyond the altar to a shrine set up in the retrochoir.

Almost rivalling the High Altar in importance, the shrine of the local saint usually consisted of three parts, the pedestal or substructure, the feretrum and the canopy. The pedestal, or throne as it was often termed, was built of Purbeck marble or of stone, architectural in character, and was enriched with carving and adorned with images of gold or silver. In the lower part were a number of recesses or niches into which pilgrims seeking the healing virtues of the saintly remains could crouch or place a limb, for miraculous powers were believed to permeate the whole structure. On the throne rested the feretrum or chest containing the remains of the saint, overlaid with plates of gold or silver and enriched with precious gems. Above the feretrum was a wooden ark-shaped canopy suspended from the roof by means of chains, and raised on the occasion of an exposition. In the roof above the shrine of S. Alban are to be seen the holes made by the pulleys. Attached to the west end of the shrine was an altar dedicated to the saint whose relics were preserved therein.

The shrine of S. Hugh in Lincoln cathedral was of 'silver and gilt standing upon four pillars . . . with one steeple in the height of the covering, ornate with red stones and a round beryl containing the finger of S. Katherine in a long purse ornate with jewels.' It was protected by an iron grille, wrought by Simon the smith. The head of the Saint was enclosed in a golden reliquary studded with jewels and was placed on a pedestal 7 feet high, now at the east end of the Angel Choir. Its northern face has three ogee-arched niches in which pilgrims could kneel, and in the spandrels are shields carved with the instruments of the Passion. In Lichfield also there was a separate shrine for the head of the Saint (S. Chad), that is mentioned in an inventory of 1345. The head-reliquary or *chef* of S. Chad was made of wood and coloured, and was kept in an iron-bound coffer in the Chapel of the Head above the sacristy.

In the south aisle of the choir is the chapel gallery from which the chef was shown to pilgrims.

'The shrine of S. Thomas of Canterbury was the richest in the land; the glory of England, almost the common property of Christendom. The princes of Christendom vied in laying upon it the most precious products of the mine and the loom, the fairest work of the most skilful artificers.'[1] A description of Becket's shrine in Stow's Annals, 1592, conveys some idea of the wealth of precious metal and stones lavished upon it. 'Temp. H. VIII. All above the stonework was first of wood, [with] jewels of gold set with stone [covered with plates of gold] wrought upon with gold wire; then again, with jewels, gold, as brooches [images, angels, rings], ten or twelve together, cramped with gold into the ground of gold, the spoils [of which filled two] chests such as six or eight men could but convey out of the church. At [one side] was an angel of gold pointing thereto, offered there by a king of France.' The silver-gilt finials of the canopy weighed in all 200 ounces. Of the shrine of S. Thomas not a vestige remains, but it is depicted in a window on the north side of the Saint's chapel. At one end of the feretrum is seen a glazed opening that afforded a glimpse of Becket's bones. The pavement between the shrine and the High Altar at Canterbury is laid out with marble inlays of Opus Alexandrinum, in which appear emblems of the Virtues and Vices and the signs of the zodiac. The Corona chapel, entered from the ambulatory at the east, enshrined the scalp of S. Thomas and was known as the Chapel of the Head.

Bedecked with images of gold and silver, and with precious stones, these costly shrines needed some protection against thieves. In 1364 the golden head-reliquary of S. Hugh was stolen from Lincoln cathedral by thieves who threw away the head and sold the container in London. On their way back to Lincoln, they were robbed of the money and were eventually hanged; the head was miraculously recovered and set in a new reliquary. At Canterbury, a small chamber above S. Anselm's chapel to the south of the Saint's chapel was used as a watching chamber. From a window by day and by night monk-guards overlooked the shrine of S. Thomas and further protection was afforded by a number of bandogs that were kept within call. Early in the fifteenth century the monks of S. Albans built a timber watching house on the north side of the Saint's chapel in the abbey church. It is a two-storeyed structure, 17 feet high, built of oak, and at the east end is a stairway leading to the upper loft, whence the watchers commanded a view of the whole of the Saint's chapel. The lower stage

[1] *History of the Church of England*. R. W. Dixon.

46. Chichester; the retrochoir

48. Lincoln; capital of a pier in Hugh's choir

47. Canterbury; capital in the Saint's chapel

49. Canterbury; the eastern crypt

50. Wells; piers in the nave

51. Wells; north side of the nave

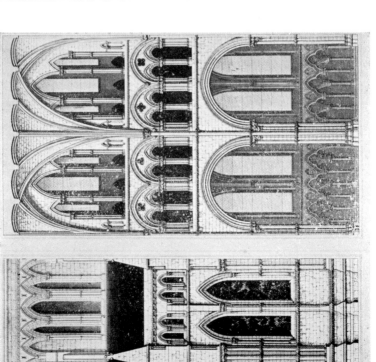

53. Lichfield; bay design of the nave

52. Lincoln; bay design of Hugh's choir

55. Rochester; north side of the presbytery

54. S. David's; north side of the nave

56. Southwark; the retrochoir

57. Lincoln; high vault of the nave

58. Ely cathedral from the west

59. Chichester cathedral from the north-west

60. York cathedral from the south-east

61. York; the Five Sisters window

62. Hereford; triforium of the north transept

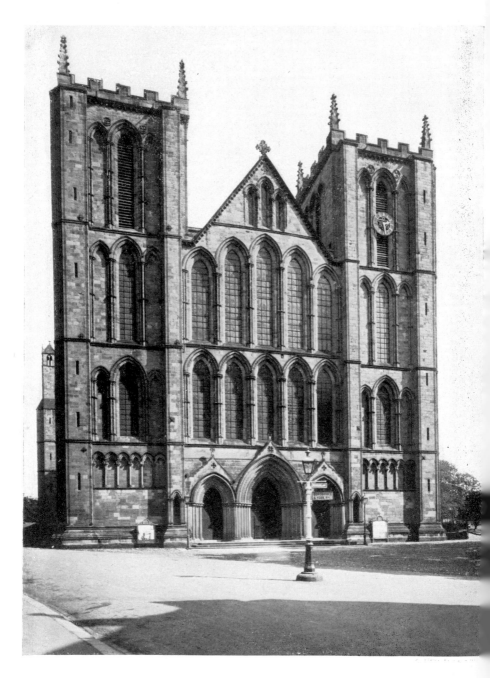

63. Ripon; the west front

64. Wells; stairway of the chapter house

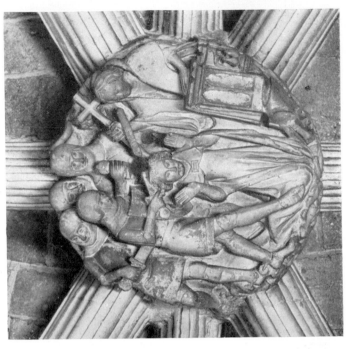

65 & 66. Exeter; bosses in the nave vault

consists of cupboards for storing palls, vestments, relics and other valuables.

In Oxford cathedral, between the Lady Chapel and the Latin chapel is a two-storeyed erection, the lower stage of stone, and above a timber gallery that served the dual purpose of a chantry chapel and a watching loft for the shrine of S. Frideswide. The door to the upper floor is at the west.

Most of the shrines in English cathedrals and churches were dismantled and broken up at the Reformation, but the thrones have in some cases been preserved, though mutilated; others that were smashed have since been pieced together. All the feretra were destroyed, the jewels wrenched from their setting, the sheets of gold and silver cast into the melting pot, and the relics scattered to the winds. The relics of S. Chad at Lichfield were removed from the shrine and after passing through many hands are now preserved in an oaken reliquary above the High Altar in S. Chad's (R.C.) cathedral, Birmingham. The original shrine at Lichfield, built by Bishop Stretton in the middle of the fourteenth century, had a pedestal of marble; the metals and jewels that garnished the shrine were granted to the chapter at the Reformation. When it was first erected, the treasurer of the cathedral was required to furnish two wax tapers, and to maintain a lamp always burning before the altar of S. Chad attached to the shrine.

Of the shrine-pedestals now preserved in our cathedrals, that of S. David is probably the earliest, dating from the first half of the thirteenth century. It stands on the north side of the sanctuary of S. David's cathedral, beneath the third arch from the east (Fig. 21), but it is doubtful whether this was the original position. In each side of the throne are three shallow recesses and beneath them three small arched apertures. The reconstructed pedestal of S. Frideswide's shrine at Oxford, first installed *c.* 1280, is but a fragment of the original; only the open arcading enriched with carved foliage is mediaeval. In a far better state is the Purbeck marble throne of the Cantelupe shrine at Hereford cathedral, dating *c.* 1287, which takes the form of an altar tomb, surmounted by a low open-arcaded stage, within which was formerly a brass depicting Bishop Thomas de Cantelupe d. 1282. The sides of the lower part are faced with niches containing fourteen figures of Knights Templars, of which Order the bishop was Grand Master (Pl. 6).

The other surviving shrine-pedestals are of the fourteenth century. That of S. Alban, erected *c.* 1308, is constructed of Purbeck marble and is 8 ft. 3 in. in height and about the same in length. On each side are four gabled niches and beneath are quatrefoiled

E

panels, two of which are pierced with lozenge-shaped openings into which the crippled could thrust a limb in the hope of a cure. The masonry above the niches is carved with foliage, and in the gables are sculptured representations of the life and death of S. Alban. The pedestal is crowned with cresting and around the shrine are the bases of fourteen detached shafts that probably supported images. The structure was broken up at the Dissolution, but in 1872, more than two thousand fragments were found in the retrochoir and with amazing skill were re-assembled by the clerk of the works. Though bereft of its original splendour and magnificence, it presents the form of the mediaeval throne almost in completeness. In the north aisle of the presbytery is an imperfect replica of the pedestal of another shrine in S. Albans cathedral, that of S. Amphibalus, which was enclosed within an iron grille in the new retrochoir c. 1350. There are two gabled recesses in the sides, and at the western end a few letters of the saint's name are carved in the stonework.

The much-prized treasure of Ely cathedral was the shrine of S. Etheldreda. On the north side of the choir is a lofty two-storeyed structure of stone that Gilbert Scott pronounced to be the pedestal of the shrine, constructed c. 1330 (Pl. 27). The silver-plated feretrum that rested on it was embossed with many figures, and adorned with a golden statue of Christ in Glory and a multitude of precious stones, of crystal and pearl, onyx and beryl, and amethyst and topaz.

A considerable portion of the throne of S. Werburgh's shrine, that has been pieced together with some ingenuity, remains in Chester cathedral at the west end of the Lady Chapel. It is a rectangular structure, nearly 6 ft. in length, 3 ft. wide and about 14 ft. high, and is of the late Decorated period. Of its two stages the lower is opened up with two ogee-arched niches on each side and one at each end. The upper stage has cusped and gabled arches in the sides and ends, and at the angles are buttresses that are panelled in the upper part and crowned with gabled niches containing figures of the royal line of S. Werburgh. The pedestal is enriched with carved ornament, crockets and finials, and is indeed a valuable relic.

All that remains of the shrine of S. Osmund at Salisbury is the so-called Stourton monument in the south arcade of the nave. Obviously it was never designed as a tomb, for in the sides are three almost circular openings, and internally the 'tomb' is divided by a wall running lengthways. This unusual monument is built of light grey marble, and is 7 ft. long, 3 ft. wide and 2 ft. in height. Probably it was the base of the pedestal on which was placed the feretrum containing the bones of S. Osmund and originally stood in the retrochoir of the cathedral. On certain festivals the feretrum was carried in procession by the clergy, and at the west door of the cathedral was held aloft by the bearers as the procession passed beneath. After being dismantled at the Reformation the pedestal was thrown out, but was reused as the tomb of Charles, Lord Stourton, who was hanged in the market place at Salisbury in 1556.

Many shrines have disappeared entirely, leaving no trace of their existence; of others, a few fragments are all that survive. In the south choir-aisle of Lincoln cathedral are the base and a few stones of the shrine of Little S. Hugh, a Christian boy of nine years who was believed to have been crucified by the Jews of Lincoln in 1255, a myth born of the popular prejudice of the time. In the museum at S. Mary's abbey, York, are considerable portions of the pedestal of the shrine of S. William, formerly Archbishop William Fitzherbert d. 1154. They are of slate-coloured stone from the Tees valley, and the architectural character of the three niches in the museum would date them as early fifteenth century. The niches which probably occupied one side of the throne are adorned with panelling and cresting and have imitation lierne vaults; in the mouldings are diminutive heads, some wearing crowns. The head of S. William was preserved in a silver-gilt reliquary in the form of a head, encrusted with jewels.

But not all cathedrals possessed the whole body of a saint. Many had to rest content with a limb or a piece of apparel. It became the practice to dismember the body and display the portions in various places in the church; thus the interest was distributed and the pilgrims had more to see. When Bishop Cantelupe of Hereford died on his way to Rome in 1282, his remains were divided; the bones went to Hereford cathedral, the heart to Ashbridge in Bucks., and the flesh was sent to a church near Orvieto in Italy. The acquisition of such relics became an obsession, particularly in the monastic cathedrals. Not infrequently all scruples were thrown to the winds in securing relics that would bring fame and revenue to a pilgrimage church. The trafficking in saintly relics led to reprehensible practices. On his appointment to the abbacy of Peterborough in 1176, one of the Canterbury monks, Benedict by name, purloined and carried off to his new home two flagstones torn from the spot where Becket had been slain, and there re-used them for making two altars.

As a rule saintly relics were encased in caskets or reliquaries made of precious metals and inlaid with gems. Their shape and size varied as much as their contents; they might be fashioned like

a church, and often were shaped like the limb or object enclosed.
In the Victoria and Albert Museum is a silver-gilt reliquary 4 in.
high in the form of a human finger. An inscription round the base
reads 'Os digitus S. Theodore' (the finger bone of S. Theodore),
and the small bone is visible through tiny Gothic piercings.

Canterbury cathedral possessed a veritable museum of saintly
relics and *disjecta membra*, more than fifty in number, consisting
mostly of bones and dust of the martyrs, that were displayed in
various parts of the cathedral. Generally the most valued reliquary
was housed in a tabernacle above the reredos of the High Altar,
and others were displayed on a beam above the altar or in some
other conspicuous position. In 1448 the reliquary of S. Feologeld,
a seventh-century archbishop, was removed from the High Altar
at Canterbury and placed upon a beam that spanned the arch
opening into the Corona chapel. In the muniments of Lichfield
cathedral is an inventory of the treasures stored in the sacristy in
1345; they include a painted casket of wood that contained the
head of S. Chad, an arm of the Saint, a portable shrine enclosing
other of his bones, a fragment of the Holy Sepulchre and a part
of S. Peter's cross. At Hereford cathedral is a small ark-shaped
reliquary of oak, measuring about 7 in. long, covered with copper
plates overlaid with Limoges enamelling (Pls. 28, 29). The front
depicts the Martyrdom of Becket and on the sloping roof is the
entombment of S. Thomas; each of the gabled ends bears the figure
of a saint and the back is decorated with quatrefoils. In all probability the *châsse* was made to hold some relic of S. Thomas of
Canterbury.

In the mediaeval cathedral all the chapels in the retrochoir and
in the choir-transepts where such existed were fenced with screens
of timber or stone. At Winchester the Lady Chapel and those on
either side of it retain their timber parclose screens, and at Ely,
the easternmost bays of the choir-aisles which were appropriated
by Bishops Alcock and West for their chantries, are enclosed by
stone screens that are virtually solid walls encrusted with tabernacled niches. Before the disastrous fire of 1829 at York cathedral,
the altar of Our Lady beneath the great east window and the
chapels flanking it on either side were fenced with wooden screens;
on the north was the chapel of S. Stephen and on the south, All
Saints chapel. The seven chapels in the choir-arm of Exeter cathedral retain their mediaeval screens more or less in their original
condition. The five in the retrochoir are of stone and Perpendicular Gothic in style. The screens of the Lady Chapel and of the
lateral chapels of S. John the Evangelist and S. Gabriel are of the
same general design and date from the end of the fourteenth cen-

tury. The stonework bears traces of colour and gilding. Projecting from the north choir-aisle near the east is the chapel of S. George, founded for the chantry of Sir John Speke in 1506, and on the south is the chapel of S. Saviour, both of which are enclosed with stone screens. Farther west the chapels of S. Andrew on the north side of the choir and of S. James on the south have parclose screens of wood, dating from the late fourteenth century (Fig. 22).

Prior to the Reformation, the most arresting feature in the nave of a cathedral church was the Great Rood, a wooden crucifix appropriately coloured with attendant figures of the Virgin Mary and S. John Evangelist. The Rood stood on a stout beam or was suspended from the roof by iron chains. In the secular cathedrals it was raised above the pulpitum, and in the monastic churches above the rood-screen. It was customary for lights to be burned before the Rood group. In 1324 when the pulpitum at Exeter was almost complete, a rood-beam of iron was fixed above it at a cost of 12s. 4d., and the following year £3 4s. was spent on gold leaf and colours for painting the Rood. When Archbishop Roger of York rebuilt the choir of the cathedral, 1160–70, a Rood was set up over the pulpitum, and within the figure of Christ were enclosed relics of the Holy Apostles, Peter, Paul and Matthew and of other saints. During the reconstruction of the choir, 1361–1405, a new Rood appears to have been carved, and in 1415 a beam was purchased to carry it. In 1419 bottles of oil were bought at a cost of 4s. 6d. for 'the lamp burning before the Cross in the nave'. Yet another Rood was made at York in 1516 and two years later a veil of painted canvas was provided to hang before it during Lent.

Early in the thirteenth century 'the incomparable painter and sculptor', Walter de Colchester, made and erected a Rood group at S. Albans 'at the cost of the sacristy, yet by his own efforts and industry'.[1]

The position of the Rood group at Canterbury is not easy to determine. The rood-screen consisting of an open iron grate was beneath the western arch of the crossing, and above it was the strainer arch of stone. Probably the Rood was suspended at an unusually great height from the western crossing. At Old S. Paul's the Rood stood above the cornice of the pulpitum, between the eastern piers at the crossing, but its fame was eclipsed by the northern Rood or Crux Borealis, situated near the door of the north transept. It was reputed to have been carved by Joseph of Arima-

---

[1] Walter de Colchester subsequently entered the monastery and in 1213 he became sacrist of S. Albans. His fame as an artist spread, for the convent at Canterbury employed him to make the shrine of S. Thomas Becket.

thea, and became the object of popular devotion amongst London citizens.

In a sacrist's Roll of Norwich cathedral, reference is made to the curious ceremony of 'letting a man down from the roof, habited as an angel, to cense the Rood'. In the high vault of the nave, immediately above the site of the rood-screen, is a large circular hole that apparently was used for this purpose. The antiquary, Lambarde, 1536–1601, who lived through the Reformation period, witnessed as a boy a similar ceremony at Whitsuntide in Old S. Paul's. 'The coming down of the Holy Ghost was set forth by a white figure that was let to fly out of a hole in the roof of the great aisle,' and a large silver censer 'descending out of the same place almost to the very ground, was swung up and down to such a length that it reached almost to the west gate of the church'.

All the roods and the many altars and images that were affixed to piers in the naves of English cathedrals, as well as the screens enclosing aisle chapels were swept away at the Reformation. Less than a century ago when the Reformation whitewash was cleaned off the Norman piers on the north side of S. Albans nave, several reredos paintings were revealed. On the western faces of five of the piers are two paintings of the thirteenth century, one above the other, depicting the Crucifixion and an episode in the life of the Virgin Mary. In the fourteenth-century figures of Edward Confessor, S. Thomas of Canterbury and other saints, all now very indistinct were painted on the southern faces of the same piers. In other cathedrals there is documentary evidence of the former existence of altars in the nave, whose dedications are known, as at Old S. Paul's where the names of seven nave altars have been established.

Except for the choir stalls, the sedilia and the stone wall benches occasionally found in the aisles of the nave, as at Salisbury, or at the bases of the nave piers as at Exeter, there were no seats as permanent fixtures in the cathedrals of the Middle Ages.

Denuded of their altars and reredoses, screens and images, hangings and lights; robbed of the glass of varied hues that filled the traceried windows; bleached of the colour-painting that was an essential finish, and scraped down to the bare bones of the structure, the cold grey interiors of our cathedrals present a vastly different aspect today from that of the Middle Ages. William of Malmesbury, describing the interior of Conrad's choir at Canterbury, wrote: 'Nothing like it could be seen in England, either for the brilliancy of its coloured glass windows, the beauty of the marble pavement, or the many-coloured pictures that led the wandering eye to the very summit of the ceiling.'

The vision of the mediaeval mason was of interiors rich in colour and decoration, not the grey drab structures to which we are accustomed today. The ancient craftsman was gifted with a sense of colour, 'a secret simple as innocence', by which brilliant reds, greens, blues and gold were applied in juxtaposition to masonry, capitals, carvings, spandrels, vaults, screens and furniture, and monuments, which in conjunction with the jewelled glass of the windows attained a polychromatic harmony that defies description and may never be recaptured. 'Nothing of crudity found place in the colour schemes of the Middle Ages. Have we not their illuminated manuscripts in evidence? . . . and we cannot doubt that the same mastery was shown in the colour schemes of cathedral painting.'[1] The extent to which painting formed an integral part of the decoration of mediaeval churches has only been recognized within recent years.[2] In few cathedrals are not to be found some vestiges of mediaeval colour, slight though they may be. Regrettable is it that with the exception of York, nearly all our cathedrals have lost most of their ancient glass.

From the seventh century it was the practice to paint the interior walls of churches, whatever the size. Bishop Wilfrid's church at Hexham was 'decorated with pictures and colours of great and wonderful variety', and the Normans used colour profusely to enrich the architecture of their vast cathedrals. At S. Albans, the plastered walls and piers were relieved by horizontal red lines to simulate courses of masonry, and the outer order of the Norman arches of the tower and nave are painted with red and blue *voussoirs* alternately. On the soffits of the nave arches are painted chevron patternings of red and blue and of other motives such as the star and lozenge.

In the chapel of S. Gabriel in the crypt of Canterbury are some paintings that 'can be ranked amongst the finest examples of Western European art of the twelfth century' (*Tristram*). Enough remains to indicate that the walls, the vaulting, the central column and its capital were all originally covered with paintings of brilliant colours. In the apse, which was walled up late in the twelfth century, is a series of paintings on the surface of the vault, the centrepiece being a large figure of Christ in Majesty supported by four angels. Arranged in tiers, four on the north and the same number on the south wall, are paintings portraying the story of the archangel Gabriel's mission. On the soffit of the arch above the site of the altar, in allusion to the Heavenly Host, are figures of the

---

[1] *The Cathedral Builders in England.* E. S. Prior.
[2] In the present century Prof. E. W. Tristram has uncovered and preserved countless examples of mural paintings in the churches of this country.

angels of the seven churches of Asia, each holding a candlestick, and an eighth figure depicts S. John Evangelist writing the Apocalypse. To the right and left of the apse are two seraphim, each with six wings spotted with eyes. On the groined vaulting in the western part of S. Gabriel's chapel are a number of large roundels containing figures of bishops; smaller medallions of demi-figures of kings, angels and prophets are encircled by interlacing scroll-work in places. The transverse arches springing from the central column are decorated with vesica-shaped patterning. High up on the wall of S. Anselm's chapel, above the chapel of S. Gabriel, is a painting of S. Paul shaking the viper into the fire at Melita (Pl. 25). The technique of the figure-painting in both chapels shows marked Byzantine influence, particularly in the treatment of the drapery, and 'has something of the perfection due to a long and fine tradition' (*Tristram*). On the vaulting of the Trinity chapel, in which stood Becket's shrine, and on that of the ambulatory were paintings of various prophets and saints, that radiated from the central boss of each bay. All traces of them have vanished, but drawings made by George Austin early in the nineteenth century are preserved in the cathedral library.

As part of the general scheme of colour decoration at Canterbury, the walls of the Corona chapel also were adorned with paintings. Less than two centuries ago a figure of S. Christopher was discernible above the tomb of Cardinal Pole at the north-west; and at the west end of the north choir-aisle was a large mural painting of the Apocalypse. In the recess of a blocked-up window of the same aisle near the north transept is a remarkable painting of the Legend of S. Eustace, a subject that is rarely found in English churches. In the crowded composition with a winding river on whose banks are woodlands and towns, are represented several episodes in the life of the Saint. Prominent in the lower part of the picture is a large white stag, between whose antlers is a crucifix; and at the top is the martyrdom of S. Eustace, showing a brazen bull with a furnace below into which the Saint is being thrown.

When Gilbert Scott lowered the choir stalls at Rochester to their original level, he brought to light heraldic diaper patterning that once covered the whole length of the walls. The design consists of a series of red quatrefoils containing golden lions, and in the blue interspaces were golden fleurs-de-lis. At the bottom was a border of interlacing ribboning and yellow-petalled roses. Beneath a string course at the top were traces of a broader band of ribbon-work alternating with green panels, each bearing a shield. The decoration was probably executed after 1340. The lions of England and the fleurs-de-lis of France in juxtaposition indicate

Edward III's ambition to unite the two realms. Of the same period are the remains of a mural painting nearly 6 feet high representing the Wheel of Fortune, on the north wall of the choir opposite the episcopal throne. The central figure, Fortune, is pictured as a queen, wearing a crown and robed in yellow. With her right hand she is controlling the movement of the wheel, and on the left are two slumbering figures of men attempting to gain a hold. At the top is seated a man arrayed in a rich robe, apparently one of Fortune's favourites. The background was originally diapered with small flowers.

Painted decoration was applied alike to the roofs and vaults of mediaeval cathedrals. The flat timber ceiling of the Norman nave of Peterborough is covered with three rows of diamond-shaped panels framed in many colours. Those in the central row bear seated figures, some of which are sacred and others of a grotesque nature. During the restoration of the ritual choir of S. Albans in 1870, the cleaning of the flat wooden ceiling revealed paintings in the sixty-six panels, consisting of the sacred monogram IHS, alternating with the heraldic arms of Edward III and his kinsfolk. Later examples of decorative painting occur on the roofs of the presbytery and the central tower of S. Albans. In the fifteenth-century roundels were painted on the cells of the wooden vault of the presbytery, presenting figures of the Lamb, the symbol of S. John Baptist, and the eagle of S. John Evangelist. The decorative effect is enhanced by the leafage above and below the roundels. The painted ceiling of the tower, dating from the sixteenth century, is divided into sixteen panels bearing coats of arms and the Red and White Roses.

At Ely cathedral are preserved the accounts of the materials and colours, and the wages paid to the workmen for painting the timber vaulting of the Octagon. The Fabric Roll of 1339 records the employment of Walter, the master painter for forty-two weeks; he was paid 9d. a week, receiving also his keep and a robe. Remnants of the colouring were revealed in 1850, when the roof was cleaned of yellow wash. The compartments of the vaulting were treated with painted tracery, consisting of a series of quatrefoils in stone colour, outlined in black and filled with green. On some of the mouldings of the ribs, traces of brilliant red remained.

Colour decoration was applied to stone vaulting, though as a rule somewhat sparingly. The painted roundel seems to have been a favourite motif. On the high vault of the choir of Salisbury cathedral are roundels portraying prophets, apostles and figures representing the months of the year. They were probably executed shortly after the consecration of the cathedral in 1258, and the

E*

specific arrangement of the subjects depicted indicates the original position of the High Altar. The series in the western half of the choir depicts twenty-four prophets and personages of the Old Testament, but in the bay flanked by the choir-transepts is a central vesica of Christ in Majesty surrounded by roundels of the four Evangelists, which mark the focal point of the choir where stood the High Altar. Eastwards of this bay, smaller roundels are devoted to secular subjects emblematic of the months of the year. The paintings were buff-washed in the eighteenth century but were renewed by Clayton and Bell about seventy-five years ago. On the vaulting of the choir-transepts are faintly visible similar paintings that have not been recoloured.

At Winchester cathedral, the whole of the vault of Bishop Orleton's chapel on the north side of the Lady Chapel is covered with painted decoration; and in each of the four cells are two large and three small medallions of angels knit together with a running pattern of foliage. Less well-preserved are the paintings in the Chapel of the Holy Sepulchre, between the northern piers of the crossing. On the east wall above the altar is the Deposition and below it the Burial of Our Lord, and on the surface of the vault immediately above is a demi-figure of Christ. The other cells of the vault have the remains of painted medallions. A group of mural paintings in the Lady Chapel at Winchester are of unique interest, for, being in monotone and set within a painted architectural framework, they were intended to simulate sculpture in relief. The paintings, twenty-two in number, portray the miracles and legends of the Virgin Mary, and are disposed in two tiers on the lower parts of the walls in the eastern half of the Lady Chapel. One of the paintings represents Prior Silkstede kneeling before the Virgin and beneath him in a scroll with the inscription 'Prior Silkstede caused these polished stones, O Mary, to be ornamented at his expense'.

The recolouring of carved bosses in the high vaults of some cathedrals during the last thirty or forty years brings home to us the importance of colour in defining the sculpture. If left 'in the white', the subject of a carved boss sixty feet or more above eye level is indistinguishable from below, but when coloured the carving takes on a form at once clear and definite. In the opinion of Prof. E. W. Tristram, under whose direction innumerable bosses in our cathedrals have been cleaned and repainted, colour played so important a part in mediaeval art, partly because it served this definite practical purpose.

In the Fabric Roll of Exeter cathedral for 1308–9 are detailed the expenses incurred in colouring the bosses and ribs of the choir vault. The total cost of oil and colours, exclusive of gold, amounted to 29s. 7¾d. The bosses were primed to receive the gold; and for painting them, 31 lb. of white lead, 1½ lb. of red lead, 1 lb. 1 oz. of cinople (vermilion), 7¼ gallons of oil and 3½ lb. of varnish were purchased. The ribs and the cells of the vault were distempered with size, the operation being committed to the care of 'one daubeouer', whose wages run on for several weeks. The predominant colour used for the bosses and ribs was vermilion, together with other shades of red. In 1316–17 several painters of varying grades were employed in decorating the reredos, the sedilia and the pulpitum of Exeter cathedral, their wages ranging from 1s. 1d. to 2s. a week. A colour-grinder named Richard received 1s. a week, and for his use a marble stone and twelve round slabs with flat bases were bought, for reducing the pigments to powder. An ell of woven linen was purchased for straining the colours.

Carved corbels, stops, and figure sculpture were also painted in many colours. The magnificent corbels supporting the vaulting shafts in the choir and nave of Exeter retain much of their decoration, and the figures in the triforium stage of the Angel Choir at Lincoln cathedral were brought to life by the application of rich colours. The saints and kings in the pulpita of our cathedrals, and in reredoses such as those at Durham and Winchester took on an inconceivable splendour from the gold and the pigments lavished upon them.

The sculptured imagery on the exterior of mediaeval cathedrals was similarly treated. In its original glory, the great western façade of Wells cathedral, with its array of saints, apostles, kings and queens, blazed in illumination; the figures and the arcading were resplendent in colour and gold. Considerable traces of the decoration remain in various parts of the front.

Parclose screens, whether of stone or timber, were fitting objects for polychromatic decoration. The stone screens behind the choir stalls at Canterbury and the eastern face of the pulpitum *c.* 1304–5 were richly painted and gilded, and were described by Gilbert Scott as 'the most valuable example of the decorative painting of the fourteenth century'. Above the stalls the openings of Eastrey's screens were boarded to a height of 3 feet with oaken panels spangled with golden rosettes, and above was a red band with gilded heraldic leopards and fleurs-de-lis.

A rare example of the colour treatment of stone screens in the late Perpendicular period is seen in the chantry chapel of Bishop Audley, 1492–1502, on the south side of the Lady Chapel at Hereford cathedral. An elaborate scheme of decoration was applied to the two tiers of rectilinear panelling that compose the front of the screen. The slender shafts dividing the panels are painted with spiral bands of black and white in the manner of a barber's pole, and other colours are applied to the tracery and mouldings; in each of the twenty panels of the upper tier is a painting of an apostle or saint, with one of Our Lord, and the figures stand beneath a canopy adorned with crockets. The panels of the lower tier were treated in the same way, though only four of the figures now remain.

Of special interest is the series of paintings on the backs of the choir stalls of Carlisle cathedral that were executed c. 1484. Thirteen of the panels, illustrative of the life of S. Cuthbert, bear so great a resemblance to certain miniatures in a twelfth-century copy of Bede's *Life of S. Cuthbert*, once owned by the convent at Durham, as to warrant the assumption that the painter either made or was given sketches of the subjects depicted in the manuscript.[1] The stall paintings are not exact copies, but the composition, particularly in the grouping of the figures, is much the same. At the time they were made, the Bishop of Carlisle was Richard Bell, formerly the prior of Durham.

No less resplendent in colour were the shrines and monuments that graced many English cathedrals. Tomb effigies of wood, stone, and of alabaster were all picked out in appropriate colours. In the niched recesses of the shrine of S. Alban, vermilion and blue can easily be distinguished. Few mediaeval tombs retain anything of their original colours, for most have been scraped at one time or another by wrong-headed restorers. Close scrutiny in a good light may often detect slight traces of pigments.[2] The panels, the tracery and mouldings of tombs and canopies were painted in many hues and gilded, as also were the effigies, the heraldic shields and the figures of 'weepers' that often filled niches in the sides. On monuments of royal personages the heraldic devices were often enamelled. In panels on the sides of the tomb of Edward, the Black Prince at Canterbury are sixteen enamelled shields displaying the Prince's arms for peace and for war.

Effigies of wood or stone were thinly coated with gesso, a mixture of size and whiting, that provided a smooth surface for painted decoration; but in the fourteenth century when alabaster was in general use for effigies, the preparatory coat of gesso was dispensed with. In a remarkable state of preservation is the coloured effigy in Rochester cathedral of Bishop John of Sheppey, 1353–60,

---

[1] *Burlington Magazine.* LXXIII. Bertram Colgrave.
[2] On the tomb of William Longspée, first Earl of Salisbury, d. 1226, in the nave of Salisbury cathedral, green and blue are visible on the stone effigy, and vestiges of colour are to be made out on the arcading beneath.

which was discovered in the wall of the presbytery in 1825. The colour and gilding retain much of their former brilliance and afford a good example of a painted figure in its mediaeval state. The figure is carved in clunch and the bishop's robes are coloured in red, brown, gold and green. The alb, the amice and the maniple on the left arm are embroidered in gold; the head rests on two cushions treated with a diapered pattern and the face is painted in natural colours. At the feet are two dogs, each wearing a red collar with golden bells and the bishop's gloves are white with jewelled backs.

When Archbishop Chicheley founded All Souls College, Oxford, in 1438, the Fellows provided a sum of £7 a year for the maintenance of the magnificent tomb of their benefactor in Canterbury cathedral, which has ever since been the object of their care. Today the colour and gilding is as fresh as it was in the fifteenth century.

Above mediaeval tombs that lacked a canopy, wooden testers were often set up, the undersides of which served as fields for paintings. On the tester over the tomb of the Black Prince at Canterbury is a representation of the Trinity, the main feature being a large figure of God the Father and a crucifix. In the four corners are symbolical figures of the Evangelists. 'In a perfect condition this painting would rank as one of the masterpieces of Northern art' (*Tristram*). In the same cathedral is a painted tester above the tomb of Henry IV, the decoration consisting mainly of heraldic devices, but attached to the pier at the head of the tomb is a large wooden panel on which is a painting, not easily discernible, of the Martyrdom of Becket. At the other end of the tomb hangs a framed panel bearing only slight traces of a painting that has been identified as the Coronation and the Assumption of the Virgin.

The practice of painting tombs and effigies did not cease at the Reformation. In Gloucester cathedral the Renaissance monuments of Thomas Machen d. 1614, Elizabeth Williams d. 1622 and of Margaret Clent d. 1623, together with the effigies and kneeling figures were decked out in colours, which were renewed after cleaning in 1948.

In the majority of English cathedrals, mediaeval glass is as rare as colour decoration. Stained or painted glass was an essential finish to a church; it was part of the scheme of colour decoration embracing the whole of the interior and its fittings and furniture. Depicted in glass, figures and pictorial subjects were but a means to that end, their didactic character being of secondary importance.

When a church was built in the Middle Ages, the windows were filled with canvas, linen or plain glass, until some benefactor came forward to provide the painted glass or until the fabric fund permitted.

The zeal of the iconoclasts of the sixteenth and seventeenth centuries swept away the ancient glass in most English cathedrals, but exceptional in this respect is York, a veritable treasury of pre-Reformation glass of all periods from the twelfth to the sixteenth century. In all no less than one hundred and twenty windows of York cathedral retain their original glass, now in the process of re-insertion after its removal during the Second World War. In quantity and quality the earliest glass there is not to be compared with that at Canterbury, where splendid specimens dating c. 1220, though far from complete, remain in the aisles of the choir, in the Saint's chapel, and in the Corona chapel. Originally, the fourteen windows in the choir-aisles depicted incidents in the life of Our Lord, but in the north aisle two only retain their medallions, several of which have been transferred from other windows in the aisle. Of the forty-nine single-light windows in the clerestory of the choir, sixteen are mediaeval, each having two figures illustrating the ancestry of Our Lord. The twelve windows in the ambulatory of the Saint's chapel were originally filled with medallions portraying miracles wrought by the intercession of S. Thomas the Martyr, but only portions of the present glass are ancient. Notable is the medallion in the head of the window opposite the shrine of S. Thomas representing the Martyr clad in pontifical robes issuing from the shrine, the only representation of the shrine now existing. The glass would not be earlier than 1220, the year in which the body of S. Thomas was translated from the crypt to the new shrine in the Trinity chapel. Of the five windows in the Corona, the central one contains fragments of thirteenth-century glass, depicting the Crucifixion, the Burial, the Resurrection and the Ascension, and Pentecost, surrounded by incidents from the Old Testament.

Contrasting with the thirteenth-century medallion glass at Canterbury is the grisaille (grey background) glass of the Five Sisters window at York, the largest and best-preserved of its kind in the country, dating c. 1250. In the nave of York and in the chapter house and vestibule are more than forty windows filled with glass of the Decorated period. Those in the nave windows are an admixture of grisaille and canopied figures of saints with coloured borders. The glass in the great west window was mainly the gift of Archbishop Melton in 1338, and displays three tiers of figures; the lowest are of eight Archbishops of York, the middle row of eight saints, including SS. Peter and Paul, and in the top row are smaller unidentified figures, associated with the Coronation of the Virgin. Archbishop Melton gave 100 marks for the glazing of the west window. 'On Monday next after the Feast of S. Agatha [Feb. 6], 1338, it was covenanted by indenture that Thomas de Boneston, vical-choral, should at his own proper costs glaze two windows of this Cathedral Church, viz., on each side one, find all the glass for the same, and pay the workmen their wages for the finishing thereof.' The Keeper of the Fabric, Thomas de Ludham, paid Boneston 22 marks out of the Archbishop's gift for 'his proper costs'. Another indenture of the same year was made between Robert —— and Thomas de Boneston for the 'making of a window at the west gable of this Cathedral Church, and to find all sort of glass for the same, and for doing the work the said Thomas was to pay him 6d. a foot for white and 12d. a foot for coloured glass'. In the windows of the chapter house are alternate panels of grisaille and medallions, the latter illustrating the lives of various saints, and the heads of the Geometric tracery are occupied by heraldic shields dating from c. 1300.

The glass in the choir is almost wholly Perpendicular, belonging to the early part of the fifteenth century, the golden age of glass-making. The canopied niche of Gothic masonry furnished the glasswright with a motif that dominated window design of this period. Typical are the canopied saints, apostles and bishops figured in the rectilinear panels of Perpendicular windows; ranged in rows one above another, they form horizontal bands of variegated colour.

For the glazing of the great east window of York a contract was drawn up on 10 December 1405, between the dean and chapter and John Thornton of Coventry. The master-glazier undertook to 'portray the said window with his own hand, and the histories, images and other things to be painted on it'. The work was to be executed in the chapter workshop; Thornton was to provide the glass, the lead, and the workmen at the expense of the chapter. He was to receive 'for every week wherein he shall work in his art, 4s., and each year, £5 sterling, and after the work is completed, £10 for his reward'. It was to be finished within three years. Thornton was responsible for the design, and he supervised the workmen who actually made the window and the leading from his cartoons. In 1410 Thornton was made a freeman of the City of York and had a shop in Stonegate, where most of the York glaziers and glass-painters lived and worked. The city was a famous centre for glass-painting; the names of more than a hundred craftsmen are recorded. The cost of making the east window, the glass of which is mainly original, was borne by Bishop Skirlaw of Durham d. 1405. In all there are some two hundred panelled figures. At the top is God the Father, and three rows below contain scenes from the Old Testament, from the Creation to the death of Absalom. Lower tiers depict illustrations of the Book of Revelations, and in the bottom row are saints and kings.

The clerestory lights in the western part of the choir of York comprise an assembly of thirty-eight figures of the saints and apostles who were instrumental in spreading the Christian faith in the north of England. In the outer wall of the north choir-transept is the famous S. William window of five lights, 73 feet in height, filled with glass representing the miracles of S. William of York. The glass was given by the Roos family of Helmsley castle, portrayed at the base of the lights. The corresponding window in the south choir-transept pictures scenes from the life of the Durham Saint, Cuthbert; the cost was defrayed by a bequest of Bishop Langley of Durham d. 1437. At various times since the Reformation, the glass at York has been taken from its setting and re-assembled in a careless and haphazard manner, resulting in a jumble of ancient and modern work. 'It is no great exaggeration to say that, apart from extraneous insertions, there are scraps of most windows in every other' (*Times*, 18 Feb. 1949).

Earlier and rather larger than the east window at York is that at Gloucester cathedral, with row upon row of rectilinear panels filled with canopied figures of Our Lord, the Apostles, Saints and Kings. From the heraldic shields the glass can be dated between 1347 and 1350, and is said to commemorate Edward III's victorious campaign in France, that culminated in the battle of Crécy.

Though less fortunate than York, Wells perhaps possesses more ancient glass than most English cathedrals. The east window above the High Altar, dating *c.* 1340 presents the Tree of Jesse, a genealogical tree showing the descent of Our Lord from Jesse, the father of King David. At the base of the seven-light window is a reclining figure of Jesse, from which issue twining branches of vine. The central stem bears the Virgin and Child beneath a golden canopy, and in the top panel is a representation of the Crucifixion. On either side intertwining branches enclose tiers of figures, including three kings, David, Solomon and Jechonias, together with three prophets of the Old Testament. In the choir-aisles and chapels is much early fourteenth-century glass, though some of the windows are composed of fragments put together at random and the windows of the Lady Chapel are also filled with similar glass jumbled together with modern insertions.

II. The Cathedral Precincts and Buildings in the Close

❡ THE NORMAN SUBJUGATION of Saxon England was not without
its impress upon the environment of our mediaeval cathedrals, in
particular upon that of the secular foundations. The cathedral
priories such as Canterbury and Norwich, with their cloisters and
the extensive buildings that housed the monks, differing little from
other monastic establishments, stood within walled precincts entered by stately gatehouses and were to all intents and purposes
isolated from the outside world. In the nature of ecclesiastical
garrisons also were the secular cathedrals, many of which stood in
a spacious walled enclosure or Close in a secluded spot away from
the centre of the city. Within the Close were erected the Bishop's
Palace, the dwellings of the canons, the vicars-choral, the chantry
priests, and not infrequently unnecessary cloisters.

The planning of the conventual buildings attached to the monastic cathedrals followed the normal method of other Benedictine
houses. To the south of the nave were the cloisters, consisting of
four covered walks enclosing a square garth and lighted by open
arcading or traceried windows. Ranged about the cloisters and
entered from the east, south and west walks were the main monastic apartments. To the east were the chapter house and the *calefactorium* or warming house, with the monks' *dorter* or dormitory
above; on the south was the *frater* or refectory, with a kitchen and
other offices adjoining it at the west; and the western range was

145

the cellarer's building. At Canterbury (Fig. 16), Gloucester (Fig. 9), and Chester (Fig. 18), the cloisters and monastic buildings lay to the north of the nave, away from the noise of the city; and at Rochester, owing to the restricted space south of the nave, the cloisters stood on the south side of the choir. Though there were slight variations in the planning of the conventual buildings, the relative arrangement remained constant. At Durham, where the buildings are fairly intact, the dorter occupied the upper floor of the western block, a very spacious and noble apartment (Fig. 11).

In addition there were other buildings within the precincts of a cathedral priory, such as the *farmery* or infirmary, the guest hall, the prior's lodging, stables and barns. The Aula Nova at Canterbury with its Norman staircase is a remarkable survival of a monastic guest hall; and Prior Crauden's chapel at Ely, a delightful specimen of Decorated Gothic bears witness to the importance of the head of the monastery attached to Ely cathedral in the Middle Ages.

Amongst the mediaeval gatehouses of the monastic cathedrals now standing are the Ely Porta *c.* 1396, a huge three-storeyed building that has served the varied purposes of prison, chapel, brewery and grammar school since the Dissolution, and Prior Goldstone II's Gatehouse built *c.* 1517 that is the main entrance to the precincts of Canterbury cathedral for the pilgrim of today.

The precincts of the secular cathedrals were used by the laity who, in some instances seemed to claim a right of way through the Close during the hours of daylight; at night-time undesirables were wont to frequent the surroundings. At Old S. Paul's a precinct-wall was erected by Bishop Richard de Belmeis, 1108–28, and in 1280 the city fathers complained that the gates were closed at times inconvenient to the citizens. They claimed the eastern part of the churchyard as the assembly place of their folk-motes and the western end of the Close was the rendezvous of the armed bands that were trained for the defence of London. By letters patent of Edward I, the wall of S. Paul's churchyard was strengthened in 1285. 'By the lurking of thieves and other bad people in the night-time within the precincts, divers robberies, homicides and fornications had been committed therein; for the prevention of the like for the future . . . and also for the better security of the canons and officers [Edward I] granted unto the dean and canons licence to enclose the churchyard with a wall on every side, with fitting gates and posterns thereto, to be opened every morning and closed every night' (*Dugdale*). That same year the chapters of Lincoln, Exeter and Wells were granted licences to erect walls round their Closes and churchyards. At Lincoln the cathedral precincts were haunted by desperadoes who were a menace to the personal safety of the clergy, especially when on their way to and from the choir for the midnight office. The clerics built a wall 12 feet high and another licence of 1319 empowered them to put up towers and gatehouses. Of the five gatehouses that formerly gave entrance to the Close at Lincoln two remain; the fourteenth-century Pottergate at the south-east and the Exchequer Gate, a large three-storeyed building at the west of the cathedral.

A tragic event that occurred in the Close of Exeter in 1285 is evidence of the need of protective measures in the purlieus of cathedrals in the Middle Ages. On his return from matins at two in the morning, the precentor, Walter Lechlade, was murdered in the precincts. Edward I and his Queen who spent Christmas in the Bishop's Palace 'were very industrious in finding out the murderers', and the ex-Mayor of Exeter who was implicated in the crime was hanged. Further, the King ordered the cathedral Close to be forthwith walled and rendered secure with gates.

When the episcopal palace at Lichfield was rebuilt by Bishop Walter Langton in 1299, the cathedral and the dwellings of the ecclesiastics were surrounded with a wall and a foss, as if it were a baronial castle. The wall remained standing until the Civil War, 1643.

In 1327 the dean and chapter of Salisbury received a licence from Edward III to crenellate the Close; and three years later, to provide material for the walls, they obtained leave to use the masonry of Old Sarum cathedral and of the buildings which the canons had occupied in the abandoned city. Embedded in the wall of Salisbury Close in Exeter Street are lumps of masonry carved with Norman mouldings and ornament that betoken their place of origin. Of the mediaeval gatehouses at Salisbury, King's Gate of the Perpendicular period and the fourteenth-century S. Anne's Gate remain almost intact.

By the middle of the fourteenth century few of the secular cathedrals were unprotected by walls. Although Hereford cathedral from its position in the Welsh marches was particularly vulnerable to attack by bands of marauders, the walling of the Close was deferred until 1389.

Unlike the brethren of the cathedral priories, the residentiary canons and clerics of the secular cathedrals did not live in common but dwelt in houses assigned them in their Close. The various dwellings were not disposed on any regular plan; their arrangement and site were governed by considerations of space and convenience. In general the bishop's palace stood to the south of the cathedral; at Lichfield it is on the north and was so at Old S. Paul's. Usually the deanery also was in the north of the Close, but at Chichester it is on the south.

Many of the secular chapters followed the lead of the monastics in providing themselves with cloisters and chapter house, that normally occupied the same relative position as in the cathedral priories. The chapter house was as indispensable in the one establishment as in the other, but secular cloisters were a superfluity, an architectural extravagance of little use save for processional purposes and as shady promenades for meditative clerics on a hot summer's day. With the exception of York and Lichfield all the secular cathedrals were furnished with cloisters, generally built south of the nave, a vestibule from the east walk leading into the chapter house. It is truly remarkable that the largest cloisters in the land are those at Salisbury, where there was no need for them. The four walks enclose a garth measuring 140 feet square. The cathedral must have been practically complete before the chapter resolved upon the costly luxury of cloisters, for the north walk which is invariably built against the aisle wall beneath the windows, is separated from the church by a wide court or yard open to the sky, an arrangement that was necessitated by the low sills of the aisle windows, which would otherwise have been blocked up by the cloister roof (Fig. 1). In the middle of the fifteenth century an upper floor was built over the east walk of Salisbury cloisters, the northern half being used as a Divinity School and the southern as a library. The latter was taken down in 1775, and the books removed to the northern part, a commodious chamber about 70 feet long.

At Lincoln cathedral the cloisters and chapter house are situated to the north of the choir. The Galilee porch attached to the south transept, the south-western transept and the episcopal palace to the south precluded the erection of cloisters in the normal position (Fig. 20).

As regards their shape and position the cloisters of Chichester cathedral are quite exceptional. There, they are laid out as an irregular quadrangle and there is no north walk.[1] The south transept of the cathedral projects into the middle of the garth; the eastern walk is entered by a door in the south aisle of the choir, and the western alley leads into the south aisle of the nave (Fig. 10). At Hereford are the remains of two cloisters. To the south of the nave are the eastern and southern walks of the canons' cloisters, and connecting the south choir-transept with the College of the Vicars-Choral is one walk of the Vicars' cloisters (Fig. 15).

[1] At Wells and Hereford also the north walk was omitted.

Common to all the monastic houses, secular cathedrals and collegiate foundations of the Middle Ages was the chapter house, in which the members of the establishment met to discuss all matters relating to the administration of the house. In the cathedral priories the chapter of monks was convened every morning before the celebration of High Mass, but in the secular cathedrals the canons sat in chapter once a week. Whatever the plan of the building the seating accommodation took the form of stone wall-benches. The chapter house was usually built off the east walk of the cloisters and was entered by a passage or vestibule. At Wells it stood to the north of the choir, the usual site being occupied by an earlier chapel (Fig. 17); and at Old S. Paul's the chapter house stood in the middle of small cloisters on the south side of the nave (Fig. 19). In the absence of cloisters, the chapter house may be a detached building situated to the north of the choir, as at York, Lichfield and Southwell; or an outbuilding of the choir. That at Llandaff is of an uncommon form, being a square apartment projecting from the south wall of the choir and having an octagonal storey above that was used as a treasury. At Glasgow cathedral the chapter room is the lower chamber of a two-storeyed building at the north-east angle of the choir, and above was the sacristy. The apsidal chapel (?) of the Norman period attached to the choir of Ripon cathedral on the south side was subdivided into a chapter house and sacristy in the fourteenth century (Fig. 23).

In the cathedral priories the chapter house was generally rectangular on plan, a form that entailed no difficulty in building the monks' dorter above it. All those of the Norman period were of this type, though sometimes as at Durham and Norwich, they terminated in an apse at the east. That at Bristol is entered from the east cloister walk by a three-aisled vestibule of exquisite Norman architecture (Pl. 21) and a similar vaulted vestibule of the thirteenth century opens into the chapter house of Chester cathedral.

Architecturally, the English chapter house attained its most glorious expression in the unrivalled series of polygonal buildings that belong to the thirteenth century. This form, of monastic origin, appeared first at Worcester cathedral, where, the original chapter house erected c. 1130 was circular on plan but was made decagonal c. 1400. It was the prototype of the ten-sided chapter house of Lincoln, c. 1230, and of the octagonal chapter houses at Westminster abbey, c. 1245, and Salisbury, c. 1265 (Pl. 30). The secular chapters greatly favoured this form as there was no difficulty in fitting it on to the east cloister walk. Standing free of cloistral buildings, it was possible to open up the sides of a polygonal chapter house with large windows that would flood the interior with light. Those of Westminster and Salisbury proved an inspiration for several that followed later in the thirteenth century, viz., Lichfield, Wells, York and Southwell. The chapter house at Lichfield, to the north of the choir, is an eight-sided building, but is longer east to west than north to south (Fig. 19). It has an upper floor that was intended to be a chapel.

The majority of polygonal chapter houses were roofed with ribbed vaulting springing from a central pier, affording an opportunity for an architectural *tour-de-force* that anticipated the complex rib-structure of later Gothic. In the chapter houses of York and Southwell the central pier was dispensed with.

The chapter house at Wells, *c.* 1285, is notable for the vaulted undercroft which is divided by eight piers into two concentric aisles. In the later example at Old S. Paul's, 1332, the chapter room was raised upon an open storey; of the ten-sided chapter house of Hereford cathedral, *c.* 1360, only parts of the walls remain. Exeter and Chichester were the only secular cathedrals that did not adopt the polygonal form.

In no secular cathedral of the Middle Ages are the residentiary buildings in the Close so complete and so well preserved as at Wells. The Liberty of S. Andrew, as the precincts were called, was enclosed with battlemented walls by licence obtained in 1285, but the two gatehouses in the market place of Wells were much later, being built by Bishop Beckington, 1443–65. Penniless Porch, where a dole was distributed daily to the needy, opens on to what was the lay cemetery at the west of the cathedral, and the more splendid Bishop's Eye, a few yards to the south is the entrance to the episcopal palace. The principal buildings in the Close are the palace, the deanery, the archdeaconry, the residences of the canons, and the Vicars' Close. The palace, some distance south of the cathedral, is virtually a fortified manor house occupying an area of about fourteen acres and surrounded by embattled walls and a moat. At the angles are bastion towers and the palace is entered by a fortified gatehouse at the north-west. Externally the palace presents the aspect of a mediaeval castle. The buildings of the main block are ranged round three sides of a quadrangle; in addition was the Great Hall, a magnificent thirteenth-century apartment, 112 feet in length, of which only the shell remains. To the north-west of the cathedral is the deanery, a substantial building mainly of the fifteenth century with crenellated parapets. Having been modernized the exterior has lost much of its mediaeval aspect. The archdeaconry retains its hall, with a fine open timber roof, but the exterior is modern, and the adjoining dwel-

lings of the canons have likewise undergone improvements. Farther east, opposite the chapter house is the Vicars' Close, a delightful little Gothic thoroughfare of the fifteenth century, with twenty-
one stone houses on either side. Each house has a garden in front
and a small one at the rear, and originally consisted of an upper
and a lower chamber. The Vicars' Close is entered at the southern
end by a gatehouse, the upper floor of which is the vicars' dining-
hall, with kitchen and other offices adjoining. In the injunctions
issued by Bishop Beckington, it was ordained that 'every vicar
going out or going in at the Close Gate shall say a paternoster and
an ave for the soul of Bishop Ralph of Shrewsbury, founder of the
Close and for the souls of his predecessors, for benefactors and for
all Christian souls'. The Vicars' Close communicates directly with
the cathedral by the covered bridge known as the Chain Gate
dating *c.* 1450, that spans the roadway and connects the Vicars'
Hall with the chapter house staircase. At the northern end of the
Close is a small rectangular chapel with a chamber above, that
was used by this little self-contained community at Wells.

No English cathedral possesses the advantages of site and space
to the same extent as does Salisbury. Covering an area of half a
square mile, the Close with its wide stretches of green sward provides a perfect setting for the massive pile that has weathered
seven centuries. To the south of the cathedral stands the bishop's
palace, founded by Bishop Richard Poore, 1217–29, but altered at
various times since. Several buildings in the Close retain their
ancient character and others of a later age are vested with a charm
and dignity worthy of their environment. Due west of the cathedral is the deanery, and next to it is a building called the King's
House, that was used by royalty in their progress through the
south-west. Farther north is the Wardrobe, used as such on the
occasion of royal visits. The dwellings of the canons and clerics
stood north of the cathedral, extending eastwards to S. Anne's
Gate. When the see was removed to New Sarum, each of the
canons who fulfilled his duty of residence was under the obligation
of building his own house in the precincts. In 1219 a decree was
issued in chapter ordaining that on the death of a canon his heir
should be awarded two-thirds of the value of the property that
reverted to the chapter, the remainder being surrendered as valua-
tion of the land on which it stood. Some of the canons, amongst
whom were Robert Wykehampton and Walter Scammell, both of
whom became in succession Bishops of Salisbury, presented their
houses to the chapter. By a deed of 1277 Wykehampton gave the
house he had occupied as dean, for the use of future occupants of
that office; and in the same year Scammell who was promoted to

the deanery, in like manner surrendered his former dwelling, which was to be assigned to a canon nominated by the bishop.

Differing in character from the Vicars' Close at Wells but of no less interest is the Vicars' Court at Lincoln, a quadrangle to the south of the choir of the cathedral and entered by a gateway of the late fourteenth century. In the houses ranged round the Court, which was begun towards the end of the thirteenth century, resided the vicars-choral attached to the cathedral. Between the gateway and the choir stands a stone chantry house built for the warden and the priests who served the chantry of Nicholas, Lord Cantelupe, at the altar of S. Nicholas in 1355. On the slope of the hill south of Lincoln cathedral was the bishop's palace, a stately mansion with a great hall and chapel dating from the twelfth century. A modern palace has risen close by. Some ancient walling in Eastgate is all that is left of the mediaeval deanery on the north side of the Close, also of the twelfth century. After the Civil War the building became ruinous and was swept away in 1847, to give place to the present deanery a little to the west.

At York, the Bedern College of Vicars-choral, founded in 1252, with its hall, chapel and dwellings survived until the middle of the eighteenth century. The chapel, largely restored in the present century, is all that remains. To the east of the cathedral is a quadrangular building, S. William's College, established in 1461 for the twenty-four chantry priests who served the many altars in York cathedral. By the end of the fifteenth century a corporate body of thirty-six priests resided in the College buildings that are now used as a church house for the northern province.

The Close at Lichfield was formerly surrounded by an artificial moat that has long since been drained and replaced by gardens and gravel walks. Of the walls that encircled the Close only fragments are now to be seen. The episcopal palace erected by Bishop Walter Langton, 1296–1321, at the north-east of the cathedral was demolished after the Civil War, and was rebuilt in 1687 by Bishop Thomas Wood, the task being imposed upon him as a penalty for his neglect of the diocese.

12. The Architecture of English Cathedrals

In this and the three following chapters, the chief works that were carried out in cathedral churches during the successive periods of mediaeval architecture are surveyed in broad outline. A word should be said about the dating of the various buildings and rebuildings. Documentary records made at the time work was executed are invaluable, as for example Gervase's account of the rebuilding of the eastern arm of Canterbury cathedral; but where such evidence is lacking, it is only from the architectural character that an approximate date can be fixed, by comparing it with dated work of the same period. Such deductions however must be accepted with caution, for in some parts of England advance was rapid at a given period; in other centres masons were much behind the times, employing forms and methods long since abandoned elsewhere. Moreover, specious restoration has rendered the task of dating mediaeval work increasingly difficult. A note on the Phases of Mediaeval Architecture is given in Appendix D

I. NORMAN AND TRANSITIONAL

Upon Saxon England the Norman ecclesiastics and masons imposed a form of architecture, massive, robust, and on occasion monumental, truly the material embodiment of the heavy hand on the Conqueror. Once the newcomers had secured a permanent footing in this country and had settled down in their new environment, the cathedrals and greater monastic churches were rebuilt on a vast and magnificent scale in the Romanesque style[1] of Normandy, a style that was foreign to Saxon England. It was essentially Benedictine, for the great building era in Normandy during the early part of the eleventh century had received its impulse from the revival of Benedictine monasticism, the influence of which was paramount at that time. A few years before the Conquest, Edward the Confessor's abbey church at Westminster had been built in the Norman style. The Confessor who had been brought up in Normandy sent across the Channel for masons and

---

[1] The term Romanesque is applied to all the phases of round-arched architecture that derived from the debased forms of the Classic Roman style, and were being evolved in Western Europe from the fourth century until the beginning of Gothic in the twelfth.

material, but the abbey church he built was an isolated instance of Norman architecture in pre-Conquest England.

So it is that the majority of our mediaeval cathedrals are Norman churches that have been subjected to alterations, additions or rebuilding in the centuries that followed. Durham, the greatest of our Romanesque cathedrals has undergone little change; Norwich is largely Norman architecture of the late eleventh century, and Ely, Peterborough and Gloucester retain much of their Norman fabric. On the other hand, York cathedral is an aggregate of all the mediaeval styles, and only a fragment in the crypt betokens its Norman origin. A small part of the west front of Lincoln proclaims the parentage of the greatest of all English Gothic cathedrals.

Firmly established in the sees from which the Saxon bishops had been ejected, the Norman hierarchy set about rebuilding in real earnest, in a style that was a provincial version of the Romanesque of Normandy. 'Quantity not quality' was their slogan. They vied one with another in rearing vast and imposing cathedral churches that in sheer bulk give the impression of prodigious strength. In their vehement haste, their masons built walls of tremendous thickness and piers of immense massiveness. At Winchester cathedral the Norman walling is in parts 10 feet thick; the aisle walls of the choir of Durham are nearly 7 feet thick, and the clerestory wall 6 feet 3 inches. This seeming solidity is however deceptive, for the method of construction was defective. Usually Norman walls and piers were composed of thin external facings or shells of masonry, with a filling of rubble grouted with mortar that was invariably of inferior quality. Reporting on the state of the Norman nave of Old S. Paul's cathedral after the Great Fire, Sir Christopher Wren wrote that 'the piers were only cased without with small stones not greater than a man's burden; but within is nothing but a core of small rubbish-stone and much mortar, which easily crushes and yields to the weight'. It was the enormous proportion of solid to void in Norman cathedrals that rendered the interiors so dark and gloomy.

The Norman practice with regard to foundations was inconsistent and varied considerably. At Durham cathedral the foundations of the parallel apses of the choir were sunk about 14 feet to solid rock beneath; but the masons of S. Albans, probably goaded by an impatient abbot, scamped the foundations of the aisle walls, for in 1936, during a heavy thunderstorm, water entered the building through some holes that had been dug outside and on investigation it was discovered that the foundations had been sunk to a depth of only 6 inches. Sooner or later, unsound methods of construction and inadequate foundations spelt disaster; towers crashed without warning (p. 105), and walls heeled over. In 1323 several bays of the south arcade of the Norman nave of S. Albans collapsed and in their fall wrecked the south aisle and the cloister walk outside.

The Norman masons brought with them the problem that had long taxed the ingenuity of the Romanesque builders of Western Europe, viz., the covering of a lofty church with a stone vault instead of a timber roof, as a safeguard against the ever-present danger of fire. Outbreaks were frequent in towns and cities, then largely composed of wooden houses, and when the flames spread to a church, the timber roof readily caught fire; its collapse meant a blazing mass that wrought great damage to the walls and columns of the interior. Two kinds of vaults were in use at the time of the Conquest; the barrel vault, a round-arched tunnel, the finest example of which is in S. John's Chapel in the Tower of London;

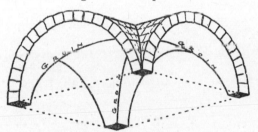

FIG 8. Diagram of groined vault

and the groined vault, with intersecting surfaces at right angles to each other. The groin or the edge of intersection is an elliptical curve crossing diagonally, and carrying the weights and thrusts of the vault to isolated points of support at the four angles.

Neither of these two forms was structually suitable for vaulting the nave or the choir of a cathedral, though the groined vault was commonly employed in Norman crypts and aisles.

The construction of walls of immense thickness was a means to this end, and eventually the problem of the high vault was solved by the Norman builders of Durham cathedral, and their achievement paved the way for Gothic architecture.

Before the end of the eleventh century the Norman ecclesiastics had embarked upon the rebuilding of all the cathedrals in the land save Exeter and Wells. Other than Old Sarum and Old S. Paul's, which have been swept away in their entirety, and York and Lichfield, they all retain substantial portions of the eleventh-century fabric.

CANTERBURY CATHEDRAL, 1070–77

Christ Church, Canterbury, was the first to be erected after the Conquest. When Abbot Lanfranc of S. Etienne, Caen, was translated to the primatial see in 1070, he found the Saxon cathedral in ruins after its total destruction by fire three years before. Immediately he set to work building a new cathedral which was completed in 1077. It was by no means a stately or imposing structure; no other Anglo-Norman cathedral was built in so short a time. Normally the eastern arm and transepts of a great church would take twenty years or longer, especially when the choir was built over a new crypt; often the building of the nave was deferred for a long period. But the design of a cathedral dates in the main from its commencement. Advances might be made in structural science and in the development of architectural form during building operations, for Norman architecture was essentially progressive in character.

Lanfranc's cathedral was a cruciform building, with a short choir-transepts with apsidal chapels at the east, an aisled nave of nine bays, a tower at the crossing and twin towers at the west (Fig. 4). The total length was about 285 feet. Of this early Norman church much of the masonry of the transepts is embedded in later work.

LINCOLN CATHEDRAL, 1074–1145

In 1067 the see of Dorchester-on-Thames fell vacant by the death of the Saxon Bishop Wulfwig, and the Conqueror installed Remigius, the almoner of Fécamp abbey, who had promoted the fortunes of Duke William by furnishing a vessel for the invasion of England. Five years later Remigius transferred the see of Dorchester to Lincoln, and on the hill within the Roman wall of the city and close by the castle, he erected the cathedral, which was begun in 1074 and finished, all but the upper parts of the west front and towers, by c. 1093. Excavations made at various times show that the Norman cathedral was cruciform on plan, 310 feet in length, with a low tower at the crossing and towers at the west. Of that building, only the central portion of the west front, together with the lower stages of the western towers remain *in situ*. In the vestibule of the nave, between the towers are to be seen the arches of the Norman triforium and traces of the clerestory windows above, which show that the three stages of the bay design of the nave were about equal in height.

The three tall cavernous recesses in the Norman walling of the west front are a striking and original feature of Lincoln cathedral

(Pl. 32). The outer recesses retain their Norman round arches, but the central one was heightened and finished with a pointed arch in the thirteenth century. This early Norman work is extremely plain and severe; the stones are small and wide-jointed and there is an absence of ornament. In 1141 the cathedral was damaged by a disastrous fire, and Bishop Alexander 'the Magnificent' lost no time in restoring the church. He roofed the building with stone vaulting and added another stage to the western towers. At the same time the bareness of the west front was relieved by applying an arcade of intersecting arches above the lateral recesses, and by inserting richly ornamented portals and the unique frieze of relief-sculptures above them. The jamb-shafts of the doorways are covered with surface decoration, and the arch-mouldings with chevron and other Norman ornament, though much of the detail is a modern renovation. The frieze, which is 3 ft. 6 in. in height, depicts incidents from Genesis and Old Testament history, and the Last Judgment, but the haphazard arrangement of the subjects suggests that the sculptures were brought from elsewhere. The Expulsion of Adam and Eve, Entering the Ark, Daniel in the Lions Den, and the Torments of the Wicked, the crowded figures of which are portrayed in lively fashion, are outstanding examples of Norman pictorial sculpture.

S. ALBANS CATHEDRAL, 1077–88

Only a few years later than Lanfranc's Canterbury was the great abbey church of S. Albans, for the building of which the Benedictine monk, Paul of Caen, who was made abbot in 1077 brought over from Normandy a band of masons to demolish the Saxon church and replace it by an imposing church 380 feet in length, of which the transepts, the central tower and portions of the nave are invaluable survivals (Fig. 13). The walls and piers are largely built of Roman bricks from the ruins of Verulamium, coated with plaster; in their stark severity and absence of ornament they are characteristic of early Norman architecture. The central tower, which has no equal in any Norman church in the country is built almost wholly of Roman bricks, originally faced with plaster. It is designed in three stages, lighted by round-arched windows and the angles are strengthened with pilaster-buttresses in the lower part, and with circular turrets in the belfry stage. The tower is carried by four huge piers 43 feet in height, and the internal walls have galleries of Norman arches. In the transepts the most interesting feature is the triforium stage, the sub-arches of which spring from Saxon baluster-shafts, re-used by the Norman builders (Pl. 31). The three-storeyed bays of the nave are de-

fined by broad pilasters that rise from pavement to roof. The triforium, which is about one-half the height of the nave arches,
consists of a single arch in each bay, and a smaller round-arched
opening pierces the clerestory wall.

The architectural treatment of the Norman work at S. Albans,
simple in the extreme, was conditioned by the nature of the
material; hence the massive piers with recessed angles but devoid
of mouldings or ornament, the chamfered imposts that serve as
capitals, and the square-edged orders of the nave arches that correspond with the angles of the piers. Originally the choir, the
transepts and the nave were roofed with flat timber ceilings, like
that of Peterborough nave.

ROCHESTER CATHEDRAL, 1077–1150

Of an entirely different character is the Norman work at Rochester cathedral. In 1076 Archbishop Lanfranc appointed his cham-
berlain, Gundulf, formerly a monk of Bec, to the see of Rochester,
and soon after the consecration, Gundulf erected a massive tower
or keep of which the lower part to a height of 40 feet stands to the
east of the north transept of the cathedral. It was undoubtedly
built for defensive purposes, but was being used as a campanile in
1154. In 1082 Lanfranc converted the secular foundation at
Rochester into a cathedral-priory to be served by Benedictine
monks, and Gundulf at once started to 'build entirely anew the
church of S. Andrew which was almost ruined by age'. Of the
eleventh-century cathedral, portions of the crypt, and of the choir
and nave still exist, but the greater part of the nave and the west
front belong to the twelfth century and were not completed before
1140 or 1150 (Fig. 11).

Of the crypt, probably the earliest extant of this period, the
western part two bays in length with north and south aisles, are
all that remain (Fig. 7). Typical of early Norman work are the
circular monolith shafts with their rude cushion capitals, and the
groined vaults devoid of transverse arches. As at S. Albans, the
choir was separated from the aisles by solid walls, the masonry of
which is incorporated in the present dividing walls (Fig. 11).
The nave of Rochester, begun by Gundulf, was reconstructed
after 1114, in which year Ernulf, abbot of Peterborough, was consecrated Bishop of Rochester. The eastern bays were re-cased with
Caen stone and the arches of the nave and triforium were enriched
with chevron ornament. Ernulf's nave is marked by certain features that are peculiar to Rochester. In the first place, all the piers
on one side differ in form, but have their counterparts in the
opposite arcade. Again, the aisles were not vaulted and therefore

there is no triforium chamber. Instead, the builders constructed a narrow passage in the thickness of the triforium wall, and the openings, which consist of two sub-arches beneath a large containing arch, are built in two planes, with the passage between. Originally the spandrels of the triforium were open, but in the middle of the twelfth century, they were filled with masonry enriched with diaper ornament. The Norman clerestory was taken down in the fifteenth century to improve the top-lighting of the nave.

The west front of Rochester cathedral, with its flanking turrets, was completed *c.* 1150. Save for the Perpendicular window above the western door, the façade is late Norman architecture, faced with tier upon tier of wall-arcading, the most favoured form of enriching plain surfaces. The nave portal, one of the most splendid of the period, is noteworthy for the sculptured ornament lavished on the arch-orders, and for the relief carving in the tympanum, that represents Christ in Majesty supported by an angel on each side and surrounded by four beasts emblematic of the Evangelists. Attached to the jamb-shafts of the doorway are figures of a king and queen, probably of Solomon and the Queen of Sheba (Pl. 33).

WINCHESTER CATHEDRAL, 1079–1120

Whilst the Norman masons were busy at Rochester, a more mighty church was rising at Winchester, the ancient metropolis of the West Saxons and the capital of Norman England. At a council held there in 1070 the Conqueror deposed the wealthy and avaricious Stigand from the see of Winchester and installed Walkelyn the Norman, who in 1079 began the cathedral that was surpassed in size only by Old S. Paul's. The Norman nave of Winchester was 40 feet longer than the present nave. Of Walkelyn's church, the crypt and the transepts, that were completed by the end of the eleventh century, are intact to this day.

Indicating in its lay-out the disposition of the eastern arm of the Norman cathedral, the crypt is of the utmost importance. The central area beneath the choir is divided from the aisles and ambulatory by arcades of huge piers set closely together and sufficiently massive to carry the piers of the superstructure. The unusual circular capitals and slab-abaci of the columns suggest a debased form of the Doric order. Prof. Willis was of opinion that the aisles of the crypt were squared at the east in order that towers should be built to flank the central apse of the choir (cf. Hereford, Fig. 4). The identical character of the architecture of that part of the crypt beneath the retrochoir and of the transepts proves them to be of the same period (Pl. 37). The whole of Winchester crypt is roofed with groined vaults, each compartment being divided from the adjacent bays by broad transverse arches that enabled the masons to vault each bay separately.

The earliest Norman work above ground at Winchester is in the transepts, although they were partly rebuilt after the fall of the central tower in 1107. Each transept has aisles at the east and west and a return aisle at the end, an arrangement that was undoubtedly copied from S. Etienne, Caen. In the arcades of the transepts the triforium and the clerestory each occupy about one-third of the total height. Of the same design and proportions were the bays of the Norman nave and choir.

The partial reconstruction of the transepts after 1107 wrought changes that afford evidence of the progressive character of Anglo-Norman building. The original work was very plain and the masonry had wide joints, whereas in the portions that were rebuilt nearest to the tower, the fine-jointed masonry is as good as at any subsequent period. The piers of the tower and those adjoining were strengthened by piling on more masonry; those at the crossing are the largest tower piers in England, in proportion to the span of the arches they carry. In playing for safety the builders wasted both labour and materials. The transept aisles of the early period were roofed with groined vaulting, but the bays of the eastern aisles that were rebuilt have ribbed vaults, a significant advance in construction. In general, the architecture of the transepts at Winchester is plain, bold Romanesque. The piers with attached shafts and cushion capitals, the arches of one or two stepped orders barren of mouldings, the severe triforium of two sub-arches and the small open arches flanking the clerestory lights, are characteristic of early honest-to-goodness Anglo-Norman building. The central tower, rising 35 feet above the cathedral roof, was completed c. 1120 but calls for no special notice. In each face are three round-arched windows with recessed orders that spring from the cushion capitals of the jamb-shafts.

HEREFORD CATHEDRAL, 1080–1145

In 1079 the ancient see of Hereford was conferred on Robert de Losinga, and upon him fell the task of rebuilding the Saxon cathedral that had been 'utterly burned' some years before by the Welsh invaders. To what extent the Norman work in Hereford cathedral can be attributed to Bishop Losinga, who held the see for sixteen years, it is difficult to say. Undoubtedly he built the choir, which was renovated if not reconstructed in the first half of the twelfth century. The eastern wall of the south transept, with its tiers of wall-arcading and diminutive triforium seem to date from the eleventh century. In their sheer bulk the compound piers of the choir point to early Norman work, but the refined enrichment of the capitals and arch-orders and the surface decoration of the triforium belong to the twelfth century. The piers are faced with broad pilasters that stop short at the triforium and were probably intended to carry transverse arches spanning the choir.

After the dedication of the choir in 1110, work proceeded on the nave, so drastically restored by Wyatt in 1786, that the piers and arches alone are of the twelfth century; the triforium and clerestory were swept away in their entirety. The Norman piers are massive cylinders, with slender coupled shafts attached on the north and south sides; the capitals are richly carved and the arch-orders adorned with the ubiquitous chevron, executed with a degree of refinement that marks late Norman detail. The nave was completed by c. 1145.

WORCESTER CATHEDRAL, 1084–1130

The Saxon Bishop Wulstan of Worcester, 1062–95, who retained the see after the Conquest, and who deplored the demolition of the pre-Conquest cathedral (p. 78), lived to see the crypt and part of the choir of the Norman cathedral erected. It was begun in 1084, and the *Annals of Worcester* record that in 1092 Wulstan summoned a synod to meet him in the crypt which he himself had dedicated. Other than the walls of the main transepts, now overlaid with Perpendicular work, and inconsiderable fragments in various parts of the cathedral, the crypt, which is one of the loveliest in England, is all that is left of Norman building in the cathedral church. The peri-apsidal plan, that may have had radiating chapels, is evidence of the lay-out of the Norman choir. Although the central area of the crypt is only 30 feet wide, it is divided into four aisles by arcades of slender columns with cushion capitals, from which spring the transverse arches of the groined vaults (Pl. 34). Before the ambulatory was blocked up and the northern outer aisle taken down, there was a forest of more than seventy Norman pillars in the crypt of Worcester (Fig. 6).

In cathedral priories such as Winchester, Durham and Worcester, the big schemes of reconstruction undertaken by the Normans embraced the cloisters and the conventual buildings in addition to the cathedral churches. The cloister walks at Worcester are mainly fourteenth-century work, but the outer walls are substantially Norman. From the eastern walk a doorway opens into the circular chapter house (Fig. 22), a unique feature of Norman architecture, dating c. 1130 and the prototype of the later polygonal chapter houses that became so popular in secular cathedrals.

F

This at Worcester has a diameter of 56 feet, and in the centre is a circular column which supported ten compartments of groined vaulting. About the year 1400 the walls on the south side showed signs of being thrust outwards by the vaulting, and in order to stabilize the building the exterior was refaced and made decagonal with buttresses at the angles, and at the same time the Norman windows and vaulting were replaced by Gothic.

ELY CATHEDRAL, 1083–1190

Before its elevation to a cathedral in 1109, Ely was the Benedictine church of a religious house that had been founded as far back as 673. The building of the present cathedral was commenced in 1083 by Abbot Simeon, brother of Bishop Walkelyn of Winchester, where Simeon had been prior. Beneath the pavement of the choir of Ely are the foundations of the apse of Simeon's choir that were laid bare by Prof. Willis in 1850. The eastern arm of the Norman church must have been fairly complete by 1106, for in that year the remains of S. Etheldreda were translated to the choir, a ceremony that was the occasion of much pomp and circumstance. Thereafter followed the building of the transepts, the central tower and the nave, but progress was so slow that the western tower and transepts were not completed until the last quarter of the twelfth century. Of that great Norman church, the transepts and the nave are standing today (Fig. 19). Like those at Winchester, the transepts three bays deep were planned with eastern, western, and return aisles, but the last-named were removed at a later period.

The nave of Ely is typical of the South-eastern 'School' of Anglo-Norman architecture, exemplified at Peterborough, Norwich and S. Albans. An outstanding feature of these churches is the enormous length of the nave. Before the easternmost bay was absorbed into the Octagon, the nave of Ely cathedral, 208 feet long, comprised thirteen bays. Again, the proportions of the three stages of the bay design are common to the south-eastern group. The triforium stage in Ely nave is little less in height than the pier arcade beneath, and the undue size was not effected at the expense of the clerestory stage. The bays are defined by triple vaulting shafts that are incorporated in the piers and rise to the roof. The arch-orders of the nave and triforium spring from slender shafts with cushion capitals; the compound piers alternate in form, and only in the transepts are there cylindrical piers. No attempt was made to erect a high vault, but the aisles have groined vaults with transverse arches (Pl. 38). Noteworthy is the abundant use of wall-arcading, which occurs in the main transepts, the aisles of the nave, the western transepts and on the lower part of the west front. The profusion of ornament and of surface decoration is a sign of late Norman architecture.

In the wall of the south aisle of the nave is the famous prior's doorway, the jamb-shafts, capitals and arch-orders of which are sumptuously carved with interlacing ornament. On the pilasters flanking the portal are medallions containing animals, birds and flowers, and the tympanum has a figure of Christ in a vesica supported by an angel on either side.

GLOUCESTER CATHEDRAL, 1089–1150

In striking contrast to Ely is Gloucester cathedral, a contemporaneous work, which, prior to 1540 was the abbey church of S. Peter, founded in 681. For four centuries its chequered history was marked by periods of decline and recovery. When the last Saxon Abbot Wilstan died in 1072, there were two monks and eight novices in the abbey, but under the rule of his successor, Serlo, William I's chaplain, S. Peter's prospered as never before. In 1089 Serlo embarked on an entire rebuilding of the church and monastery.

Gloucester cathedral ranks high amongst the architectural creations of the Middle Ages. In the twelfth century and again in the fourteenth, the builders founded schools of masoncraft distinguished by their own local characteristics. With regard to dimensions Gloucester does not compare with other of the great Norman cathedrals, being inferior in length to Winchester, Ely and Norwich, to name a few. Despite the changes that have been wrought in the fabric the plan of Gloucester cathedral remains much the same as in the twelfth century, and the church is substantially a Norman building. Commenced in 1089 it was consecrated in 1100, though probably only the crypt, the choir and the transepts had been built in eleven years. During the early part of the twelfth century the building of the nave dragged on, interrupted in 1102 and 1120 by outbreaks of fire. Not later than 1160 this impressive nave, one of the glories of Anglo-Norman architecture, was finished. The cathedral is unique amongst the greater churches of this country as being a three-storeyed church. In the triforium stage as well as in the crypt and on the ground level, is an amulatory with radiating chapels together with transeptal chapels.

The central area of the crypt is divided into three aisles by arcades of circular columns about 6 feet high. So negligent were the Norman masons of sound foundation, that settlements occurred in the crypt soon after the superstructure was built. The sinking of the massive piers disturbed the groined vaulting in the south

aisle of the crypt and necessitated recasing the piers and reinforcing the vaults by applying stout ribs to the groins. There is very
little architectural ornament in the crypt; here and there in the
ambulatory is to be seen Norman chevron that was added when
the vaults were strengthened.

When the choir and transepts of Gloucester were refashioned in
the fourteenth century, the Norman walls and piers were not torn
down but were faced with a skin-deep vesture of Perpendicular
masonry (p. 255), and that being so, the piers, the arches and
vaults in the aisles and in the triforium are revealed in their
original form. To permit of a lofty triforium chamber, that serves
as an ambulatory for the upper chapels, the Norman builders kept
the arcades of the choir very low. The squat cylindrical piers,
7 feet in diameter, are only 8 feet high. The choir aisles are roofed
with groined vaults, as also are the radiating chapels; and the triforium chamber and chapels retain their Norman vaulting. Much
of the original fabric of the transepts is visible beneath the Perpendicular casing. The piers at the crossing carried a low Norman
tower that was taken down in the thirteenth century.

The columnar nave of Gloucester differs entirely from those of
the South-eastern School. The Norman masons of the Western
School set out the nave on basilican lines. To impart an impression
of great height to the interior they built cylindrical piers more than
30 feet in height and about 7 feet in diameter, and the arches were
thrown up to a height of 40 feet from the pavement (Pl. 35). Not
being needed for ritualistic purposes, the triforium stage of Gloucester nave was almost entirely eliminated. The clerestory was
rebuilt when the nave was vaulted in 1242, thereby destroying the
proportions of the interior. Equally unfortunate are the two western bays of the nave, that are remodellings of the fifteenth century.
Mediaeval bishops and abbots had little antiquarian respect for
Norman architecture as such. There are no vaulting shafts attached to the piers; the masons preferred the basilican effect of
a long unbroken range of columns, and a roof of timber sufficed.
The aisles of the nave, however, had simple *ribbed* vaults, denoting
the structural advance of the twelfth century. The north aisle is
almost untouched Norman, whereas the southern was remodelled
in the fourteenth century.

The Gloucester type of basilican nave with its tall cylindrical
piers was adopted also at Tewkesbury abbey, almost an exact
replica of Gloucester, and again at Pershore abbey, Worcestershire.

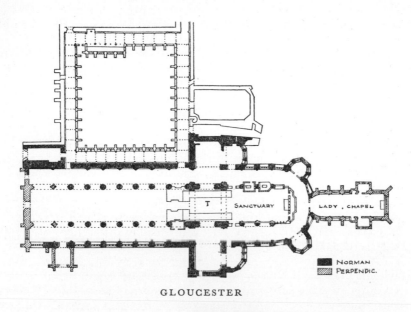

GLOUCESTER

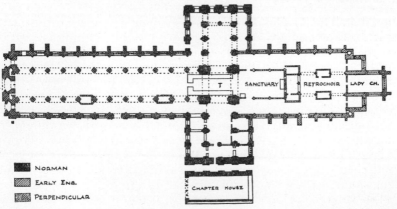

WINCHESTER

FIG 9. Plans of Gloucester and Winchester

CHICHESTER CATHEDRAL, 1091–1140

Generally it is the monastic cathedrals that have preserved the greater part of their Norman structure. Amongst the secular cathedrals, Chichester is to a great extent an eleventh-century building. Further, except for the extension eastwards of the Lady Chapel and the chapels that were tacked on to the aisles of the nave, the cathedral was as complete when first erected as at the present day. The see of the South Saxons was first established at Selsey on the Sussex coast by S. Wilfrid c. 680, and in 1082 was removed to Chichester. Nothing is known of the pre-Conquest cathedral at Selsey. In 1091 Radulph was appointed to the bishopric and he at once commenced to build a cathedral on the new site. Most of the Norman work now at Chichester was executed during the thirty-two years Radulph held the see, despite the fire of 1114 that held up building operations and damaged the nave. Without doubt the four western bays, which are out of alignment with the eastern part and display differences of detail, were erected after the fire.

The Norman cathedral of Chichester was cruciform on plan, with a peri-apsidal choir, unaisled transepts, a low tower at the crossing, a nave of eight bays and western towers (Fig. 4). The building extended almost as far east as the present cathedral, for three of the five bays of the Lady Chapel retain their Norman walling. The arcades of the nave and choir are remarkable for the piers, of such immensity that they are virtually chunks of walling, with half-round shafts and cushion capitals to carry the inner order of the arches. From the west end of the nave the arcades appear as solid walls, pierced at intervals with a series of round arches. Whence the design derived is not easy to say, nor was it repeated in any other Anglo-Norman cathedral. Both the triforium and the clerestory are original Norman work, though refaced. With its two sub-arches, the triforium is a considerable feature in the bay design; the spandrels of the western bays are enriched with diaper decoration. Attached to the piers are vaulting shafts, but the high vault was not put up until after the fire of 1186 (p. 190). The Norman cathedral had a timber roof with a wooden ceiling beneath.

CARLISLE CATHEDRAL, 1092–1125

More normal as regards proportions were the cylindrical piers of the Norman nave of Carlisle cathedral, only two bays of which survive (Fig. 14). The church was founded in 1092 by Walter, a Norman priest whom William I had appointed Governor of

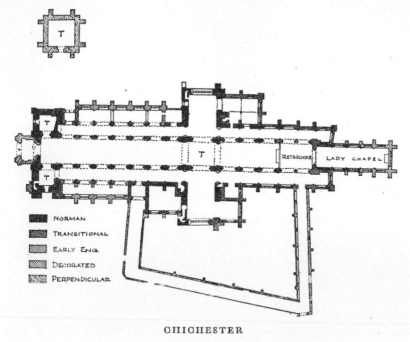

NORMAN
TRANSITIONAL
EARLY ENG.
DECORATED
PERPENDICULAR

CHICHESTER

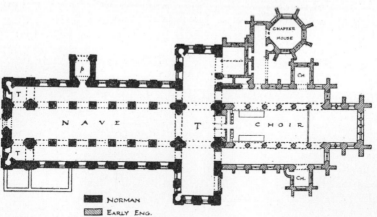

NORMAN
EARLY ENG.
DECORATED

SOUTHWELL

FIG 10. Plans of Chichester and Southwell

Carlisle, and was completed by Henry I, who converted the establishment into a priory of Augustinian canons. In 1133 Carlisle was made the seat of a bishop, and was the sole episcopal chapter of the Augustinian Order in mediaeval England. Of the Norman church, the south transept and the two eastern bays of the nave escaped destruction in the seventeenth century. The Norman work at Carlisle is severe and devoid of ornament. The cylindrical piers, not unlike those at S. John's, Chester and Hereford cathedral, have coniferous capitals and support arches of two orders. The triforium is opened up with a single arch in each bay, comparable with that of the nave of Southwell, and the clerestory wall is pierced with a window flanked by small Norman arches. The nave and transepts were probably finished by 1125 or soon afterwards.

CHESTER CATHEDRAL, 1093–1140

More scanty are the Norman remains of the Benedictine abbey church of S. Werburgh, Chester, which after the remodellings of four centuries was made a cathedral by Henry VIII. The abbey was founded in 1093 by Hugh Lupus, Earl of Chester, and of the church he reared the existing portions are the north transept, the wall of the north aisle of the nave and the basement of the north-western tower. The coarse masonry in the north transept, the irregular coursing of the small stones, and the wide joints are an indication of its early date. In the eastern wall of the north transept is a pseudo-triforium or blind arcade, reminiscent of that in the transepts at S. Albans. In 1930 the Norman arch below was opened up and the lower parts of the walls of the apsidal chapel to the east are now visible within. At the east end of the north aisle of the nave is the cloister doorway dating c. 1100, and in the south wall of the cloisters is a series of Norman recesses. In the pavement of the north aisle of the choir are some bases of the cylindrical piers that formed part of the peri-apsidal choir of the eleventh century.

Amongst the remains of the cloistral buildings is the undercroft of the Norman cellarium, a long apartment occupying the western block. Six bays in length, it is divided into two aisles by stout piers supporting the transverse arches of the groined vaults.

DURHAM CATHEDRAL, 1093–1175

No great English church of the Middle Ages occupies so commanding a situation as Durham cathedral, standing on a precipitous mass of rock almost encircled by the Wear that winds in horseshoe fashion about its base. Architecturally it has no equal amongst Anglo-Norman buildings; not only is it the least altered, but in the process of its erection was solved the problem of roofing a church with a stone vault. The Norman masons at Durham were the first in these islands to put up ribbed vaults of stone over every part of a mighty cathedral, and by employing the pointed arch in solving the problem, they laid the foundations of Gothic architecture.

The early history of Durham is associated with S. Cuthbert, Bishop of Lindisfarne in the seventh century. After his death in 685 his remains were a treasured possession of the monastery on Holy Isle. When the Danes sacked Lindisfarne in 875, the monks fled to the mainland with his body and finally settled at Durham in 999, where a church was built to enshrine the Saint. The history of the present cathedral begins in 1081, when the Norman Bishop, William of S. Carileph, refounded the establishment at Durham as a cathedral-priory of Benedictine monks, and then commenced to rebuild the church on Norman lines in 1093. On plan, Carileph's cathedral was a cruciform structure, with a parallel-apsed choir, north and south transepts, a tower at the crossing, an aisled nave of eight bays and twin towers at the west. Except for the eastern end of the choir and the central tower, Durham cathedral is almost wholly a Norman building (Fig. 11).

After seven years' work, the eastern arm and the transepts were approaching completion, and in 1104 the shrine of S. Cuthbert was installed in the apse behind the High Altar. Less speedy was the building of the nave, but by 1140 the whole of the cathedral was finished excepting the western towers.

In the structural system underlying its building, Durham cathedral was far in advance of contemporary architecture in England and Normandy. The system embodied principles that went to the making of the more organic and economical Gothic style. For the purpose of vaulting the cathedral, the Durham masons planned the choir, the transepts and the nave in large square compartments; massive compound piers were built alternating with cylindrical piers, the intention being that only the compound piers should support the high vaults, the intermediate piers being structurally subordinate (Fig. 11). This system of alternating piers was an invention of the Romanesque builders of Lombardy, and is to be seen in the churches of S. Ambrogio, Milan, and S. Zeno, Verona. After Durham it appears at Selby abbey, Yorks., begun c. 1110, the nave of which was undoubtedly the work of the Durham masons. By 1096 considerable progress has been made by roofing the aisles of the choir with ribbed vaults, the diagonal ribs

F*

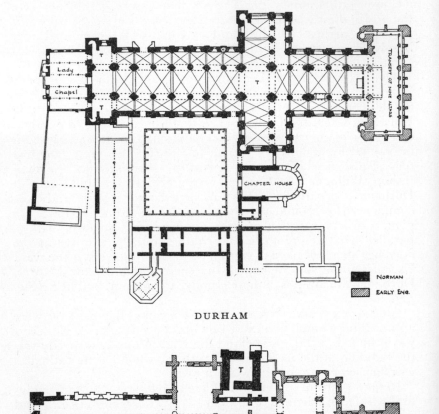

DURHAM

ROCHESTER

FIG 11. Plans of Durham and Rochester

forming a framework on which the infilling or web was laid. These four-celled or *quadripartite* vaults of the choir aisles are the earliest in England. The new principle was then applied to the high vaults, but though the choir had been laid out with compound piers forming square bays, the vaulting was actually built in oblong bays, the difficulty of which was overcome by using the pointed arch, a momentous innovation. All the diagonal ribs of the high vaults are semicircular in form, but the transverse arches are pointed. The vault of the choir was completed by 1104, that of the transepts by *c.* 1110 and twenty-five years later the nave and its aisles were roofed with ribbed vaults (Pl. 39).

The achievement of the northern masons appears greater still when we consider the means by which their high vaults were rendered stable. Stone vaulting exerts an outward thrust against the wall from which it springs, and some form of counteracting the thrust is needed. In the aisles at Durham the walls were strengthened by external buttresses, the construction of which presented no difficulty. But the thrusts of the high vaults had to be carried *over the aisles* on to the wall buttresses, by arches that were built in the triforium chamber. Those supporting the choir vault are semicircular, but for the vaulting of the nave, the *flying buttresses* are quadrant in form and are therefore more logical and effectual.

On entering Durham cathedral the first impression is one of rocky solidity, so huge are the masses of masonry composing the piers. Logically, the compound piers take their shape and form from the members of the superstructure, so that the angles and shafts correspond with the arch-orders, the vaulting shafts and the ribs of the aisle vaults. The cylindrical columns are noteworthy for the various channellings in their surfaces. Those in the choir and transepts have spiral groovings, whereas the columnar piers of the nave are incised with network striations, chevron patternings and vertical flutings with beadings (Pl. 39). The walls of the aisles are faced with Norman arcading that appears also on the external walls of the western towers. Less than forty years after the cathedral was finished, Bishop Hugh Pudsey of Durham resolved upon adding a Lady Chapel. Attempts to erect the chapel at the east end of the choir having proved futile (p. 87), a site in the cramped space between the west front and the steep cliff was chosen. Pudsey's Galilee, as it was called, begun *c.* 1175, is a rectangular building, 48 ft. long and 75 ft. wide, divided into five aisles. The round arches of the arcades, richly decorated with chevron ornament, spring from clustered piers of Purbeck marble and stone, the stone shafts being added in the fifteenth century. The arcades carry large areas of blank walling and the chapel has a timber roof;

there is nothing to show that stone vaulting was intended. This late piece of Norman architecture is marked by a lightness and grace that was an earnest of the Gothic of the next century.

CANTERBURY CATHEDRAL, 1096–1126

Long before the end of the eleventh century, Lanfranc's unambitious cathedral at Canterbury was outclassed in scale by great Benedictine churches such as S. Albans, Winchester and Ely, that had arisen or were in process of reconstruction. After standing for twenty years Lanfranc's cathedral was showing signs of instability. Amongst the monks of Christ Church was one Ernulf, who had come from Normandy with Lanfranc, and on his election to the office of prior in 1096, he inspired the convent to undertake the building of a more spacious and splendid choir. The funds for this project were derived from rents and profits of the manor of Peckham, which Archbishop Anselm granted the convent for the purpose. In 1107 Ernulf left Canterbury to become the Abbot of Peterborough, and his successor, Conrad by name, completed the reconstruction by 1126. Such was the magnificence of the new eastern arm of the cathedral, that it was always spoken of as 'Conrad's Glorious Choir'. William of Malmesbury wrote: 'Nothing like it could be seen in England.' It was in fact a complete church built to the east of Lanfranc's nave and transepts (Fig. 4), and was reared on a crypt extending beneath the whole of the new building (Fig. 6). The 'Glorious Choir' was destroyed by fire in 1174, but the crypt, completed c. 1105, is intact and is the most ancient portion of the cathedral now standing. The central area is divided into three aisles by ranges of circular columns with cushion capitals, from which spring the transverse arches of the groined vaults. Sixty or seventy years later some of the capitals were carved with grotesque subjects.

NORWICH CATHEDRAL, 1096–1150

The diocese of Norwich is one of the most ancient in England. Its origin dates back to the year 630 when the see was founded at Dunwich in Suffolk. After about forty years the diocese was split into two, with sees at Dunwich and Elmham. Late in the ninth century the bishopric was suppressed,[1] and Elmham remained until 1070, when the see was removed to Thetford by Bishop Herfast, William I's chaplain. In 1091 Herbert de Losinga, the prior of Fécamp abbey in Normandy, purchased the bishopric for £1900, a huge sum in those days, and in 1095 he transplanted the see to

[1] In 1934 after many centuries of obscurity the town of Dunwich was made the seat of a bishop-suffragan in the modern diocese of Bury S. Edmunds and Ipswich.

Norwich. The following year Bishop Losinga laid the foundations of Norwich cathedral, to which he attached a priory of Benedictine monks.

In plan and substance no Anglo-Norman cathedral has suffered less change than Norwich. Save for the War Memorial chapel at the eastern extremity and other chapels that flank the choir-arm, the plan is that of the twelfth century cathedral (Fig. 12). Norwich is one of the few great mediaeval churches that possessed no saint's shrine, and therefore the necessity never arose for remodelling or extending the choir-arm. The eastern arm consists of a choir of four bays terminating in an apse with an encircling ambulatory. Of the three chapels off the ambulatory, the eastern which was horseshoe in shape was replaced by a Lady Chapel in the thirteenth century and was demolished in 1580. Most unusual are the radiating chapels at the north-east and south-east, being on plan double segments of circles. The lay-out of Losinga's choir was without doubt copied from the abbey church of Fécamp, begun c. 1082, itself a rare instance of the peri-apsidal plan in Normandy. Of the apsidal chapels that projected from the transepts only the northern survives. The Norman nave of fourteen bays with a total length of 252 feet dates from c. 1120 and was completed by the middle of the century.

Architecturally Norwich cathedral is one of the foremost achieve-

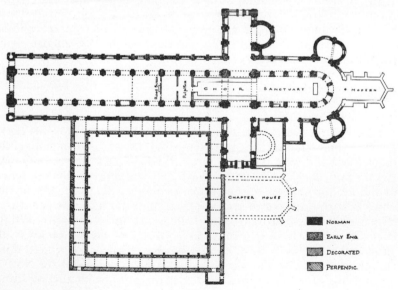

FIG 12. Plan of Norwich

ments of the South-eastern School of Anglo-Norman building. The inordinate length of the nave, the proportions of the bay design and the general use of compound piers are characteristic. When the masons started to build the eastern part of the nave, they adopted the alternating-pier system of Durham cathedral. The fifth pier on each side of the nave west of the crossing is cylindrical, and it has been found that the first and third pairs also were originally cylindrical but were recased as compound piers after the fire of 1171. These cylindrical piers alternated with compound piers. However, as the nave progressed the scheme was abandoned and in the nine remaining bays compound piers were built. On the two cylindrical piers appear spiral channellings in the Durham manner. In the five western bays, the arches are enriched with broken billet ornament, and those of the triforium with chevron.

In the bay design, the nave arcade, triforium and clerestory are 25, 24, and 25 feet high respectively. To admit the maximum light, windows were pierced in the outer wall of the triforium chamber, and the single broad arch of that stage was constructed without sub-arches. In preparation for high vaults, vaulting shafts were attached to the piers, but timber roofs were put up. The aisles are roofed with groined vaults; the Durham masons had constructed ribbed vaults over their aisles *before* the foundations of Norwich cathedral were laid.

In Norman peri-apsidal choirs, the piers of the apse were commonly cylindrical, whereas those at Norwich are compound. Here the masons had a liking for slender shafting with cushion capitals, a feature that is abundantly employed, and they revelled in wall arcading both externally and internally.

The three-storeyed wall design of the transepts is a masterly adaptation of the bay design of the choir (Pl. 44).

SOUTHWELL CATHEDRAL, 1108–50

Early in the twelfth century Thomas II, Archbishop of York, promoted a scheme for the rebuilding of the Saxon collegiate church of Southwell, Notts., a pro-cathedral in the diocese of York. All through the Middle Ages Southwell was a favourite residence of the archbishops of the northern province. To the south of the church lie the ruins of the palace, first built in the twelfth century. The pre-Conquest history of the collegiate church is scanty. Whatever the Saxon building may have been, it was swept away in 1108 and in its place arose a great Norman church, of which more than half is still *in situ*. In a pastoral letter to the people of Notts., Archbishop Thomas appealed for contributions to the building fund, 'and that ye may more willingly do this, we release you, so that you need not visit every year the Church of York as other parishioners do, but the church of S. Mary of Southwell instead, and there have the same pardon as at York'. Sums of money were also given by the Jewish moneylenders of York and Lincoln.

The Norman choir-arm, a variant of the parallel-apsed plan, was remodelled in the thirteenth century, but the transepts, the nave and the three towers date from the middle of the twelfth century. Originally a two-storeyed apse projected eastwards from each transept. The internal length, little less than that of Rochester, reaches to 306 feet (Fig. 10). The nave of seven bays, measuring about 180 feet east to west, is almost undiluted Norman and is of cathedral design, with a lofty triforium stage surmounted by an insignificant clerestory. The interior effect is one of horizontality, due to the absence of vaulting shafts or vertical divisions, and to the bold string courses dividing the three stages (Pl. 40). From the squat cylindrical piers, 9 feet in height and with a diameter of about 5 feet, rise arches of two orders enriched with unobstrusive ornament, such as the broken billet; the wide arches of the triforium lack sub-arches, though little blocks of masonry projecting from the inner arch orders are proof that sub-arches were intended. So narrow are the round-arched openings in the clerestory wall that little light is admitted through the outer circular windows.

The Norman nave of Southwell was roofed in timber; the present waggon roof is modern. Ornament is used somewhat sparingly. The great arches at the crossing are enriched with cable moulding, an ornament that also occurs in the transepts. Externally a string of chevron is carried round the Norman church. Of particular interest is the north-western porch, one of the finest of the period. It is roofed with a barrel vault and the internal walls are overlaid with intersecting wall-arcading. The inner doorway, like the western entrance of the nave, wreathed in a wealth of shafts and arch-orders, is typical of late Norman masoncraft. The most striking feature of the exterior is the west front, which seems to have been modelled on that of S. Etienne, Caen. The twin towers are effective in their simplicity, and the angle pilasters impart a feeling of stability; wall-arcading is applied to the upper stages of the towers, and the design of the central is in perfect harmony with those at the west. The Norman character of the west front has been marred by the large Perpendicular window that was inserted in 1450 to improve the lighting of the nave.

Exeter Cathedral, 1110–1200

At the close of the eleventh century the only secular cathedrals that had not been or were not being rebuilt were Exeter and Lichfield. More than forty years elapsed after the Conquest before the Saxon cathedral of Exeter was pulled down to give place to an imposing Norman church. In 1050 the see of Devon was moved from Crediton, an unfortified 'vill', to the walled town of Exeter, where the Saxon Bishop Leofric set up his throne in the abbey church of SS. Mary and Paul. The monks were dispersed and secular canons were installed. On Leofric's death in 1072, Osbern, a Norman, was appointed to the bishopric, and it was his successor, William Warelwast, 1107–36, a nephew of William I, who undertook the reconstruction of Exeter cathedral, the transeptal towers of which are his enduring monument. Warelwast's church, which was 240 feet in length, consisted of a parallel-apsed eastern arm, a nave and choir uninterrupted by a crossing, and flanking transeptal towers, each with an apsidal chapel at the east (Fig. 4). Norman masonry in the walls of the aisles of the nave and in the western wall afford evidence that Warelwast's nave was of the same width as the present cathedral and extended as far to the west. But the nave was not completed until the time of Bishop Marshall, 1194–1206, who 'finished the building according to the Plat and Foundation which his predecessors had laid'.

The towers of Exeter are unique in Anglo-Norman ecclesiastical architecture. Being outside the body of the cathedral, they rid the chapter of anxiety that would result from raising a tower at the crossing. For half their height the tower walls are as plain and severe as the keeps of Norman castles. When Exeter was besieged in Stephen's reign, the northern tower (Pl. 45) was badly battered and may have served as a fortress. In the upper parts the walls are faced with tiers of blind arcading and are pierced with a row of circular windows. The angles are strengthened with flat pilasters that are carried up above the parapets as square turrets. When first built, the towers opened into the cathedral by small arches, but late in the thirteenth century, the inner walls were taken down to the full height of the interior, and the towers were thus converted into transepts (p. 229).

PETERBOROUGH CATHEDRAL, 1118–1200

To the South-eastern School of Anglo-Norman building belongs the cathedral of Peterborough, formerly the church of a Benedictine abbey known in ancient times as Medeshamstede. It was founded by King Penda in 656, and after devastation by the Danes was refounded by King Edgar in the tenth century. 'Peterborough the Proud' as it was termed in later days was held in such veneration in the Middle Ages, that 'all of what degree soever who entered the great gate, were required to do so barefoot'. At least

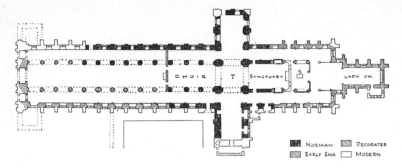

S. ALBANS

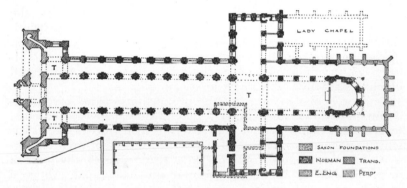

PETERBOROUGH

FIG 13. Plans of S. Albans and Peterborough

two churches had occupied the site of the cathedral in Saxon
days; about seventy years ago, the foundations of a small cruciform church of the Saxon period were uncovered below the pavement in and near the south transept of the cathedral. The church
had a square chancel, transepts and an unaisled nave, the north
wall of which almost coincides with the present south nave arcade
(Fig. 13).

Documentary evidence of the rebuilding of the abbey in the
twelfth century is lacking, but a pretty tradition has it, that the
Saxon church was destroyed by fire in 1116. On the Vigil of S.
Oswald, King and Martyr, one of the abbot's servants had been
blaspheming all day because the fire in the kitchen would not
burn. 'The devil kindle thee,' was his concluding malediction,
whereon the whole monastery burst into flames and was destroyed.
Fire or no fire, a new abbey church was begun in 1118 by Abbot

John de Sais. At his death in 1125 little of the church had been built, but by the middle of the century the choir-arm, the piers at the crossing and the lower parts of the transepts had been put up, and by 1175 the central tower and the transepts were complete. The nave also was sufficiently advanced for the stalls of the monks to be set up in the eastern bays. Under Abbot Benedict, 1177–93 the nave was lengthened by two bays and twin towers erected at the west. As an afterthought shallow transepts were built flanking the towers, and the abbey church, that had been three-quarters of a century in building was finished by *c*. 1200.

The transepts and nave of Peterborough afford a perfect example of late Norman architecture, and the choir of four bays retains much of its Norman character. The eastern apse was lighted by three tiers of round-arched windows corresponding with the arcade, triforium and clerestory of the choir. In the fourteenth century the windows of the two upper stages were enlarged, and open arches replaced the windows of the ground stage in the fifteenth century. The piers of the choir are alternately circular and polygonal and they all have cushion capitals.

In all parts of the cathedral the proportions of the bay design are similar to those of Ely (Pl. 41). The triforium has two sub-arches, the tympana being treated with varying forms of surface ornament; the chevron and billet ornament are used for arch enrichment. The three-bayed transepts have eastern aisles, the piers of the arcades being alternately circular and octagonal. Above a range of wall-arcading on the end walls of the transepts are three tiers of tall windows. The nave of ten bays with compound piers and arches of many orders and the superb triforium and clerestory are in no way inferior to those of Ely. A flat timber roof of the twelfth century covers the nave (p. 137); the aisles of both choir and nave have quadripartite vaulting with stout ribs, and wall-arcading is abundant.

Of the same period was the nave of Old S. Paul's, twelve bays in length, and perhaps the greatest of the Norman period (Fig. 19), made known to us by the drawings of the Bohemian, Wenceslaus Hollar.

Old S. Paul's and Peterborough were the last of the great Norman cathedrals. Long before their completion new forms were being evolved and structural progress was effecting changes that culminated in the Gothic architecture of the early thirteenth century. The second half of the twelfth century was a fertile period in things architectural, to which the term 'Transitional' is applied. Much of the work of this period was charged with the Gothic impulse. By inventing the ribbed vault, the masons at Durham had evolved a structural system that formed the basic principle of Gothic architecture. The use of the pointed arch, introduced as a structural expedient in vaulting Durham cathedral, prepared the way for the development of the Transitional style.

Projects such as the rebuilding of Canterbury choir, of Wells cathedral and of Hugh's choir at Lincoln show how the architecture of this phase was gradually freeing itself of the static and ponderous quality of Romanesque, and was moving towards the more organic pointed style; and in lesser undertakings, at Worcester and Chichester cathedrals, the same advance towards Gothic is manifest. That is not to say that the so-called Transitional style was universal, for in some places, diffident or conservative masons clung to forms that had long fallen into desuetude elsewhere. At Oxford cathedral, in course of erection between 1158 and 1180, there is little that foreshadows the oncoming Gothic.

An outstanding feature of Transitional building is the employment of the pointed arch in conjunction with the round arch. About 1150 the pointed arch appeared in the nave arcade of Malmesbury abbey church, Wilts., but the masons there resorted to the semicircular arch in designing the triforium. In the earlier Cistercian churches of Fountains and Buildwas, the nave arches were pointed and those of the clerestory are round. Another important feature of Transitional work was the economy that was effected in the fabric. Experience had taught the masons much concerning the qualities of building stones and of the loads they were capable of bearing. The massive piers of the Norman period gave place to shafted piers of increasing lightness, occasioned to a great extent by the use of Purbeck marble, that could be turned and cut into slender shafts for attaching to the stone core of Transitional piers. Soon after 1170 sprang up a definite industry in supplying Purbeck shafts, and by the end of the century, the Purbeck use was general in all parts of the country.

There was still much to be learned in the matter of vaulting. The difficulty of the high vault had been mastered at Durham, but elsewhere, there was some hesitancy in tackling the problems involved. Many vaults, put up long after those at Durham, collapsed soon after they were built. A fragment of an Evensong prayer of the thirteenth century is significant: 'And, deare Lord, support our roof this night, that it may in no wyse fall upon us and styfle us, Amen.' A big change came over the ornament and carving of capitals and other features. Greater refinement was possible when the chisel was substituted for the axe. Moreover, the mason turned to natural leaf-forms for his motifs; the foliage was conventionalized to serve the needs of the craftsman.

RIPON CATHEDRAL, 1154–81

Infused with the vigour and promise of Gothic was the new minster at Ripon, commenced by Archbishop Roger of York in 1154. The archbishop contributed the sum of £1000 towards the building 'which we have begun afresh'. The active part taken by the northern primates through the succeeding centuries in rebuilding schemes at Ripon is evidence of the close ties that bound the collegiate establishment to York. The minster began as a small monastic house in the seventh century and after many vicissitudes it emerged as a collegiate church in the tenth century. Apart from the crypt there is nothing that enables us to determine the architectural character of the minster at the time of the Conquest. Towards the end of the eleventh century Archbishop Thomas of Bayeux, 1070–1100, enlarged or rebuilt the pre-Conquest church. Archbishop Roger's reconstruction in 1154–81 involved the demolition *in toto* of the earlier building, with the exception of the Saxon crypt and the small apsidal chapel on the south side of the choir (Fig. 23), which is the sole remnant of the church of Thomas of Bayeux.

Roger's minster was planned with an aisled choir, square-ended at the east, north and south transepts, and a wide unaisled nave. Of that church, there remain the western bays of the north arcade of the choir, the transepts and the eastern and western extremities of the nave (Fig. 23), in which are displayed the finer qualities of Transitional architecture. The choir was co-extensive with the present one, though it was largely rebuilt in the thirteenth and the fifteenth centuries. The bay design is unsurpassed by any of the same period in England, as regards proportions; the choir arcade occupies about one-half of the total height, and round and pointed arches appear in juxtaposition (Pl. 42). The arches carried by the slender clustered piers are pointed, but above, the main arches of the triforium and clerestory are semicircular, as also are windows of the aisles. In the triforium, the two pointed sub-arches are flanked on each side by a blind pointed arch, a design that is repeated on a larger scale without sub-arches in the clerestory; vaulting shafts rise the full height of the bays, though the intention to build a high vault was abandoned before the clerestory was completed. The choir aisles are roofed with quadripartite vaulting.

The design of Roger's transepts corresponds with that of the choir. In the upper stages of the bay design occurs the same mingling of the old with the new, the round with the pointed arch. The exterior of the end wall of the north transept furnishes a rare instance of a Transitional façade.

Of the Transitional nave of Ripon, eastern and western bays alone survive. It was of abnormal width for an unaisled nave, being 40 feet across. The two bays at the west render possible a reconstruction on paper of the interior of Roger's nave. To a height of about 16 feet the walls were quite plain, but the upper parts, that were divided by vaulting shafts into wide and narrow bays alternately, were treated with a blind quasi-triforium and a clerestory of lancet arcading opened up as windows in the wide bays. Unfortunately this Transitional nave was transformed in the Perpendicular period when the aisles were added. The grand scheme inaugurated by Archbishop Roger was probably not completed before the turn of the twelfth century.

York Cathedral, 1154–81

Whilst the masons at Ripon were breaking new ground in the realm of architecture, others less receptive of new ideas were busy remodelling York cathedral, a project that was initiated by the same archbishop, Roger. The new eastern arm then planned was more than twice the length of the Norman choir of Thomas of Bayeux.[1] It was raised on a crypt, of which four piers are *in situ*; the lesser circular columns were re-used in the fourteenth century to support the platform of the High Altar. Judging from the piers of Roger's crypt, the York masons were far behind the times, for there is nothing to show that the superstructure compared with the Transitional work in the choir of Ripon. The squat Norman piers have reticulated designs incised in their surfaces, the capitals are the old-fashioned coniferous type, and the arches are enriched with chevron ornament. In style, Roger's crypt at York with its ribbed vaults was unadulterated Norman.

Oxford Cathedral, 1158–85

Equally loth to cast aside traditional forms and methods were the builders of the priory church of S. Frideswide, now the cathedral of Christ Church, Oxford, which is almost purely Norman in style, regardless of the innovations that were accepted elsewhere.

Oxford cathedral is largely a creation of the later years of the twelfth century. The aisled choir of four bays with a short square sanctuary at the east, the aisled nave curtailed by Wolsey to four bays, and the transepts originally aisled at the east and west (Fig. 14), were commenced *c.* 1158, and the church was finished soon after 1180. The early history of the church takes us back to

---

[1] On his translation to York in 1070, Thomas of Bayeux embarked upon a rebuilding of the cathedral from its foundation. Of that Norman church, that was finished within thrity years, some stonework in the western part of the crypt is all that remains.

the seventh century when a nunnery was founded on the site; in 1111 the house was refounded as a priory of Augustinian canons. A puzzling discovery was made in 1887, the foundations of three small parallel apses being unearthed to the north of the sanctuary. In the eastern walls of the north choir-aisle and of the Lady Chapel were found the remains of rough arches that apparently opened into the apses. It may be reasonable to assume that the diminutive apse whose total width was less than 30 feet was part of the choir of a Norman church that existed before the present cathedral was built.

The most arresting feature of the Norman architecture of Oxford is the bay design, an eccentricity by means of which the master mason ensured an interior effect of height in a three-storeyed church that was abnormally low. The internal height is about 42 feet, or less than half that of the nave of Ripon or Norwich. But the master mason would not dispense with the useless triforium stage in the bay design; therefore to increase the apparent height of the nave and choir arches, he carried the cylindrical piers up to the triforium level, and heavily moulded arches were made to spring from the capitals, *beneath* which is the triforium stage (Pl. 36). Below the triforium less bold arches rise from corbels attached to the piers. As a result, the triforium arcade seemingly lies below the nave arcade, though structurally this is not so. At first glance the impression is one of a well-proportioned bay design, embracing only a lofty nave arcade and a clerestory, so relatively unimportant are the corbelled arches of the real nave arcade.

In the choir and transepts all the piers are cylindrical, whereas those in the nave are alternately octagonal and cylindrical. In the nave alone appears the pointed arch, and there only in the clerestory windows. The aisles are roofed with quadripartite vaults, but no preparation was made in the twelfth century for high vaults in the choir or nave. In one respect, the masons at Oxford were looking forward, for the exquisite carving of the capitals was truly an earnest of the foliated capitals of Early English Gothic.

WORCESTER CATHEDRAL, 1170–5

So pronounced is the Transitional character of the two western bays of the nave of Worcester cathedral, that they may be said to constitute 'a landmark in the history of English Gothic'. The building of the Norman cathedral, begun by Bishop Wulfstan in 1084, had been retarded by a conflagration in 1113, and during the troublous reign of King Stephen, when Worcester was raided by the King's enemies, work was brought to a standstill. The cathe-

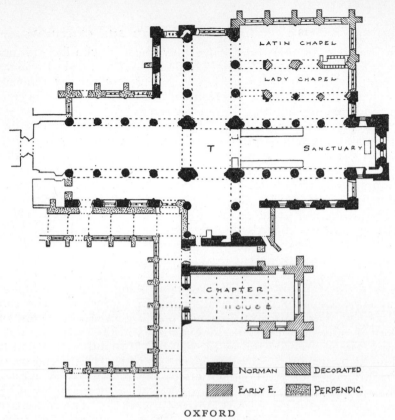

LATIN CHAPEL

LADY CHAPEL

T

SANCTUARY

CHAPTER HOUSE

| NORMAN | DECORATED |
| EARLY E. | PERPENDIC. |

OXFORD

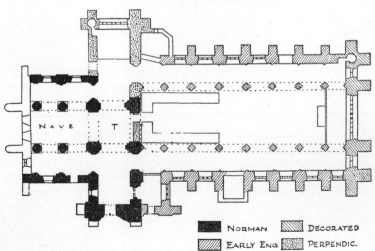

NAVE   T

| NORMAN | DECORATED |
| EARLY ENG. | PERPENDIC. |

CARLISLE

FIG 14. Plans of Oxford and Carlisle

dral became the resort of terrified townspeople, who fled thither for safety. Florence of Worcester, a monk of the cathedral priory, wrote: 'Behold! the house of God . . . seems now but a warehouse for furniture; the principal conventual church of the whole diocese in converted into quarters for the townsmen.'

The years dragged on and not before *c.* 1170 was the completion of the nave taken in hand. To the seven Norman bays were added two at the western end, which together with Roger's work in the choir of Ripon, though different in many respects, furnish valuable examples of Transitional architecture (Pl. 43). Here is the same mingling of the old with the new. In the bay design the triforium stage maintains its traditional importance as regards both height and treatment. The compound piers are composed of slender shafts with cushion capitals, from which spring pointed arches. The arch-orders are well defined in relation to their supports. The triforium stage of each bay has two pointed containing arches, with three semi-circular sub-arches springing from the cushion capitals of slender shafts. The sub-arches are adorned with chevron ornament. The pairing of the containing arches was a promise of the triforium design that became common in the thirteenth century. The clerestory window in each bay is round-arched and is flanked by a blind pointed arch on each side. Having mastered the principles of vault construction, the masons at Worcester erected high vaults over these two bays, which were replaced by the present vaulting in the fourteenth century. The aisles are covered with the original quadripartite vaults, which have semi-circular diagonals but pointed transverse arches. The vaulting shafts provide an early instance of the clustered forms of Gothic, being composed of five shafts.

Ely Cathedral, 1170–95

The vast Norman cathedral at Ely, founded in 1083, had been in the builders' hands for well nigh a century. By 1170 all that remained to be done were the upper stages of the western tower and of the western transepts with their eastern apses. Most marked is the difference between the lower tiers of Norman wall-arcading and the two upper stages, that exhibit so rapid a change to Transitional that it is not easy to believe that the work was continuous. Probably a few years elapsed before the completion of the west end of the cathedral was resolved upon, by which time the old-fashioned Norman style was outmoded by the new Transitional vogue. The external walls are faced with five tiers of arcading that is also carried round the octagonal angle-turrets, and upon them is lavished a wealth of exuberant ornament so loved by the Benedictines.

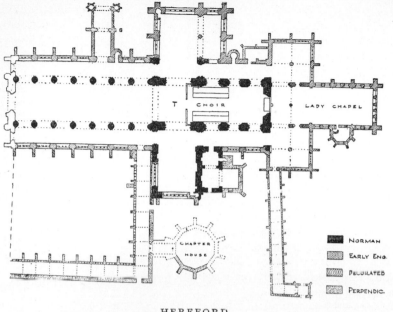

HEREFORD

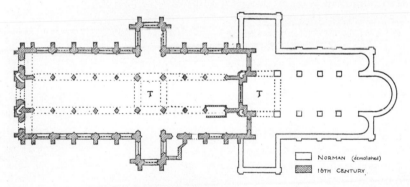

BATH

FIG 15. Plans of Hereford and Bath

In the two upper Transitional tiers, pointed and trefoiled arches are used exclusively and the chevron ornament appears side by side with the dog-tooth that was so general in the thirteenth century.

CANTERBURY CATHEDRAL, 1175–85

Foremost amongst the buildings of this period is the eastern arm of Canterbury cathedral. In 1174 the Glorious Choir of Conrad was gutted by a disastrous fire that broke out before the gate of the priory and destroyed three cottages outside the precincts. The chronicler Gervase, an eye-witness, has left an account of the conflagration. 'While the citizens were assembling and subduing the flames, cinders and sparks carried aloft by the high wind were deposited upon the church and remained there amongst the half-rotten planks; and glowing with increasing heat, set fire to the rotten rafters and was communicated to the larger beams.' All efforts to control the outbreak proved futile, and 'it was marvellous though sad to behold how that glorious choir itself fed and assisted the fire that was destroying it. In this manner the House of God, hitherto delightful . . . was made a despicable heap of ashes, reduced to a dreary wilderness and laid open to all the injuries of the weather.' Lanfranc's nave and transepts escaped serious damage, for they remained in use for another two centuries.

The brethren of Christ Church were equal to the occasion and decided upon rebuilding at once. Master masons were summoned to Canterbury to offer advice and suggests methods of reconstruction. They were of differing opinions; some advised the restoration of the burnt-out choir, others favoured clearing the site and building anew. After much deliberation the convent of Christ Church commissioned a French master mason, William de Sens to undertake the task. The new choir was to be in plan and design a replica of Conrad's choir, but in fact it turned out to be an advanced specimen of Transitional architecture. To preserve as much as possible of the old building, the lower parts of the outer walls were allowed to stand, but the central part, viz., the piers, the arches and the walls above, had to be entirely rebuilt. Work began on 6 September 1175 at the western end adjoining the Norman transepts, and the progress of the operations is detailed year by year in the chronicle of Gervase.

After little more than three years' work, whilst engaged on 'preparing the machines for the turning of the high vault', Master William de Sens fell from the scaffolding fifty feet to the ground. Despite severe injuries he continued for a time to direct the building operations from his bed, but eventually he had to abandon the work, and returned to France crippled for life. The convent thereupon chose as his successor another William, an Englishman, probably the Master's right-hand man, whom Gervase described as 'small in body, but in craftsmanship of many kinds, acute and honest'. This little fellow, 'William the Englishman', as he was called, proved in every way a worthy and capable master mason, and carried out his predecessor's design with little variation. By the end of the year 1179 he had laid 'the foundations for the en-

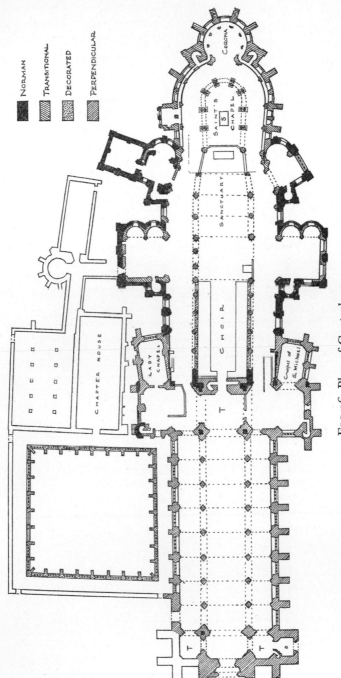

Fig 16. Plan of Canterbury

largement of the church at the eastern part, because the chapel of S. Thomas was to be built there'. Very little delay was caused by the retirement of the Frenchman, for in 1180 the monks were in possession of the new choir, which was boarded up at the east while the Saint's chapel was being built. The years 1180 and 1181 witnessed the erection of the new eastern crypt on which the Saint's chapel and the Corona were raised. Ernulf's crypt to the west was left untouched. That of William the Englishman being more lofty, the pavement of the Saint's chapel is considerably above the level of the choir. Architecturally the later crypt is a big advance on the Norman crypt of 1096; here are pointed arches, ribbed vaults and a central arcade carried by Purbeck marble columns (Pl. 49). After ten years' work the reconstruction was at an end. Our observant Gervase, who had watched the progress of the building from west to east, records the changes that marked the new eastern arm. 'The pillars of the old and the new work are alike in form and thickness but different in length; for the new pillars are elongated by almost twelve feet. In the old capitals the work was plain, in the new ones exquisite in sculpture. There, the circuit of the choir had twenty-two pillars, here are twenty-eight; there, the arches and everything else was plain or sculptured with an axe and not with a chisel. But here almost throughout is appropriate sculpture. No [Purbeck] marble columns were there, but here are innumerable ones. There, in the circuit around the choir the vaults are plain [groined], but here they are arch-ribbed and have keystones [bosses]. There, was a ceiling of wood decorated with excellent painting, but here is a vault beautifully constructed of stone and light tufa,' and he wisely concludes: 'All this will be better understood from inspection than by any description.'

In this magnificent Transitional work at Canterbury, the heaviness of the Anglo-Norman style is thrown off; piers and capitals are less ponderous, mouldings are richer and capitals more delicately carved. Semicircular and pointed arches are not used indiscriminately. In the aisles the western parts of which are in the main those of Ernulf's choir, the windows, the wall-arcading and the vaulting ribs are round-arched, but in the choir itself the pointed arch predominates; only in the triforium is the round arch consistently employed, and even there the sub-arches are pointed. Curiously, the Norman chevron ornament appears side by side with the dog-tooth of early Gothic. For the first time in English architecture, Purbeck marble was lavishly employed for the slender shafting attached to piers and for vaulting shafts. As Purbeck marble could only be quarried in short lengths, annulet rings were inserted at the joints. From the first, Purbeck was used by William de Sens; there was no precedent in his country, so it must have been introduced by the English masons working under him.

The eastern arm of Canterbury has definite French affinities. At once apparent is the influence of the cathedrals of Sens and Noyon, with which the French master-mason was well acquainted. The apse-and-ambulatory plan of the Saint's chapel, long abandoned in this country, was the normal lay-out of French cathedrals of the period, and the coupled columns that occur nowhere else in England were copied from Sens cathedral; the Corinthianesque capitals (Pl. 47) exquisitely sculptured are quite un-English too, though common enough in the contemporary churches of France.[1] The arches of the apse are stilted in the French mode, and the sexpartite or six-celled vaults of the choir also derive from France. It was in the high vault of the choir, that the carved boss at the intersection of the ribs was definitely established as part of the architectural design. The practice of carving the keystones of ribbed vaults originated in the Norman period, an early example occurring in the Norman treasury at Canterbury. But it was the bosses in the choir vaulting, mostly of conventional foliage, that set the fashion that prevailed through the Gothic phases. In the vault above the eastern crossing of Canterbury choir is a boss carved with the Agnus Dei, a Lamb bearing the Cross and banner of the Resurrection, a rare subject in English boss-sculpture. The flying-buttresses supporting the high vault of the choir are probably amongst the earliest to be exposed above the aisle roofs, and not as hitherto, concealed in the triforium chamber. The influence of the momentous undertaking at Canterbury was almost immediate.

CHICHESTER CATHEDRAL, 1187–99

In November 1186 the city of Chichester was visited by the dread enemy, fire, that involved the Norman cathedral and necessitated extensive reparations that culminated in the remodelling of the eastern end of the choir. The roofs of the cathedral

---

[1] The masons who sculptured the capitals must have assumed that Purbeck marble shafts were to be attached to the coupled piers, for a smaller capital is tucked between the main capitals; but there is no provision in the bases of the piers for additional shafts. It seems therefore that the Corinthianesque capitals were carved before the bases were in position. Probably the sculptors were well ahead of the masons, who were at a standstill awaiting the delivery of the columns. Two whole columns and two halves are of a reddish-brown or pink Sicilian marble and were the gift of William the Good of Sicily, to Henry II, whose daughter William had married in 1176. He had presented drums of marble for *all* the columns in the Saint's chapel, but the bulk of them got no farther than the seaport Marsala in Sicily. It may have been that all the capitals were carved whilst the masons were awaiting the load of Sicilian columns, and when the latter failed to arrive and building was resumed, it was decided by William the Englishman to dispense with Purbeck shafting and the bases were moulded accordingly.

caught fire and in their fall the burning timbers calcined and fractured the masonry of the piers and arcades. The work of reparation was at once taken in hand by Bishop Siegfrid II, 1180–1204. The damage which was largely superficial was made good by refacing the piers and the lower parts of the walls with Caen stone, and rebuilding the inner face and arcade of the clerestory. The arches of the nave and the choir were remoulded and slender shafts of Purbeck marble were attached to the piers; the three stages of the bay design were emphasized by inserting string courses of Purbeck, and shafts of the same material were used in the new clerestory. To avert the risk of future damage by fire, the whole cathedral was roofed with quadripartite vaulting, and the stability of the high vaults was ensured by building external flying buttresses as well as those in the triforium chamber.

Evidently there was no lack of funds, for Bishop Siegfrid tore down the apse and ambulatory of the Norman choir, which may or may not have been rendered unsafe by the fire, and in its place was built a squared retrochoir, two bays long, the Lady Chapel beyond being preserved in its entirety (Fig. 10). The east end of Chichester cathedral, thus converted into a work of singular beauty, is generally attributed to masons of Canterbury who found their way to Chichester when there was no more work for them at Christ Church. Dating from the closing years of the twelfth century, the two bays of the retrochoir afford a choice example of Transitional architecture on the very verge of Early English Gothic. The Purbeck marble piers are composed of four detached shafts grouped about a cylindrical column, the capitals of which are richly carved with trefoil foliage (Pl. 46). Rarely, if ever, were Gothic piers designed whose beauty compares with these at Chichester. The main arches of three orders are semicircular, and in the triforium a pair of pointed arches are contained within a round arch. The spandrels of the triforium openings in the east wall are adorned with sculptured figures, an anticipation of the Angel Choir of Lincoln. Centrally placed is Christ in Majesty and in the adjacent triforia are figures of angels set within clusters of foliage. In the clerestory stage all the arches are pointed. But for the round arches in the arcade and the triforium the retrochoir would be a piece of fully developed Early English Gothic.

WELLS CATHEDRAL, 1185–1240

It was inevitable that sooner or later the round arch would be completely ousted by the pointed arch. All important in this respect is the cathedral church of S. Andrew, Wells, the first great church in England to be built throughout in the pointed style, Early English Gothic born before its time.

Of the Saxon and Norman cathedrals no vestige remains. The present cathedral, which was erected on a new site, owes its inception to Bishop Reginald de Bohun, 1174–91. To him and the masons he employed must be ascribed the planning of the cathedral and a great part of the fabric. In a document prepared before 1180, Bishop Reginald acknowledged that 'the honour due to God should not be tarnished by the squalor of His house', and he negotiated with the chapter for 'a substantial grant to the fabric fund until the work be finished'. Building operations commenced *c.* 1185–90. Reginald's cathedral was planned with an aisled presbytery of three bays, beyond which was a squared ambulatory (Fig. 5), transepts with eastern and western aisles, an aisled nave of ten bays and a north-west porch. There were to be twin towers at the west and a tower at the crossing. In the absence of fabric rolls, it is impossible to determine how much of the church had been accomplished when Bishop Reginald was translated to Canterbury in 1192, but by the end of the century the choir, the transepts, the central tower up to the roof level, and the eastern bays of the nave had been built, all of which are now standing, save the eastern part of the choir which was extended in the fourteenth century (Fig. 17). The western half of the nave and the flanking towers were completed by Bishop Jocelin Trotman, 1206–42, though for the first few years of his episcopate the work was in abeyance. The reign of King John was not favourable to the vigorous prosecution of church building anywhere in England. During the Interdict Bishop Jocelin fled the country and was an exile for five years. On his return the building of the nave was resumed; in 1220 the youthful Henry III gave sixty great oaks 'from our woods at Cheddar to make a kiln for the work of the church at Wells', and four years later he granted five marks a year for a period of twelve years to the fabric fund. Enough of the cathedral had been raised for its consecration to take place in 1239, and by about 1245 it was fairly complete, although the west front lacked its full complement of statuary.

Wells was the product of the closing years of the Transitional period, when the masons had thrown off the last vestiges of Anglo-Norman architecture. There is not a single round arch anywhere in the cathedral, though the bulky piers and the angular abaci of the capitals are a Romanesque heritage. The Gothic of Wells did not spring up spontaneously; it owed nothing to Canterbury, not even Purbeck shafting; rather was it a development of the Transitional mode emanating from Worcester and Glastonbury.

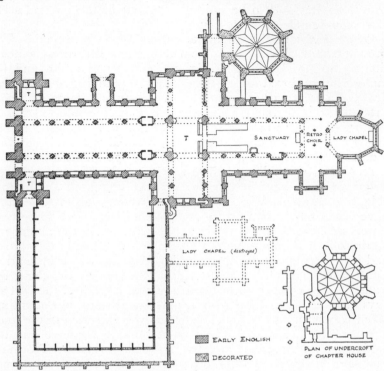

FIG 17. Plan of Wells

With slight modifications the bay design is constant from east to west, and only in minor details does the later differ from the early work. The triforium is reduced to barely more than one-sixth of the total height, but the clerestory is only two feet less than the arches of the ground stage. In form the bulky piers are composed of twenty-four clustered shafts, arranged in triplets (Pl. 50). The foliage capitals are an earnest of the stiff-leaf capitals of Early English Gothic. Unfortunately the earliest bays, those of Reginald's choir, were altered in the fourteenth century, though the piers and main arches are the early work. Architecturally, the transepts are on the very threshold of Early English; in each bay of the triforium are two wide lancets, and in the clerestory is a single lancet light. The capitals of the western piers of the transepts seem to be later than those at the east, and may have been carved when the transepts were repaired in the thirteenth century. Those of the eastern piers are sculptured with foliage, and the western capitals, especially in the south transept are remarkable for the lively little

67. Exeter; bay design of the choir

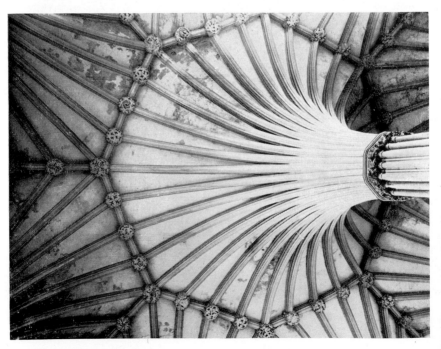

70. Ripon; the choir

71. Southwell; capital of the chapter house portal

72. York; eastern bays of the nave

73. Bristol; the south choir aisle

74. Lichfield; the Lady Chapel

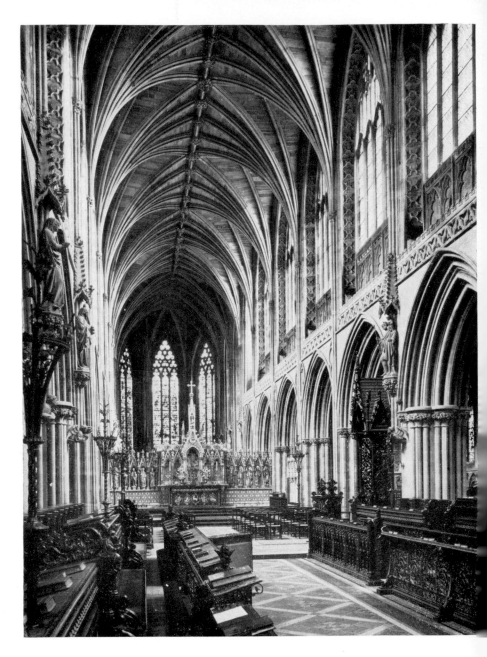

75. Lichfield; the choir looking east

76. Wells; the retrochoir and Lady Chapel

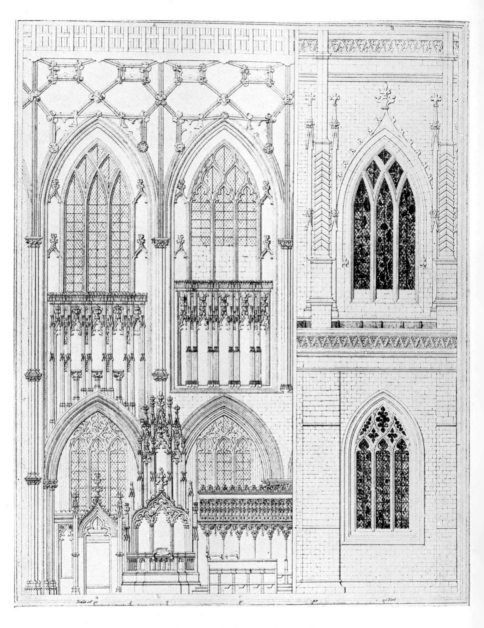

77. Wells; bay design of the choir

78. Wells; the scissor-arches from the south transept

79. Ely; interior of the Lady Chapel

80. Ely; detail of wall arcading in the Lady Chapel

81. Ely; the Octagon from the nave roof

82. Ely; the Octagon from below

83. Gloucester; the central tower

figures intermingled with the foliage. One of them portrays two men in the act of stealing fruit and being belaboured by farmers; another depicts a cobbler mending shoes and a woman extracting a thorn from her foot. There are also several 'toothache' capitals that became associated with Bishop Bytton d. 1274, whose tomb was believed to possess curative powers for sufferers of toothache.

The nave, 161 feet in length, was laid out in ten bays so as to impart an impression of length to so short a nave, the bays were not demarcated by vaulting shafts, and the triforium was designed as an uninterrupted range of lancets, three in each bay (Pl. 51).

About midway up the nave is a definite break in the character of the masonry, in the size of the stones, and this together with the different treatment of the carved capitals clearly indicates work of the two periods, before and after the Interdict. The north-west porch is a choice example of Early Gothic. The jambs of the entrance are packed with marble shafts, and the interior is a storehouse of ornament, lavished unsparingly on the three tiers of wall arcading. The porch was indeed a promise of greater things that reached fulfilment in the design of the west front of the cathedral.

The claim of Wells to be the earliest Gothic cathedral in England rests to a great extent on the vaulting. The high vaults as well as those of the aisles are quadripartite, and all the ribbed arches are pointed. To support the high vaults the masons built flying-buttresses within the triforium chamber and partly relied upon the thickness of the clerestory walls to absorb the thrusts, a tradition of wall-support that persisted in the early Gothic of this country.

S. David's Cathedral, 1180

The builders of York and Oxford in the second half of the twelfth century were not alone in the tardy adoption of new forms. More than twenty years after Oxford was commenced, a reconstruction of S. David's cathedral, Pembroke, was undertaken by Bishop Peter de Leia, 1176–98, the third Norman prelate to occupy the see. The present cathedral, embodying a great part of de Leia's building was the fourth to be erected on the site. Founded in the sixth century, S. David's was the foremost of the four Welsh sees in the Middle Ages. Llandaff, S. Asaph and Bangor were at one time suffragans to the Archbishopric of S. David. Its remote situation on the Welsh coast may account for the predominantly Romanesque character of the cathedral that was commenced in 1180. The whole of the nave, the western parts of the crossing and of the transepts belong to the last twenty years of the twelfth century (Fig. 21).

G

Of exceptional interest and beauty is the nave of six bays. From the bulky piers, alternately cylindrical and octagonal with attached shafts at the cardinal points, rise semicircular arches of three orders elaborately moulded. The scalloped capitals, richly carved and of great variety, are a big remove from the Norman cushion type. In the westernmost bay, which is of smaller span than the others, the pointed arch appears. Unique in every respect is the design of the upper stages of the nave (Pl. 54). The clerestory arcade of two round arches absorbs the triforium stage, the wall of which is pierced with coupled pointed arches, and has the appearance of a clerestory parapet. Although vaulting shafts rise from the triforium level, the nave was originally covered with a timber roof, vastly different from the ornate roof put up in the fifteenth century. Apart from the pointed arches in the triforium and that of the western bay of the nave, the semicircular arch is employed throughout. It is the carved detail of exceptional refinement, rather than the few pointed arches that mark the Transitional character of the nave of S. David's.

HEREFORD CATHEDRAL, 1189–1200

Retaining much of its original aspect is the Transitional retrochoir of Hereford, begun by Bishop de Vere, 1189–99. Here are pointed arches and quadripartite vaults, the ribs of which are enriched with chevron ornament. The work was retarded by the Interdict of John's reign, and the Lady Chapel that was part of the project was not commenced until c. 1222.

LINCOLN CATHEDRAL, 1192–1200

The Norman cathedral of Lincoln, restored and finished by Alexander the Magnificent after the fire of 1141, was to suffer a more dire calamity in less than fifty years. The historian, Roger of Hoveden, relates that on Palm Sunday, 1185, 'the mother church of Lincoln was cleft from top to bottom' by an earthquake. So severe was the damage that, with the exception of the west front and the twin towers, the whole of the cathedral needed reconstruction. The following year the illustrious Hugh of Avalon was advanced to the bishopric of Lincoln, where the task of building a new cathedral awaited him. His tenure of the see from 1186 to 1200 marks a new era in the history of Lincoln, for the reconstruction initiated by him, which was of a century's duration, was in effect the substitution of a super-Gothic cathedral for the Norman church of Alexander. To obtain the necessary funds for the building, Bishop Hugh founded a Gild of S. Mary whose brethren pledged themselves to contribute, the fund thereby benefiting by

1,000 marks a year. Henry II granted letters patent to Hugh's successors for the maintenance of the Gild. 'But how incongruous it would be that such a noble work should be unfinished. And inasmuch as it needs your help and aid, we beg of you all, we admonish and exhort you in the Lord . . .'

The master mason engaged to direct the building operations was an Englishman, Geoffrey de Noiers, one of a family long seated in Northants. The foundations of the new choir were laid in 1192, and Bishop Hugh himself lent a hand in fetching and carrying materials. The plan (Fig. 5) shows the extent of Hugh's choir. The three-sided apse and ambulatory were swept away when the Angel Choir was built (p. 210), but the foundations were revealed in 1791 and again in 1887. Otherwise Hugh's choir and in particular the eastern transepts are fairly intact, and provide the earliest example after Wells of Lancet Gothic. At the time of Hugh's death, the masons were at work in the main transepts.

Architecturally, the choir of Lincoln cathedral was far ahead of any contemporary building in the land; so much so that Gilbert Scott regarded it almost as an anachronism (Pl. 52). In the fashioning of the shafted piers, composed of four Purbeck shafts grouped about a stone column, in the pointed arches and the wall arcadings, in the carving of the stiff-leaf capitals and in the chiselling of the mouldings, Bishop Hugh's masons discarded every trace of Norman tradition, and in doing so they evolved the initial phase of Gothic architecture (Pl. 48). It might be assumed that the new choir at Lincoln would have been influenced by the work of William de Sens and his successor at Canterbury, finished some six years before. The coupled apses of the eastern transepts may have been copied from Canterbury, and the Purbeck use at Lincoln may have derived from Canterbury. The Transitional building at Canterbury was largely of French inspiration, but the new choir of Lincoln owed nothing to France in form, detail or ornament. Advanced it certainly was; so much so, that both Gilbert Scott and Viollet-le-Duc found difficulty in accepting readily so early a period as 1192–1200 for its erection.

The western bays of Hugh's choir were robbed of much of their original form by the indifferent restoration that followed the fall of the central tower. The third pair of piers east of the crossing seem to be the only ones that remain as Hugh's masons left them; the others were rebuilt and the triforium was replaced by one that resembles that of the nave. In the clerestory are lancet lights fronted with a tall arcade carried by Purbeck shafts. The choir and its aisles were roofed with timber ceilings, the stone vaults being erected later. In the choir transepts, which escaped the havoc of 1239 (p. 208), the work of Hugh's masons is better preserved. The clustered piers of Purbeck and stone shafts have capitals of stiff-leaf foliage and in some of the piers carved crockets are ranged vertically between the shafts. A sure sign of Gothic is the circular abacus; in Norman and Transitional work the abacus is invariably square or angular. In some bays the triforium openings, consisting of two main arches, each enclosing two sub-arches, have simple plate tracery, merely circular piercings of the spandrels.

Hugh's choir at Lincoln shares with Wells cathedral the distinction of being the first great churches to which the term Gothic can be applied, though they differ so utterly in their expression.

LICHFIELD CATHEDRAL, 1195–1210

Bishops, abbots and chapters who were bent on enlarging or rebuilding their churches showed scant respect for the work of their predecessors. A church might be an outstanding monument of Norman architecture, but if inadequate to the needs of the day, down it came. When Bishop Reginald de Bohun rebuilt Wells, every stone of the pre-existing cathedral was cleared away, and the same drastic measures were adopted at Lichfield in the last decade of the twelfth century. The Norman cathedral was far less than a century old when the eastern arm was torn down to give place to a much larger choir with a squared ambulatory, similar to Roger's choir at York cathedral. Owing to subsequent alterations, only the piers and the pointed arches of the three western bays and the sacristy on the south side of the choir that was begun in 1195 are now standing. The triforium and the clerestory were altered in the fourteenth century. In form the clustered piers consisting of twenty-four shafts arranged in triplets, bear a strong resemblance to those of Wells, and the arches above are moulded with bold rounds and hollows, a feature common to thirteenth-century Gothic. The carved foliage of the capitals lacks the vigour of those at Wells.

Entered from the south choir-aisle of Lichfield is the sacristy, over which is the chapel of S. Chad, drastically restored in the nineteenth century. The triple lancets of the chapel are original, but the vault is modern. In a book of the Chapter Acts under the date 1481 is an entry: 'Two monstrances given to the cathedral, in the charge of William Hukyns, custodian of the Head of S. Chad, by Dean Heywood, for keeping relics.' At one time a doorway in the west wall of the sacristy opened into a small square treasury that is now entered from the aisle (Fig. 19).

13. The Architecture of English Cathedrals

II. EARLY ENGLISH GOTHIC

⟪ By the close of the twelfth century the Transitional phase was at an end, and the potentialities of Gothic lay ahead. The round arch was everywhere rejected in favour of the pointed arch with its unlimited span and height. The principles of vault-construction and of abutment had been mastered, and an economy was being effected in material; walls and piers were less massively built, and a greater refinement was manifested in the cutting of mouldings and in the carving of capitals and ornament. Now that the thrusts generated by ribbed vaults were met at isolated points by buttresses, the wall spaces between the buttresses could be converted into windows for the display of coloured glass. Gothic architecture has been spoken of as 'the stained glass style'. The architectural historian Fergusson, writing nearly a century ago, claimed that the invention of painted glass was the formative principle of Gothic. 'All windows in all churches after the twelfth century were designed to receive painted glass, and the principal and guiding motive in all the changes subsequently introduced into Gothic was to obtain the maximum space for its display.' This is but half the truth, for the underlying principle of Gothic derives from the structural system of thrust and counter-thrust. It was the employment of wall-buttresses and 'fliers' that enabled the walls of churches to be converted into screens of glass.

The use of Purbeck marble at Canterbury and Lincoln set the fashion for piers with detached shafts, so marked a feature of Early English Gothic. All through the thirteenth century Purbeck was in favour, notably at Salisbury and Lincoln, and was extensively used in the fourteenth century at Exeter cathedral.

Significant were the changes in the forms of windows. It now became the practice to group two or more lancet lights beneath a containing arch, leaving a blank spandrel above the heads of the lights, and before long the spandrel was pierced with a circular or a foiled opening to which the name 'plate tracery' has been given. As early as 1145, in the triforium of Peterborough choir, the spandrel above the sub-arches was perforated with small circular openings three or four in number, and in the choir-transepts at Lincoln cathedral, c. 1192, the piercings take the form of trefoils and quatrefoils. During the Lancet period the perforations became more complex in design; the intervening masonry was fined away until it was reduced to a patterning of 'bar tracery', and the walls dividing the lights were thinned down to vertical bars or mullions. By the middle of the century the heads of Gothic windows were being filled with geometric forms, usually circles enclosing trefoils or quatrefoils, whence derives the term Geometric that is generally applied to the Gothic style of the second half of the thirteenth century. The fully developed Geometric window appeared at Westminster abbey c. 1250, the earliest of its kind in England. Some authorities are of opinion that Geometric tracery was an importation from the Ile de France, where many great cathedrals were rising and where Gothic was making rapid progress.

Advances were also made in the construction of ribbed vaults. To strengthen the jointing at the top of the vault, horizontal ridge ribs were applied both longitudinally and transversely, thereby effecting a unity in the structure of the vault from end to end. The high vault of the choir of Ely cathedral is an early example, dating 1235–50. A further elaboration of vault construction followed almost at once, by the introduction of tierceron ribs, that were made to spring from the same points as the diagonals and abutted against the ridge ribs. The tierceron vault of Lincoln nave dates c. 1240. The multiplication of ribs afforded the carver of bosses ample opportunities for the exercise of his craft, and before the end of the thirteenth century, still more ribs, decorative rather than structural, and more carved bosses, made the English vault a distinctive feature of our insular Gothic.

There was great building activity in the thirteenth century; it was the age of choir remodelling and extension (p. 86), and the eastern arms of our cathedrals that were rebuilt at this time provided admirable specimens of Early English, the purest and most vigorous phase of Gothic.

S. Albans Cathedral, 1198–1290

For more than a century the Norman abbey church of S. Albans remained undisturbed, but under the rule of John de Cella, 1195–1214, alterations were begun at the west end. Probably the abbot desired a more dignified façade embracing twin towers and deep portals. The work commenced with the building of a new west front thirty feet beyond the old front, and therefore involved lengthening the nave by three bays. The convent was badly served by the master-mason, Hugh de Godelif, 'an untrustworthy and deceitful man but a consummate craftsman'. By the time the foundations were sunk the sum of 100 marks, bequeathed by the abbot's predecessors, had been squandered; and the extravagance and dishonesty of Master Hugh caused a complete stoppage of the work in the winter of 1197–8. The walls were then only a few feet above ground, and the masons, who saw no prospect of receiving their wages downed tools and departed. In desperate need of money the abbot sent forth one of the monks on a begging mission, and when the operations were resumed, one of the convent, Gilbert of Eversholt, was appointed *custos operis*. Abbot John seemed doomed to frustration and disappointment, and at his death in 1214 only the north porch of the west front had been finished. It fell to his successor, William of Trumpington, 1214–35, to complete the work so grossly mismanaged. When the west front was in an advanced stage, the old Norman façade was demolished and a start was made on the nave-extension. Working from west to east, the masons built four bays on the north side of the nave and five on the south (Fig. 13). The existence of vaulting shafts shows the intention of erecting a high vault, but all concerned were so anxious to bring the long-drawn-out project to an end that the vaulting shafts were stopped short at the triforium and the new bays of the nave were roofed in timber. The idea of building twin towers at the west was abandoned. Beneath the turf outside, lie the foundations of the towers, 40 feet square, and at the end of the south aisle is to be seen the lofty arch, richly moulded and shafted, that was to have opened into the south-western tower. The western elongation imparted an internal length of 275 feet to the nave of S. Albans, the longest in any mediaeval church in England.

The new west front was drastically altered in the fifteenth century and Lord Grimthorpe spared little of what remained. Only the inner parts of the porches, with wall-arcading carried by Purbeck shafts, and the quadripartite vaults are of the thirteenth century. Abbot Trumpington's bays differ in proportions from the Norman bays to the east, the main arches being of greater height at the expense of the triforium. The Early English piers, octagonal in form with four attached shafts, are wholly of stone; no Purbeck shafting was employed, so that the piers should harmonize with the Norman plastered piers. The mouldings of the nave arches are multiplied to an uncommon extent for such early work. The triforium stage is treated with two arches in each bay, with subarches that spring from clustered shafts and are enriched with dog-tooth ornament.

Of greater consequence was the new eastern arm of the abbey church, commenced about twenty years later. The old Norman apses had long been outmoded; they were inconvenient for the monks' processions and for the crowds of pilgrims that surged into the church. A special chapel for the shrine of S. Alban was an urgent necessity as also was a Lady Chapel, that was then regarded as an integral part of every great church. In 1257, owing to the unsafe condition of the Norman apses, the chapter decided to remodel the choir-arm on the lines of that at Winchester, then half a century old. The plan embraced a spacious sanctuary, a Saint's chapel, a retrochoir and ambulatory and a Lady Chapel (Fig. 13). This ambitious scheme, formulated by Abbot John de Hertford, 1253–63, was more than sixty years in fulfilment, progress being held up at various times through lack of funds. The Lady Chapel therefore belongs to the early years of the fourteenth century.

From considerations of cost, the stout clustered piers of the choir are devoid of Purbeck shafts. In each bay of the triforium is a range of six blind panels with trefoiled heads, and the clerestory has three-light windows of the nineteenth century. A high vault of stone was intended, the springers of which are to be seen in the clerestory walls. Instead, a quadripartite ceiling of wood was put up. Of the fabric of the thirteenth-century retrochoir little has survived, for the restoration of 1874 practically amounted to a rebuilding. Roofed at a lower level than the choir, as at Winchester, the retrochoir is divided into a nave and aisles by arcades of two arches carried by octagonal columns. As soon as the retrochoir was ready, Abbot John de Maryns, 1302–8, 'moved and adorned the Shrine of S. Alban'. A new pedestal was in fact made for the feretrum (p. 129).

CHESTER CATHEDRAL, 1200–40

At the opening of the thirteenth century, the Norman choir of the Benedictine abbey church of S. Werburgh, Chester, now the cathedral, was taken down and a new eastern arm was planned, embracing a presbytery, a squared ambulatory and a Lady Chapel (Fig. 5). The monks also resolved upon rebuilding the conventual apartments off the east and north walks of the cloisters. Small wonder that the scheme fell short of fulfilment for more than a century. By 1240 or soon afterwards, the Lady Chapel, three eastern bays of the presbytery including the ambulatory, and the aisles had been rebuilt; and of the same period are the chapter house and its vestibule, the slype, the sub-dorter in the eastern block and the monks' frater at the north, all of which are in good preservation today (Fig. 18). The masons were evidently in desperate haste for the Lady Chapel was erected without foundations of any kind. It has been much restored; the lancet windows of graded heights were inserted by Scott, but the tierceron vault is original.

Of the three eastern bays of the choir, the main arcade and the triforium stage alone are of the early thirteenth century; the lofty clerestory was not added until forty or fifty years later. The piers are composed of eight attached shafts with corresponding archorders boldly moulded above; and the diminutive triforium, that is out of all proportion to the clerestory, is fronted with trefoiled arcading. From corbels above the capitals rise triple vaulting shafts, but the high vault of oak is modern.

Off the eastern walk of the cloisters and immediately adjoining the north transept is the square vestibule of the chapter house, one of the loveliest productions of Early English Gothic. It is entered through a trefoiled portal and is divided into nine bays by four clustered piers that take their form from the ribs of the quadripartite vaults that are carried down to the bases without intervening capitals. The rectangular chapter house is roofed with three bays of simple tierceron vaulting; each bay is lighted by three lancet windows, in front of which are detached shafts with annulet rings.

ROCHESTER CATHEDRAL, 1200–90

The remodelling of the eastern arm of Rochester cathedral, begun c. 1200 (p. 90), was part of a grand scheme for rebuilding the whole of the Norman church. The scheme fell short of accomplishment and was halted at the eastern end of the nave. The new sanctuary and the choir transepts were raised on an Early Gothic crypt, the finest of its kind in the land (Fig. 7). From the circular and octagonal columns in the crypt spring the ribs of the quadripartite vaulting, and attached to the major piers are half-round and semi-octagonal responds.

The Early Gothic of the superstructure is remarkable in many respects. The internal elevation is of two storeys, the triforium stage being omitted. Most effective but uncommon is the treatment of the walls of the unaisled sanctuary, in the lower parts of which is a series of tall recesses each pierced with a lancet window. The lengths of walling between the recesses have the appearance of isolated piers, and thereby the effect of flatness is avoided (Pl. 55). In the clerestory stage is a pointed window in each bay, fronted with an arcade of three arches carried by Purbeck shafts.

In the choir transepts which have eastern aisles an unbroken
G*

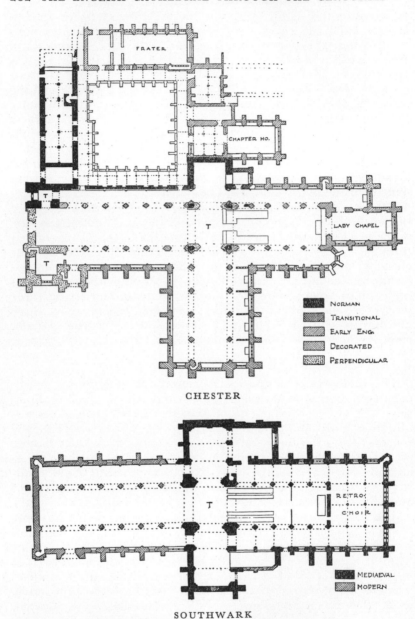

FRATER

CHAPTER HO.

LADY CHAPEL

NORMAN
TRANSITIONAL
EARLY ENG.
DECORATED
PERPENDICULAR

CHESTER

RETRO
CHOIR

MEDIAEVAL
MODERN

SOUTHWARK

FIG 18. Plans of Chester and Southwark

range of wall-arcading takes the place of clerestory lights. The solid walls of the Norman choir were not removed but were refaced with ashlar. Above the stalls is a blind arcade surmounted by a clerestory similar to that of the sanctuary, and enriched with dog-tooth ornament, which is also applied to the ribs of the high vault. The new choir-arm of Rochester is roofed with sexpartite vaulting, probably copied from William de Sens' choir at Canterbury. Purbeck marble, as might be expected, is used profusely for shafts of the wall-arcading, for string courses and for vaulting shafts.

From contemporary records we learn that Prior Radulf 'roofed and leaded the greater part of the Church'. Whilst he held the office of sacrist, Radulf's successor, Helias, never spent less than £20 a year upon the *novum opus ecclesiae*. The 'new work' was paid for out of the offerings made at the tomb of S. William, and proceeded under the direction of William de Hoo, the sacrist. In 1227 the monks were using the sanctuary for the Divine offices; and the whole of the eastern arm was completed in 1240 and was dedicated in November of that year. The rebuilding of the north transept was then taken in hand. Here again the design is two-storeyed, Purbeck shafting is abundant and the vaulting is sexpartite. About twenty-five years later the south transept was reconstructed and a start was made on the piers at the crossing and on the eastern bays of the nave. Though much altered in the fifteenth century, the two eastern bays of the nave testify to the ambitious project that, for lack of funds had to be abandoned before the end of the century.

ELY CATHEDRAL, 1200–52

The masons of the Early English period positively revelled in wall-arcading and seem to have seized every opportunity to enrich large areas of wall surface with this form of decoration. Attached to the west front of Ely cathedral is a lofty Galilee porch, *c.* 1200, clad in wall-arcading ranged in four tiers, that are broken only by the portal and the three tall lancet lights in the west wall (Pl. 58). The interior one is of the most perfect things in English Gothic. The two-storeyed arcades of the lateral walls, the inner portal flanked by innumerable shafts carrying richly carved archorders, the foliage of the capitals and the profuse dog-tooth ornament are witness of the enormous progress in masoncraft since the Transitional period, and were an earnest of the magnificent Early English Gothic of the choir extension carried out by Bishop Northwold, 1229–54. The six aisled bays of the retrochoir begun *c.* 1235 added 100 feet to the length of the eastern arm of Ely (Fig. 19), and furnish one of the loveliest examples of Early

English Gothic, exquisite in every detail. The proportions of the bay design were governed by that of the Norman bays left standing at the west; hence the abnormally large triforium stage. Attached to the cylindrical piers are eight Purbeck marble shafts with annulet rings and richly carved capitals. In each bay of the triforium are two openings with trefoiled arches, and the clerestory has an arcade in front of three lancet lights in the outer wall. The spandrels of the choir arcade and the triforium are relieved with sunken trefoils and quatrefoils. The mouldings, the carved corbels of the vaulting shafts, and the ornament are unsurpassed in refinement. 'Lovelier detail was never wrought by the hand of man.' The choir is roofed with a tierceron vault in which are many carved bosses. Above the High Altar is one representing S. Etheldreda crowned, and another depicts the Coronation of the Virgin. There are double flying-buttresses; those within the triforium chamber abut the high vault, and others in the open counteract the spread of the timber roof. The aisles were originally lighted by lancet windows but later were replaced by four-light windows.

After seventeen years the choir extension was completed in 1252. It was built at a cost of £5,040 18s. 7d., the greater part of which was found by Bishop Northwold, though small sums were contributed by the prior and convent and other persons. On 15 October 1252 the shrine of S. Etheldreda was installed in the new retrochoir in the presence of Henry III, nobles, prelates and ecclesiastics, and the cathedral, on ground plan as it is today, was rededicated to S. Etheldreda, S. Mary and S. Peter.

PETERBOROUGH CATHEDRAL, 1200–25

The Galilee porch that was tacked on to the west front of Ely cathedral pales into insignificance before the amazing western façade of Peterborough cathedral dating c. 1200–15, that has been fittingly described as 'the noblest version of a Classic portico in terms of Gothic'. Built outside the western wall of the nave it is a gigantic porch rather than a façade, consisting of an open arcade of three colossal arches carried by clustered piers and flanked by lofty square towers. Though at first glance the triple arches appear to have little reference to the internal ordonnance of the church behind, the narrower central arch relates to the span of the nave, and the lateral arches embrace the western transepts. The flanking towers are in the nature of buttresses whose purpose is to absorb the thrusts of the outer arches, and were subsequently weighted with stone spires. The design was certainly the conception of an architectural genius whose name is not known.

The moulded orders of these great arches spring from clustered

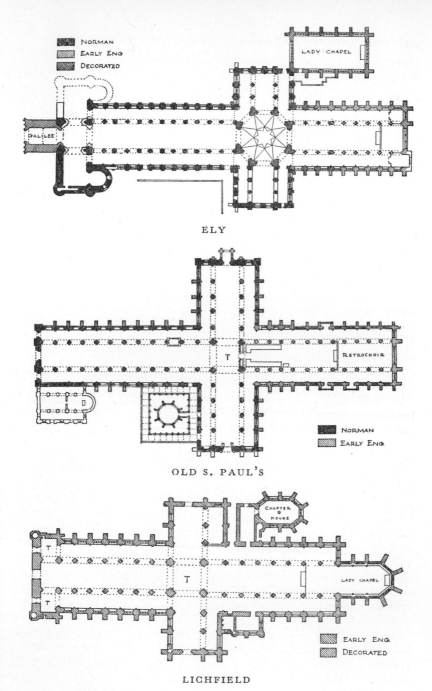

FIG 19. Plans of Ely, Old S. Paul's and Lichfield

piers having six banded shafts on each side; between the shafts of
the central arch are series of crocketed and dog-tooth ornament,
and the arches themselves are enriched with chevron and billet.
The gables are pierced with wheel windows, below which is a
range of niches tenanted by figures of the Apostles; the spandrels
also are occupied by niched figures. The towers are faced with six
tiers of wall-arcading of varying heights, which are in perfect harmony with the general design, as also are the arcadings of the inner
wall that range with those of the towers. The two-storeyed porch
squatting beneath the middle arch was inserted late in the fourteenth century (p. 277).

SOUTHWARK CATHEDRAL, 1215–30

Early in the thirteenth century the church of the Augustinian
priory of S. Mary Overie at Southwark, now the cathedral, was
rebuilt by Peter de Rupibus, Bishop of Winchester, 1205–38, after
its destruction by fire in 1213. From the ninth century when S.
Swithun refounded the religious house there as a college of secular canons, the bishops of Winchester were closely associated with
S. Mary Overie. Their London palace lay immediately to the west
of the church. In 1106 the establishment was converted into an
Augustinian priory and a new church was erected in the Norman
style, traces of which remain in the north transept and in the north
aisle of the nave. At the east end of the latter is the Norman portal
that once opened into the cloisters. Of the church that was built
after the fire of 1213, the whole of the Early English choir and
retrochoir, after centuries of maltreatment and neglect, are now
restored to something of their original condition (Fig. 18).

The choir of three bays is flanked by aisles that lead to the
splendid retrochoir beyond, roofed at a lower level than the choir.
The piers of the choir, alternately circular and octagonal, have
triple vaulting shafts attached to them; those on the north side
have additional shafts to carry the innermost orders of the arches,
and on the south side corbels are made to serve the purpose. The
capitals are merely moulded and there is an absence of Purbeck
marble. In the triforium is a range of pointed arches carried by
slender shafts, four to each bay, the continuity of which is broken
by vaulting shafts, and behind them is a solid wall. The clerestory
is marked by triple arcading and the high vault is quadripartite.

The priory possessed no saintly relics and a Saint's chapel not
being needed, the retrochoir was planned on simple lines as a low
eastern annexe, with 'the Little Chapel of Our Lady', since
destroyed, extending eastwards. The Early English work of the
retrochoir is more mature and graceful than that of the choir

THE ARCHITECTURE OF ENGLISH CATHEDRALS 207

(Pl. 56). Originally it was lighted on all sides by triple lancet windows like those now in the east wall. The slender piers are composed of four attached shafts with concave hollows between them, and from the bell-capitals rise the ribs of the quadripartite vaulting.

The retrochoir of Southwark cathedral is a noble specimen of thirteenth-century Gothic in planning and in design. The rebuilding of the church continued throughout the century. In the north transept the lofty wall-arcading has shafts of Purbeck marble, and attached to the wall of the south aisle of the nave at the western end are remnants of late Early English arcading.

LINCOLN CATHEDRAL, 1220–80

The early Gothic of Hugh's choir at Lincoln, 1192–1200, was promise of the glorious maturity of the thirteenth century. At the time of the bishop's death in 1200, the innermost bays of the main transepts of the cathedral had been put up, the double arcading of the aisle walls being of that period. The reconstruction made steady progress, although the cathedral establishment was passing through difficult times. In 1216 when the city of Lincoln was captured by the barons in their struggle against King John, the cathedral treasury was despoiled of 11,000 marks, a sum amassed by the precentor for the building operations. Nevertheless, the main transepts and the chapter house that had been commenced c. 1220, were completed by 1235, and the central tower was slowly rising, an amazing achievement considering the circumstances.

The bay design of the transept arcades is similar to that of Hugh's choir, but the clustered piers consist of eight stone and the same number of marble shafts. The particular glories of the transepts are the large circular windows, 24 feet in diameter, in the end walls. That in the north transept, popularly called 'the Dean's Eye', is an advanced example of plate tracery, dating c. 1225. In the centre of the window is a huge quatrefoiled circle set within a ring of sixteen circular openings filled with thirteenth-century glass. The corresponding window in the south transept belongs to the fourteenth century (p. 242).

From the east walk of the cloisters to the north of the choir a lofty vestibule leads to the chapter house, one of the earliest of the polygonal type. On plan it is a ten-sided building, having a diameter of 62 feet. In each wall are two lancet windows, below which a wall bench is carried round the interior and is surmounted by arcading. From the central pier of clustered shafts spring the ribs of the vault, a complex design remarkable for so early a date. The external flying-buttresses spread out like colossal fingers, were added in the fourteenth century to counteract the thrusts at the angles of the building (Fig. 20).

In the early years of the episcopate of Robert Grosseteste, 1235–53, was built the Galilee porch at the west of the south transept; it served as a state entrance for my lord bishop whose palace lay to the south of the cathedral. This little cruciform building exhibits Lancet Gothic at its best. A portal on the east side, ornate with carved foliage, gives entrance to the transept, and the other sides of the porch have open arches. The walls are overlaid with choice arcading supported by clustered shafting and the dog-tooth ornament is prolific. The Galilee has a quadripartite vault, and above is a chamber lighted by lancet windows that served as a Court Room of the chapter.

A work of greater importance was the building of the nave; the scaffoldings were moving westwards by 1239, a year that was marked by an unforeseen calamity, viz., the collapse of the new central tower. The bays of the choir and transepts adjoining the crossing sustained grievous damage and the restoration that followed was so hastily and clumsily carried out, that much of Hugh's work was obliterated. The piers of the tower were reinforced with additional masonry to which were attached twenty-four shafts, twelve of stone and the others of Purbeck marble. The choir was in part remodelled, the piers in the transepts rebuilt and in place of the timber roofing, stone vaults were put up in the choir and transepts. The high vault of the choir is quinquipartite (five-celled), an eccentric form that was not repeated at Lincoln or elsewhere. To support the vault transverse arches were constructed in the triforium chamber, in addition to flying-buttresses, a system of double abutment that was resorted to later in the nave and the retrochoir. When the aisles of the choir were vaulted, the walls were doubled in thickness; the wall-arcading of Hugh's aisles were faced with a trefoiled arcade, above which the plain walling was recased. The double planes of arcading, a feature of extraordinary beauty, also occurs in the two chapels of the main transepts next the crossing and in the dean's chapel to the west of the north choir-transept. The main transepts were covered with sexpartite vaulting.

Apparently the building of the western arm of Lincoln cathedral was not retarded by the fall of the central tower, for it is generally held that the nave, the western transepts and the arcaded 'framing' of the west front were completed in Bishop Grosseteste's time, i.e. not later than 1253. To ensure stability, the nave arcades were built on continuous foundations, and sleeper-walls were laid from the piers to the aisle-walls. The bay design conforms with that of the transepts, though all the nave piers have eight clustered shafts. Purbeck marble was used for all the shafting, except for one pair of piers near the west, where marble alternates with stone. The triforium design with its foiled plate tracery so strongly resembles that of the transepts as to leave no doubt that the building operations were continuous. The tierceron vault of the nave with its bosses of foliage and figure-subjects shows the progress that marks the Gothic of Lincoln cathedral (Pl. 57).

The addition of transepts at the west end of the nave converted the west front into a gigantic screen, adorned with tiers of arcading. Between the towers was erected the lofty gable of the nave and the central recess was heightened, a pointed arch being substituted for the Norman round arch. Unsatisfactory as the façade may be as an architectural composition, it was a bold conception and remains a striking feature of the exterior. For more than sixty years the cathedral that had been planned by Bishop Hugh had been in course of erection, and three years after the death of Bishop Grosseteste, the chapter embarked upon an ambitious extension of the eastern arm.

In 1220 a Papal bull was issued authorizing the canonization of Bishop Hugh, whose tomb stood in the chapel of S. John Baptist in the north choir-transept, a most inconvenient position for pilgrim visitations; and Pope Innocent III directed that the Saint's

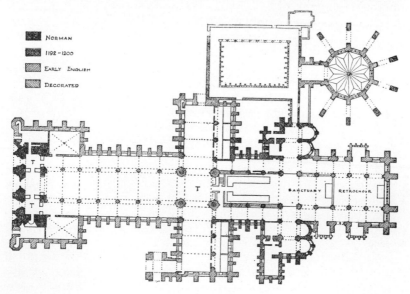

FIG 20, Plan of Lincoln

remains should be translated to a more honourable place in the cathedral. With no more ado, the three-sided apse and ambulatory of Hugh's choir were pulled down and the choir was lengthened by five bays beyond the eastern transepts (Fig. 20). Henry III granted a licence to the chapter in 1255 to remove part of the city wall that stood in the way at the east. The Lincoln planners laid out the new extension as an aisled rectangle, modelling it upon the choir arm of Ely cathedral that had been completed in 1252. The Angel Choir of Lincoln, so called from the thirty sculptured angels in the triforium, was the culminating achievement of the masons of the thirteenth century at Lincoln, an architectural creation of surpassing loveliness and a Geometric version of the Lancet retrochoir of Ely (Pl. 8). The Purbeck marble piers, the traceried windows and the wall-arcading, the sculptured figures, capitals and corbels and the refined mouldings render the Angel Choir a supreme monument of mediaeval Gothic. The piers have eight engaged shafts with annulet rings, and the foliage of the capitals and corbels are carved with the utmost delicacy. In the triforium are two main arches each containing a two-light opening with a quatrefoiled circle in the head, and the spandrels are occupied by sculptured angels with spreading wings and bearing musical instruments, scrolls and crowns. The clerestory is one of the wonders of Gothic architecture, a marvel of stone cutting. The four-light windows of Geometric tracery are constructed in inner and outer planes of masonry, a method that not only ensured maximum top-lighting but also effected an economy in stone. From the triforium rise the ribs of the tierceron vaulting, notable for the carved foliage of the bosses, and in the aisle vaults are a number of figure subjects as well as leafage. Of exceptional beauty is the Geometrical wall-arcading beneath the three-light windows in the aisles, though much of it was mutilated when chantry chapels were built off the aisles in later centuries. The eight-light window in the east wall, 34 feet wide, is one of the largest of its kind and is designed as a multiple of two-light units.

All glorious within the Angel Choir demanded a majestic entrance from the south. Between the buttresses of the third bay from the east is the noble Judgment Porch, so named from the sculptured Doom on the tympanum. The gabled front is brought forward so as to be flush with the buttresses, thereby providing deeply recessed jambs for figure sculpture. Prof. Lethaby has shown that the Porch was a study of the central portal of the north transept of Westminster abbey. On the trumeau dividing the two doors is a modern statue of the Virgin and Child, and in the tympanum is a quatrefoil containing a figure of Our Lord attended

by censing angels, all much restored. On the left angels receive
the resurrected dead, and on the right the condemned are con-
signed to the mouth of Hell. The arch-orders are richly carved,
the innermost order bearing niches tenanted by figures of kings
and queens, and in other rings of the arch are the Ten Virgins and
the Tree of Jesse.

In October 1280, Edward I, Queen Eleanor, nobles and ecclesiastics were present in Lincoln cathedral to witness the translation
of the remains of S. Hugh to a new shrine in the Saint's chapel
behind the High Altar. The Angel Choir, however, was not completely finished until early in the fourteenth century. In 1305 a
contract for the *Novum Opus* (Angel Choir) was drawn up between
the chapter and Richard of Gainsborough, *cementarius*, the plain
work to be done by measure, and the carving and sculpture by the
day. After its completion, no reconstructions were made that involved changes in the plan of the cathedral which was now perfectly suited to its mediaeval purposes.

SALISBURY CATHEDRAL, 1220–66

When Bishop Richard Poore removed the see of Old Sarum in
1219, the builders of the new Salisbury cathedral had the advantage of rearing a great church on virgin ground. Standing on their
own feet, Poore's masons produced a fully developed plan for the
cathedral (p. 90), that also affords a complete embodiment of the
architectural ideals of the Lancet period. It was begun in 1220 and
with the exception of the tower and spire was erected within the
space of fifty years, and is therefore homogeneous in style. From
end to end of the great church, there is uniformity and consistency
in the design, the variations being so slight as not to affect the harmony of the building as a whole. Bishop Poore's enthusiasm for
the project was shared by the canons, who agreed to contribute
one-fourth of their emoluments for seven years to the building
fund. At a general chapter in August 1220, it was decreed that if
any canon defaulted, the corn of his prebend should be seized as
payment of his due. To swell the funds the Dean, William de
Wenda, toured the diocese of London soliciting alms of the faithful.

The architecture of Salisbury cathedral is characterized by a
severe restraint and sobriety; detail is subordinated and fussy and
exuberant ornament avoided. Externally its impressive grandeur
lies in the well-balanced disposition of its several parts, and in the
expression of repose and stability, that is largely due to the bold
base mouldings carried round the building at every point. The
horizontal lines emphasize the stability of the footings on which

the huge pile rests. In sheer masoncraft the utmost precision was observed in the cutting of the stones and in the regular coursing and jointing. To quote Prof. Willis: 'The regularity of the size of the stones is astonishing. The masonry runs in even bands and you may follow it from the south transept eastwards round to the north transept, after which they [the masons] have not taken such great pains in the regularity.' The bonding of the courses and the jointing are so close that the cathedral might have been hewn out of one mighty block. Nor were the masons less consistent in the fenestration. Other than a few in the transepts and the west front, all the windows are lancet lights. The aisles are lighted with large coupled lancets, and in the clerestory the lancets are triple. A variant occurs in the transept-ends and in the west front, where plate tracery makes its appearance. There, the spandrels above the grouped lancets are pierced with quatrefoiled openings. Most satisfactory are the triple lancets in the Lady Chapel as well as in the eastern walls of the choir-aisles and in the west front.

The Salisbury masons put their faith in Purbeck marble; there are piers with two, four and eight shafts respectively, and those at the crossing are clustered with no less than twenty shafts. The variation in pier forms is a distinctive feature of the interior; only in the main transepts are there piers devoid of marble shafts. From end to end of the cathedral the piers stand on low stone platforms that form a continuous base 6 feet wide. The foundations were sunk in a bed of gravel, and being in the low-lying valley of the Avon, the site was subject to flooding. As recently as 1925 the nave was under water.

In the Lady Chapel, the earliest and most lovely part of the cathedral, elegance and lightness were achieved by dividing it into a nave and aisles with slender shafts of Purbeck marble some 30 feet in height. The piers in the choir consist of a stone core, quatrefoil in section, with eight detached shafts and the arch mouldings are enriched with dog-tooth ornament. The least happy feature of the bay design is the triforium, the main arches of which sprawl in an ungainly fashion and give the effect of being squeezed out from above; the closely packed shafts of this stage are all of Purbeck marble with none of stone by way of contrast or to relieve the cavernous darkness of the triforium chamber. On the other hand the clerestory with its triple lancets and slender shafting is of singular beauty. The design of the nave differs little from that of the choir, the minor importance of this part of the church being reflected in the simpler detail. The quatrefoil piers have only four shafts, and no less significant is the absence of dog-tooth ornament in the arch mouldings. The whole of the cathedral is roofed with quadripartite vaulting. The ribs of the high vaults spring from corbels on the clerestory level that are supported by triple marble shafts. In the vault of the choir are several carved and gilded bosses and the web surfaces are decorated with painted roundels (p. 137). Thr high vaults are supported by flying-buttresses concealed in the triforium chamber and thus protected from the weather. The external fliers were added in the fifteenth century.

By 1250 the nave was completed and the masons were at work on the west front, the frontispiece of the cathedral and therefore of prime importance. The design is somewhat disappointing, being a haphazard arrangement of windows, arcadings, niches and other features. Bold buttresses define the nave and its aisles, but the end walling of the aisles is carried up to the level of the nave gable, far above the aisle roofs and is therefore an architectural deceit. Wanting in size and dignity are the stair turrets at the angles, the sole purpose of which was to give greater width to the façade. A definite scheme of iconography was prepared to set forth the story of the Christian faith, the statuary being disposed in six tiers of niches, most of which are now occupied by modern figures. In the gable of the nave is Christ in Majesty, beneath which is a range of niches tenanted by angels, seraphim and cherubim. The second tier presents patriarchs of the Old Testament, and below are figures of the Apostles and Saints of the New Testament bearing their emblems; in the fourth tier are doctors of the Church, together with Virgins and Martyrs, and the range of niches above the nave portal contains figures of S. Barbara, S. Roch, S. Sebastian, S. Ursula and other saints of the Early Church. The bottom tier consists of worthies of the English Church, particularly those of local fame, including Bishop Giles de Bridport and Bishop Poore. Above the doorway within the central portal is a figure of the Virgin Mary, to whom Salisbury cathedral was dedicated.

The main entrance to the cathedral is the lofty two-storeyed porch at the north-west of the nave, the inner walls of which are adorned with fine wall-arcading. The chamber above was probably used as a scriptorium.

A note in the *Book of Statutes* of Bishop Roger de Mortival, 1315–30, states that the cathedral was completed on 25 March 1266, the cost of the fabric up to then amounting to 42,000 marks, a sum equivalent to more than a million pounds of our money.

The resources of the chapter were by no means exhausted, for they had already resolved upon the costly project of building cloisters and a chapter house. In 1263 the north and east walks of the cloisters were begun, and by 1284 the whole undertaking, comprising the four walks, each 181 feet long, together with the chapter house and its vestibule, had been accomplished. In the half-century that had passed since the foundations of the cathedral had been laid, the Lancet phase of Gothic had developed into Geometric.

Deeply projecting buttresses divide the bays of the cloisters, and in each bay is a four-light window consisting of paired couplets with foiled circles in their heads—Geometric tracery at its best. Originally the shafts were of Purbeck marble, but were replaced by stone in the nineteenth century. The inner walls of the walks are overlaid with blind arcading, petrified shadows as it were of the cloister windows, and to make a perfect whole the masons covered the walks with quadripartite vaulting. No cloisters of the thirteenth century compare with these at Salisbury. From the east walk a vestibule opens into the chapter house, an octagonal building modelled upon that of Westminster abbey. A central pier clustered with Purbeck shafts supports a ribbed vault of intricate design; the Geometric windows of four lights make the chapter house a veritable lantern. Above the wall-bench runs a wall-arcade, in the spandrels of which is a remarkable series of relief sculptures, depicting sixty incidents from biblical history. Unfortunately the carvings were wantonly mutilated in the seventeenth century and the heads of most of the figures were hacked away, though they have since been restored. The vaulted vestibule is a worthy appendage to the chapter house. The arch of the inner portal is adorned with fourteen niches containing figures of the Virtues and Vices in combat.

WELLS CATHEDRAL, 1225–60

The west front of Salisbury is a modified version of the façade of Wells cathedral, that had been commenced *c.* 1225 and was in the final stages of construction twenty years before Salisbury cathedral was consecrated in 1258. The Purbeck use had been ignored at Wells until the masons reached the west front, which is so vastly different in character from the nave that Bishop Jocelin may have imported 'outside' masons who were experienced in Purbeck shafting to execute the work. The interior of the west wall of the nave is faced with an arcade of five arches carried by Purbeck shafts, and externally the same material and blue lias were extensively used for shafting, all of which have long since been removed and Kilkenny marble substituted.

The west front of Wells was conceived as a vast open-air reredos peopled with innumerable sculptured figures. From north to south the front is 147 feet wide and incorporates the two towers around which the tiers of imagery are carried. This wonderful façade should be judged as a screen and not as a western wall revealing what is behind it. The architectural treatment is definitely subordinated to the sculptured statuary, which provides the finest collection of figure-sculpture in England. Here are saints and apostles, kings and ecclesiastics, nobles, ladies and other personages, both biblical and legendary. In all there are some three hundred and fifty statues, nearly half of them life-size or larger, that fill the niches ranged tier upon tier. In the canopy above the portal of the nave is a sculptured group, much mutilated, representing the Coronation of the Virgin and on the tympanum within is the Madonna and Child. These two sculptures may afford a clue to the subject matter of the array of statuary above, which was considered by Prof. Lethaby to represent 'the ever-renewed Feast of the Assumption of the Blessed Virgin'. In the selection and the arrangement of the figures there was nothing of caprice; one may assume that Bishop Jocelin summoned the foremost theologians of the day to prepare the whole scheme of iconography; the sculptors did not fail them, though who they were and whence they came is not known. The master-mason, perhaps the designer of the west front was Adam Lock d. 1229, who was succeeded by a Master Norreys, but it is unlikely that either had anything to do with the sculpturing of the figures. When Bishop Jocelin died in 1242, few of the statues were in position, and it was probably another thirty or forty years before the niches were fully occupied. The statues were disposed in seven tiers, the two main tiers ranging with the long lancet windows in the front. In the absence of emblems, the identification of all the figures has never been satisfactorily established. In the topmost stage, above the three central windows, is a vesica containing a figure of Christ in Majesty, only the lower part of which remains, and on either side are niches that formerly housed figures of the Virgin Mary and S. John Baptist. Immediately beneath the Majestas is a tier of the twelve Apostles, and below are nine angels in niches representing the Heavenly hierarchy. The stage beneath depicts the Resurrection of the dead, naked figures awaking from their long sleep with varying expressions of hope and despair. The two main tiers, comprising more than a hundred figures, 8 feet and more in height, are of kings and queens, bishops and saints, from early days to the time of Henry II. The lower of these ranges contain what are believed to be the twenty bishops of Wells from its foundation to Jocelin. The sixth tier is composed of a series of forty-eight high reliefs set in quatrefoiled panels and portraying biblical incidents, those on the south from the Old Testament, and on the north the life of Our Lord. The bottom stage, above the plinth consists of

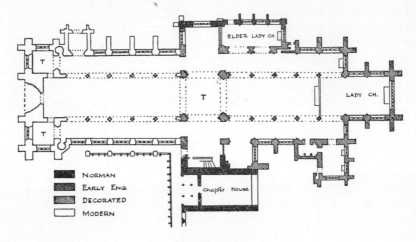

BRISTOL

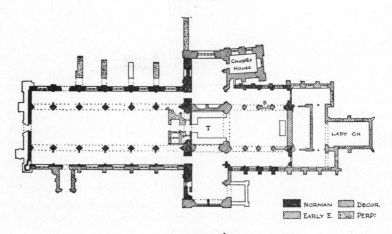

S. DAVID'S

FIG 21. Plans of Bristol and St. David's

sixty-two niches arranged in pairs beneath gables, but less than twenty retain their figures, so far unidentified; and in the spandrels of the gables are quatrefoils that were once occupied by demi-figures of angels bearing crowns and scrolls in their hands.

BRISTOL CATHEDRAL, 1220

The cult of the Virgin Mary that was so widely adopted in the thirteenth century induced the canons of S. Augustine's abbey,

Bristol, to provide themselves with the so-called Elder Lady Chapel, commenced *c.* 1220. The Chapel on plan is an unaisled rectangle, four bays in length, and stands outside the choir, to the east of the north transept (Fig. 21). It was a separate building before the choir was remodelled in the fourteenth century. There are triple lancet windows in each bay with an inner plane of Purbeck arcading, and the walls below are adorned with arcadings of trefoiled arches. The carved capitals and the lively grotesque sculptures of the spandrels are choice specimens of Early English masoncraft. On a spandrel of the south wall is a representation of an ape playing on Pandean pipes accompanied by a ram with a violin; a goat blowing a horn and carrying a hare slung on a pole is the subject of another carving, and amongst others is the legend of the fox and goose.

Originally the Elder Lady Chapel was built with a timber roof, but in the last decade of the thirteenth century, the quadripartite vault with ridge ribs and bosses carved with foliage was put up, and at the same time the five-light Geometric window was inserted in the east wall.

LICHFIELD CATHEDRAL, 1220–1300

The new choir of Lichfield cathedral (p. 88) was completed shortly after 1210, and ten years later the chapter undertook the rebuilding of the south transept. Thenceforward, for more than a century building operations were continuous in some part or other of the cathedral. Excepting the three western bays of the choir, an entirely new cathedral had risen by the middle of the fourteenth century, and not a stone of the Norman church was left above ground.

Both transepts were planned with eastern aisles two bays deep. When the southern was rebuilt *c.* 1220, the width of the aisle was restricted by the wall of the treasury that flanks the south aisle of the choir (Fig. 19). The reconstruction of the north transept followed, *c.* 1230. The transepts of the Norman cathedral must have been aisleless, for when the aisles were added in the thirteenth century, the westernmost window of the north choir-aisle was no longer in the open but looked into the adjoining transeptal chapel. Later, both transepts lost much of their Early English character by the substitution of Perpendicular windows for lancet lights; the western wall of the south transept alone retains its original windows. The five lancets above the portal in the north wall are modern replicas dating from the restoration of 1892; the thirteenth-century stonework that was recovered when the Perpendicular window was taken out was largely re-used.

In 1235 and again in 1238 the chapter was granted licence to dig Hopwas stone for 'the new fabric of the church at Lichfield', and in 1243 Henry III issued a warrant to Archbishop Walter de Grey of York to expedite the works at S. George's Chapel, Windsor, in which he orders a lofty timber roof 'like the roof at the new work at Lichfield, to appear to be stonework with good ceiling [celatura] and painting'. The 'new fabric' and the 'new work' referred to must be the transepts which were roofed with wooden vaults when first built. The present tierceron vaults were erected by Bishop Walter de Langton who occupied the see of Lichfield from 1296 to 1321.

Of the same period as the transepts are the chapter house and vestibule on the north side of the choir (Fig. 19). The vestibule which is entered from the north aisle has a range of thirteen arcaded seats against the western wall, and there is an upper chamber, formerly a chapel dedicated to S. Peter. On plan the chapter house is an irregular octagon, its length east to west exceeding its width. Beneath the two-light windows the walls are faced with trefoiled arcading that rises above the stone bench all round the interior. In the centre is a clustered pier of ten shafts with annulet rings and carved capitals that are merged into an encircling band of stiff-leaf foliage. From the capitals the ribs of the tierceron vault diverge in sheaf-like form to meet others springing from the walls. The vault is supported by bold buttresses crowned with gablets.

The chapter house and vestibule being completed by 1250, the bigger task of rebuilding the western arm of the cathedral lay ahead, and for the next thirty years the nave of seven bays with north and south aisles, a noble example of Geometric Gothic, was slowly taking shape. The shaftiness of the piers of the nave and the triforium arcades, and the vaulting shafts that demarcate the bays emphasize the verticality of Lichfield nave; and typical of Geometric work is the multiplication of the arch-mouldings and the coupled two-light openings of the triforium stage that have quatrefoiled circles in the heads (Pl. 53). The windows of the clerestory take the form of spherical triangles containing three trefoiled circles, a design that was probably copied from the windows in the outer wall of the triforium at Westminster abbey. The spandrels of the nave arcade are filled with blind foiled circles, a form of surface decoration that occurred earlier in the retrochoir of Ely. The foliage capitals of the nave piers are excellent specimens of the carver's art in the Early English period. From the vaulting shafts rise the ribs of the tierceron high vault, an anticipation of the vaulting of Exeter cathedral. The windows of the aisles are of three lights with trefoiled circles in the heads, and below runs a continuous wall arcade above a low stone bench. The aisles have quadripartite vaulting with ridge ribs. By the close of the thirteenth century the lower portion of the west front up to the sill of the great window had been built. It is faced with Geometric arcading and cinquefoiled circles; the three portals are to a great extent modern restorations. The greater part of the west front of Lichfield cathedral belongs to the early years of the fourteenth century.

OXFORD CATHEDRAL, 1220–50

In the second quarter of the thirteenth century additions were made to the priory church of S. Frideswide, Oxford. The funds at the disposal of the chapter permitted the building of a Lady Chapel and a new chapter house, and the raising of the central tower together with the stone spire.

As there was no space east of the priory church, the Lady Chapel, begun *c.* 1220, was built as an outer aisle on the north side of the choir (Fig. 14), and at the west it absorbed the central bay of the eastern aisle of the north transept. The outer wall of the north choir aisle was knocked down, and an arcade of three wide bays was built, the clustered piers of which retain the Norman responds of the north choir aisle. The piers have stiff-leaf capitals, from which spring richly moulded arches, and the four bays of the chapel have quadripartite vaults. The new chapter house, rectangular on plan, stands to the east of the cloisters; it was roofed with a stone vault and was adorned with Early English wall arcading carried by Purbeck shafts.

By the middle of the thirteenth century the upper stage of the tower and the spire were completed. In each face of the tower are a pair of two-light windows. There is no parapet but at the angles are tall pinnacles. The cardinal sides of the octagonal spire, with dormer windows at the base, rest on the walls of the tower thickened by corbel courses, and the oblique sides are carried by squinch arches that span the interior angles of the tower. The Oxford spire was a promise of the more graceful spires that were to rise at Salisbury and Lichfield in the Decorated period.

HEREFORD CATHEDRAL, 1222–70

The Lady Chapel of Hereford cathedral that formed part of the scheme of remodelling initiated by Bishop de Vere was begun in 1222. It was built over a crypt, the last of the Gothic period now existing in an English mediaeval cathedral. The interior of the crypt, that is 50 feet in length, is divided by ranges of octagonal columns into a central area with aisles on either side; the capitals of the columns are moulded and the stout ribs of the quadripartite vault are chamfered.

The chapel above is a good example of Lancet Gothic. Each of three bays is lighted by two large windows; the wall of the central bay on the south side was altered when Bishop Audley's chantry chapel was erected *c.* 1500. In the east wall are five narrow lancet lights above which are blind quatrefoiled openings. The jambs of the windows are clustered with shafts, and the chapel is roofed with a quadripartite vault having a ridge rib. A curious feature of the exterior is the Norman arcading of intersecting arches on the walls above the windows, that must be the latest occurrence of this early form of enrichment in mediaeval architecture.

No sooner was the Lady Chapel completed, *c.* 1240, than the canons decided to improve the lighting of the Norman choir that had always been intolerably dark. The immense piers blocked out light from the aisle-windows, and the only means of providing more light was by inserting large windows in the clerestory wall. Accordingly the Norman top-lights were replaced by two-light windows with plate-traceried heads and a graceful inner arcade. By the middle of the thirteenth century the choir of the cathedral had been vastly improved by the new clerestory and the high vault. This was followed by a more important work, viz., the rebuilding of the north transept, *c.* 1260, the design of which is unique in many respects. The two bays of the main arcade open into the eastern aisle by almost straight-sided arches rising from a clustered pier and richly moulded. The central arch-order is undercut with dog-tooth ornament (Pl. 62). To eyes accustomed to the easy curvature of two-centred arches, the triangular effect of these arches and of those in the triforium stage is more singular than pleasing. In each bay of the triforium is a pair of three-light openings with quatrefoiled circles in their heads, and the spandrels are diapered with leaf ornament. The windows of the clerestory are spherical triangles enclosing eight-foiled circles. In the aisle of the transept are Geometric windows of three lights, above which are circular windows with octofoiled tracery that light the triforium chamber. The six-light window in the end wall and two unusually tall windows with straight-sided arches in the west wall flood the interior of the north transept with light. By 1265 the transept and its aisle were roofed with quadripartite vaults, notable for the fine foliage bosses.

Towards the end of the century vast numbers of pilgrims wended their way to Hereford to visit the tomb of Bishop Cantelupe d. 1282, at which miracles were reputed to occur; their offerings brought untold wealth to the cathedral treasury, and as a result important additions and alterations were made in the fabric. To Bishop Richard de Swinfield, 1283–1316, is attributed the planning of the eastern transepts, though only the northern was put up during his rule. Further improvements were made in the lighting of the cathedral, by raising the walls of the aisles of the nave and choir to a greater height and inserting large four-light windows of early Decorated character. Bishop Swinfield also built what is now the inner bay of the north-west porch.

WORCESTER CATHEDRAL, 1224–50

Bishop Wulstan's Norman cathedral at Worcester with the Transitional bays at the west end of the nave (p. 184), stood un-impaired until the early part of the thirteenth century, although disaster had befallen the church in 1176 when the central tower collapsed. In 1202 a destructive fire wrought great havoc to the fabric, and extensive repairs were undertaken, the nature of which is not known. Twenty years later a violent storm wrecked part of the apse of the Norman choir; the western part of the choir con-tinued in use for a time. In 1224 Bishop William de Blois effected a 'compositio' with the convent, that resulted in the building of the *novum opus frontis*, viz., the stately Lady Chapel some distance east of the Norman choir with which it was ultimately to be joined up. Thus was initiated a scheme for reconstructing the whole of the eastern limb of Worcester cathedral as it exists today. The cost was met largely by the liberal offerings that were made at the tomb of Bishop Wulstan after his canonization in 1203. In for a penny, in for a pound! The Gothic impulse was not to be resisted and the old Norman choir was pulled down. Begun in 1224 the new choir-arm was more than twice the length of the old, and thus provided more accommodation for the monks and facilities for visiting pilgrims.

In the general layout the *novum opus* of Worcester (Fig. 22) re-sembles the eastern arm of Rochester cathedral and in both churches the retrochoir and its adjuncts rise to the full height of the choir. The presbytery was built over the Norman crypt, and everything to the east of it is paved at a lower level and is reached by a descent of six steps. The piers and arches of the retrochoir are therefore more lofty, whereas the triforium and the clerestory range respectively with those of the choir. The whole structure is a most graceful product of the Lancet period. All the piers are octagonal each having eight detached shafts of Purbeck marble; the capitals are richly carved with foliage and the arch-mouldings are grouped in orders corresponding with the shafts below. In-fluenced by the work at Salisbury, the masons at Worcester made

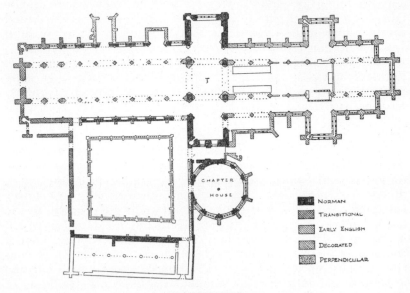

WORCESTER

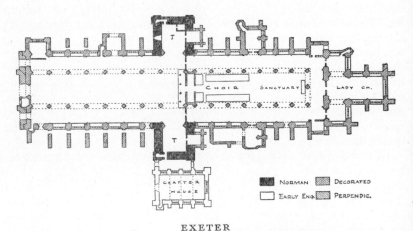

EXETER

FIG 22. Plans of Worcester and Exeter

prolific use of Purbeck marble. It was the mediaeval practice not
to put the shafts of Purbeck marble in place for a few years,
until the walls and piers had had time to settle. Those in Worcester choir were not added to the stone piers for thirty years or
more. The shafts were seated in lead and the joints were often

encircled with bronze rings to keep the lead from being squeezed out. At Worcester and Salisbury bronze rings are much in evidence in the Purbeck shafting; there are also annulet rings of marble that are coursed into the piers.

In each bay of the triforium stage are two main arches with two sub-arches, all of which spring from marble shafts, and the wall behind is faced with a small blind arcade. The two planes thus give depth to the triforium. The clerestory wall is pierced with triple lights in front of which is a tall Purbeck arcade. The high vault is notable for the longitudinal ridge rib that rarely makes its appearance before *c.* 1230. Round the walls of the choir transepts and the east end runs a trefoiled arcade with exceptionally beautiful detail, particularly the sculptures in the spandrels exhibiting biblical subjects and animals from the bestiary; one in the north aisle depicts Bishop William de Blois offering a model of the cathedral at an altar. Most of the carvings have been restored and a few are modern. Another feature of interest is the wall design of the choir transepts with two tiers of triple lancet lights above wall-arcading. The Early English windows in the choir aisles are largely restorations, and the east wall of the choir opened up with two tiers of lancets is a reconstruction of 1857.

SOUTHWELL CATHEDRAL, 1225–50

By the second quarter of the thirteenth century the Purbeck use, so readily adopted by the masons at Lincoln and Salisbury after its inception at Canterbury had become the widespread fashion. Notwithstanding, there were centres up and down the country where marble shafting was not in favour, possibly on account of the cost and the difficulty of transport. The choir-arm of Southwell dating from *c.* 1225 is a notable instance.

For more than a century the dark and incommodious Norman choir of Southwell cathedral had met the requirements of the canons of the collegiate establishment, as it was then. Other great churches had promoted schemes of choir-extension that left Southwell far behind the times; in 1220 the canons of Beverley minster, that like Southwell, served as a pro-cathedral in the diocese of York, ventured on the rebuilding of a new and glorious choir, embellished with Purbeck marble, a work that must have excited the envy of the establishment at Southwell. Some time before 1230 the canons of Southwell therefore entered upon the task of rebuilding their choir-arm, the interior of which remains much the same as when the masons left it in 1250. In 1233 Archbishop Walter de Grey of York issued an indulgence of thirty days to all who made offerings towards 'the completion of the fabric, begun some time ago', a like indulgence having been granted previously by the Pope. From the phrase 'some time ago' it may be assumed that the new work had been commenced between 1225 and 1230. As regards the plan, the thirteenth-century choir of Southwell has much in common with that of Beverley; each is six bays in length with an ambulatory leading to the Lady Chapel and both have eastern transepts (Fig. 10). In little else does Southwell compare with Beverley. Several distinctive features however are of absorbing interest. Due to its low altitude the bay design seems to be of two stages only; to all appearances the triforium stage is eliminated as an integral part of the bay design. Actually it is contained within the lofty double arches of the clerestory, the jambs of which are brought down to the string courses above the choir arches. The two windows of the clerestory and two blind lancets of the triforium are thus combined in one stage. The double containing arches supported by clustered shafts reach to the high vault, and are profusely enriched with dog-tooth ornament.

The choir arcade that is more than half of the total interior height consists of piers of eight engaged shafts with moulded bell capitals, and the dog-tooth is again conspicuous in the arch mouldings. The builders showed a great liking for the fillet, a flat moulding that was applied vertically to the curved surfaces of shafts and columns. The high vault is quadripartite with a longitudinal ridge rib that springs from corbels uncommonly low down. The triple vaulting shafts are seated on corbels in the spandrels of the choir arcade. In the east wall of the Lady Chapel are two tiers of four lancet lights, and curiously the ridge rib of the vault is brought down to a shaft between the middle windows of the upper tier.

CHICHESTER CATHEDRAL, 1225–75

The sombre gloom of the Norman nave of Chichester cathedral was relieved to some extent by the large Geometric windows of the chapels that were built flanking the aisles, 1225–75 (p. 95). The addition of these outer chapels incidently enhanced the spatial effect of the interior of the western limb of the cathedral. The chapels attached to the south aisle, with Geometric windows of four lights, were the earlier; those on the north, a little more advanced in style, are of three lights. They are all covered with quadripartite vaulting, and in the southern chapels the ridge of the vault is tilted upwards to permit of a larger window area. In the easternmost chapel on the north, dedicated to S. Thomas, is a wall reredos of the thirteenth century consisting of a triple arcade

84. Ely; design of the western bays of the choir

85. Winchester; bay design of the nave

86. York; design of the eastern bays of the choir

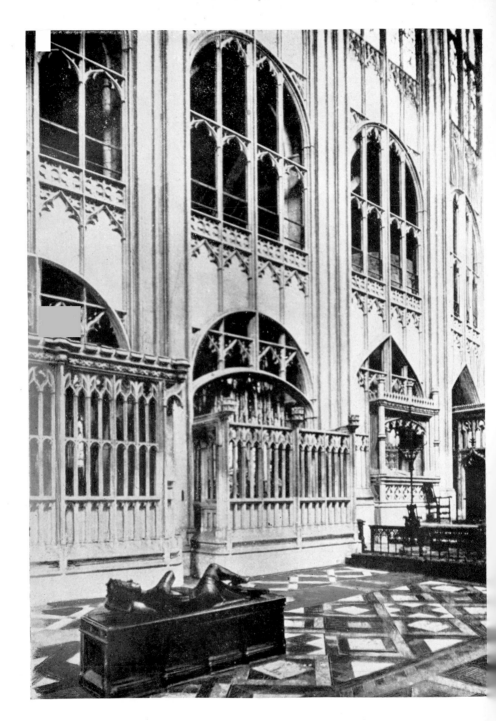

87. Gloucester; north side of the choir

88. Winchester; view across the nave

89. Norwich; high vault of the nave

90. Norwich cathedral from the west

91. Peterborough; the retrochoir looking north

92. Canterbury; the central tower

93. Hereford; the north-west porch

94. Hereford cathedral from the south-east

95. Hereford; east walk of the cloisters

96. Exeter; screen of the west front

97. Oxford; detail of the choir vault

98. Salisbury; consecration cross on the outside of the Lady Chapel

99. Bath; the west front

with Purbeck shafting, and above are two quatrefoiled panels containing figures of winged angels. Whilst this work was in progress the central tower was carried up and completed *c.* 1250. The present tower, a rebuilding of 1866, rises one stage above the cathedral roof; each face is pierced with a pair of two-light windows with plate-traceried heads, that are replicas of the originals (Pl. 59).

YORK CATHEDRAL, 1230–60

At the dawn of the thirteenth century York cathedral consisted of the nave and transepts of the Norman church built by Thomas of Bayeux and the twelfth-century choir of Archbishop Roger (p. 84). Of that cathedral nothing survives other than a portion of Roger's crypt. The architectural history of the cathedral now standing properly begins in the year 1230, three years after the canonization of Archbishop William Fitzherbert, the great-grandson of William the Conqueror, d. 1154. The offerings at the shrine of S. William of York, together with the wealth of the arch-see put huge sums of money at the disposal of the chapter for the reconstruction of the entire cathedral in the thirteenth and fourteenth centuries. By the year 1405, York cathedral as we know it today had arisen, save for the western towers.

This ambitious project was launched by Archbishop Walter de Grey, 1215–55, who in 1230 set about remodelling the south transept. The scale on which it was planned was out of all proportion to the rest of the cathedral then standing, a proof that from the first the intention was to rebuild the whole church. In superficial area and in height the new south transept literally swallowed up the diminutive Norman transept, and was planned with eastern and western aisles, the final instance in an English mediaeval cathedral (Fig. 23).

In the bay design of the transept, the main arches occupy nearly one-half of the elevation, and the unduly large triforium, a most prominent feature, has reduced the clerestory to comparative insignificance. The latter is of less height than the triforium and is faced with an arcade of five arches in each bay. The complex design of the triforium shows how loth were the masons to dispense with what was a useless stage in the bay design. Spanning each bay is a large containing arch that is all but semicircular in form, with two pointed sub-arches, each of which is again sub-divided into two recessed and acutely pointed arches. All the spandrels are pierced with blind foiled circles. In the three stages of the design Purbeck marble is used for the clustered shafting and for the vaulting shafts. Above the clerestory string are the

H

stone springers of a high vault that was never put up. The timber vault dates from the fifteenth century. In this Early English work of the south transept, the carved capitals and corbels, the dog-tooth and billet ornament, the arch mouldings and the detail are rich in the extreme and leave little to be desired. Strangely, the builders scamped the actual construction. In 1871 when the transept was falling into a state of dilapidation Mr. G. E. Street was called in to investigate, and he reported that the walls were built of two thin shells of masonry with a filling of loose stone chippings without cement binding.

The south front is designed in three storeys, composed of lancet windows and arcadings (Pl. 60). The two lower stages are 'broken' by a central porch with triple gables, above which is the main storey of tall lancet windows. In the gable is a large wheel window with radiating foiled arches that is flanked by a triple arcade on each side. There is an abundance of dog-tooth ornament particularly in the upper part of the front. On his death in 1255 Archbishop Grey was buried in the eastern aisle of the transept he had been instrumental in building; he had lived to see much of the north transept erected. Commenced c. 1241 it was designed on the same lines as the other, with aisles at the east and west (Fig. 23). In the north wall of the transept are the famous 'Five Sisters' windows, a range of five lancet lights each 54 feet high and 5 feet wide, the largest of the kind in England (Pl. 61). Beneath them runs Early English wall-arcading, and a tier of five graduated lancets fills the gable of the wall. By 1260 the north transept was finished, and thirty years or more elapsed before the next stage, the reconstruction of the nave was undertaken (p. 234).

RIPON CATHEDRAL, 1233–60

To Archbishop Walter de Grey is also attributed the west front of Ripon cathedral, that was in progress at the same time as the transepts of York (Fig. 23). In 1233 and 1258 indulgences were granted to benefactors who contributed to the building fund. Originally the twin towers flanked the west end of the unaisled nave of Ripon. The design of the façade that owes much to Gilbert Scott's restoration is not an unpleasing example of Lancet Gothic (Pl. 63). The central part, viz., the western wall of the nave, has three gabled portals with two tiers of lancet windows above, surmounted by three small lancets in the gable. In 1379 mullions and tracery were inserted in the windows of the two main tiers but were taken out by Scott. Important from an architectural point of view are the broad buttresses at the angles of the towers, that not only enhance the effect of stability but relieve the flatness of the façade as a whole.

DURHAM CATHEDRAL, 1242–80

After the Norman period the need in all cathedrals and greater churches was for altars and yet more altars, especially in the choir-arm. Parallel-apsed choirs did not lend themselves to expansion to this end, and were invariably swept away to make room for commodious choirs with many chapels. In 1240 the convent at Durham cathedral, unwilling to tear down the whole of the eastern arm, decided to build a spacious eastern transept, modelled upon that at Fountains abbey, Yorks., then all but complete. Athwart the east end of the choir of Durham was erected a lofty hall, 129 feet from north to south, now spoken of as the Transept of Nine Altars (Fig. 11). The master-mason who supervised the work was Richard de Farinham, probably a kinsman of Nicholas de Farinham, Bishop of Durham at the time. Owing to the fall of the ground at the east, the pavement of the transept is 3 feet lower than that of the choir, the proportions of the interior being thereby improved. The building is a fine example of Early English Gothic. The clustered wall-piers composed of slender shafts of sandstone and Frosterley marble, the long lancet lights in the east wall, the magnificent Geometric window of six lights in the north wall, the graceful wall-arcading beneath the windows, the high vault enriched with carved bosses and sculptured ornament—all these features combine to render the interior of the Nine Altars transept one of the most satisfying of the thirteenth century.[1] The easternmost bay of the choir had to be rebuilt, but is in perfect harmony with the architecture of the transept. When the masons came to vault this bay they found it necessary to reconstruct all the choir vaulting which was then in an unsafe condition.

OLD S. PAUL'S CATHEDRAL, 1256–1316

One of the foremost works of the Geometric period, the loss of which is to be deplored, was the choir-arm of Old S. Paul's cathedral, commenced in 1256, and comparable with the Angel Choir of Lincoln. When completed sixty years later, it was the longest and greatest in the land. The piers of the choir arcades were of freestone with eight detached marble shafts; the pointed arches were richly moulded. In each bay of the triforium were a pair of two-light openings, and the clerestory windows were of three lights. In the east wall was a splendid rose window, 40 feet in diameter, below which were seven tall windows constructed in

[1] The rose window in the central bay was inserted by Wyatt in 1792.

double planes. The choir was roofed with a tierceron vault. The internal walls of the aisles were faced with wall-arcading, and a number of tomb-recesses were hollowed out of the thickness of the walls. Beneath the choir was an Early English crypt divided into four aisles by massive piers (Fig. 7).

The Geometrical phase, which was English Gothic in its maturity, was of short duration. Towards the end of the thirteenth century certain changes were coming over architectural design that foreshadowed the less direct and more ornate Decorated style of the early fourteenth century. In the construction of the clustered piers there was a tendency for detached shafts to sink back into the body of the pier, as had been anticipated in the choir of Southwell early in the thirteenth century; the foiling of Geometrical windows was gradually reduced to cusping, and the pointed lobe ousted the circle in the tracery of windows. Further, the stiff-leaf and conventional foliage of capitals and corbels approximated to more naturalistic leafage. In effect such changes marked the transition from Geometrical Gothic to the Decorated style. By comparing the eastern arm of Exeter cathedral with the Angel Choir of Lincoln the transition is at once evident.

WELLS CATHEDRAL, 1275–1320

Of this period the chapter house of Wells cathedral provides a work of rare and distinctive beauty. Situated to the north of the choir it is an octagonal building, 52 feet in diameter, with an undercroft that served as the cathedral treasury, the heavy timber doors of which are evidence of its use as a strong room. The chapter room above is reached from the north transept by a stone stairway, and the treasury that is on the ground level is entered through a passage from the north aisle of the choir. The undercroft is divided into two concentric aisles by eight cylindrical piers and has a central pier of great mass with eight attached shafts (Fig. 17); the columnar piers have plain bell capitals, of which one is adorned with dog-tooth. The chamber is vaulted in triangular cells with unmoulded ribs, and is lighted by deeply splayed windows. The entrance passage has three bays of quadripartite vaulting with several grotesque bosses and corbels. Whilst the undercroft and passage were in course of erection, masons were busy on the wonderful stone stairway (Pl. 64), entered by a portal in the north-east angle of the transept and leading up to a chamber above the Chain Gate. The stairway is lighted by two four-light windows of Geometric Gothic, and has wall-shafts of blue lias. After an ascent of eighteen steps, the stairway branches off to the portal of the chapter room, work on which was begun *c.* 1292 when the stairway was fairly complete. The design of the portal is that of a large two-light window with a segmental triangle in the head. Each wall of the chapter room has a four-light window, the long-lobed trefoils of the tracery indicating early Decorated work. Beneath the windows runs a gabled arcade carried by shafts of blue lias and enriched with crockets, finials and head-stops; the stone wall-bench afforded seating for fifty canons. From the central pier of the chapter room, composed of sixteen clustered shafts of Purbeck marble spring thirty-two closely packed ribs of the vault and at the ridge are the same number of carved bosses (Pl. 68). The thrusts of the vault are borne by stout angle buttresses. The chapter house was finished *c.* 1320.

EXETER CATHEDRAL, 1280–1350

The transformation of Warelwast's Norman cathedral of Exeter into the great Gothic church that we have today was the conception of Bishop Walter Bronscombe, 1257–80, his protégé and successor, Peter Quivil, being the prime mover in the project that occupied more than a century in fulfilment. Warelwast's transeptal towers alone were spared; the Fabric Roll of 1285 records that the inner wall of the north tower was 'thrown down' and opened up with a broad and lofty arch that gave access to the transept, and the following year the same was done to the southern tower.

'In 1288 our new church was founded by the venerable father, Bishop Peter [Quivil]' states the *Exeter Chronicle* of the fifteenth century. The choir-arm that was then planned is little less than the nave in length (Fig. 22). The metamorphosis commenced at the east with the building of the Lady Chapel and the square retrochoir, but little had been done at Quivil's death in 1292. The work was pushed on by Bishop Thomas de Bytton who practically completed the sanctuary and the retrochoir. In the Fabric Roll of 1301–2 we read of payment for the glazing of the east window, and £26 was disbursed for the painting of eight corbels (of vaulting shafts?) and forty-nine bosses of the high vault, with gold, silver, azure and other colours. Bytton's successor, Bishop Walter de Stapledon, 1308–26, finished the eastern arm of the cathedral, even to the glazing of the windows. During his episcopate he contributed the large sum of £1,800 out of his own purse towards the reconstruction. The master-mason Roger, who supervised the building operations is designated *cementarius* in the Fabric Roll of 1299.

The Exeter masons had definite ideas of their own. They were enamoured of the Purbeck use but with a difference. The clustered piers of the choir have no detached shafts but are composed of sixteen shafts compactly arranged diamond-wise, and built up of horizontal slices of Purbeck marble from 9 to 15 inches thick. The arches are of local sandstone with innumerable mouldings. The triforium stage, reduced to relative unimportance, is faced with arcading of clustered marble shafts and is surmounted by a balustrade pierced with quatrefoiled openings (Pl. 67). In the clerestory walls are windows of four lights with varying forms of tre-foils, quatrefoils and cusped openings in the heads, an anticipation of Decorated tracery. No two windows are of exactly the same design. The multi-ribbed tierceron vault rises from marble vault-ing shafts seated on corbels above the pier capitals and exquistely sculptured. The corbels and some of the bosses of the high vault were carved by Master William of Montacute; the vine and grape, and the oak and acorn are sculptured with fidelity to nature. Some difficulty arose in transforming without pulling down the Norman bays at the west end of the choir, for the walls of the Norman arcade were thicker than those of the new retrochoir. Boldly grappling with the problem, the masons constructed wider and loftier arches in the old walls, which were then recased, and they erected clustered piers of greater bulk than those at the east to support the new arches. As far as possible the builders retained the aisle walls and inserted wide windows of five lights with traceried heads similar to those in the clerestory. Adequate lighting of the *Novum Opus* was an all-important consideration.

By the year 1326, the eastern arm, the pulpitum, the piers at the crossing and probably one bay of the nave were finished. In a letter to the Pope, Bishop Grandisson, 1327–69, wrote: 'The church of Exeter is finished to just about the middle,' a glorious work of fine intelligence that had been the life's labour of three bishops; and it was reserved to Grandisson to dedicate the *Novum Opus* on 18 December 1328, and thereafter to rear the six bays at the western end of the nave and to commence the west front of the cathedral. Bishop Stapledon had left quantities of materials and building gear for re-casting the nave. In 1324 fifteen poplar trees had been purchased for the nave scaffoldings and one hun-dred alder trees at a cost of 13s. 6d., and ample stocks of timber and masonry were at hand. Funds also for the furtherance of the scheme were available; a final donation of 1,000 marks from Bishop Stapledon and £60 contributed by Bishop Grandisson relieved the chapter from monetary anxieties.

By the middle of the fourteenth century, this grand project initiated by Bishop Quivil fell little short of completion. The funds also permitted work on the north walk of the cloisters.

Except in unimportant detail, the builders of Exeter nave adhered to the design and proportions of the choir. The marble piers, the triforium arcade and balustrading, and the tierceron vaulting (Pl. 69) are precisely those of the earlier work, with the result that a unity of design and architectural character pervades the cathedral from east to west. As there is no central tower, the high vault presents an unbroken vista from end to end of the building. In the vaulting is a magnificent series of carved bosses; of birds and beasts, human heads and foliage. One of the finest represents the murder of Thomas Becket (Pl. 66), and another displays a seated figure of Bishop Grandisson (Pl. 65).

RIPON CATHEDRAL, 1290

The transition from Geometrical to Decorated Gothic is again perceptible in the noble east window of Ripon choir, dating c. 1290. A year or two earlier, the two eastern bays had collapsed, and on rebuilding, the enormous seven-light window was constructed, occupying almost the whole of the eastern wall (Pl. 70). The masterly design is a compound version of a two-light Geometrical window, in the head of which is a huge circle containing six trefoiled openings, three with pointed lobes. The major lights below are sub-divided into three lights surmounted by three foiled circles.

14. The Architecture of English Cathedrals

———————————————————————————————————

III. DECORATED GOTHIC

❡ EXETER WAS THE last mediaeval cathedral to be built entirely anew, but partial reconstructions of many others took place in the fourteenth and fifteenth centuries, testifying to the ever-changing ideals of mediaeval masons and to the continuous development of Gothic form. Before the close of the Early English period, the Geometric style was feeling its way towards the opulent and less restrained Decorated or Curvilinear phase. Decorated it truly is; a style of ornament for the sake of ornament; of tracery twisted into graceful and fanciful shapes; of crocketed canopies, niches and pinnacles; and of vegetation sculptured with an almost botanical exactitude.

The crisp and rigid tracery of Geometrical windows gradually gave place to forms branching into flowing and sinuous lines, as if woven together like a net. The change was deplored by Ruskin who declared that curvilinear tracery, undulating like the threads of a cobweb lifted by the wind, lost its essence as a structure of stone. 'Reduced to the slenderness of threads, it began to be considered as possessing their flexibility,' thereby sacrificing the great principle of truth. Infinite are the patternings of tracery in Decorated windows; and not uncommon is the reticulated design, the repetition of an ogee-shaped unit in the head of the window. In shape, the ogee arch had an immense vogue in this period, but being unconstructional in form, it was usually confined to ornamental features such as wall-arcading, niches, canopies and especially the hood-moulds of doorways. Invariably it was enriched with crockets and finials that took the form of carved clumps of foliage. Characteristic was the ogee-arched niche, a canopied recess in wall or buttress designed to take the sculptured image of a saint or martyr. The pet architectural ornament of the masons was the ball-flower that was often sown in abundance in the mouldings of arches and windows.

A further elaboration occurred in the rib-structure of vaults, solely for the purpose of ornament. Hitherto all ribs had been of structural importance, and now in the Decorated phase, further

232

ribs known as liernes were added as decoration. These short ribs thrown from boss to boss, produced a patterning of squares, hexagons, octagons and other shapes in a regular if not symmetrical design.

A marked feature of fourteenth-century cathedral design was the change from the three-storeyed interior by the suppression of the triforium stage. Its elimination permitted of larger clerestory windows and interiors became much better lighted. The change did not affect such cathedrals as Ely, where it was necessary in the interests of uniformity to conform with the proportions of the Norman cathedral of which so much remained. Again, Decorated bays are well defined by the treatment of the vaulting shaft that generally rises from a bold corbel above the capital of the arcade.

SOUTHWELL CATHEDRAL, 1290

In the last decade of the thirteenth century the canons of Southwell provided themselves with a chapter house, built on the north side of the choir. At a Visitation in 1294 John de Romaine, Archbishop of York, decreed that canons of the college who failed to repair their houses within a year should be subjected to a heavy fine, the proceeds of which should be devoted 'ad fabricam novi capituli'. The chapter house is reached from the north aisle of the choir by a passage 54 feet long, that is noteworthy for the lovely wall-arcading with capitals of naturalistic foliage and carved stops. On the eastern side the arcade formerly opened on to a little court, but was walled up to the level of the capitals to keep out the weather. The northern end of the passage forms a lofty ante-room with a quadripartite vault. The chapter house of Southwell is one of the supreme achievements of mediaeval building. Octagonal on plan, it has a diameter of about 30 feet and is roofed with an intricately ribbed vault unsupported by a central pier. The interior is lighted by Geometrical windows of three lights. The vestibule, the entrance portal, and the trefoiled wall-arcading beneath the windows present a wealth of sculptured detail that is lavished on the arch-orders, capitals, spandrels, crockets, finials and bosses (Pl. 71). Of infinite variety, the leaves of the buttercup, the oak, the vine, the hawthorn and maple, together with birds, animals, and heads are executed with a rare delicacy and a close rendering of the natural forms.

CHICHESTER CATHEDRAL, 1290–1304

One of the best examples of early Decorated Gothic is the Lady Chapel of Chichester cathedral, which was lengthened eastwards by two bays during the episcopate of Gilbert de S. Leofard,

H*

1288–1304. The three Norman bays at the western end of the chapel were transformed to bring them into harmony with the new work (Fig. 10). The eight windows of three lights in the side walls have trefoiled lobes in the traceried heads, and straight-sided gables appear in the five-light window of the east wall. Tierceron vaults with carved bosses were put up over the new bays, whereas the older bays have quadripartite vaulting. The ribs of the vaults spring from triple wall-shafts, the foliage capitals of which are naturalistic.

York Cathedral, 1291–1354

After the completion of the Early English transepts at York *c.* 1260, building operations in the cathedral were at a standstill until 1291, when Archbishop Romaine laid the foundation stone of the nave. Materials were furnished by Robert le Vavasour, who granted the chapter the free use of his quarries at Tadcaster, and by Robert Percy who gave a wood at Bolton for the timber of the roof. Offerings at the shrine of S. William and indulgences granted by successive archbishops helped to defray the cost of the building operations, and in 1338 Archbishop William de Melton contributed the sum of 500 marks to the fabric fund.

The new nave was planned on a far larger scale than the old Norman nave. Eight bays in length it rises to a height of 100 feet and has a span of 45 feet, the loftiest and widest in any English mediaeval cathedral. As the aisles were widened, new arches had to be built opening into them from the transepts, and this entailed a rearrangement of the innermost piers of the transepts, and accounts for the solid walling between the new and the old piers (Fig. 23).

In style and proportions the bay design of the nave is vastly different from that of the transepts. The nave arches occupy more than half the height of the elevation and the triforium is well-nigh eliminated, the openings being no more than unglazed panels in the lower part of the clerestory windows. To all appearances the interior elevation is two-storeyed. In the eastern bays of the nave which were the first to be erected (Pl. 72), Geometric forms occur in the traceried windows, and as the work progressed westwards curvilinear tracery appears and dominates the design of the great west window, *c.* 1345, one of the finest of the Decorated period. Purbeck marble had fallen into disuse at York when the nave was built. The clustered piers are composed of attached shafts of varying sizes, and thinly moulded arches spring from the foliage capitals. Significant are the heraldic shields in the spandrels of the nave arches, 'symbolizing the religion of chivalry rather than that

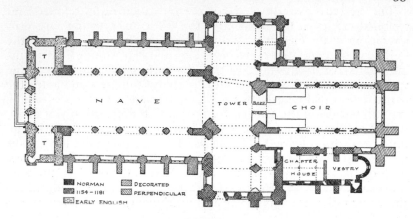

RIPON

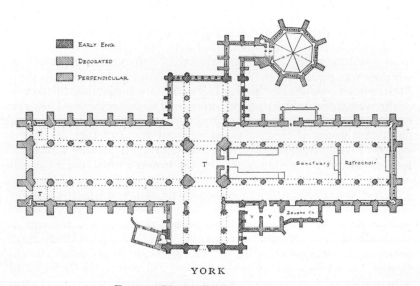

YORK

Fɪɢ 23. Plans of Ripon and York

of sacred story'.[1] The fourteenth century was the age of chivalry and of aristocratic ostentation; so, the heavenly host of the Angel Choir of Lincoln found no place in York nave. Instead were sculptured the coats of arms of great families, of the Cobhams, Beauchamps, Bohuns and Percies, who may or may not have been benefactors of the fabric.

[1] *The Cathedral Builders in England*. E. S. Prior.

The clerestory windows are of five lights with quatrefoiled and trefoiled circles in the head, and the triforium openings are prolongations of the clerestory lights. There can be no doubt that the builders contemplated erecting a high vault of stone. Bold vaulting shafts rise from the bases of the nave piers, and the stone springers for a high vault remain; preparations were made for the construction of flying-buttresses and pinnacles, vestiges of which are still visible on the south side. Probably the intention was abandoned on the grounds of cost, and the nave was roofed with an imitation vault of wood. The aisles, that are unusually lofty, have quadripartite vaults of stone and are lighted with simple windows with quatrefoiled circles in the heads. The walls beneath the windows are faced with Decorated arcading; ornate in the extreme is the west wall of the nave, overlaid with five tiers of gabled arcading.

The great west window of the nave, a superb example of Curvilinear Gothic, is composed of eight lights grouped in pairs. The main lines of the tracery consist of two ogee-arches that glide upwards into a large centrepiece filled with leaf-like panels sprouting from a central stem, and above is a vesica with similar panels. The window was glazed in 1338, towards the cost of which Archbishop Melton gave 100 marks (p. 142). The boldly projecting buttresses of the west front define the ordonnance of the interior, and like the masonry flanking the windows and portals, are faced with tiers of niches surmounted by crocketed gables typical of the Decorated period (Pl. 15). By 1360 the new nave was roofed, but the west front had to await the upper parts of the towers until the fifteenth century (p. 262).

A few years after the commencement of the nave, the canons must needs have a chapter house, which was accordingly erected to the north of the choir, from which it is entered through a vestibule attached to the north transept (Fig. 23). The chapter house is an octagonal building, modelled on that of Southwell, though on a much larger scale, having a diameter of 64 feet and a height of 68 feet. In common with Southwell it has no central pier. The external buttresses at the angles suggest that a stone vault was intended, and not the imitation wooden vault that was erected. The steeply pitched octagonal roof over the vault is a most complicated structure, with a massive central post and transverse beams from which the ribs of the wooden vault are suspended. The five-light windows of the chapter house are Geometrical in style and have three nine-foiled circles in the head, and beneath are forty-four prebendal seats set beneath canopies that are a great advance on flat wall-arcading. The three-sided canopies, an early form of Gothic tabernacling are supported by slender Purbeck shafts and are faced with gabling enriched with sculptured ornament, including many delightful human heads as stops. Above the canopies a passage runs all round the chapter house through the walling between the windows. An ancient Latin inscription put into English reads:

As the rose is the flower of flowers
So is this the house of houses,

a legend that Prof. Lethaby pointed out was borrowed from the pavement tiles of the chapter house of Westminster abbey dating from 1253.

The vestibule, which was an afterthought, is a lofty passage entered through a double portal surmounted by a Geometric gable, in the north-east angle of the north transept of the cathedral. Beneath the Decorated windows of the vestibule runs a traceried wall-arcade with capitals of carved foliage and curious animals.

CARLISLE CATHEDRAL, 1292–1380

About the year 1240 the canons of Carlisle embarked on the building of a new choir-arm of their cathedral. It was planned as an aisled rectangle, seven bays in length, and was more lofty and 12 feet wider than the Norman choir. Hardly had the work been completed, when the building was reduced to a shell by a great fire in 1292; only the aisles which were vaulted and the arches of the choir arcades escaped serious damage. At once extensive restoration was undertaken and the choir was lengthened by an eastern bay (Fig. 14). New piers were built without disturbing the arches, a feat that was executed by the process of underpinning. As a consequence Decorated piers of clustered shafts support Early English arches enriched with dog-tooth ornament. The sculptured capitals of the piers portray 'the best mediaeval representation of the Seasons' (*Francis Bond*). The unimportant triforium stage is opened up with three two-light Curvilinear windows in each bay, and above the string course are corbels carved with naturalistic foliage, on which are seated triple vaulting shafts. In the clerestory are three Decorated windows, fronted by an arcade of three arches, at the base of which is quatrefoiled balustrading. A timber ceiling was put up over the new choir; the waggon roof is modern. The prime glory of Carlisle cathedral is the nine-light window that almost fills the whole of the east wall and is unrivalled amongst Decorated windows. The branching and sinuous tracery of the window is struck from two hundred and sixty-three centres.

From the sill to the apex of the arch the window measures 51 feet and is 26 feet wide.

BRISTOL CATHEDRAL, 1298–1350

A new era in the architectural history of S. Augustine's abbey, Bristol, opened in the first half of the fourteenth century. In 1298 the old Norman choir was taken down and a new eastern arm was begun, comprising an aisled choir of four bays, a single-bayed retrochoir and a Lady Chapel (Fig. 21). The canons were hard put to in finding the money for the reconstruction. A chronicler wrote: 'They were in such want that when the hour of dinner came, they were compelled to send to the burgery of Bristol asking for necessary victuals as a loan or gift.' In 1313 to relieve their wants they secured the appropriation of Wotton church, thus adding £30 a year to the revenue of the house.

Architecturally the choir of Bristol stands in a class apart, characterized as it is by structural eccentricities that are a measure of the enterprise and ingenuity of the master-mason employed by the convent. The traditional three-storeyed bay design was discarded, the triforium and clerestory were dispensed with, and the aisles were built the same height as the choir. The very motive underlying the interior ordonnance of the new eastern arm was the provision of abundant side-lighting in preference to top-lighting. Hence the unusually lofty four-light windows, strengthened by transoms, in the aisle walls. The arches of the choir are carried up the full height of the interior and are the loftiest (52 feet) in any English mediaeval choir; the supporting piers are no longer bundles of clustered shafts but are moulded, and the capitals are almost non-existent. The lierne vaulting of the choir, with central kite-shaped cells, is the earliest of its kind. The aisle vaulting is a triumph of structural skill. Spanning the aisles from pier to wall are horizontal stone girders that act as buttresses to the vaulting of the choir and are supported by transverse arches. From the centre of the girders spring the ribs of the aisle vaults, so that the whole vaulting has the appearance of a series of ribbed conoids poised on horizontal beams. It was a novel and masterly experiment in the technique of skeleton construction that more properly belongs to the craft of carpentry (Pl. 73).

The Lady Chapel at the east, two bays in length (Fig. 21), is vaulted and roofed at the same level as the choir. In the side walls are lofty three-light windows and in the east wall is one of nine lights. At the base of the windows is a pierced parapet, beneath which is a string course enriched with ball flower ornament. The vaulting is similar to that of the choir. In the walls of the choir aisles and the Lady Chapel are a number of star-shaped recesses, whose arch-mouldings are enriched with crockets and finials of naturalistic carving, of the vine, the oak, the hawthorn and the maple-leaf. Similar stellate recesses occur also at S. Mary Redcliffe, Bristol, at S. David's cathedral and in Berkeley parish church, and were obviously designed to house tombs. They were an original contribution of the Bristol masons to fourteenth-century Gothic.

Near the east end of the south choir aisle is the monastic sacristy (Fig. 21), a small chamber that serves as a vestibule to the Berkeley chantry chapel; it is entered by a Decorated doorway in the south aisle, and is notable for the remarkable vault, consisting of a skeleton framework of ribs with no web that supports a flat stone roof above. A small portal at the east opens into the chapel founded in 1348 by Thomas, Lord Berkeley for his wife Margaret, d. 1337. The chapel has two altars and was dedicated to the Blessed Virgin Mary. Of exceeding beauty are the carved bosses of the vault, the foliage capitals and the ball-flower ornament. In the wall dividing the chapel from the choir aisle is a large arch beneath which is the tomb of Thomas, 2nd Lord Berkeley, d. 1321.

Alterations in the Elder Lady Chapel that stood detached from the old choir were occasioned by the building of the new and wider choir in the fourteenth century. The intervening space was filled in and the south wall of the Chapel was reconstructed; the two large openings in the wall reveal its great thickness.

The new eastern arm of Bristol cathedral was finished c. 1340. Rather later than the choir was the Newton chapel, that replaced the Norman apsidal chapel to the east of the south transept. It is an interesting work of late Decorated Gothic verging on Perpendicular (Fig. 21).

LICHFIELD CATHEDRAL, 1296–1345

There was considerable building activity at Lichfield cathedral during the first half of the fourteenth century. About the year 1296 work was resumed on the west front and on the raising of the central tower, both of which may have been completed by c. 1325. The three tiers of canopied niches on the façade are in the main restorations of the nineteenth century and the Geometrical window is modern. The stone spires of the central and the south-western towers followed the west front,[1] and that of the north-western tower was put up in the fifteenth century. All three spires are octagonal and are banded at intervals, each stage being pierced with two-light windows (Pl. 10). There is a profusion of ball-flower ornament, and the pinnacles at the base of the spires are laden

[1] The central spire was destroyed in the Civil War and was rebuilt by Wren.

with crockets and finials. The parapet beneath is overlaid with Decorated quatrefoils.

At the other end of the cathedral the early Gothic choir had already proved inadequate to the ritualistic requirements of the fourteenth century. Prompted by the great remodellings in other cathedrals, Bishop Walter Langton of Lichfield, 1296–1321, embarked upon the building of a much more stately eastern arm. Here as elsewhere the desiderata were a chapel for the adoration of the Blessed Virgin and a worthy setting for the shrine. A new shrine for the remains of S. Chad was in the making. Operations started *c.* 1310 with the erection of the Lady Chapel some distance to the east of the old choir. No low rectangular annexe would content Bishop Langton; the Chapel was to be a lofty building terminating at the east in a three-sided apse (Fig. 19), undoubtedly inspired by the polygonal chapter house of the thirteenth century (Pl. 74). The immensely tall windows show the increasing importance of light and of glass in the development of Gothic architecture. In height the Lady Chapel is only a few feet less than the choir; a special feature of the windows, which are mostly of three lights, is the rather formal build-up of the six or more trefoils in the traceried heads. Less obvious are the ogee-arched drip-stones of the exterior. Beneath the windows internally runs a canopied arcade supported by shafts with carved capitals. The ogee-arches of the canopies bow forward as in the Lady Chapel of Ely and are enriched with crockets and finials. The Lady Chapel which has a tierceron vault with many carved bosses was completed by 1326. Little progress having been made in his lifetime, Bishop Langton left £80 13s. 3d. for its completion. In 1323 his executors and the chapter came to an agreement that each should pay half the cost of finding a quarry for the stone that was needed.

From 1326 the work proceeded westwards and in alignment with the Lady Chapel, the axis of which deviated slightly to the north. Moreover, the new bays were given the same width as the Lady Chapel, and were therefore 2 feet narrower than the three bays that were retained at the west end of the choir. At this stage, *c.* 1337, the chapter called in William Ramsey, the King's mason, as a consultant architect, and this distinguished master devised means for effecting the junction of the old and the new work, whereby the irregularities would be rendered imperceptible to the eye (p. 293).

The choir-arm of Lichfield cathedral had been lengthened by the addition of the Lady Chapel and of one bay connecting it with the east end of the old choir. As regards the interior lighting, the old choir compared ill with the Lady Chapel and the chapter

therefore resolved upon further reconstruction that would flood
the whole of the choir with light. Accordingly, all the Early English bays, excepting the piers and arches of the three westernmost
which were altered to make them uniform with the new work,
were torn down. In the bay design of the new choir the triforium
stages was represented by unobtrusive blind panelling at the base
of the five-light windows of the clerestory, after the fashion of York
nave (Pl. 75). The elevation is thus virtually two-storeyed, and the
large clerestory windows are as lofty as the choir arches below.
Unfortunately only two of the Decorated windows, distinguished
by flowing tracery and pointed lobes, survived the Civil War.
The splays of the windows are decorated with quatrefoil ornamen-
tation carried up to the top of the arches. The aisle windows of the
same curvilinear character also sustained grievous injury during
the sieges of Lichfield in the seventeenth century. The high vault
of the choir is similar to the tierceron vault of the Lady Chapel
(Pl. 75).

LINCOLN CATHEDRAL, 1296–1380

The chapter house at Lincoln had been in use for about seventy
years before the small cloisters were built to the north-west of the
choir, on a site previously occupied by the canons' stables. The
eastern walk that is entered through a passage from the north
choir transept was commenced in 1296. Bishop Sutton, 1280–99,
made a gift of 50 marks towards the cost of building and by the
year 1310 all the walks enclosing the quadrangular garth were
complete. They were, however, built without foundations and the
arcades soon showed signs of insecurity; so much so, that the north
walk, on the verge of collapse, had to be taken down.[1] The traceried openings of the cloister arcades mark the transition from Geometric to Decorated Gothic, and the walks are roofed with timber
vaulting, enriched with carved bosses of foliage, grotesque heads,
sacred subjects, and others representing the occupations of the
months.

To the early years of the fourteenth century also belong the upper stages of the central tower, the pulpitum (p. 116), and the
timber choir stalls of Lincoln. In 1307 Bishop Dalderby offered
indulgences to further the erection of the tower, which was finished
four years later, the loftiest central tower of any English cathedral,
268 feet in height. Countless crockets adorn the tall windows, pro-
ducing an effect of richness unsurpassed in any other cathedral

---

[1] The Doric arcade with library above was built on the site of the north walk in
1674 from the designs of Sir Christopher Wren. The other walks were reconstructed
stone by stone about seventy years ago.

tower. At the angles are octagonal turrets; the pinnacles and the pierced parapets are renovations of the eighteenth century. The vault, 125 feet above the pavement at the crossing, is typical of the complex rib-structure of vaults of this period and dates *c.* 1380.

To do honour to the memory of 'Saint' John de Dalderby, d. 1320, the enormous circular window known as 'the Bishop's Eye' was inserted in the end wall of the south transept. Within the circle are two vesicas, each having a central stem from which curvilinear tracery branches out in leaf-forms, an unusual design for a window of that form. The chapter was indebted to John Welbourn, treasurer and *custos operis*, 1351–85, for the glorious stalls, and to him is ascribed the range of canopied figures of English kings from William I to Edward III above the central portal of the west front. These eleven bearded and seated monarchs all of the same type were originally coloured and gilded (Pl. 32).

S. ALBANS CATHEDRAL, 1308–60

Few of the monks of S. Albans who had witnessed the laying of the foundations of the new choir-arm *c.* 1260 lived to see its completion. Fifty years had passed, and the walls of the Lady Chapel had risen to a height of only 6 feet. The chronicles relate that Abbot Hugh of Eversden, 1308–26, 'brought to a praiseworthy completion the Chapel of the Virgin in the eastern part of the Church'. In its original state the chapel, some 57 feet long and 24 feet wide, was a fine piece of Decorated Gothic, lighted by curvilinear windows, the jambs and mullions of which yet retain small figures of saints, kings and queens, as well as much ball-flower ornament. The five-light window in the east wall is a combination of flowing tracery with crocketed gabling. The arcading below the windows was so badly mutilated by the grammar-school boys of three centuries, that the walls were refaced with new arcading in the nineteenth century. A wooden vault was put up over the chapel, since replaced by the modern tierceron vault of stone.

In 1323 when the Lady Chapel was fast approaching completion, the fourth and fifth piers of the south nave arcade west of the crossing crashed outwards, and the collapse of the superstructure wrecked the south aisle of the nave and the adjoining cloister walk. Without delay reparation was put in hand under the direction of Henry Wye *magister operum*. Five bays on the south side of the nave, the fourth to the eighth inclusive, together with the aisle and the cloister walk had to be rebuilt, though the work dragged on for twenty years and was not finished until *c.* 1345. Abbot Michael de

Mentmore, 1335–49, acquired the quarries of Eglemount for the supply of stone. The junction of the Early English and the Decorated bays is marked by a massive pier with a broad pilaster attached to it that is carried up to the roof. In general design the fourteenth-century bays of the nave are similar to the Early English bays to the west. Necessarily the proportions of the three stages are the same, but as to detail the advance to Decorated Gothic is at once apparent. The new piers are of the same size and form; the arch mouldings are thin compared with the bold rounds and hollows of the thirteenth century. From east to west the hood-moulds terminate in carved heads that represent Abbot Hugh, Queen Isabella, Edward II, and master-mason Geoffrey, and in the spandrels are shields bearing the arms of England, Edward the Confessor, Mercia and France. In the triforium the sub-arches are cusped, the hood-moulds have head-stops, and in place of the bell capitals and dog-tooth of the Early English triforium appear foliage capitals and ball-flower ornament.

Had Abbot Michael de Mentmore not been carried off by the Black Death in 1349, he would probably have erected a new rood-screen in the nave to replace the one damaged in 1323. To his successor, Thomas de la Mare, is attributed the splendid rood-screen that stretches across the nave in the third bay west of the crossing (p. 114). During his long rule of forty-seven years at S. Albans he also built the Great Gatehouse to the west of the cathedral and the cloister portal in the south aisle of the nave, an ornate specimen of Decorated Gothic with rich carvings in the arch-mouldings and the lateral niches.

WORCESTER CATHEDRAL, 1317–27

The costly rebuilding of the eastern limb of Worcester cathedral, that was fast approaching completion by the middle of the thirteenth century, had drained the resources of the convent, and the raising of the central tower was therefore deferred. In 1281 Bishop Nicholas bequeathed the sum of 60 marks for the tower, and the convent secured the appropriation of Wolverley church for the same purpose. However, there is no record of further building at Worcester until the episcopate of Thomas Cobham, 1317–27, when work was started on a new nave. The five eastern bays of the north nave arcade, the lower parts of two bays farther west, and the north aisle of the nave were erected. Then the work came to a sudden stop, and the building of the nave was not resumed nor was the central tower put up until after the Black Death, by which time Gothic was passing from the Decorated to the Perpendicular phase. The cessation was undoubtedly caused by the lack of funds.

Offerings at the shrine of S. Wulstan or Worcester had long been a profitable source of revenue, but after 1330 the tomb of the murdered Edward II at Gloucester proved a far greater attraction to pilgrims, and Gloucester's gain was Worcester's loss.

The Decorated bay design of the north nave arcade is a compromise between that of the Early English choir and of the Transitional bays at the west end of the nave. The proportions of the three stages conform with those of the choir; in form, the bulky piers are modifications of the Transitional piers and are composed of clustered shafts; the capitals are encircling bands of carved foliage. The triforium openings are copied from those of the choir, and consist of two containing arches with two sub-arches; but the clerestory, in which a lofty central light is flanked by smaller openings, is a Decorated version of the Transitional clerestory.

Projecting from the second bay of the north aisle of the nave is a small chantry chapel (much restored) that was founded by Bishop Cobham and was dedicated to the Holy Name of Jesus (Fig. 22).

GLOUCESTER CATHEDRAL, 1318–29

Early in the fourteenth century the monks of Gloucester gained first-hand knowledge of the unsound methods of Norman building, when the wall of the south aisle of the nave heeled over and threatened to collapse. Between 1318 and 1329 the aisle was transformed into Decorated Gothic; the walls were strengthened with buttresses, three-light windows were inserted, and a new vault erected. The windows are noteworthy for the profusion of ballflower ornament in the arch mouldings and the jambs, and even the tracery is studded with ball flower.

WELLS CATHEDRAL, 1320–65

Of exceeding splendour is the Decorated Gothic of the choir arm of Wells cathedral, the building of which followed hard upon the chapter house (Fig. 17). The Lady Chapel is octagonal on plan, the outer walls comprising five sides, and the three western walls are carried by lofty arches that spring from clustered piers of Purbeck marble. The chapel has large five-light windows of reticulated tracery, and from triple wall-shafts rises the wondrous lierne vaulting, woven with multitudinous ribs. Of the many carved bosses in the vault, the central one presents a figure of Christ enthroned.

The master-mason responsible for building the Lady Chapel was William Joye, a Somerset man, who had been commissioned by the chapter in 1315 to raise the central tower, that was then barely above the roof of the cathedral. To minimize the load on the piers at the crossing, the tower was built with hollow walls which the master-mason braced together with iron ties and with bands of masonry. In each face of the tower he inserted three pairs of tall lancet windows; the angles were originally built without buttresses, but the design was subsequently modified. By the year 1321 the tower was being roofed. Meanwhile, work on the Lady Chapel was forging ahead, and the retrochoir with low transeptal chapels on either side was taking shape. The four clustered piers in the retrochoir are composed mainly of Purbeck shafts with foliage capitals that support the ribs of the elaborate lierne vault (Pl. 76). Incidentally the vault of the retrochoir is lower than that of the Lady Chapel. In 1325 an indulgence of ten days was granted to all who subscribed to the 'New Work'.

The next stage in the operations was to remove the eastern end of the twelfth-century choir in preparation for the eastern extension of three bays. The lofty wall at the east end of the new choir rises well above the retrochoir and is opened up with three arches behind the High Altar. The choir arcades were built the same height as those of the twelfth century to the west, and triple vaulting shafts rise from the bases of the piers. There is no triforium as such, the walling above the arches of the choir being faced with niches and tabernacling. The eastern wall is of the same design, and above the tabernacling is a Jesse window of seven lights filled with fourteenth-century glass depicting the descent of Our Lord from King David.

When the three bays of the presbytery were up, the older bays at the west were recast in the same style (Pl. 77). Only the piers and the arches remained untouched; the triforium stage was cased with tabernacling, Curvilinear windows were inserted in the clerestory wall, and Decorated windows of three lights were substituted for lancets in the aisles. The whole of the choir thus enlarged was covered with a pointed barrel vault, 67 feet high, the surfaces being ribbed with a patterning of squares and hexagons. Tierceron vaults were erected over the aisles. Flying-buttresses, that had been concealed in the triforium chamber in the old choir, were now exposed above the aisle roofs and the upper parts were pierced with tracery. This grand scheme of remodelling at Wells was brought to a conclusion c. 1340.

As happened so often in other great churches, the central tower had been piled up on piers incapable of bearing so mighty a load, and fifteen years after the scaffolds had been removed much anxiety was caused by the sinking of the four piers at the crossing and by fissures that appeared in the arches. Towards the work of stabilizing the tower the canons in residence contributed the large sum of £1,000, and the non-residentiaries were required to pay £200 'still owing'. In 1337 an emergency meeting of the chapter was convened to decide upon measures to arrest further subsidence of the tower piers. The method devised by the master-mason, the same William Joye who had built the tower, was a sensational *tour-de-force*, an engineering feat that was structurally sound but unspeakably ugly. Beneath each of the arches at the crossing except the eastern, a huge scissor-like framework of masonry was constructed, consisting of a pointed arch surmounted by an inverted arch. In the spandrels are enormous circles that to some extent relieve the ponderous character of the design (Pl. 78). The same form of strainer-arch had been employed seven years before in the choir transepts at Salisbury. The central tower of Wells cathedral was strengthened still more by the building of flying-buttresses in the triforia and clerestories adjacent to the tower. Emboldened by their success the masons proceeded to pile more weight on the piers by sundry additions to the tower. The tall lancet windows were converted into two lights, the lower halves being filled with panelling; and a traceried parapet together with angle pinnacles was added.

Finally the walls of the clerestory and the aisles throughout the cathedral were crowned with parapets pierced with curvilinear tracery.

WINCHESTER CATHEDRAL, 1320–50

The building of the retrochoir of Winchester cathedral in the early part of the thirteenth century (p. 89) had not disturbed the old Norman presbytery and its eastern apse, which remained until *c*. 1320. The apse was then taken down to permit of a remodelling of the choir. A minor difficulty arose in connecting the choir with De Lucy's retrochoir, the central area of which was of less width than the Norman presbytery. The new bay between the High Altar and the east window was therefore narrowed, forming a three-sided termination (Fig. 9). This eastern bay was used as the Saint's chapel in which was duly installed the shrine of S. Swithun. The three-staged elevation of the Norman choir was converted into a two-storeyed design and the piers and arches were remodelled. Evidently the building operations were delayed by the Black Death, 1349, and it is not easy to say how much of the new choir was finished in the fourteenth century. The upper parts of the presbytery walls, the wooden high vault and the choir aisles are the work of Bishop Fox, 1500–28 (p. 270). To the Decorated period, however, belongs the low wall enclosing the Saint's chapel at the east; the front is adorned with nine tabernacled niches, each containing two pedestals on which were formerly small statues of Saxon kings and bishops. The ogee-arched canopies are enriched with crockets and finials of exquisitely sculptured leafage.

Ely Cathedral, 1321–70

The craft of chiselling ornament in stone reached its climax in the Decorated Gothic of Ely cathedral, the virtuosity of which is perhaps overshadowed by the structural inventiveness displayed in the famous Octagon.

Seventy years after the dedication of the Early English retrochoir in 1252, the Norman tower at the crossing of the cathedral fell, and ruined the western bays of Abbot Simeon's choir. Only the previous year, 1321, the foundations of a magnificent Lady Chapel had been laid to the east of the north transept and parallel with the choir (Fig. 19). Scant honour would have been conferred upon the 'Queen of Heaven' had the monks set up an altar to Our Lady in the retrochoir, where S. Etheldreda reigned supreme. The site chosen for the Lady Chapel was probably suggested by the position of the Lady Chapel erected at Peterborough fifty years before. The Chapel at Ely is approached through a doorway in the north-eastern angle of the transept.

In a less wealthy establishment than Ely, the collapse of the central tower would have been a disaster of appalling magnitude, for a three-fold task faced the convent, viz., the erection of the Lady Chapel, the rebuilding of the tower and of the three ruined bays of the choir. Notwithstanding the prodigious cost, these three works proceeded simultaneously on a lavish scale and regardless of expense, and were all completed within thirty years, save for the east window of the Lady Chapel.

Rectangular on plan and 100 feet in length, the Lady Chapel is the widest stone-vaulted building of single span in our mediaeval churches, having a width of 46 feet (Pl. 79). It is divided into five bays, and is lighted by expansive windows; those in the side walls, richly traceried are of four lights, in the east wall is a window of seven lights and in the west is an eight-light window. Beneath the windows runs an arcade of elaborate tabernacled and gabled niches, with ogee-cusping, and exuberant with sculptured flowers and dainty leafage (Pl. 80). The canopies of the tabernacling bend forwards and the spandrels are filled with diaper-work and with sculptured subjects depicting incidents in the life of the Virgin Mary, and the story of Julian the Apostate. The backs of the niches and other parts of the building retain traces of colouring. In its original state the chapel was a veritable storehouse of imagery and tabernacle work, the high-water mark of Decorated Gothic. The lierne vault was painted in rich blue studded with silver stars and the many bosses were carved with emblems of the Nativity, the Crucifixion, the Virgin Mary, flowers, foliage and grotesques, all brilliantly coloured and gilded.

On the Vigil of the Feast of S. Eormenilda, 1322, the central tower fell 'with such a shock and so great a tumult, that it was thought an earthquake had taken place'. The catastrophe was not wholly unforeseen; owing to the unsafe condition of the tower, the monks had already abandoned the ritual choir in the crossing and celebrated the Divine offices in a chapel off the east walk of the cloisters. The new tower that was then built was the work of a constructive genius, and was without precedent in English medi-aeval architecture. This masterly conception, which is attributed to Alan of Walsingham, the sacrist and later the prior of Ely, involved the erection of an octagonal stone tower over the whole breadth of the nave and transepts, including aisles, and covering an area more than three times that of the Norman tower (Fig. 19). 'With great labour and expense', wrote the chronicler, 'he [Alan] caused to be removed from within the church the stones and timber that had fallen in the ruin; and at the place where he was about to construct the new tower, he by architectural skill measured out eight positions in which the eight stone columns were to stand supporting the whole building . . . and caused them to be dug out and examined, until he had found the solid rock on which the foundations of his work might be securely fixed. These aforesaid eight places having been firmly consolidated with stones and sand, he then began the eight columns and the superincum-bent stone work . . . which was brought to a conclusion after six years in the year of Our Lord 1328.' The record seems to imply that Alan of Walsingham took an active part in the building operations and needs to be accepted with some reserve. The four main arches at the crossing are flanked by the narrower sides of the Octagon, the walls of which are designed in three stages, con-sisting of arches opening into the aisles, a blind triforium with three trefoiled niches, and above, a large Decorated window of four lights. About half-way up each of the vaulting shafts is a canopied niche resting on a sculptured corbel representing an incident in the life of S. Etheldreda.

Within the stone Octagon rests the octagonal lantern, a gigantic wooden tower suspended at a height of 94 feet above the pave-ment (Pl. 81). It is recorded that to find eight sufficiently large and sound oak trees for the angle posts of the lantern, Alan of Walsingham went 'searching far and wide, and with the greatest difficulty finding them at last, paying a great price for them, transported them to Ely by sea and land'. The eight angle posts, each 63 feet long, that form the skeleton of the lantern, are framed into an octagonal curb, and attached to each post are two radial struts, the lower ends of which are seated on corbels in the walls of the stone Octagon. At a further height of 18 feet is another series of radial struts that also carry the roof of the outer Octagon. Due to the system of framing, the faces of the lantern are set obliquely and not parallel to those of the stone octagon. From below, the oaken timbers are concealed by wooden vaulting and the lantern is roofed in the same way (Pl. 82). Above is a bell chamber, carrying the lantern up to a height of more than 180 feet. At the base of the lantern is a gallery with panelled front and above are eight spacious traceried windows of four lights. The wooden vaulting was originally painted with conventional scroll-work of leafage and flowers. The stone Octagon was completed by 1328, but another fourteen years were to pass before the lantern was finished. The total cost of the Octagon amounted to £2,046 6s. 11d. With the exception of £206 12s. 0¼d. the whole sum was found by the convent of Ely.

Whilst the Octagon was slowly rising, the three ruined bays at the west end of the choir were rebuilding, at the expense of Bishop Hotham, d. 1337. He also bequeathed money for the work. Each bay cost £680. These new Decorated bays are remarkable for the abnormally large triforium stage and for the 'ornament for the sake of ornament' that is lavished on every feature. Necessarily the proportions of the bay-design conform with those of the thirteenth century bays to the east, thus accounting for the lofty triforium, that is of unusual height in the eastern bays (Pl. 84). The arches of the Decorated bays are carried by piers that are modified forms of the Early English piers, and sunk in the arch-mouldings are clumps of foliage, an ornament that is repeated in the triforium arches. The elongated corbels of the vaulting shafts are profusely carved with foliage, and the cusped tracery of the two-light triforium openings is almost lace-like in character. In the spandrels of both stages are cusped trefoils. Each bay of the clerestory has a large curvilinear window of four lights, and from the level of the clerestory string rise the ribs of the lierne vault, enriched with sixteen carved bosses in each bay. These three Decorated bays of the choir were erected at a cost of £2,034 12s. 8¾d., which was defrayed by Bishop Hotham. To improve the lighting of the eastern part of the choir, the outer walls of the triforium chamber of two bays adjoining the new work were taken down, the aisles were covered with flat roofs and the triforium openings were glazed after the insertion of Decorated windows.

A contemporaneous work of minor importance at Ely is Prior Crauden's Chapel, a two-storeyed building some distance south of the cloisters. This little gem of Decorated Gothic is rectangular on plan, 31 feet in length and 15 feet wide. The chapel proper occupies the upper floor, that is reached by a vice in the north-west angle. It is divided into four bays by clustered wall-shafts from which spring the ribs of the vault. In the east wall is a five-light window and there are two-light windows in the side walls, all curvilinear in style. The undercroft beneath the chapel is vaulted.

CHESTER CATHEDRAL, 1323–49

The extensive reconstruction of the conventual buildings at the east and north of the cloisters at Chester had retarded work on the choir. As a result, the clerestory stage of the western bays of the choir, with its wide windows of four lights, was not completed until early in the fourteenth century. Then the convent put in hand the re-building of the south transept, the most singular feature of Chester cathedral. It was planned on a scale out of all proportion to the nave and choir; of equal length to the choir, and nearly as long as the nave the south transept is considerably broader than either, and has aisles at the east and the west, a rare arrangement in any but cathedrals of the first rank such as York (Fig. 18). The re-building brought the convent into conflict with the parishioners of S. Oswald, whose church that stood on the site of the transept was swept away. They duly claimed the transept for parochial worship and made an entrance in the western wall; for the con-venience of both parties it was walled off from the rest of the monastic church.

In addition to the south transept, a new nave was begun, though the work on both ceased at the time of the Black Death, 1349, and was not resumed before late in the fifteenth century. As far as can be determined, the piers and arches of the transept arcades, the aisles and the southern part of the nave were in course of erection by 1349. The bay design is two-storeyed, for the tri-forium as a separate stage is non-existent. Above the transept arcades is a parapet pierced with quatrefoils, masking the wall passage that runs beneath the clerestory windows in lieu of a tri-forium. The arch-orders of the transept arcade correspond with the shafts of the piers, and in each bay of the aisles is a large four-light window of curvilinear tracery. The clerestory windows were inserted when the transept was completed in the fifteenth century.

HEREFORD CATHEDRAL, 1325–70

Within a few years of his accession to the see of Hereford, Bishop Adam Orleton obtained from Pope John XXII a grant of the revenues of two parish churches in Berks. for the rebuilding of the central tower of the cathedral, which had fallen into a state of dilapidation. The new tower, begun *c.* 1325, was raised on the Norman piers and arches at the crossing, and to minimise the load, the interior walls of the tower were carried by grids of vertical stone stanchions, 26 feet in height. The two stages of each face of the tower have ranges of four two-light windows, and at the angles are pinnacled buttresses, there is a profusion of ball-flower ornament on the masonry. The squat appearance of the tower is due to the removal of the timber spire by Wyatt in 1790, who also added the battlemented parapet (Pl. 94).

After the Black Death, the building or rebuilding of the south transept of the choir was undertaken. Hereford suffered grievously from the effects of the pestilence that reappeared in 1360. To allay the fears of the townspeople, the feretrum containing the remains of S. Thomas Cantelupe were carried in procession through the streets. The chapter was short of funds for building and skilled masons were scarce. Small wonder that the work on the south choir transept was inferior in quality, as witness the tracery of the four-light Decorated windows.

SALISBURY CATHEDRAL, 1330–80

Bishop Poore's Early English cathedral at Salisbury had been forty-six years in the building, and at the crossing was a dwarf tower that rose but a few feet above the cathedral roof. The exterior elevation, however, demanded a lofty central tower about which the main masses of the great church would be grouped. Accordingly, about the year 1330 on the low stump at the crossing were raised a tower and spire soaring to a height of 404 feet, designed and erected by Richard Farleigh, a Wiltshire man. The piling up of 6,000 tons of masonry on the piers at the crossing was certainly not contemplated by the masons of the thirteenth century, or the supports would have been more massively built. To take the additional weight, flying-buttresses were constructed at the external angles of the tower and in the triforium and clerestory of the adjoining bays; and the masonry of the octagonal spire was built up of courses only 2 feet thick at the base and 9 inches at the summit. To afford greater rigidity, the timber scaffolding within the spire was not removed after completion. Despite such cautionary measures, settlements occurred during the actual operations, and in the fifteenth century, when further signs of instability appeared, girder-arches had to be inserted beneath the north and south arches at the crossing.

The Decorated Gothic of the graceful and well-proportioned tower and spire of Salisbury are in perfect harmony with the more restrained Lancet forms of the thirteenth century. The two stages of the tower are well defined by bands of quatrefoil tracery, and three similar belts adorn the faces of the spire. Four gabled windows of two lights pierce each stage of the tower, and in the upper part as also on the arrises of the spire occurs the ball-flower ornament, so unobtrusively as not to be easily discerned from ground level. The design was unified by grouping pinnacles above the parapet of the tower, thus masking the transition from square to octagon.

ROCHESTER CATHEDRAL, 1342–50

The most noteworthy piece of Decorated Gothic at Rochester cathedral is the lovely doorway, *c.* 1342, in the eastern aisle of the south choir-transept, that now forms the entrance to the chapter room. In the deeply moulded jambs are two large figures symbolizing the Christian and the Jewish dispensations, and in the archmouldings above are two canopied figures on either side representing Doctors of the Church seated at reading-desks. In the apex of the arch is a little naked soul of the founder, and the outer ogeearch is studded with ornament and enriched with crockets. The cost of the doorway was met by Bishop Hamo de Hythe, d. 1352. The two windows with flowing tracery on either side of the portal are of the same date. Bishop Hamo also 'caused the new steeple of the church of Rochester to be carried up higher with stones and timbers, and to be covered with lead'. In other words the Bishop added an upper stage to the central tower and capped it with a timber spire.

OXFORD CATHEDRAL, 1350–55

Light and yet more light being needed in S. Frideswide's, Oxford, large traceried windows were substituted for the small Norman openings in various parts of the church, improvements in fenestration that were continued in the fifteenth century. In 1350 or shortly afterwards, was built the chapel of S. Katherine, commonly known as the Latin chapel, flanking the Lady Chapel on the north (Fig. 14). Rectangular on plan and four bays in length, the chapel is noteworthy for the Curvilinear windows of four lights, all of different design, in the north wall; and for the carved bosses of the vault, including a squirrel and a king's head.

15. The Architecture of
English Cathedrals

IV. PERPENDICULAR GOTHIC

⟨ BEFORE THE MIDDLE of the fourteenth century, English Gothic was passing from the exuberant Decorated style into a more economic and disciplined phase, to which the name Perpendicular is applied and which prevailed for more than two centuries. The transition to Perpendicular or Rectilinear Gothic became general in all parts of the country after the Black Death, the terrible pestilence that spread throughout the land in 1349–50. No special dispensation of Providence afforded immunity to masons, craftsmen and labourers, who suffered equally with all classes of the community. Building labour became scarce and works that were in progress in cathedrals and other churches were brought to a halt. For some years after the scourge the services of skilled masons were monopolized by royal undertakings at Westminster and Windsor; in the year 1362 proclamations were issued in London and in twenty-four counties forbidding the employment of hewers and layers of stone except by the King's leave.

Perfectly appropriate is the name Perpendicular, deriving from the predominance of the vertical line in window design of the period. The flowing curves of Decorated Gothic straighten themselves and become rigid, the mullions rising from the sill to the arched head of the windows. In every possible way, the masons sought to emphasize verticality in their designs; craftsmen of moderate skill could cut the straight-line forms of rectilinear windows. The frills and fancies of the Decorated style were dispensed with, architectural features were simplified and shorn of over-elaboration, although the ogee-arch and the crocketed pinnacle persisted through the Perpendicular period, mainly as decorative adjuncts. The niche was succeeded by the flat rectilinear panel, the unit of design for wall decoration and for windows. The enormous increase of window area and the reduction of walling are characteristic. The craze was for well-lighted interiors; large Perpendicular windows were inserted in the west fronts of Rochester, Norwich and other cathedrals, and in the end walls of the transepts of Durham and Chichester, and elsewhere. Exeter cathedral must needs have a nine-light window in the east wall of the choir, and rectilinear windows appeared in the transepts and the west front of Lichfield, and in the three lofty recesses of the Lincoln façade. At Peterborough, more than seventy Norman windows were replaced by Perpendicular windows in the fifteenth century. By the use of transoms, vast windows of many lights were divided into tiers of rectilinear panels, which were treated by the glass painter as niches to be filled with translucent figures of prophets, saints and apostles.

Usually Perpendicular piers are composed of semi-shafts and shallow mouldings, and insignificant capitals appear on the shafts.

Many wonderful vaults, triumphs of structural skill, were built in the greater churches in this period, in particular the so-called fan vault, built up of inverted trumpet-shaped conoids, the surfaces of which were enriched with panelling arranged in the fashion of a fan. In the Tudor period the obtusely pointed four-centred arch made its appearance in arcades, doors and windows. Significant is the importance of the central tower in cathedral-building of the Perpendicular period, notably at York, Gloucester and Canterbury, each of which expresses the highest ideals of the local school of masoncraft.

GLOUCESTER CATHEDRAL, 1331-74

The cradle of Perpendicular Gothic was the abbey church of S. Peter, Gloucester, and the creation of the new style by the western masons from 1331 onwards is one of the romances and marvels of mediaeval building. After the murder of Edward II at Berkeley castle in September 1327, Abbot Thokey, an opportunist of great courage and foresight brought the remains of the king to S. Peter's abbey, where they were laid to rest on the north side of the choir, near the High Altar. His laudable act proved a godsend to the convent; popular sympathy for the murdered monarch exalted him to the rank of a saint and martyr, and pilgrims flocked to Gloucester from far and wide. An era of prosperity set in for the abbey. In 1329 a wondrous tomb for the remains of the king was erected in the presbytery and by the middle of the century the oblations made thereat amounted to a sum sufficient to rebuild the whole of the abbey church. The monument of Edward II, crowned with a mass of dazzling tabernacling is unsurpassed in English Gothic art. The tomb itself is constructed of Purbeck marble, and on it lies the recumbent effigy of the king, the first important alabaster figure that was made for an English monument, dating c. 1332 (Pl. 7).

The offerings that poured into the abbey treasury were put to good purpose. The old Norman choir was deemed unworthy of the 'shrine', the most popular resort of the day for pilgrims and sightseers merited a more up-to-date setting; and so it was that the convent embarked upon a scheme that transformed the dark Norman choir into a Perpendicular glasshouse. The method was unprecedented in mediaeval building practice, a recasing of the Norman structure with a Perpendicular veneer. The operations commenced in the south transept *c.* 1332, the side walls of which were carried up to a height of 86 feet to permit of top-lighting; the end wall was opened up with an eight-light window. Ever receptive of new ideas, the Gloucester masons cemented a veil of traceried panelling on to the interior walls of the transept, and the dark voids of the Norman triforium were overlaid with similar panelling. This new work marks the inception of Perpendicular Gothic; curvilinear forms linger in the tracery of the windows and panelling, and it was but one step further to Perpendicular, viz., to carry the mullions straight up to the heads of the windows and panels. By 1337 the high vault of the south transept was being built, one of the earliest lierne vaults in England. The complicated network of ribs is jointed with singular precision and is devoid of bosses.

The stylistic architecture of the south transept of Gloucester subsequently altered the whole trend of English Gothic; the recasing was an earnest of the spectacular refashioning of the choir-arm, where the method employed by the masons was more audacious. There, the Norman piers and walling were reduced to a skeleton structure which was then clothed in Perpendicular vesture. This was effected by paring down the piers to a flat surface, to which vaulting shafts were then attached and a screenwork of stone panelling applied to the intervening walling. In the arches of the choir and of the triforium the four-light panelling is open, but is blind in the spandrels and glazed in the clerestory stage which was raised to a greater height as in the south transept (Pl. 87). The Norman apse at the east was pulled down and was replaced by a square east end two bays in length. The great east window, a vast screen of glass, 72 feet by 38 feet, is the largest in any mediaeval church of this country. To admit the maximum of light, the easternmost bay was widened by 5 feet and the east window of fourteen lights was canted. The window is divided by transoms into eight tiers of panels that were glazed *c.* 1350 (p. 144). The fenestration of the remodelled choir converted the sanctuary into a veritable stone lantern. As if to demonstrate their consummate skill, the masons roofed the choir with a lierne vault, tangled with innumerable ribs and enriched with sculptured bosses figuring Our Lord and the angelic choir. The high vault of the two new bays at the east is supported by three flying-buttresses arranged tripod-wise in the triforium chamber.

When the Norman apse was removed, a narrow tunnel-like passage, now known as the Whispering Gallery, was contrived to join up the triforium-ambulatories on each side of the choir. Standing clear of the east window, it appears externally as a closed-in bridge carried by flat arches on either side of the Lady Chapel.

The name of the master-mason who conceived and executed the amazing transformation of Gloucester choir is unrecorded; he was certainly an architectural genius of the first order.

There can have been no shortage of money, for when the choir was finished the area at the crossing was covered with a vault similar to that of the choir. For its support, skeleton arches dangling in mid-air were constructed beneath the north and south arches of the tower. Then followed the recasting of the north transept, the same method being employed as in the south transept, although the panelling is more advanced Perpendicular in character. The total cost of the work in the north transept amounted to £781, of which Abbot Thomas Horton, 1351–77, contributed £444.

By 1374 the labour of forty years had converted the greater part of the abbey church into something rich and strange. Further reconstruction lay ahead, for c. 1370 the convent had decided upon rebuilding the cloisters to the north of the nave. The Norman walls were faced with panelling, a Perpendicular window was inserted in each bay, and the four walks were roofed with fan vaults, the earliest extant. The southern bays of the east walk were the first to be built, and fifty years passed before the cloisters were finished (Fig. 9). In the south alley that served as the monks' scriptorium are twenty little recesses or carrels, originally fitted up with desks for the monk-scribes, and the north walk is remarkable for the fan-vaulted lavatorium that projects into the garth at the western end. In the long stone trough the brethren washed their hands before meals, and in the wall opposite the lavatorium is a recess that contained the towel cupboards. The cloisters at Gloucester, the finest of the Perpendicular period, have survived intact to this day.

No further change occurred in the fabric of the abbey church until the time of Abbot Morwent, 1421–37, who contemplated a rebuilding of the nave. 'He built the west part of the church, and made the porch and west frontispiece from the ground, *designing*, *if he had lived, to have made the whole body of the church of like work,'* (*Monasticon Anglicanum*). The old west front was showing signs of weakness, and was taken down to make way for the present undistinguished façade with its nine-light Perpendicular window; and two western bays of the nave were rebuilt, their feeble design contrasting unhappily with the columnar piers and round arches of the Norman bays to the east. The proportions differ; the piers are thinly shafted and moulded and the arches are more lofty. The westernmost bay is of an enormous span, and the triforium stage, a piece of blank walling, does not range with the Norman triforium. The much-restored porch at the south-west of the nave has an upper chamber, the front of which is faced with niches containing modern statuary. Abbot Morwent's scheme to reconstruct the whole of the nave was fortunately abandoned at his death in 1437.

Under the rule of Abbot Thomas Seabroke, 1450–7, arose the magnificent tower at the crossing, the prime glory of the exterior of Gloucester cathedral (Pl. 83). Perfect in its proportions and clothed in Perpendicular full-dress, the central tower rises to a height of 225 feet and dominates the main masses of the church. In each of its two stages is a pair of two-light louvred windows, and a distinctive feature of the design is the elongated and crocketed gabling of the panelling that is applied to the whole of the wall surfaces, and of the window heads. The parapets and the pinnacled turrets at the angles are pierced with rectilinear panels.

Another costly work that followed the erection of the tower was the Lady Chapel at the extreme east (Fig. 9). The old chapel dedicated to the Virgin was small and incommodious, and the convent were in need of a more splendid chapel in keeping with the new choir. It was commenced by Abbot Hanley, 1457–72, and is one of the largest in the country, rectangular on plan, 90 feet long and 25 feet wide. It has diminutive transepts and beneath the east end is a vaulted tunnel, by which the monks could pass from the north side to the cemetery on the south. So as not to obscure the east window of the choir, the Lady Chapel was narrowed at the west end; internally the narrowed bay serves as a vestibule, above which is a chapel entered from the whispering gallery and supported by a four-centred arch. The stone screen enclosing the upper chapel at the east repeats the design of the nine-light window above the altar of the Lady Chapel. The whole building presents Perpendicular Gothic in full flower. The walls are almost all glass, and vertical lines predominate, leading the eye up to the lierne vault with its multitudinous ribs and wealth of carved bosses of foliage, and of strange animals and fishes.

I

Old S. Paul's Cathedral, 1332

A rival school of Perpendicular building sprang up in London at Old S. Paul's cathedral, when the small cloisters and the octagonal chapter house in the garth were erected *c*. 1332 (Fig. 19). The master mason engaged by the chapter for this work was William Ramsey, who for six years had been employed in S. Stephen's Chapel of the Palace of Westminster. It was an important undertaking, for in 1332 the mayor and aldermen of the city of London granted Ramsey exemption from serving on juries and inquests 'as long as he shall be in the service of the church [cathedral]'. Both the cloisters and the chapter house were two-storeyed buildings. The rigid tracery of the windows of the upper stages of the cloisters and chapter house, together with the rectilinear panelling portrayed in Hollar's drawing clearly indicate the Perpendicular character of Ramsey's work, that was contemporaneous with the remodelling at Gloucester.

Durham Cathedral, 1345–1495

It was in the greater Norman churches that the crying need for light was most urgent; the fashion now was for wide and lofty windows of many lights, filled with painted glass of saints and martyrs innumerable. At Durham, the nave, the transepts, and the Galilee Chapel had long been in a state of perpetual gloom. To remedy this, Bishop Hatfield, 1345–81, inserted a Decorated window of seven lights in the west front, wherein was pictured 'the Rute of Jessie in most fyne coloured glass'.[1] In due course the transepts were similarly fenestrated. A large six-light window was pierced in the end wall of the north transept in 1359, and early in the fifteenth century the south transept was opened up with a Te Deum window of six lights. 'As every verse of the Te Deum is sung or said, so it is pictured in the window with the nine orders of angels, and the picture of Christ as he was upon the Cross crucified.'

A more urgent undertaking at the time was the restoration of Pudsey's Galilee Chapel, which had fallen into disrepair. The western wall needed shoring up, the Purbeck piers required reinforcing, and the roof was ruinous. A thorough restoration was begun in 1428 by Cardinal Thomas Langley, who held the see of Durham from 1406 to 1437. The western wall was strengthened with stout buttresses, shafts of sandstone were added to the piers, the chapel was re-roofed, and the lighting was vastly improved by the insertion of Perpendicular windows in the western wall.

[1] The present glass in the window dates from the nineteenth century.

An unforeseen calamity befell the convent in 1429, when the wooden belfry of the squat tower at the crossing was fired by lightning, and the masonry was damaged beyond repair. Being hard pressed for funds the convent sent forth the proctor to solicit alms, carrying with him a silver-gilt crucifix and a piece of cloth in which the body of S. Cuthbert had been wrapped. Nothing seems to have been done until 1455, by which time the tower was in so perilous a condition that its removal brooked no delay. An entire reconstruction was imperative and work began at the internal gallery, the walls above being faced with tall panelling The new central tower, rising to a height of 218 feet, is divided into two stages by an external gallery that may have served as a parapet to the tall lower stage, completed by 1474. The upper stage was not finished for another twenty-five years. Both stages have two windows with ogee-arched dripstones. Though not comparable with the Angel Steeple at Canterbury, the central tower of Durham is a well-proportioned specimen of late Perpendicular Gothic, and its erection closes the story of mediaeval building at the mighty minster of the north.

Bishop Hatfield had undertaken the rebuilding of the cloisters c. 1370, but so drastic were the alterations in the eighteenth and nineteenth centuries, that little remains of the mediaeval work except the oak roofing of the walks.

YORK CATHEDRAL, 1361–1500

The long series of building operations at York cathedral, broken by intervals of inactivity, was advanced another stage by Archbishop John of Thoresby, 1352–73, who in real earnest set about the reconstruction of the choir-arm. Only a few days before the death of his predecessor, Archbishop Zouche, in 1352, the chapter had sanctioned the erection of the Zouche chantry chapel on the south side of the choir, and William Hutton was appointed as master-mason (Fig. 23).

On 20 July 1361, Archbishop Thoresby declared to the canons assembled in the new chapter house that 'it was right that every church whatsoever should agree in the fitting decoration of each several part, and that the choir in particular, where the Holy Sacrifice of Mass took place, should be especially rich in ornament'. But the lack of ornament in the old choir was not the sole reason. There was no Lady Chapel in Roger's choir, nor was there adequate provision for the shrine of S. William of York. The reconstruction being resolved upon, Archbishop Thoresby immediately advanced £100 for the work and engaged himself to contribute £200 a year until the choir, which was to be the most grandiose in England, was finished. He also made a present of the stone from his ruined manor house at Sherburn-in-Elmet. The building of the new choir-arm occupied sixty years; it was planned as an aisled rectangle (Fig. 23), and is the largest and loftiest in England, 100 feet high and, including the aisles, 99 feet wide. Its length of 224 feet exceeds that of the nave.

The work falls into two periods; the first, 1361–70, to which belongs the retrochoir of four bays, comprising the Saint's chapel, ambulatory and Lady Chapel;[1] and secondly, 1380–1400, when the five western bays forming the sanctuary and ritual choir were erected (Fig. 23). In this new eastern arm the proportions and general design of the Decorated nave were adhered to.

Building operations started some 70 feet east of the old choir, and being longer and wider, the eastern bays were put up without disturbing Roger's choir, which remained in use for Divine worship for some years. Even when the four new bays had arisen at the east, the aisles of the ritual choir were built outside the old aisles. The transeptal chapels or towers(?) of Roger's choir were pulled down and were replaced by the present eastern transepts or transeptal bays, that consist of one bay of the choir-aisle carried up the full height of the choir. They do not project as in the case of normal transepts, but are open to the choir from top to bottom.

Incorporated in the clustered piers of the choir are vaulting shafts, attached to which, below the capitals of the piers, are brackets and canopies for statuary, and in the spandrels of the arches are shields bearing the arms of kings, saints and of noble families associated with the cathedral. Not the least interesting feature is the treatment of the triforium, which is absorbed into the five-light windows of the clerestory. In the retrochoir, i.e. the four eastern bays, the clerestory windows and the triforium openings are flush with the inner face of the wall, and the triforium passage is *outside*; externally, each bay of the clerestory is of a screen-like design, consisting of two stout mullions crossed by a transom in the lower part, a unique design evidently adopted to provide maximum lighting (Pl. 86). But in the ritual choir, i.e. the five western bays, the clerestory is recessed and the triforium passage is therefore inside.

The new choir-arm of York fell short of perfection, in that it was roofed with a timber vault, a makeshift that was far less costly than a high vault of stone. In the three-light windows of the aisles curvilinear and rectilinear traceries intermingle, an indication of the transition from Decorated to Perpendicular Gothic. The wall

---

[1] The High Altar now stands in the Saint's chapel but was originally in the next bay to the west.

beneath the windows is faced with rectilinear panelling, and externally the windows have ogee-arched dripstones enriched with crockets and finials. The aisles have quadripartite vaults of stone with ridge ribs. In the outer walls of the quasi-transepts are huge Perpendicular windows of five lights, divided by three transoms into panels filled with splendid glass; in the spandrels of the arches opening into the choir and its aisles are heraldic shields.

The great east window of nine lights, 78 feet high and 32 feet wide, and second in size to that of Gloucester choir, presented an immense field for the display of painted glass that was executed by John Thornton of Coventry (p. 143). The lower half of the window is constructed in two planes, with passages between them at the sill level and at the top. The east front of the cathedral is an immature example of Perpendicular Gothic, retaining as it does several features of Decorated. The great window is crowned with an ogee-arched gable, and the adjoining wall-surfaces are overlaid with panelling; the parapet is pierced with crocketed gables as also are the eastern parapets of the choir aisles, and the buttresses flanking the window are decorated with six stages of niches.

Archbishop Thoresby lived to see the retrochoir completed, but after his death in 1373, some years elapsed before the ritual choir of five bays was begun, the delay doubtless being occasioned by the lack of funds. The retrochoir had been built in less than ten years, but the simpler task of rearing the five bays of the ritual choir lasted thirty years, from 1380 to 1410, and the work proceeded so slowly that at an archiepiscopal Visitation in 1390, it was averred that 'due to negligence, the construction of the church is retarded'. The date of the glass in the western bays points to the completion of the ritual choir between 1410 and 1423. All traces of Curvilinear Gothic disappear in this later work, and the style is mature Perpendicular.

The erection of the new eastern arm of the cathedral had brought about settlements in the crypt that necessitated a reconstruction of that part beneath the High Altar. Though the Norman materials were reused, the outer piers in the crypt are Perpendicular and the transverse arches of the ribbed vault are four-centred.

By the year 1420 only the central and western towers were needed to make the vast church a stately and harmonious whole. In preparation for the central tower, the piers at the crossing had long before been reinforced in parts. The core of the piers is Norman, and had been recased with Decorated and Perpendicular masonry as the rebuilding of the nave and the choir had progressed. When both were completed, the process of recasing was also finished.

Imposing in the extreme, the central tower rises one stage above the cathedral roofs, and the interior being open to a height of 180 feet, the tower is a lantern that lights the crossing. Externally, each face has two tall rectilinear windows of three lights, surmounted by ogee-gables, and between them are three niches, one above another (Pl. 15). The angle buttresses are faced with panelling. In the spandrels of the arches at the crossing are shields with armorial bearings, and the tower is roofed with a lierne vault. The enormous bulk of the lantern, that has an internal width of 93 feet, the simplicity of the design and the absence of pinnacles, impart a dignified restraint and breadth that render it one of the glories of late Gothic architecture in this country.

About 1433 work was commenced on the south-western tower. The lower portions of both western towers, together with the projecting buttresses, being parts of the west front, followed the building of the nave, and belong to the first half of the fourteenth century; so that only the belfry stages above the parapet of the façade are later Perpendicular in character. In design they differ greatly from the central tower. In each face of the belfry stage is a three-light window with an outer ogee-arch and the wall above is overlaid with gabled panelling. Crocketed pinnacles rise from the parapets at the angles and intermediately, in contrast with the parapets of the lantern. Work on the south-western tower was at an end by 1447, and though twenty-five years later the north-western tower is a replica of the earlier. Both are 2 feet less in height than the lantern at the crossing.

The new Gothic cathedral of York was consecrated in 1472, and the same year William Hyndley, the famous mason from Norwich undertook the erection of the pulpitum that encloses the choir at the west (p. 117). By the end of the fifteenth century, the cathedral had been entirely rebuilt as it now stands, and since then it has suffered few changes other than those rendered necessary by fire and decay.

The mistake the mediaeval builders made was to cover the church with timber vaulting, a shortcoming that was to spell disaster sooner or later. One night in February 1829, a maniac named Martin secreted himself in the cathedral after evensong, and when all was quiet, he set fire to the choir. The woodwork, the stalls, the organ and the wooden high vault were totally destroyed and much of the masonry was calcined. The cost of restoration amounted to £65,000. In May 1840, a less disastrous fire that broke out in the south-western tower, wrought considerable damage to the stonework and destroyed the timber vault of the nave. Another £23,000 was needed for restoration.

NORWICH CATHEDRAL, 1362–1520

Uninfluenced by the eastern extensions that had been effected in many Norman cathedrals during the thirteenth century, the peri-apsidal choir of Norwich cathedral remained untouched for two and a half centuries, save for the elongation of the Lady Chapel. But in 1361 the timber spire that had been added to the central tower in the preceding century was blown down by a violent gale of wind, and falling eastwards it ruined the clerestory of the Norman choir. Here was an opportunity not to be lost of dispelling the darkness of the choir, by erecting a lofty clerestory that would be a wall of glass. Accordingly, a new top stage was built, pierced with tall windows of four lights that are Decorated to Perpendicular in character. Above the clerestory, which added 11 feet to the height of the choir, was built a timber roof; the high vault was yet to come. At the same time, square-headed windows of four lights were inserted in the outer wall of the triforium chamber, above the small round-headed Norman lights.

So effectual was the new fenestration of the choir, that a few years later the desire for a lighter nave led to the construction of curvilinear windows in the walls of the aisles, and the outer wall of the triforium was raised several feet to permit of large windows that would cast light across the upper part of the western arm of the cathedral.

Further reconstructions were carried out at Norwich in the fifteenth century. The cloisters were remodelled, the west front was subjected to alterations, and high vaults were built over the nave and the choir. The original Norman cloisters had been destroyed in 1272, when the turbulent citizens of Norwich besieged and set fire to the monastic buildings. The work of rebuilding was commenced by Bishop Ralph Walpole in 1297, but was held up for a long period by the Black Death of 1349. As a result the cloister walks were not completely finished until c. 1430. In their design is displayed the development of Gothic from the Geometric to the Perpendicular period; it is mainly in the traceried arcades and in minor detail that differences in style are apparent. The cloisters are situated to the south of the nave, the four walks enclosing a garth 145 feet square (Fig. 12). Above the eastern, western and southern walks are apartments that were put to various uses by the monks. In each bay of the arcading is a three-light opening; in the east walk, which is the earliest, completed c. 1325, the tracery is Geometric and is supported by slender shafts with capitals and bases. The so-called prior's door that opens into the south aisle of the nave in the north-east angle of the cloisters is a veritable masterpiece of Decorated Gothic, remarkable for the seven canopied figures that radiate across the arch-mouldings. In the centre is a seated figure of Our Lord, and on either side are S. John Baptist, S. Peter, S. Edmund and Moses. The arcades of the south walk, dating from 1327–50, are Curvilinear Gothic, and those of the western walk which were completed c. 1430 are Perpendicular.

The Norman cloisters had timber roofs but the present Gothic walks are covered with tierceron vaults of stone. In the forty-nine bays there are more than three hundred figure-bosses, exhibiting a great variety of subjects. In the east walk is a series forming a definite scheme, illustrative of the Passion of Our Lord together with many foliage bosses; no less than a hundred in the south and west walks represent subjects from the Apocalypse, probably inspired by illuminations of the East Anglican School; and in the north walk is a sequence of post-Resurrection incidents as well as other bosses portraying the Virgin Mary and legends of the saints. In 1428 when the cloisters were all but complete, James Wooderoffe was master-mason and his assistants were John Horne and William Reppys, both of whom received payment for carving six bosses in the north walk.

Despite the larger windows in the aisles and in the triforium of the nave, the lighting of that part of the cathedral was far from satisfactory, and steps were taken to remedy the defect by Bishop Alnwick, 1426–36. Before his translation to the see of Lincoln, he constructed the central doorway in the west front and made preparations for inserting a lofty window above it, the full width of the nave. The bishop made provision in his will for the west window which was finished by his successor. Of mature Perpendicular design, the window is of nine lights crossed by a transom (Pl. 90).

In the newly lighted interior, the timber roof of the nave showed up badly, and ever present was the menace of destruction by fire. Realizing that safety lay only in a stone vault, the convent took down the wooden roof, and in its place was put up a lierne vault of elaborate design (Pl. 89). At his death Bishop William Lyhart, 1446–72, made a bequest of 2,000 marks to further the work. In the high vault of the nave are two hundred and fifty-five bosses, carved with subjects from the Creation to the Last Judgment, arranged in series about incidents depicted on the central bosses, and comprising an epitome of Scripture history.

In the year 1463 whilst the masons were busy on the nave vault the timber spire of the central tower was fired by lightning, and the blazing mass fell eastwards and destroyed the wooden roof of the presbytery. The spire was rebuilt in stone, after which Bishop Goldwell, 1472–99, erected the lierne vault of the choir. There are few figure-bosses in the high vault, but of note are the Assumption of the Virgin and the Trinity. Flying buttresses were built at an acute angle to support the vault, the choir piers that had suffered damage from the fire were recased with Perpendicular masonry, and the Norman arches of the choir arcades were replaced by four-centred arches.

In 1509 Norwich cathedral was again visited by fire, and the roofs of the transepts were burned out. It fell to Bishop Nykke, 1501–35, to complete the fireproofing of the cathedral by covering both transepts with stone vaulting. Of the hundred and fifty bosses in the lierne vaults of the transepts, the majority portray scenes in the early life of Christ, such as the Shepherds, the Nativity and the Flight into Egypt, as well as incidents from New Testament history.

An exquisite specimen of Perpendicular work of the sixteenth century is the stone screen in the south transept that fills the Norman arch opening into the south aisle of the choir. The screen is composed of eighteen lights grouped in threes, and at the base is a doorway with a four-centred arch. The design is in perfect harmony with its setting.

WORCESTER CATHEDRAL, 1360–1504

The building of the nave of Worcester cathedral had come to a sudden halt about 1330 (p. 243), and the work was not resumed until after the Black Death. By c. 1375 the two unfinished bays of the north nave arcade and seven on the south side were built. Bishop Henry Wakefield, 1375–94, pushed on with the work energetically, and during his rule the high vault of the nave, the north-west porch and the central tower were erected. To him also are attributed the cloisters that had been commenced in 1372. By the end of the century the cathedral was complete.

The bays of the nave dating from c. 1360 are early Perpendicular in style, the design of the piers, the triforium arcade and the clerestory lights following in the main that of the earlier bays, though minor differences appear. In the south arcade the shafts of the piers are less pronounced and each has its own capital, unlike the encircling foliage of the Decorated piers on the north. The three-light windows of the clerestory and the openings on either side have straight-sided arches, a peculiarity that is less marked here than in the north transept of Hereford cathedral. The triforium arcade consists of two main arches with two sub-arches.

1*

The curious treatment of the springers of the tierceron vault on the north side make it evident that the masons of the early fourteenth century intended covering the nave with a quadripartite vault. As the south aisle abutted on to the north walk of the cloisters, the wall was raised so that windows could be inserted above the cloister roof; a lierne vault was erected over the aisle. The west front was rebuilt, the chief feature of which was an eight-light Perpendicular window, now replaced by a nineteenth-century substitute. The porch at the north-west, vaulted in two bays, has an upper chamber; the north front of the porch was entirely renewed a century since.

The central tower dating from 1374 rises to a height of 196 feet. Early in the present century, the external masonry had crumbled and decayed to such an extent that the whole of it had to be renewed. It is designed in two stages; the lower is faced with panelling, and in the upper are a pair of two-light windows with crocketed gables. At each angle of the parapet is a crocketed pinnacle.

The cloisters, that lie to the south of the nave, form an irregular quadrangle, the eastern walk being 5 feet longer than the others. The outer walls are substantially Norman, but the cloister arcades with five-light Perpendicular windows, and the vaults date from late in the fourteenth century. An uncommon feature is the flowing tracery that is applied as ornament to the soffits of the arcades; and the lierne vaulting is of singular interest, for the number and variety of the carved bosses. In the centre of the south walk is one representing the Coronation of the Virgin, surrounded by smaller bosses of kings and angels, and at the western end is the Tree of Jesse. In the vault of the north walk is the Madonna and Child, encircled by angels and archangels.

On the south side of the choir of Worcester cathedral, in the bay adjoining the High Altar, and seen to advantage from the choir transept, is the stately chantry chapel of Prince Arthur, the eldest son of Henry VII, who died at Ludlow castle five months after his marriage to Princess Katherine of Aragon in 1501. The chapel is a sumptuous example of Tudor Gothic, begun in 1504 and in its architectural character it bears affinity to Henry VII's chapel at Westminster abbey, and was probably the work of Westminster masons. The enclosing stone screens are divided into compartments by slender paired buttresses faced with tiers of niched figures, the intervening spaces being filled with open rectilinear panels, which are blind at the angles of the chapel. Less than halfway up is a range of solid panels, each embellished with a Tudor badge—the rose, the portcullis, the falcon and open fetterlock, the rose-en-soleil and the sheaf of arrows. The whole is surmounted by a parapet of open panels, with pinnacles rising from the buttresses. The interior of the chapel is richly overlaid with panelling and against the east wall is the reredos of the altar, four niches of which retain their figures, somewhat mutilated. The vaulting of the chapel is almost flat and is covered with traceried panelling, into which a flying-arch cuts at the east and west. In the centre stands the granite tomb of Prince Arthur, with no other ornament than the arms of England and France in the panels on its sides.

Winchester Cathedral, 1367–1450

The adventurous spirit of Gothic that had draped the choir of Gloucester in a mantle of Rectilinear masonry is again manifest in the 'Perpendicularing' of the nave of Winchester cathedral. Its structural core from pavement to roof is the Norman building of Bishop Walkelyn's time, though it presents to the eye a perfect specimen of Penpendicular Gothic.

In the middle of the fourteenth century, the north side of Walkelyn's nave was falling into disrepair and Bishop William Edingdon, 1346–66 embarked on the remodelling a few years before his death. He tore down the old Norman west front and erected the present façade, together with the western extremities of the aisles. By his will, dated 1366, the bishop made provision for the furtherance of the rebuilding, which for some reason made little progress for nearly thirty years. Edingdon's successor, the famous William of Wykeham, had been Surveyor of the King's works at Windsor castle since 1356, and by virtue of his office was empowered to impress masons, artisans and labourers, and to provide stone, timber and other materials for the rebuilding in progress there. On his election to the see of Winchester, he immediately set about repairing the twelve episcopal palaces, upon which he expended the enormous sum of 20,000 marks. In 1394 Wykeham resumed work on the cathedral nave that was pursued with vigour until his death in 1404. His patronage of the scheme and his lifelong interest in architectural works led his biographer to assert the nave was William of Wykeham's work and that 'the designs were mainly due to him'. His will, dated 24 July 1403 (p. 301), furnishes information concerning the progress of the nave and of the mode in which the building operations were organized. 'I will and ordain that my executors shall cause to be constructed the body or middle part (of the cathedral), between the north and south aisles, from the west door of the choir as far as the west end, in its walls, windows and vault, handsomely and well, according to the form and manner of the new work of the aisles now begun ... and they shall complete the said aisles through the same extent in length (as the nave). And they shall expend upon the works as much as 2,000 marks, if so much be required for its completion.' Bishop Wykeham also bequeathed 500 marks for the glazing of the windows in the south aisle and the clerestory, and 'if then any portion of the sum remains, I will that it be expended upon the windows of the north aisle'. A good part of the nave had risen at the time of Wykeham's death in 1404, and to his executors fell the task of completing the aisles, the clerestories and the high vault. The bosses of the nave vault bear the heraldic devices of Cardinal Beaufort and Bishop Waynflete, the immediate successors of William of Wykeham, and afford evidence that the high vault was not finished before 1450.

The method of converting the Norman bay design of three equal stages into a Perpendicular elevation of two storeys without demolishing the whole of the Norman masonry was a daring conception, executed with consummate skill, and constitutes one of the marvels of mediaeval building (Pl. 85). Without disturbing the old piers, the low Norman arches of the nave arcades were taken down, the sub-arches of the triforium were knocked out, leaving the containing arch which is hidden behind the balustrading of the Perpendicular clerestory. Ingenious and unprecedented were the methods employed in remodelling the piers. The eight western piers of the south nave arcade were merely re-chiselled with Perpendicular mouldings, a task that proved so laborious that all the other piers were recased with Caen stone that had been cut with Perpendicular mouldings.[1] The stout Norman vaulting shafts however were retained and rise above the vault to the top of the clerestory walls. Twelve bays in length, the nave of Winchester is Norman in bulk and largely in substance, but is Perpendicular in form. The piers are twelve feet thick, only one foot less than the width of the aisles. In the two-storeyed bay design, the balustrade at the base of the clerestory is all that remains of the triforium. The three-light windows of the clerestory have arches that are almost straight-sided and the lierne vault of the nave is remarkable for the absence of diagonal ribs and for the innumerable bosses. Of undistinguished design for a great cathedral is Edingdon's west front, the main feature of which is the Perpendicular window of nine lights. Beneath is a projecting porch with a gallery above. The gable of the nave and the turrets flanking it are adorned with rectilinear panelling.

[1] The lower parts of the second pair of piers from the crossing retain their Norman shafts and capitals, which were buried in the masonry of the rood screen that spanned the nave at this point. Only the upper parts of these piers therefore were recased with Perpendicular masonry (Pl. 88).

Very fitting is it that Bishop Edingdon and William of Wykeham should erect chantry chapels in the nave that they had transformed. That of Bishop Edingdon stands in the second bay from the crossing on the south side, and is the earliest of its kind in Winchester cathedral. It is of comparatively small dimensions and the enclosing screens of stone are simple in design, consisting of two ranges of open panelling above a low plinth. Within the chapel is the tomb of the bishop with his effigy in pontificalibus. On a more imposing scale is the elegant chapel of William of Wykeham, in the fifth bay from the west on the south side. A clause in his will shows that it was built during his lifetime. 'Item, I desire that my body be buried in the middle of a certain chapel by me newly erected on the south side of the nave.' He directed that three chantry monks should recite masses at the altar in the chapel thrice daily, each of whom was to receive one penny a day; the boy choristers who sang there nightly were to be paid 6s. 8d. a year. Wykeham's chapel fills the whole of one bay of the nave, from the pavement to the balustrade of the clerestory, and is thus half the height of the nave. The screen-walls of the chapel are conceived as large three-light windows with slender mullions, the lower part consisting of two tiers of Perpendicular lights above a range of blind panels. The altar in the chapel is backed by a reredos of two tiers of canopied niches tenanted by modern figures, and the lierne vault is enriched with gilt bosses. In the middle of the chapel stands the tomb of the founder, on which rests an effigy clad in episcopal vestments; two angels support his head and at his feet are three seated figures. In the sides of the tomb are niches containing heraldic shields, including the arms of the see and of Bishop Wykeham.

Towards the close of the fifteenth century the Early English Lady Chapel at Winchester, being too small to accommodate all the brethren for the daily Mass of Our Lady, was doubled in length by the addition of an eastern bay (Fig. 9). The rebus bosses in the lierne vault show that the extension was the work of Priors Hunton and Silkstede, c. 1487–1500. In the northern, eastern and southern walls is a large seven-light window and the vault is of a complex design. On the walls are the remains of paintings that were executed under the direction of Prior Silkstede in 1489 (p. 138).

Preoccupied as were Bishops Edingdon and Wykeham in the second half of the fourteenth century with the remodelling of the nave of the cathedral, they left the presbytery that had been transformed to a large extent early in the century, in an unfinished state. Much remained to do, and strangely enough the choir was still incomplete when Bishop Fox was translated to Winchester in

1500. He at once set to work on the choir, the completion of which bears witness to his interest in the fabric. The eastern gable was rebuilt smothered with Perpendicular panelling and a seven-light window was constructed in the wall beneath; the Norman aisles were covered with lierne vaults and the walls opened up with four-light windows. The flying-buttresses that span the aisle-roofs are evidence that a high vault of stone was intended for the choir. To save expense an imitation lierne ceiling of wood was erected, remarkable for the brilliantly coloured bosses including arms and badges of the Lancastrian and Tudor families. In the easternmost bay all the bosses bear emblems of the Passion or are carved with subjects connected with the sufferings and death of Our Lord, such as the betrayal by Judas and Peter's denial. The central and most arresting feature of the choir is the Fox reredos (p. 120), elaborate in design and exquisite in its carved detail. Of particular interest are the stone screens dividing the choir from its aisles, erected by Bishop Fox. Carved in low relief on the frieze is a band of antique ornament, evidence of the oncoming of the Renaissance. In the bay adjoining the High Altar on the south is Bishop Fox's chantry chapel, the most ornate in Winchester cathedral.

The dignity of the choir is enhanced by its elevation above the level of the nave, due to the Norman crypt below. There is an ascent of eight steps from the nave, and several more eastwards up to the sanctuary.

EXETER CATHEDRAL, 1370–1520

By the middle of the fourteenth century the whole of the Norman cathedral of Exeter had been swept away, with the exception of the transeptal towers, and in its place had arisen a Gothic church of single and unified design. The west end of the nave having been completed by Bishop Grandisson, the same prelate began the screen of imagery, unparalleled in any English cathedral, that was tacked on to the west front (p. 111). It was finished by his successor, Bishop Brantynham, c. 1390. In the Fabric Roll of 1375, an entry headed 'ad frontem ecclesie', relating to the screen, records payments to John Pratt, *imaginator*, for 9½ weeks' work at 9d. to 10d. a day. The screen, which is crowned with a battlemented parapet, is about one-third of the height of the west front and exhibits an assemblage of niched statues disposed in three tiers, the lowest of which consists of angelic figures. In the topmost tier, uninterrupted by the portals of the nave and aisles, are thirty-five figures of saints, apostles and kings of Wessex, and one of Richard II; and in the row beneath are thirty statues, mainly of

English kings from Canute to Edward III. Between the screen and the west wall of the nave, to the south of the central portal is a cavernous recess that was the chantry chapel of Bishop Grandisson, d. 1369. It was roofed with a pointed barrel vault and the tomb of the bishop was set up in a recess in the east wall, but was thrown out in Elizabeth I's reign.

In the last decade of the fourteenth century, more light being needed in the sanctuary, the large nine-light Perpendicular window in the east wall was substituted for the existing window; the cost was borne by Henry Blakeborn, one of the canons.

To the early years of the sixteenth century belong the fine series of Perpendicular screens of stone that were built to enclose the many chapels in the choir-arm of the cathedral.

CANTERBURY CATHEDRAL, 1363–1495

The earliest Perpendicular Gothic at Canterbury cathedral is in the paired apsidal chapels of the Norman crypt, beneath the south choir transept. In 1363 the chapels were appropriated by Edward the Black Prince, son of Edward III, for the two chantries he founded in pious acknowledgment of the Papal dispensation granted for his union with his cousin Joan, the Fair Maid of Kent. At Prince Edward's expense, the Norman masonry of the chapels was clothed in Perpendicular garb and altars were dedicated to the Holy Trinity and the Blessed Virgin. The walls of the apses were pierced with three-light windows, the piers were cased with clustered shafts, and lierne vaults enriched with carved bosses replaced the Norman vaulting. One of the bosses is a female head, said to represent the Fair Maid, and another is a lively rendering of Samson, with the head of a lion or an ass beneath his arm. The Black Prince died in 1376 and by his will ordained that he should be buried in the chapel of Our Lady Undercroft in the crypt; he also left precise details for the making of his tomb. His wish to be buried in comparative obscurity of the crypt was however disregarded by the convent, who opined that the tomb of so illustrious a prince should be set up on a more hallowed spot, near the shrine of S. Thomas. Accordingly it was erected between the coupled columns on the south side of the Saint's chapel, and with its magnificent bronze effigy presents a superb example of fourteenth-century craftsmanship.

Other than the re-fashioning of the crypt chapels for the chantries of the Black Prince, the fabric of Canterbury cathedral was subjected to no substantial changes until the last quarter of the fourteenth century, when the Norman nave of Lanfranc's cathedral was falling into a perilous state. A new nave, more in scale and harmony with the choir-arm was long overdue. The undertaking involved the rebuilding of the Norman transepts and strengthening the piers at the crossing. In 1377 Archbishop Sudbury issued an appeal for funds throughout the diocese, granting an indulgence of forty days to all benefactors. The new nave and transepts constitute one work; they are uniform in style and furnish an example of early Perpendicular Gothic, contemporaneous with the nave of Winchester. The work commenced in 1377 with the reconstruction of the transepts, the Norman apsidal chapels to the east of which were not removed. Noteworthy are the expansive Perpendicular windows of eight lights in the end walls of the transepts.

The rebuilding of the nave was begun at the western end and for twenty-five years proceeded eastwards. The Norman piers and arcades were pulled down; only the plinths of the aisle walls and the piers at the crossing were spared. In the design of the new nave the verticality of Perpendicular Gothic is triumphant. In order to gain an effect of enormous altitude, the masons threw the arches of the nave up to an abnormal height at the expense of the clerestory; the main lighting is therefore provided by the unduly lofty windows of the aisles, and the top-lighting is of secondary importance. Characteristic of Perpendicular Gothic is the suppression of the triforium, the shafted and moulded piers and their insignificant capitals. The transepts, the nave and its aisles have lierne vaults with multitudinous bosses, many of which display heraldic devices. In the western wall of the nave is a Perpendicular window of seven lights. In preparation for a new tower the piers at the crossing were recased with masonry. The major part of the Perpendicular transformation was executed during the priorate of Thomas Chillenden, 1391–1411, who is described by Leland as 'the great setter-forth of the new body of the building of the church'.

Prior Chillenden also erected the pulpitum at the entrance to the choir (p. 116), and before the end of the century he had persuaded the convent of Christ Church to rebuild the cloister walks and enlarge the chapter house. Here, as at Gloucester, the cloisters lie to the north of the nave, away from the noise and bustle of the city. A partial reconstruction of the walks had taken place in the thirteenth century, remnants of which are to be seen in the wall-arcading of the north walk and the doorway opening into the north transept. In the main the cloisters are work of the Perpendicular period, begun c. 1397. The arcades consist of four-light openings, the arches of which are surmounted by curved gables. Outstanding is the magnificent series of heraldic and other bosses, eight hundred and eleven in all, that occur in the lierne vaulting. The coats of arms there displayed are those of persons and places connected with the history of Christ Church, and of the many benefactors who contributed to the cost of the rebuilding. The pristine splendour of the vaulting has been revived by Professor Tristram, who recoloured and gilded the bosses about eighteen years ago. The rectangular chapter house is a mixture of Early English and Perpendicular Gothic. The lower parts of the walls, faced with thirteenth-century arcading are the work of Prior Eastrey, and above is the walling of Prior Chillenden's masons. In the east and west walls are seven-light windows, and the building has a waggon roof of timber smothered with an intricate network of panelling, richly coloured and gilded.

Prior Chillenden's scheme for rebuilding the nave of the cathedral had embraced the rearing of twin towers at the west, in place of Lanfranc's Norman towers, but after his death the convent was burdened with a legacy of debt, and more urgent was the completion of the cloisters. Several years passed before work was started on the south-west tower, and the Chicheley steeple as it is called, was not finished before c. 1458. The master-mason who supervised its erection was Thomas Mapilton of Westminster abbey. At the base of the tower is a two-storeyed porch, the front and sides of which are faced with two tiers of niched figures. The lierne vaulting within the porch has twenty-nine heraldic bosses, of which the central one bears the shield of Henry VI. Until 1834, the Norman tower at the north-west remained untouched, a somewhat incongruous partner of the Chicheley steeple.

Whilst work on the south-west tower was in progress, alterations were taking place in Chillenden's transepts, which had retained the Norman apses at the east. About the year 1430, the widowed Lady Margaret Holland, desirous of founding a memorial chapel for herself and her two husbands, John, Earl of Somerset, and Thomas, Earl of Clarence, was granted permission to take down the apse of the south transept and erect a larger chapel on the site, dedicated to S. Michael and All Angels.[1] It was begun in 1439, only a few days before the founder's death. Curiously the chapel is not set square with the transept but inclines to the south (Fig. 16). In the east wall is a Perpendicular window of five lights and the ornate lierne vault has bosses carved with the arms of Lady Holland and her husbands. On the slab of the huge monument in the centre of the chapel are alabaster effigies of all three.

The new chapel roused the envy of the monks of Christ Church,

---

[1] It now serves as the chapel of the Royal East Kent Regiment, and the reredos of oak was erected as a War Memorial of the Buffs,

who had long felt the need of a more conveniently situated Lady Chapel. 'Our Lady Undercroft' in the crypt was cold and draughty in winter, nor was it easy of access. The only altar dedicated to the Virgin above ground stood within a screened enclosure in the north aisle of the nave. The brethren therefore decided to build a new Lady Chapel to the east of the north transept on the site of the Norman apse (Fig. 16). It was commenced in 1448 and within seven years the chapel was finished. It is noteworthy for its recti-linear windows, the fan vault and the Perpendicular screen fenc-ing it at the west.

A minor work, built at the expense of the Crown, was the tiny chantry chapel of Henry IV, d. 1413, which was inserted between two buttresses off the north ambulatory of the choir (Fig. 16). Henry IV breathed his last in the abbot's house at Westminster, but had no love for the monks of S. Peter's, and by his will dated 1409, the King ordained that his body should be buried in Can-terbury cathedral, and left specific instructions for the building of a chapel near to his tomb, where was to be 'a chauntrie per-petuell with twey prestis for to sing and pray for my soul'. The chapel was not erected for many years after his death. The altar was dedicated to Edward Confessor in 1437, and scratched on the wall is an item referring to the cost of the reredos. 'Ye middel image was 19s. 11d.' The little building is lighted by two Perpen-dicular windows in the outer wall and is roofed with a fan vault. Close by, on the north side of the Saint's chapel stands the royal tomb with alabaster effigies of Henry IV and his Queen, Joan of Navarre, d. 1437.

The supreme achievement of the fifteenth-century masons at Canterbury is the graceful central tower known as the Angel Steeple, so called from the gilded figure of an angel that formerly crowned one of its pinnacles. Unrivalled amongst the central towers of our mediaeval cathedrals, it rises to a height of 235 feet (Pl. 92). In anticipation, the piers that carry it had been strengthen-ed by Prior Chillenden but the actual construction was deferred until c. 1433. The master-mason who designed the upper stages of the tower and supervised the operations was Richard Beck. A letter from Prior Selling, 1472–94, to Cardinal-Archbishop Morton is not without interest. 'Most reverend father in God, the master surveyor and I have communed with John Wastell your mason, to preserve what form and shape he will keep in raising of the pinnacles of your new tower here. He drew unto us two patterns of them. . . . I think he might provide that these pinnacles may be finished this next summer following. Then your tower outward would appear perfect.' And a perfect work it is today, the outstanding glory of the exterior of the cathedral. The angle turrets with their slender radiating buttresses were the conception of a master mind, and emphasize the verticality eagerly sought by the architects of late Gothic. From the crossing is seen the lovely fan vault of the tower, above which is a loft containing a large wheel that was used for hauling up the building materials. The core of the walls above the loft consists largely of red brick, a material that is mentioned in the records of 1458 and 1477. The Angel Steeple imposed a tremendous load on the piers at the crossing, and before the end of the century it was found necessary to stabilize them by girder arches of masonry (p. 107).

Little more than twenty years before the Suppression of Christ Church priory, was built the Great Gatehouse on the site of an earlier gateway at the south-west of the monastic precincts. Affording a beautiful example of Perpendicular Gothic, it stands at the end of Mercery Lane, and is a three-storeyed building with octagonal turrets at the angles. In the centre of the façade is a tall canopied niche that formerly contained a figure of Our Lord, and above the four-centred archway is a row of Tudor devices, resplendent in colour and gold. Below the windows of the top storey is a band of heraldic shields supported by winged angels.

WELLS CATHEDRAL, 1370–1460

By the middle of the fourteenth century, all that the cathedral of S. Andrew, Wells, lacked was the upper stages of the western towers. Otherwise the impress of Rectilinear Gothic is stamped on features of minor importance only. The south-western tower was raised to its present height during the rule of Bishop John Harewell, 1367–86, who made a bequest of money for the work. To preserve a unity of design, the buttresses of the Perpendicular stages of the tower conformed with those of the lower and earlier stages, and the fenestration repeats that of the central tower. About forty years later, the tower at the north-west was completed, in general design a copy of the Harewell tower, though differing in detail and in height. On the western face is a niched figure of Bishop Nicholas Bubwith, d. 1424, who left a legacy towards the cost of the tower. The angle buttresses of both towers are carried up about two-thirds of the height, and there are two two-light belfry windows in the faces.

About the year 1440 the chapter of Wells embarked on the building of the cloisters, that are situated to the south of the nave, and as at Hereford, are without a northern walk (Fig. 17). Early in the thirteenth century Bishop Jocelin had erected a covered way from the south transept to the bishop's palace, and the outer wall was retained when the east cloister walk was commenced *c.* 1440, by the executors of Bishop Bubwith. Measuring 170 feet in length the east walk stops short at the south transept, and above the northern half is a library, entered from the transept by a vice. The southern part of the library is much later, the square-headed windows in the outer wall dating from 1670. The west walk of the cloisters, that is in alignment with the towers and has an upper storey, was erected by Bishop Beckington, 1443–65, who also completed the Vicars' Close. The south walk was mainly the work of Thomas Henry, the treasurer of the cathedral. By 1460 all the walks were finished. In each bay is a six-light Perpendicular window looking on to the garth and the walks have lierne vaults enriched with sculptured bosses, many of which are square-framed. Others are carved with cressets, the badge of Bishop Beckington, and with angels bearing shields of the emblems of the Passion. The Fabric Roll of 1458 records the payment of £6 11s. 3d., plus a bonus of 10s. to John Turpyn the mason, who executed vaulting in the east walk.

In the last quarter of the fifteenth century, a magnificent Lady Chapel, cruciform on plan and roofed with a fan vault, was built to the east of the cloisters (Fig. 17), but it was razed to the ground in 1552.

LINCOLN CATHEDRAL, 1370–1545

The final phase of English Gothic left comparatively little mark on the fabric of Lincoln cathedral. The principal undertaking was the addition of upper stages to the western towers, which hitherto had been dwarfed by the colossal screen-façade behind which they crouched. The Perpendicular belfry stages, commenced *c.* 1380, imparted a total height of 206 feet to the twin towers; rising far above the parapet of the façade, they have been likened to prisoners in the dock. In each face of the towers are two rectilinear windows of two lights and at the angles are octagonal turrets crowned with pinnacles. Both towers were finished with timber spires that were taken down in 1807. Whilst the work was in progress, the Early English windows in the three recesses of the west front were filled with Perpendicular tracery.

At the other end of Lincoln cathedral, Perpendicular Gothic asserted itself in three charming little chantry chapels built between the buttresses on the north and south sides of the Angel Choir. The earliest is the chapel of Bishop Richard Fleming d. 1431, on the north side, dedicated to the Holy Trinity (Fig. 20). The front facing the choir has three pendant arches, beneath which is the tomb of the bishop with his effigy thereon. Below is a cadaver to remind beholders of mortal decay. The little building is lighted with Perpendicular windows and has a timber roof, adorned with carvings of oak foliage and the vine. The two other chapels to the south of the Angel Choir, one on each side of the Judgment Porch (Fig. 20), were modelled on that of Bishop Fleming. East of the porch is the chapel of S. Blaise, founded by Bishop John Russell, d. 1495; and west of the porch is the chapel of S. Katherine, founded for the soul of Bishop Longland, d. 1547.

PETERBOROUGH CATHEDRAL, 1370–1510

Save for the Gothic portico at the west, Peterborough cathedral remained a Norman building in its entirety until late in the fourteenth century, when a two-storeyed porch was inserted in the central bay of the three-arched west front. Of the Perpendicular period also are many windows that took the place of Norman windows, and last but not least the 'New Building' at the extreme east of the cathedral.

About the year 1370, under the thrusts of the lateral arches of the colossal portico at the west, the two supporting piers showed a tendency to bulge inwards, and to avoid collapse a lofty porch was erected between the piers, 'the construction of which is extremely scientific, especially in the manner in which the thrusts are distributed through the side turrets so as to fall on the buttresses in front' (*Paley*). This 'unsightly encumbrance' as it has been called certainly fulfilled its structural purpose, and is an instance of the resources of the mediaeval mason when confronted by a problem of stability (Fig. 13).

Although the general remodelling of the choirs of Norman cathedrals was a thing long past, the conservative monks of Peterborough had contented themselves for more than three and a half centuries with the parallel-apsed choir of the early twelfth century. During the rule of Abbot Ashton, 1438–71, however, was begun the 'New Building', a squared retrochoir to the east of the apses and of the same width as the choir and its aisles (Pl. 91). The Norman lateral apses were pulled down, the walls of the aisles were continued eastwards and squared, and the central apse was pierced with three arches on the ground level (Fig. 13). The new retrochoir that provided accommodation for five altars against the east wall was flooded with light. In the east wall are five large Perpendicular windows and there are four in each of the side walls. The 'New Building' was completed by Abbot Kirton, 1496–1528, and to him is attributed the fan vaulting of exquisite detail, resembling that of King's College Chapel, Cambridge, though on a smaller scale. Amongst the bosses in the vault appear the Tudor rose, the portcullis, crowns pierced with arrows and many other devices. Externally, the massive buttresses that counteract the thrusts of the vault are surmounted by seated figures of the Apostles, and the merlons of the pierced parapet are gabled, a distinctive feature of late Perpendicular architecture.

SOUTHWELL CATHEDRAL, 1390–1450

In their desire for adequate lighting neither secular nor monastic chapters showed any scruples in disfiguring or effacing architectural features of an earlier age. Like all Norman naves, that of Southwell was intolerably dark, and to remedy this defect, rectilinear windows of three lights were pierced in the walls of the aisles *c.* 1390. Apparently the new windows left much to be desired, for in 1450 the small Norman windows in the west front of the church were removed and a large Perpendicular window of seven lights was substituted, occupying almost the whole of the wall between the Norman towers from portal to parapet.

ELY CATHEDRAL, 1395–1533

In the closing years of the fourteenth century, the convent at Ely crowned the single tower at the west of the cathedral with an octagonal lantern of stone to harmonize with the Octagon at the crossing. To pile up additional weight on a tower carried by Norman arches was a risky undertaking and new sustaining arches were therefore built at the base. The lantern, flanked at the angles by octagonal turrets, has three-light windows in each face and is surmounted by a battlemented parapet. Support is given to the lantern by small flying-buttresses. Despite the strengthening of the tower arches, the north-western transept subsequently broke away from the tower and had to be taken down (Pl. 58).

Late in the fifteenth century Bishop John Alcock, 1486–1500, appropriated the easternmost bay of the north aisle of the choir and transformed it into a Perpendicular chantry chapel, remarkable for the extraordinary richness of its architectural make-up, though it is now mutilated and shorn of many figures that formerly tenanted the niches. The chapel was enclosed on the west and south by stone screens laden with a mass of tabernacled canopies. Recurring again and again in the carved masonry is the Bishop's rebus, a cock on a globe, a device that appears in the small windows flanking the doorway. Large windows were inserted in the outer walls of the chapel and a fan vault with a central pendant was put up (Fig. 19). The corresponding bay at the end of the south choir aisle was subjected to the same process for the chantry chapel of Bishop Nicholas West, 1515–34. Less ornate than the

Alcock chapel, it is rather larger, the original eastern wall having been torn down and a new wall built farther east. The chapel is particularly noteworthy for the tiers of canopied niches with which the walls are covered, varying in form, size and decoration, and sufficient in number to house two hundred figures or more. The vault is overlaid with traceried panels and retains much of its colour. On the vault surfaces are painted the arms of the see of Ely and of Bishop West. Above the portal are panels enriched with antique ornament in low relief, heralding the advent of Renaissance art.

CHICHESTER CATHEDRAL, 1392–1500

Important additions were made to Chichester cathedral in the Perpendicular period. Towards the end of the fourteenth century, the central tower was finished with a spire, rebuilt in 1861. The transition from tower to spire is masked by octagonal pinnacles at the base, and these together with the blind dormers in the faces of the spire produce a unified design. Bands of traceried ornament are carried round the spire at two levels.

The large curvilinear window of seven lights that had been set in the end wall of the south transept in the fourteenth century had so greatly improved the lighting of that part of the church, that c. 1410 a Perpendicular window of seven lights was inserted in the north transept; so clumsily however was this done that flying-buttresses had to be built to support the upper portion of the north wall.

Within a few years of the raising of the spire, the tower betrayed signs of insecurity, and about 1410 a detached tower to hold the bells was erected to the north-west of the cathedral (Fig. 10). The design is notable mainly for the two bold buttresses in each face and for the low octagonal stage above the parapet.

A work that occupied most of the fifteenth century was the building of the cloister walks, that are grouped about the south transept (Fig. 10). They afforded covered ways from the bishop's palace at the south-west to the cathedral and to the Vicars' Close at the south-east. The arcades of the cloisters are filled with Perpendicular windows of four lights and the three walks are covered with timber roofs.

HEREFORD CATHEDRAL, 1395–1520

For nearly three centuries the unaisled south transept of Hereford cathedral remained as the Norman builders had left it. Under Bishop Thomas Trevenant, 1389–1404, the end wall of the transept was rebuilt and large Perpendicular windows of six lights were inserted in the south and west walls. The timber roof was replaced by a tierceron vault, and the sacristy to the east of the transept was enlarged (Fig. 15). A few years later the canons of Hereford set about the erection of a chapter house and cloisters. The former, commenced c. 1412, was a ten-sided building situated to the east of the cloisters; only the entrance portal and fragments of three walls remain today. In 1418 Bishop Edmund Lacy began the cloister walks to the south of the nave, towards the cost of which Bishop Thomas Spofford, 1421–48, contributed 2,800 marks. Only the eastern and southern walks are now standing; a north walk was not built, and the western was demolished in Edward VI's reign (Fig. 15). The cloister arches are filled with Perpendicular openings of four lights, the tracery of which is unusually attractive. The southern end of the east walk and the bays of the south walk have lierne vaults, with numerous armorial bosses. A unique feature is the upper chamber above the east walk at the entrance to the chapter house; a polygonal turret at the southeastern angle contains the stairway to the upper chamber, which has the appearance of a square tower (Pl. 95). What mediaeval purpose it served is not known, though the large square-headed windows of many lights suggest a book-room.

Some distance to the east of the main cloisters is the vicars' cloister, a covered way that connected the college of the vicars-choral with the south choir transept (Fig. 15). Bishop John Stanbury, 1453–74, granted the vicars a part of the garden of the episcopal palace as a site for their buildings, which were erected south of their cloister. The entrance to the college has a fan vault and the covered way has a magnificent timber roof.

Projecting from the north aisle of the choir of Hereford cathedral is the fan-vaulted chantry chapel founded by Bishop Stanbury and erected during his lifetime. On a grander scale is the two-storeyed chantry chapel of Bishop Edmund Audley, 1492–1502, a semi-octagonal structure projecting from the south side of the Lady Chapel. Enclosing it from the Lady Chapel is a stone screen faced with two tiers of rectilinear panelling, and both storeys have fan vaults. The bishop was not buried in this splendid chapel, for shortly after its completion he was translated to the see of Salisbury, and in the choir of that cathedral he built another chapel where he was interred on his death in 1524.

A later and charming example of Perpendicular Gothic at Hereford is the outer bay of the north-west porch, built by Bishop Thomas Booth, the stone work of which bears the date of his death, 1535 (Pl. 93). The new bay that has an upper chamber, is attached to the smaller porch of the fourteenth century. It has open arches on three sides and is roofed with a lierne vault. At the angles are octagonal turrets containing stairways to the chamber above; and the turrets are lighted in the upper parts by square-headed windows, giving the effect of little stone lanterns. In each wall of the chamber is a richly traceried rectilinear window.

CARLISLE CATHEDRAL, 1400–20

More often than is recorded in the Middle Ages, a building project envisaged by a cathedral chapter was brought to nought or modified by a disastrous fire, a toppling tower, or an empty treasury; Carlisle is a case in point. When the new choir-arm was rebuilding after the fire of 1292 (p. 237), an operation that lasted for almost a century, the intention was to take down the Norman tower and the piers at the crossing and raise a central tower of the same width as the choir, after which the nave was to be rebuilt. But another fire at the end of the fourteenth century wrecked the north transept and put an end to the aspirations of the chapter. The transept was rebuilt on the old foundations and the canons had to content themselves with adding an upper stage to the old tower, the cost of which was met by Bishop William Strickland between 1401 and 1419. The tower which ranges with the narrow nave is not centrally situated in relation to the choir; hence the lop-sided appearance of the oaken pulpitum that was erected beneath the eastern arch at the crossing c. 1450. The choir entrance, being opposite the middle of the choir, immediately adjoins the tower pier on the north, but on the south it is flanked by the panelled front of the pulpitum (Fig. 14). Unpretentious in design, the tower of Carlisle rises two stages above the roof of the nave but only one above the choir roof. In the lower part are two windows, each of two lights, and the upper storey has a three-light window in each face. At the north-eastern angle is a turret that is carried above the embattled parapet.

SOUTHWARK CATHEDRAL, 1405–1520

The church of S. Mary Overie, Southwark, was again visited by the dread enemy fire at the end of the fourteenth century, as a result of which the south transept, less than a century old, was subjected to an extensive restoration that was made possible by the benefactions of Cardinal Beaufort, Bishop of Winchester, 1405–47. His part in the work is commemorated by the sculptured representation of a cardinal's hat and tasselled strings enclosing his arms, on the east wall of the transept. Perpendicular windows now restored were constructed in the end and side walls.

To another Bishop of Winchester, the famous Richard Fox, was the chapter indebted for the two upper stages of the tower at the crossing. Prior to 1510 the tower rose but a few feet above the roofing of the church. The upper stages are built of flint and stone; in the faces of each stage are two Perpendicular windows of two lights, and the tower terminates in a battlemented parapet with crocketed pinnacles at the angles. As a whole the design is undistinguished. Bishop Fox also erected the reredos of the High Altar, *c.* 1520; with its three tiers of canopied niches, occupying almost the whole of the eastern wall of the choir, the screen was obviously modelled on that of Winchester cathedral.

BRISTOL CATHEDRAL, 1460–1515

During the second half of the fifteenth century important works, promoted by Abbot Newbury, 1460–73, were in progress at Bristol. In 1466 Bishop Stillington of Bath and Wells granted the abbot the lease of a quarry at Dundry, Somerset, the stone from which was probably used for the building of the central tower of the abbey church. Newbury's successor, Abbot Hunt, completed the tower; the chapter was indebted to him for £240 at his death in 1481. The piers at the crossing were recased to carry the tower, which is remarkable for the five two-light windows in each face of its two stages. The vault of the tower is similar to that of the choir.

In the Rolls of the obedientiaries of S. Augustine's, Bristol, for the year 1491, John Martyn the prior and *magister novi operis* paid for the transport of waggon-loads of stone from Dundry quarry, which had been sublet for two years on the condition that the lessee delivered forty loads at Redcliffe Hill. Apparently the stone was required for the remodelling of the transepts that had been begun in 1473 and were not completed until *c.* 1515. Both transepts were rebuilt on the original Norman walling, much of which still remains. The two bays in each transept have lierne vaults with sculptured bosses, recoloured a few years ago by Prof. E. W. Tristram. Of special interest are the bosses in the north transept, one of which represents Edward II in his death agony, and others emblems of the Trinity and shields bearing the coats of arms of Our Lord and the Blessed Virgin.

From an entry in the Register of Abbot Nailheart (or Newland), 1481–1515, it appears that he started a rebuilding of the nave. The chronicler states that Abbot Newland built 'the fundacion of the body of the church to the sailis [sills] of the wyndos of the north side and the west end'. How much of the new nave was erected it is not possible to say, for it was all swept away together with the masonry of the old Norman nave in 1543. To Abbot Elyot, 1515–25, is ascribed the building of the cloisters, of which only the eastern walk was put up several feet to the south of the original, when the nave was built in the nineteenth century (p. 331).

RIPON CATHEDRAL, 1460–1520

The most vulnerable part of a great mediaeval church was always the central tower, subject as it was to collapse, or less often to destruction by fire after being struck by lightning. In 1458 the eastern and southern walls of the central tower of Ripon minster toppled over and wrecked part of the south arcade of the choir and the aisle of the south transept. For many years the choir was in disuse, the Divine offices being recited in an adjoining chapel. To furnish funds for the restoration, Archbishop William Booth granted indulgences to benefactors in 1459 and in 1477 the canons contributed one-half of their emoluments from the common fund of the college towards repairs. The task of restoration entailed the rebuilding of three western bays of the south choir arcade and of the transept arcade, the reinforcing of the piers at the crossing and the reconstruction of the tower arches. The south-eastern pier was entirely rebuilt but those at the north-east and south-west were merely recased, and to buttress the two eastern piers, the adjoining bays on both sides of the choir were filled in with solid masonry. The western semicircular arch of the crossing was not rebuilt; in conjunction with the recased pier at the south-west it presents a decidedly incongruous appearance. Otherwise, the masons preserved a harmony with the earlier work. The granting of an indulgence by Archbishop George Neville shows that the tower was partially repaired by 1465, though it is mentioned in the Fabric Roll of 1541–2.

Of the greater churches of England, Ripon was the only one in which the nave remained aisleless until the sixteenth century. A chapter minute of 1502 alludes to the task confronting the canons, in their resolve to transform the Transitional nave of their church (p. 181) into a Perpendicular nave with aisles on either side. The Fabric Roll of the following year records the purchase of stone, and in 1512 an indulgence was offered by Archbishop Baynbridge to all benefactors. The foundations of the north aisle of the nave are mentioned in the Roll of the same year. The solid walls of the old nave were pulled down and were replaced by north and south arcades, five bays in length, extending westwards to the thirteenth century towers (Fig. 23). The bay design of the new nave is that of a late Gothic parish church. From clustered piers spring arches of three orders; there is no triforium, but a large clerestory with a passage at the base of the five-light windows. In the walls of the aisles are Perpendicular windows of three lights. The records show that the nave was roofed in timber by 1521, and the greater part of the reconstruction was finished by 1528. The present roof of the nave and the vaults of the aisles date from Gilbert Scott's restoration of 1862–70.

ROCHESTER CATHEDRAL, 1470–1510

The same measures for improving the lighting of Southwell nave (p. 278) were adopted at Rochester cathedral. In the north aisle of the nave, and presumably in the south,[1] the Norman windows were knocked out and rectilinear ones of two lights substituted, and the wall of the west front above the Norman portal was opened up with an eight-light window c. 1470. Later, the clerestory wall of the nave being in an unsound condition was rebuilt and Perpendicular windows of three lights were inserted, a reconstruction that involved the removal of the flat Norman ceiling and the erection of an open timber roof.

The final addition to Rochester cathedral in pre-Reformation days was the western extension of the Lady Chapel, dating c. 1510. From the eleventh century an altar dedicated to the Virgin Mary stood in the south transept, together with another altar of unknown dedication. After the rebuilding of the transept late in the thirteenth century, the two arches in the eastern wall containing the altars were converted into one, beneath which was placed the altar of Our Lady, alluded to in the fourteenth-century Custumale as 'the altar of the Blessed Mary in the new work (*in novo operi*)'. Thenceforth the whole of the south transept served as the Lady Chapel, but in 1510 when more room was required to accommodate the monks at the Lady Masses, a western extension was built, flanking the south aisle of the nave; the outer wall of the chapel ranges with the end wall of the transept (Fig. 11). The three new bays served as the choir of the Lady Chapel and stalls were set up therein. The extension opens into the transept by one wide arch; the aisle-wall on the north was taken down and three lofty arches were built, beneath which stone screens were erected to enclose the chapel on the north. The transept also was fenced on the north by a screen. It was contemplated that the new bays should be covered with fan vaults that were to spring from two central columns, but ultimately a timber roof was put up. The chapel was lighted by Perpendicular windows in the south and west walls.

OXFORD CATHEDRAL, 1470–1524

For three centuries the canons of S. Frideswide, Oxford, had deferred the fireproofing of their Norman church, which retained

[1] The present windows in the south aisle are modern.

the timber ceilings until *c.* 1470. Then it was decided to vault the choir, the transepts and the nave in stone. By this time lierne vaulting was well established as the normal and fashionable type. In the construction of the high vault of the choir, elongated voussoirs or pendants were dropped from the transverse ribs, thus forming square compartments that were filled with lierne vaulting of stellar design; and the narrow space flanking the central compartment on either side was roofed with a segmental barrel vault (Pl. 97). The masons relied on the thickness of the Norman clerestory wall to support the vault and therefore dispensed with flying-buttresses. In preparation for the high vault of the nave, corbels were inserted in the clerestory wall, but the chapter were more intent upon rebuilding the cloisters, and the vaulting of the nave and transepts was abandoned. The open timber roof of the nave is attributed to Cardinal Wolsey, who shortened the nave of the priory church by three bays in 1524 and tore down the western walk of the cloisters to provide room for the quadrangle of Cardinal College at the west. The cloisters to the south of the nave had been completed before Wolsey's appropriation. The arches of the walks that remain are filled with Perpendicular windows of three lights.

S. David's Cathedral, 1472–1509

In a sense parallel with the high vault of Oxford choir and of the same period is the wonderful if not unique timber roof that covers the nave of S. David's cathedral, accredited to the treasurer, Owen Pole, 1472–1509. Structurally the roof is a flat ceiling, resting on tie-beams crossed by longitudinal timbers, at the intersections of which are dropped elongated pendants. The ceiling appears to be supported by segmental arches that are thrown from pendant to pendant, but the real supports are the great beams. The cusping of the arches, the spandrels pierced with tracery, and the colour lavished on the woodwork impart an effect of Oriental richness to this singular roof.

Chester Cathedral, 1485–1530

The rebuilding of the south transept and the nave of Chester cathedral had been brought to a sudden stop by the Black Death, and probably on account of an exhausted treasury, the work was not resumed before late in the fifteenth century. The fenestration of the upper part of the south transept is rectilinear. The nave arcades were not finished before *c.* 1490; the westernmost pier of the south arcade bears the initials of Abbot Simon Ripley, 1485–92. In the bay design everything above the nave arches is extremely plain and void of ornament and detail; the triforium is merely blank walling beneath the sills of the clerestory windows. Abbot Ripley also rebuilt the tower at the crossing, remodelled by Gilbert Scott in the nineteenth century. Abbot Ripley was held in such esteem by the convent that he was commemorated by a painting on the north-eastern pier of the tower, depicting 'the story of the Transfiguration in which was introduced a figure of this Abbot under a canopy, with a book in one hand and the other lifted in the act of blessing'.

Early in the sixteenth century, the western arm of the church was completed by the addition of the south-western tower, the porch adjoining it, and the west front.

Of the Perpendicular period also were the eastern extensions of the choir-aisles, so as to facilitate the passage of processions and the circulation of pilgrims (p. 89). The three-sided apses of the aisles were taken down and the latter were extended by two bays lighted with three-light windows.[1] Finally the convent undertook the rebuilding of the cloister walks (Fig. 18), situated north of the nave. Except for the south walk, which is almost modern, the cloisters are late Perpendicular Gothic, dating c. 1500–30, although completely restored in our time. A unique feature of the west walk and the modern south walk is the double arcading, the original purpose of which was to provide a series of carrels or studies for the monk-scribes. The walks have quadripartite vaults with ridge-ribs, and amongst the many bosses are two displaying the heraldic arms of Cardinal Wolsey.

BATH ABBEY, 1500–39

For more than four centuries before the Suppression, Bath abbey had been a Benedictine cathedral-priory in the diocese of Wells. Early in the twelfth century a throne for the Bishop of Wells had been installed in the abbey church. Architecturally Bath abbey has no place in the front rank of English cathedrals, but being the last complete monastic cathedral to be erected in this country, and by reason of the advanced character of the Perpendicular style in which it was built, it merits consideration in a survey of cathedral architecture.

When Bishop John de Villula of Wells raised Bath to the status of a cathedral-priory in 1107, he began an immense cruciform church, the Norman nave of which was as long as the present building; the eastern arm terminated in parallel apses (Fig. 15). Of the changes that Villula's church was subjected to through the Gothic centuries, nothing is known; but when Bishop Oliver King was translated from Exeter to Bath and Wells in 1495 he found the

---

[1] The extension of the southern aisle was taken down by Scott.

abbey church in a ruinous state. Tradition has it, that as soon as he was installed at Wells, he beheld in a dream a vision of the Holy Trinity, with angels ascending and descending a ladder, and a voice was heard: 'Let an Olive establish the Crown, and a King restore the church.' Bishop King had been instrumental as Secretary of State in establishing the first of the Tudors, Henry VII. Interpreting the vision as a Divine injunction, he at once demolished the Norman nave of Bath abbey in 1500, and set about a complete rebuilding of the church. After his death in 1503, the work was pushed forward by Priors Bird and Holloway, but the nave was still unfinished at the Dissolution and remained roofless until 1610. The new choir was built to the west of the Norman choir and transepts, which were taken down after the surrender of the abbey to Henry VIII's commissioners.

On plan the church commenced by Bishop King when Perpendicular Gothic was at its zenith, is a cruciform building, 225 feet from east to west; it consists of a choir of three bays laid out as an aisled rectangle, a nave of five bays with aisles, unaisled transepts, and a tower at the crossing. The transepts being narrower than the nave the tower is not square but oblong (Fig. 15). In the nineteenth century extensive restorations were undertaken by Gilbert Scott, and the nave and aisles were fan-vaulted to complete the original design.

Architecturally, the abbey church is remarkable in many respects, not the least being the spatial treatment of the interior. The reduction of fabric and the substitution of walls of glass for masonry render the church a lantern of stone; the proportion of void to solid is 6 to 1, not exceeded in any aisled church of the Middle Ages. In the bay design the triforium is completely eliminated, the vast clerestory windows of five lights being brought down to a string course immediately above the main arcades. The enormous mouldings of the piers are carried up to the crowns of the four-centred arches, broken only by indifferent capitals of the vaulting and inner shafts of the piers. The choir and its aisles are roofed with fan vaulting of the early sixteenth century that were duly copied by Gilbert Scott in the nave. A peculiarity of the fan vault is the absence of transverse arches to divide the bays. The high vault is supported by acute flying-buttresses, the spandrels of which are pierced with tracery. In the east wall of the choir is a square-headed Perpendicular window of seven lights crossed by four traceried transoms, and there are five-light windows in the aisles of the choir. Carved in the stonework of the west front on either side of the seven-light window is a representation of Bishop King's vision, the buttresses are faced with ladders on which are figures of angels ascending and descending, and above the window are tiers of figures portraying the Heavenly Host (Pl. 99).

The central tower, 162 feet high, is designed in two stages, each having two square-headed windows, and at the angles are octagonal buttresses crowned with openwork pinnacles. The battlemented parapet is pierced with panelling typical of Perpendicular Gothic.

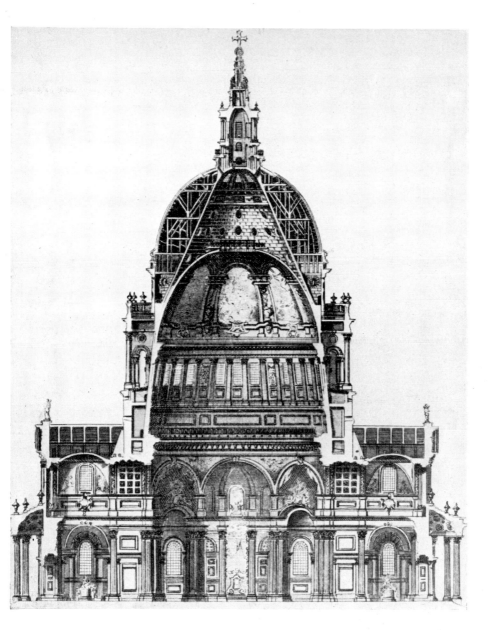

100. Section of the dome of S. Paul's cathedral

101. S. Paul's; the south transept and western end

102. Truro cathedral from the north

103. S. Paul's; interior from the south-west

104. Wakefield; the sanctuary from the west

105. Newcastle; the tower and lantern

106. Manchester; the tower and western end of the nave

107. Model of the new Coventry cathedral

108. Birmingham; the western tower

109. Bradford cathedral from the west

110. Liverpool; interior looking east

Elphin cathedral, as it will be

112. Derby; interior from the west

112. Chelmsford cathedral from the south-east

114. Guildford cathedral from the west

115. Guildford; interior of the choir

16. Cathedral Building in the Middle Ages

The Montalembert Myth · The Vault of Gloucester Nave · Lay Masons and the Evidence of Fabric Rolls · Building Projects promoted by Bishops. The Administration of Building Funds · Craftsmen named in the Fabric Rolls of Ely Cathedral · The Use of the Rebus · The Importation of Norman Masons in the Eleventh and Twelfth Centuries · William de Sens at Canterbury · Mediaeval Chapters and the Employment of Master Masons · William Ramsey at Westminster Palace, Old S. Paul's and Lichfield Cathedral · The Royal Master Mason, William of Colchester at York · The Custos Operis, Magister, Cementarius · Degrees of Craftsmanship · Freemasons, Layers, Hewers, Carpenters, Labourers · Pressgang Methods of Obtaining Craftsmen · Discipline of the Lodge at York · Banker Marks · The Master Mason's Office · Transport of Stone and Materials for Cathedral Building · Norman Building at S. Albans · The Geological Formation of this Land · The Use of Purbeck Marble · The Process of Building a Cathedral · Operations retarded by Lack of Funds and Bad Weather · Meeting the Cost · Indulgences and Gifts · Consecration of a Cathedral in the Middle Ages · The Fabric Rolls of Exeter and York · Information respecting Materials, Craftsmen, Wages, Expenditure · Details of Columns, Windows, Glass, Colours, etc. · The Decorated Window at Canterbury Cathedral, 1336

⟦ 'WHEN WE SAY that the innumerable monastic churches scattered over the whole face of Europe were built by the monks, the statement must be taken in its literal sense. They were, in fact, not only the architects but the masons of their buildings; after drawing up the plans . . . they carried them out with their own hands and in general without employing craftsmen from outside. . . . While simple monks were often the chief architects of their buildings, abbots willingly condescended to serve as common workmen.' This statement was penned by the French political authority, Charles Forbes de Montalembert in Volume VI of his great work, *The Monks of the West*, published ninety years ago, and has been accepted and repeated by English writers and scholars until the myth was exploded by the late Dr. G. G. Coulton[1] and R. E. Swartwout.[2] Foremost amongst Montalembert's 'monastic churches'

---

[1] *Art and the Reformation.* G. G. Coulton.
[2] *The Monastic Craftsman.* R. E. Swartwout.

would be the English cathedral-priories. The researches of the above-named historians have proved conclusively that the employment of monks in the building of their churches or in the ancillary crafts of sculpture, glass-painting and mural painting was exceptional. In the rare instances that occurred, monastic annalists recorded with a sense of pride the skill and achievements of their brethren. Gloucester may be cited as a case in point, where the monks, under stress of financial straits, themselves undertook the erection of a high vault. 'In 1242 was completed the new vault over the nave of the [abbey] church, not by the extraneous aid of professional workmen as before, but by the vigorous hands of the monks who resided on the spot' (*Gloucester Chartulary. Rolls Series I*). Clumsy though the high vault is, it may be questioned whether a lay master-mason was not called in to direct and supervise the actual building operations.

The evidence furnished by existing Fabric Rolls goes to prove that the building of monastic and cathedral churches was the work of lay masons. It is misleading to ascribe a building project to the bishop who occupied the see when the work was undertaken; invariably the bishop or the chapter promoted the scheme; he would devise ways and means such as offering indulgences, for finding the money for the labour and materials, but had nothing to do with the building operations or the architectural character of the prospective work. Bishop Richard Poore, the founder of Salisbury cathedral, may perhaps have had a voice in deciding the general lay-out and the magnitude of the new cathedral, subject to the approval of the dean and chapter, but the design and construction were solely the business of the master-mason and his army of craftsmen. 'Neither churchman alone, nor mason alone, could have done what churchman and mason did in harmonious partnership.'[1] The administration of the building fund and the control of the masons, craftsmen and labourers lay with the dean and chapter, one of their number usually being appointed *custos operis*. At York in the fourteenth century, the masons and other workmen were required to comply with certain regulations the chapter had ordained for their management, and once a year on the pledge-day (la pleghdai) they had to swear to observe the rules.

To credit clerics and monks with architectural projects they promoted is a misinterpretation of the chronicles of mediaeval scribes. To Alan of Walsingham, the sacrist of Ely cathedral in 1321 has been ascribed the honour of rearing the famous Octagon (p. 248). The conception may have been his, but beyond that he

[1] *Art and the Reformation*. G. G. Coulton.

did little else than 'cause' the Octagon to be erected by experienced lay masons and builders. This is confirmed by the Fabric Rolls in which occur the names of the craftsmen employed. There were the master-masons, John probably a Londoner, and Attagreene; Peter Quadraterius, who planned the eight piers to carry the Octagon; William Hurle, the master-carpenter, who constructed the timber lantern, and who may be the William Hurley, employed at S. Stephen's chapel, Westminster. He was paid a retaining fee of £8 a year for his professional services, and was assisted by master carpenters Thomas and Galfrido. Other craftsmen named include master Simoni the plumber, and William Tyler, glass worker. The sacrist's Roll of 1339 records the payment of 'two shillings, and his keep at the prior's table' to John of Burwell, for carving the central boss of the Octagon with a figure of Christ in Glory.

Similarly the nave of Canterbury cathedral is attributed to Prior Chillenden, described by Leland as 'the greatest builder of a prior that ever was at Christ Church. He was the great setterforth of the new body of the building of the church.' At his death in 1411 'the skin scarcely covered the bones of his emaciated body'. It was not, however, as an operative mason that Chillenden wore his flesh to the bone, but as the setter-forth, i.e. as promoter of the scheme.

The records of Lincoln cathedral afford a unique instance of an ecclesiastic of high rank lending a hand in building operations. When the new choir of Lincoln was in process of construction, 1191–1200, under the direction of Geoffrey de Noiers, a lay master-mason, Bishop Hugh the Burgundian 'oftentimes bore the hod-load of hewn stone or of building lime'.

From the middle of the fifteenth century it was often the practice for a bishop or an ecclesiastic who was responsible for the erection of some feature in his church to perpetuate his name by having a rebus or punning device carved in the fabric. Amongst the innumerable bosses in the high vault of the nave of Norwich cathedral, several are carved with a representation of a hart lying by the waterside, the rebus of Bishop Lyhart, during whose episcopate the vault was put up; and in the lierne vault of Norwich choir are a large number of bosses bearing the rebus of Bishop Goldwell, depicting a well and a golden bucket. On the masonry of the chantry chapel of Dr. Hugh Sugar, 1485–90, in the south nave arcade of Wells cathedral are three sugar loaves beneath a doctor's cap; and at S. Albans cathedral, the rebus of Abbot Ramryge that appears on the cornice of his chantry chapel on the north side of the sanctuary takes the form of a ram wearing a collar bearing the letters RYGE. Above the northern doorway in the reredos of the High Altar in Southwark cathedral is a small carving of a fox, commemorating the famous Bishop of Winchester who bore the cost of the reredos. Amongst the sculptured ornament of the pulpitum of York cathedral is to be seen the figure of a hind, the rebus of William Hyndley, the master-mason who journeyed from Norwich to York in 1473 to design and execute the screen.

Heraldic devices also were employed as a means of identifying the work of a bishop or ecclesiastic. Above the nave arcades at Winchester cathedral are angels supporting the arms of William of Wykeham and of the see.

Of the large number of masons who came to this country from Normandy and Burgundy in the half-century following the Norman Conquest, very little is known. In the building of the cathedrals and monastic churches, Saxon labour was undoubtedly pressed into service for unskilled tasks, for burning lime, for felling timber and for fetching and carrying. Few names of the foreign master-masons who controlled the building operations have come down to us. For the rebuilding of S. Albans abbey, a band of masons was brought over from Normandy in 1077 by Abbot Paul. Amongst them was a Master Robert, 'the most skilful mason in England', who was rewarded by the abbot with the manor of Sarret, a gift the monks disapproved of, as the property belonged to the convent. Of the Norman masons engaged in the building of the immense nave of Old S. Paul's, mention was made in 1127 of Andrew 'cementarius'; it is not unlikely that he was the master appointed by the chapter.

For the rebuildings and extensions carried out through the Gothic centuries, the procedure was similar to that adopted by the chapter of Christ Church, Canterbury after the destruction by fire of Conrad's Glorious Choir in 1174. In his tract on the burning and the reconstruction of the choir, the monk Gervase records that English and French master masons were summoned to Canterbury and expressed their opinions concerning the rebuilding. The choice of the convent fell upon William de Sens, an active and able man, and 'most skilful both in wood and stone'. The master from Champagne at once set about procuring stone from Caen; he devised ingenious machines for loading and unloading the vessels of transportation and for drawing the mortar and stones; and he delivered moulds to the (working) masons for shaping the stones, and prepared other things needed for the building operations.

In the later Gothic periods, the services of master-masons of repute were sought by the cathedral chapters when building projects requiring expert advice were taken in hand. Two instances may be quoted, both of which relate to famous masons of Westminster. In 1332 William Ramsey, one of a family of masons who had been in the King's employ at the Palace of Westminster, was commissioned by the dean and chapter of S. Paul's cathedral to design and build the chapter house and cloisters on the south side of the cathedral, and the City Corporation decreed that as 'Master William de Ramseye was assiduously giving his whole attention to the business', he should be exempted from service on juries and inquests. By 1337 under the designation of 'King's mason', Ramsey was appointed Surveyor of all the King's Works including the Tower of London, and such was his fame that in the same year the dean and chapter of Lichfield enlisted his services in linking up the new Lady Chapel of the cathedral with the choir, a problem of alignment. By his skill the two sections of the eastern arm were united without any apparent awkwardness. The contract between Ramsey and the chapter was made on 23 May 1337, his fee being fixed at 22s. a visit (equal to £60 of our money) with an allowance of 6s. 8d. for the travelling expenses of himself and his attendants from Westminster and back, then a matter of eight days for the return journey. About the year 1410, on the recommendation of Henry IV, the dean and chapter of York engaged the royal master-mason, William of Colchester, for the reconstruction of the central tower of the cathedral, then on the verge of collapse and in particular for the rebuilding of the four piers that supported it. The appointment of an outsider proved unpopular with the 'closed shop' at York; the royal mason was regarded as an interloper and on his arrival from London, master William went in danger of his life. 'Moved by envy they conspired together to kill him and his assistant.' Although he was wounded by the malcontents and his assistant was slain, William of Colchester remained at York for some years and reared the noble central tower now standing. His office at Westminster was filled by a Thomas Mapilton, who had been master of the works at Durham cathedral and who became the visiting architect of Canterbury during the erection of the south-west tower, 1423–34. Mapilton paid periodical visits to the cathedral whilst the work was in progress, and on each occasion was paid a fee and his travelling expenses.

When news of a building project in a cathedral spread abroad, masons, carpenters, artisans and workmen of varying degrees of skill who dwelt in the surrounding district and sometimes in places far distant made their way thither to offer their services. They worked under the duly-appointed master-mason and his chief assistants, but were engaged by the Warden of the Work, who also paid them their daily wages. The Warden or *custos operis* was usually a member of the cathedral chapter, a canon, a vicar or a monk as the case might be, whose duties were wholly administrative; he was the link between employer and employed. Elyas de Derham, Canon of Salisbury, who acted as Warden of the Works during the twenty-five years' building of the cathedral, has for long been regarded as the architect responsible for the design of Salisbury. Previously he had been Keeper of the Works for Henry III at Winchester and had a good deal of experience in building undertakings. As Prof. Lethaby wrote, 'he may from the employing side have had much to say on the design of Salisbury cathedral, just as Henry III had on the design of Westminster abbey'. An entry in the cathedral accounts for 1262 is nearer fact. 'Robertus cementarius rexit per XX annos.' The terms *cementarius* and *magister* were commonly applied to the master-mason, the man who was responsible for the design and who controlled the building operations throughout. The record of the twenty years' rule of Robert entitles him and not Elyas Derham to the credit of designing Salisbury cathedral.

When the remodelling of the eastern arm of Old S. Paul's was commenced in 1256, one of the residentiary canons was appointed Keeper of the Works, but at a later stage of the reconstruction, in 1312, John de Parteneye, a builder who contracted for the work still to be done, was entrusted with the fabric disbursements and accounts and was required to submit the *computus* to the chapter every quarter.

Craftsmen and labourers under the general term 'artifices' were classified and received wages according to their skill. In the highest grade were the free-masons or workers in freestone, who were capable of cutting mouldings and tracery, and of sculpturing capitals, bosses and architectural detail. From the fourteenth century the name *lathomus* was often used for free-mason. In a Register of Canterbury cathedral for the year 1429, stone-cutters and masons are named under the heading 'Lathomi de la Loygge'. Ranking below the free-masons were the rough masons, often described in fabric rolls as layers or setters, and there were the hard hewers who rough-dressed the blocks of stone. A great number of unskilled 'labourers' were employed in carting and digging, in burning lime and mixing mortar, and in rearing scaffolding. In addition were the master-carpenter and his many assistants, who made the timber centrings for arches and vaults and built the roofs; and there were wood-carvers, smiths, tylers, plumbers, plasterers, painters and glaziers. The master-mason was generally a person of some standing and substance; he owned property and sometimes had an interest in quarries that provided the stone.[1]

The Fabric Roll of York cathedral relating to the building of the choir arm, 1370, yields information respecting the discipline and the observance of regular hours that was enforced by the master-mason, Robert of Patrington[2] and the cathedral chapter. 'All their times and hours shall be revealed by a bill, ordained therefor.' From Michaelmas to the first Sunday in Lent, the masons were to be at work in the lodge within the Close 'as early as they may see skilfully by daylight; and they shall stand there truly working all day, as long as they may see skilfully for the work'. They were allowed an hour at noon for a meal, but they were not to 'stay away from the lodges nor from their work over the space of time of an hour; and after noon they may drink in the lodge'. From Lent to Michaelmas they were to commence work in the lodge at sunrise, and 'truly and busily work on the aforesaid work of the kirk all day, until it be no more space than time of a mile-way before sunset. All their times and hours shall be revealed by a bell ordained therefor.' If any man defaulted he was to be 'chastised with abating of his payment'. A new mason who sought employment was to be 'first proved a week or more upon his well-working', and after the week's probation he was required to swear upon the book to observe the rules of the lodge.

The master-mason's task was not always an enviable one. Some workmen were quarrelsome and resorted to physical violence; others were addicted to wandering away after a few weeks' work. Following a report made by an officer appointed by the chapter of York in 1344 to inquire into the progress of the nave, the master-mason and master-carpenter were summoned to appear before the chapter. Their evidence revealed negligence, idleness and indiscipline on the part of the masons and labourers, as a result of which the fabric of the nave was falling into decay. Many of the men were unruly and insubordinate and the master admitted that he had lost control over them. There were strikes amongst the labourers; timber, stone, lime and cement were stolen from the dumps in the cathedral yard; rain poured into the nave through the temporary roof; the unfinished buttresses being unprotected from the weather were breaking up, and the pulley-wheels at the west end of the nave had fallen into decay from disuse and proper

---

[1] When there was a shortage of labour in a royal undertaking, the master-mason was empowered to employ press-gang methods. On several occasions in 1441, craftsmen and artisans were rounded up for work at Eton College.

[2] In 1386 Robert was granted £10 a year and a house in the precincts of the cathedral, with the proviso that should he become blind or otherwise incapacitated he should draw his wages and retain the house, so long as he continued to bestow 'his counsel and advice as far as he is able'.

attention (*Inquisitio de Defectibus Fabricae et Custodem ejusdem*, 1344). Small cause for wonder that the building of the nave was brought to a standstill.

Incised in the masonry of the walls and piers of some cathedral churches will be found numbers of curious devices and of initial letters known as banker-marks, that were made by the masons who dressed and shaped the blocks as they lay on the bankers or benches in the sheds of the lodge. The capital letters were probably the initials of Christian names. Stone was always a costly item and master-masons would require craftsmen, particularly the inexperienced and those whose work was not known, to mark the stones with a sign-manual. By this means the taskmaster was able to identify any man guilty of faulty or spoilt stones. Large numbers of banker-marks have been obliterated by the scraping that our cathedrals were subjected to in the nineteenth century, but a considerable number remain at Ely, Winchester and Gloucester. The practice obtained from Norman times. At Canterbury cathedral marks of several periods occur, from the twelfth century to late Perpendicular Gothic. On the walls of the paired apsidal chapels in the choir transepts are numerous marks incised by the masons who worked under William de Sens and William the Englishman, 1175–84. Some of the marks, e.g. the letters A and R appear in all four chapels (Fig. 16); others reappear in the Saint's chapel, together with those of newly enlisted masons who remained to complete the Corona Chapel. On the piers of the nave is a series of marks made by the craftsmen of the late fourteenth century and in the chapels to the east of the main transepts are a number of the fifteenth century.

The master-mason who supervised the building of a mediaeval cathedral was not an architect in the modern meaning of the term. He had been trained as a mason and builder; the preparation of elaborate plans, elevations and drawings of architectural detail on paper long before the work was begun was no part of his apprenticeship. The master would necessarily sketch out a *platt* or plan on parchment, board or paper, and as the work progressed he would prepare designs for windows, doors, vaults and other features in the 'tracing-house' or drawing office on the site. In a Fabric Roll of Exeter cathedral is an entry recording the purchase of parchment for the mason 'to show the form of the work', probably an allusion to the templates that were to be made for the use of the masons; and a Roll of 1375 mentions the building of a new 'tracyng house' at a cost of about £10.

The erection of a cathedral or the rebuilding of a choir or a nave was a costly and usually a protracted business. Few of the people who witnessed the laying of the foundations lived to see its completion. Where there were no quarries in the neighbourhood, stone had often to be brought great distances by land and water; roads were bad for transport and the forests that covered much of the country were impassable for waggons laden with weighty masonry. The stone for the cathedrals of Durham and Lincoln came from quarries close by, but for the building of Norwich, Ely and Peterborough, stone from Barnack in Northants had to be conveyed in barges along the waterways of East Anglia. Water carriage was cheap compared with road haulage.

In the Norman period, before local quarries were opened up, stone was frequently imported in large quantities from quarries in the vicinity of Caen in Normandy, which produced a freestone of excellent quality. For the building of the great Benedictine abbey of Bury S. Edmund's, Suffolk, Lydgate tells us that Abbot Baldwin used

> '. . . stone brought from Kane out of Normandy
> By the sea; and set upon the strand
> At Ratlysdene, and carried forth by hand.'

The Norman cathedral of Canterbury, begun by Archbishop Lanfranc in 1070 was built mainly of Caen stone. After crossing the Channel, the laden barges discharged their freights at Fordwich, the port of Canterbury at the head of the estuary of the Stour, within two miles of the city. For the reconstruction of the eastern arm of Canterbury in 1174 William de Sens imported stone from Normandy, and throughout the Middle Ages it retained its popularity at Canterbury and was used for rebuildings and restorations. Early in the twelfth century stone from Caen was brought up the Thames for the building of Old S. Paul's and vessels entering the Fleet were granted exemption from toll and custom by Henry I. Masonry from the same source was used for the completion of the nave of Rochester cathedral from 1114, and after the fire of 1186 the Norman nave of Chichester cathedral was entirely recased with freestone from Caen.

Singularly fortunate and resourceful were the masons who built the Norman abbey that is now S. Albans cathedral. No need to import stone from Caen or to open up distant quarries, for hard by lay the ruins of Verulamium, a quarry that furnished Roman brick and stone in abundance and was accordingly ransacked for building material (p. 157). Later, limestone from Tottenhoe, Beds., known in 1396 as Egalmounde was used at S. Albans.

In the interests of economy, the stone for cathedral building was, as far as possible, obtained from local quarries, thereby saving
K*

both time and expense. Most of the stone for Exeter in the thirteenth century came from the Devon quarries of Beer, Salcombe, Heavitree and Thorveston, but stone was also brought from Caen and Portland, and quantities of Purbeck marble from Corfe in Dorset. The Purbeck was sent by sea to Topsham on the Exe estuary and thence was conveyed by road to Exeter.

Most important were the oolitic limestones composing the geological series of strata that extended in a north-easterly direction from Dorset to the Yorkshire coast. At the southern end of the great ridge were the limestones of Somerset, Wiltshire and Gloucestershire; the quarries of Doulting, Somerset, yielded the stone for Wells cathedral and Salisbury was built of limestone from Chilmark but a few miles distant.

That part of the oolitic ridge from Notts. to the Northumberland coast provided a valuable seam of magnesian limestone; quarries at Huddlestone, owned by the chapter of York, supplied the bulk of the masonry for York cathedral. In the Midlands and west, a wide area stretching to Chester and South Lancashire is geologically rich in red sandstones that were used for the building of Worcester, Lichfield and Chester cathedrals.

All through the thirteenth century the dark shelly limestone, known as Purbeck marble was quarried at Corfe in Dorset, and was used in abundance in cathedrals and churches for the shafting of clustered piers and of wall arcades and for the making of tombs and effigies. To meet the general demand the Purbeck merchants promoted an industry for fashioning shafts, piers, capitals and effigies, and wherever water carriage was possible, they shipped their products from the Dorset coast to all parts of the country. As early as 1175 Purbeck shafting was sent by sea to Durham for Bishop Pudsey's Galilee chapel, and it was also used in Bishop Hugh's choir at Lincoln in 1192. So general was the 'Purbeck use' that quantities of similar marbles were worked at Frosterley near Durham for use in the Transept of the Nine Altars; at Nidderdale in Yorkshire and in the south at Bethersden, Kent, and at Petworth, Surrey, dark-coloured marbles were quarried as a substitute for Purbeck. When polished these non-crystalline stones bore the appearance of marble and were therefore known as such.

A vast amount of timber was needed for the building of a great church. Wooden sheds or lodges had to be erected on the site for the masons; poles were needed for scaffolds when the walls were rising; timber was used for making the centrings for arches and later for vaults, and for the construction of the roofs; and wood provided fuel for the limekilns. Trees in nearby forests were felled for these purposes. According to the Annals of Winchester, William I granted Bishop Walkelyn for the rebuilding of Winchester cathedral as much timber from the Forest of Hempage, three miles distant, as his men could cut down in four days and nights. Walkelyn made the most of the gift and summoned 'an innumerable troop of carpenters' who cleared the whole forest. When the King passed the site and beheld the clearance he exclaimed in anger: 'Am I bewitched? Have I taken leave of my senses?' The Bishop assuaged the royal anger by offering to relinquish the see, and William replied: 'I was as much too liberal in my grant as you were too greedy in availing yourself of it.'

The first part of a cathedral to be erected was the choir arm, so that the High Altar could be installed and the religious offices recited at the earliest possible moment. In 1225, five years after the foundations were laid at Salisbury cathedral, Bishop Poore consecrated altars in the Lady Chapel at the eastern end of the choir, and the following day he solemnly celebrated the Divine mysteries in the new building, which was boarded up at the west so that the services should continue, uninterrupted by the noise and smother of the work in progress beyond. Gervase, the chronicler of Canterbury cathedral, records that when the new choir was ready, in 1180 and three altars had been set up therein, a wooden wall was erected transversely at the east end with three glass windows in it. Beyond the wall the masons pushed on with the building of the Saint's chapel.

The eastern arm of a cathedral having been completed, if the necessary funds were forthcoming, work began on the transepts and the nave. Though the completion of the nave might be deferred for a long period, one or two bays were generally put up to buttress the piers of the tower at the crossing. Rarely was a cathedral built from east to west without long intervals of inactivity. The nave of Old S. Paul's was almost a century in the building; the Norman arcades of the early twelfth century were not finished with their clerestory and high vault until the thirteenth century. So slow and intermittent was the rearing of the nave of Westminster abbey, begun in 1376, that a century and a half passed before its completion, and the western towers had then risen only half their present height. Some cathedrals can never have been free of building operations. From 1220 to 1475 there were but brief intervals when masons were not engaged on some part of the fabric of York cathedral and the same may be said of Lichfield from 1195 to 1350. In the depth of winter, bad weather necessarily slowed down or temporarily suspended operations, and the top surfaces of unfinished walls were thatched to protect them. At such times the layers and other men would be idle, but masons and sculptors worked in the lodges and sheds cutting mouldings and tracery, and carving capitals, corbels and ornament.

Nothing retarded the progress of building so much as the lack of funds. From all parts of the diocese gifts and bequests were made by the faithful; rents issuing from property owned by the chapter were often allocated to the Fabric Fund, which was augmented by the sale of indulgences, abundant evidence of this source being furnished by the muniments of our cathedrals. When the choir arm of Old S. Paul's was being remodelled late in the thirteenth century, an almost nation-wide appeal was made for funds. The Bishop of London granted forty days' indulgence to the citizens, and the English and Welsh bishops issued hortatory letters in their dioceses offering indulgences to benefactors. The diocese of Norwich contributed four times to the fund; Salisbury, Ely, Coventry and Lichfield thrice, and support came from across the Channel, from Bourges and Cologne. An item in the Fabric Roll of Exeter cathedral, 1349–50, specifies the hiring of a scribe for 8s. to write out eight hundred indulgences for the fabric of the church.

Frankly outspoken on the subject of the fabric indulgences at York in 1440 was Thomas Gascoigne, Chancellor of Oxford. 'I know that the officials of one cathedral church [York], enjoin and command all parish priests in their province to bid their penitents in Lententide, pay somewhat of their goods to the cathedral church; and the priest enjoins for a penance upon a poor man who has not fourpence, to pay forty pence to the Minster; and another priest has taken his own church and parish on farm from the Minster officials. I know one who pays five shillings a year to the Minster for his parish; and this very parish priest straitly enjoined upon every man in his parish that he should pay a certain sum that year to the cathedral church; so that certain poor folk paid to this priest forty pence [each] for the fabric, yet he who laid the injunction upon them had the parish to farm for five shillings' (*Liber Veritatum*, 1450).

Another means of swelling the building funds was to offer letters of fraternity 'to all benefactors who, from the goods God hath given them, pay anything to the fabric of our church'. To provide money for the erection of the new choir of Lincoln in 1186, Bishop Hugh founded a Gild of S. Mary, whose brethren pledged themselves to contribute to the Fabric Fund, which benefited by 1,000 marks a year, and as money was needed over a long period, the King granted letters patent to Hugh's successors for the maintenance of the Gild. Often a bishop would make liberal gifts from his own purse. During the eighteen years of his episcopate, Bishop

Stapledon, d. 1326, contributed in all the large sum of £1,800 towards the transforming of Exeter cathedral. Archbishop Greenfield of York, and his successor, each made a donation of 500 marks towards the building of the nave of York, 1291–1338, and Archbishop Thoresby, 1352–73, gave £200 a year to further the rebuilding of the presbytery. For the Perpendicular nave of Winchester, William of Wykeham bequeathed 2,500 marks, and by his will, 1403, ordained that 'the prior and convent of the church shall provide all the scaffold necessary and convenient for the work; also, that they shall freely and without charge permit lime and sand to be taken by the workmen sent by myself or my executors, from any part of the lands of the convent or of their tenants. Also that stones, lead, ironwork, timber, glass or any other of the materials which the old building may yield, shall be employed in the new work. And I will and ordain that the arrangement and conduct of the new work shall be entrusted to Master William Wynford [a mason of repute] and such others discreet, sufficient and approved in their art . . . Also, that Dominus Simon Membury, now supervisor and paymaster of the work, shall continue in the same offices under the supervision of John Wayte, monk of my said church and at present controller of the work on the part of the prior and convent.'

It was not unusual for collections to be made throughout the diocese by authorized messengers. When money was badly needed for the building of the western end of S. Albans nave in 1198, one of the monks was sent out on a begging mission accompanied by a young man who had been miraculously restored to life at the shrine of S. Alban. In the muniments of York cathedral is a copy of the injunctions issued by Archbishop William de Melton, 1317–40, to regularly appointed 'questores' who were sent forth on behalf of the fabric fund during the building of the nave. Twelve of these people are mentioned by name. The whole diocese of York was periodically visited by them and large sums of money were obtained; but the privilege of soliciting alms for any religious purpose was frequently abused in the Middle Ages; the country was overrun by unprincipled rogues who enriched themselves by defrauding the faithful. In 1324 Archbishop Melton warned his spiritual subjects in strong terms against such impostors.

The ritual observed at the consecration of a cathedral in the thirteenth century has been described by Durandus, Bishop of Mende in Southern France. He may have been present at the consecration of Salisbury cathedral by Archbishop Boniface of Canterbury in September 1258. On the external walls of the cathedral are twelve carved crosses that mark the spots besprinkled with holy water by the archbishop, and inside the church are three on each wall to the north, south, east and west, before which lights were burning during the ceremony of consecration. The archbishop together with other ecclesiastics and many laymen in procession made a circuit of the outside of the building three times, during which the crosses were anointed. Then the procession entered the cathedral at the west, and a cross of ashes and sand was made on the floor. The sprinkling of the crosses of the interior followed, High Mass was sung at the High Altar and the ceremony concluded with a solemn Te Deum. The consecration crosses on the outside of Salisbury cathedral, about four feet above the eye level, were of metal, probably latten (bronze) and were framed in quatrefoils that still remain (Pl. 98). Those on the walls of the interior were unframed.

The Fabric Rolls of Exeter cathedral furnish a wealth of information respecting the acquisition of building materials, the quantities and costs, the masons and other craftsmen employed, their rates of pay and often their names, and the progress of the operations through the fourteenth century. Unfortunately the Rolls of the earliest years of the reconstruction of the cathedral are missing, and of some other periods the records are scanty. An early Roll of 1284 refers to work on the chapel of S. Mary Magdalene that flanked the Lady Chapel at the north-west. Two carpenters were employed at 2s. 8d. a week and a mate at 7½d.; and in the following year 5s. 8d. was disbursed for work in the same chapel.

In 1301–2 are recorded payments for 300 stones from Silverton *ad voltam*, i.e. for the vault of the Lady Chapel, and for 1,271 feet of glass for the upper windows, viz., the east window of the choir, and two or more in the clerestory stage. Magister Walter le Verrouer was paid £4 10s. in 1303 for glazing eight clerestory windows, six aisle windows and the circular window in the gable of the east wall that lights the roof. Twenty or more masons were working in the choir in 1303–4, and Master Roger received 30s. to cover the expense of a journey to Corfe to buy stone. The same Roll has an entry 'For the purchase of 18 great blocks of stone at Portland for the keys or bosses (*claves*) together with 60 bases and capitals, including carriage by sea, £4 16s. 8d.' and £7 10s. was the cost of carving 30 bosses at 5s. each. In addition £1 1s. 0d. was paid for the carving of 6 bosses for the aisles, £1 5s. 6d. for 3 springers of the aisle vaulting and 11s. for 3 corbels.

In the Fabric Roll of 1308–9 is recorded the expenditure of 29s. 7¾d. for the purchase of red lead, white lead, priming for the gold and vermilion, colour wash and varnish, all of which were used for painting the vaults of the choir aisles. From 1308 to 1311 the expenditure was mainly for the purchase of glass for the windows of the clerestory and of the choir aisles, and as wages of Walter the glazier and his two boys. From 1309 onwards William Canon and his son, who owned the quarries at Corfe, supplied Purbeck marble for the piers and shafts of Exeter cathedral, which were fashioned at Corfe before being shipped to Topsham. In the Roll of 1309–10 appears an entry '8 marble columns bought for 32s.; 4 metal annulets for the columns, 4s.' which were probably for the transeptal chapels of the choir. In 1310 William Canon was paid 'for marble from Corfe for columns, £35 2s. 8d. and no more this year because the same William received in the past year £26 13s. 4d.' The making of the piers seems to have been by contract, the payments being for work done. Under a later agreement (1322), payments were made in three instalments. In the Roll of 1316 mention occurs of 38 columns at 5s. 6d. each, including bases and capitals, for the *aluras* or galleries of the triforium between the High Altar and the choir (*inter magnum altare et chorum*). Glass figures largely in the Rolls for the years 1317 to 1319, 629 feet of white glass being bought at Rouen for £15 4s. 9d., and 203 feet of coloured glass at 1s. a foot. It is assumed that the Rouen glass was for the windows of the Lady Chapel as the price was higher than for that of the choir windows, which averaged 5½d. to 6½d. a foot. For the seven-light window in the south transept, 2d. a foot was paid for plain glass and 3d. a foot for coloured, and the bill for the corresponding window in the north transept was slightly heavier. The glass for the windows in the aisles and the clerestory of the nave was also of the lower grade, ranging from 2d. to 3d. a foot. In the Rolls that are extant for the period 1317 to 1342, Master Thomas of Wittenaye is frequently alluded to as the *magister operis*. Prof. Lethaby was of opinion that he was the mastermason who directed the building of the nave of Exeter from end to end.

The Fabric Rolls for 1318 to 1322 testify to the splendour and costliness of the High Altar and its canopied reredos, rich with imagery, gilding and colour; 300 lb. of iron were bought, probably for the making of the rods to secure the tabernacling of the reredos, and 54 marble shafts, large and small, were used to support the canopy. John Aurifero was paid £5 18s. for 'the work of the silver tabula'. In 1324 a figure of Our Lord, probably set within a niche of the reredos, cost 3s. The total amount expended on this sumptuous altar and reredos was £319 11s. 1½, a sum equal to £25,000 in modern values. Details are given in the Rolls of 1318, 1323 and 1325 of the erection of the pulpitum at the entrance to the choir, and of the altars of S. Nicholas and S. Mary that stood on either side of the central doorway. William Canon was paid £15 3s. 7½d. in 1318 for 4 marble piers with their capitals and bases, and 243 feet of Purbeck were supplied for the steps before the pulpitum. So satisfied were the dean and chapter with the marble work executed by William Canon that they presented him 'of their courtesy' with an honorarium of £4 in 1318.

To fill the niches on the front of the pulpitum, twelve images were purchased in 1324 for £10 0s. 6d. and ten smaller figures for 15s. Hinges, bolts and locks for the door, and 5 bosses for the vault on the underside of the pulpitum cost 8s. The same year timber was bought at Norton and 48 trees at Langford, and 'a boat from Thopysham to Torre abbey for [conveying] 2 pieces of timber to the quay [at Exeter]' is entered on the Roll of 1324–5. In 1328–9, 33 stones from the Silverton quarries 'containing 80 feet run, for weatherings and gutters above the porch' were paid for, together with 100 nails and fittings for the door (of the porch). Items in the Roll of 1331–2 relate to the building of the north walk of the cloister, when 25 horse-loads of sand were purchased and 1,000 lath nails and 'helyng pinnes'.

Attached to the Roll of 1331–2 is a memorandum dated 1334 that appears to have been a final settlement with Canon of Corfe, at the same time making him responsible for repairing any defects in the marble columns resulting from injury during the building operations. On 23 January 1332 William Canon entered into an agreement with the dean and chapter to supply the Purbeck piers of the nave. 'Namely, for 11½ great columns, the price of a column £10 10s., total £124 14s. Also pairs [clusters] of columns with bases and capitals for the triforia, £15; the price of each base, with capitals and columns, 5s.; also for 29 columns for the cloister, 21s. 9d.; total of the aforesaid sums, £140 5s. 9d. Whereof the said William received by three tallies [payments] from Messrs. Shireford and Peter de Castro, wardens of the church aforesaid, £132 17s. 5d. And so there is due to the said William £7 8s. 4d., which he received on account by the hands of Master Peter de Castro. . . . And he is bound to repair the whole of the aforesaid marble, and to make good the defects of the same at the time of its placing in the work, on reasonable notice. . . . And if the said William shall have faithfully kept his covenant as concerns the repairing and making good of the said marble, the dean and chapter gave him hopes that they will satisfy him concerning 54s. for a quarter column, over and above their undertaking. Afterwards the said William caused the columns to be sufficiently repaired, and therefore the dean and chapter did satisfy the said William concerning 54s. for the quarter column; and so all was made smooth between the parties aforesaid. These last matters were done in the treasury of S. Peter's Church on Friday, the morrow of the Nativity of the B.V.M. [Sept. 9] A.D. 1334.'[1]

The inference is that if Canon made good any damaged piers, the chapter were willing to pay him for a quarter-column that was never used.

The Fabric Roll of 1346–7 records the expenditure of the large sum of £35 5s. 2½d. on the west front, but nothing is known of the costs and materials of the great screen with its tiers of sculptured images that was erected by Bishop Brantyngham. The building of the high vault of the nave figures in the Roll of 1353; trees were purchased for the scaffoldings and two carpenters were employed making ladders.

And what of the annual expenditure? During the building of the eastern arm of the cathedral, 1301–24, the cost ranged from £100 to £247 a year, but the years 1309 and 1310 were exceptional, the disbursements reaching £337 and £383 respectively. For the nave, 1325–50 the cost varied considerably each year. In 1326 which marked the end of Stapledon's episcopate, the huge sum of £325 was spent; in other years the amounts were from £100 to £194. At the end of the period they fell to £35 and £50, and never exceeded these figures during the forty-two years Bishop Grandisson held the see, 1327–69.

The cloisters reappear in the Roll of 1377–8. Robert Lesyngham, the master-mason, was employed at 7s. a week and he received an additional payment of 25s. every quarter. A dozen other masons are mentioned whose wages varied from 1s. 11d. to 3s. 4d. a week. A parchment was bought for the use of Master Lesyngham in preparing drawings of the cloisters. The name of the master carpenter, Walter Gyst, is of frequent occurrence; he and his assistants made the timber centrings for the vaults of the cloister walks. In 1398 the walks were paved with marble and the 57 bosses of the vault in the south walk were painted in 1435.

No less interesting than the Fabric Rolls of Exeter are those of York, dating from 1360 onwards. The documents shed much light on the man-power, equipment, and the transport of materials relating to the erection of the choir and the towers. Many of the Rolls are imperfect and others are missing over long intervals. Those extant bristle with names of craftsmen of all degrees, from the master-mason and master-carpenter to the unskilled labourers (*communes operarii*). The wages and other payments are entered with an exactitude that would content a modern auditor.

In the earliest Roll, *c.* 1360, which is fragmentary, occur the

[1] *The Architectural History of Exeter Cathedral.* P. Freeman.

names of the master-mason, William de Hoton, and the master-carpenter, Philip de Lincoln, both well known in their day. All the workmen were paid fortnightly, Hoton receiving 5s. and Philip 4s. The cartage of nine loads of stone from the landing place on the bank of the Ouse to the cemetery (*cymiterium*), where were the masons' dumps and lodges, cost 22s. 6d.

The next Roll that is preserved, dated 1371, deals with the building of the eastern part of the choir, the foundation stones of which had been laid ten years before. The master-mason was Robert de Patrington, and Philip was still the master-carpenter, his wages for the year amounting to £7 16s. The average fortnightly wages account reached £9 8s. 7d. A considerable number of masons were employed, and judging from the differences in the wages paid, they were of several grades. The labourers received 1s. 4d. a week and each was given an extra 3s. 4d. for a working jacket (*tunica sua*). Casual labourers earned 3½d. to 4½d. a day. Evidently the east end of the choir of the cathedral was being roofed in 1371, for there are several references to the ceiling (*celatura*) in the Roll for this year. Two large trees, 80 rigalds (timber beams?) and 500 wainscots were purchased, 5¼ roods of timber were sawn for the roof and 41s. 8d. was paid for 10,000 nails. There was also a payment of 47s. 3d. to Richard Kyng for painting the timber ceiling above the High Altar with stars. Amongst the *expensae minutae* is an entry: 'For besomns and wengges [wings for sweeping] bought for cleaning the church, 6d.' The total expenditure for 1371 was £622 9s. 4d., but the *custos fabricae* had £177 19s. 9½d. in hand at the end of the year.

An interval of twenty-eight years elapses before the next Roll is forthcoming, but in the interim the chapter acquired an eighty-years' lease of a quarry at Huddlestone. In 1399 Hugh of Hedon was master-mason, and he with Laurence de Broghton were allowed the expenses of a journey to the quarries at Stapleton and Thovedale to select stone.

Of unusual interest is the inventory of the stores and equipment written on the back of the Fabric Roll of 1399. The tools and instruments in the masons' lodge included 69 stone axes, 1 large hammer, 96 iron chisels, 24 mallets bound with iron, 400 iron fourmers or moulds for stone cutting, a pair of iron compasses, 2 tracynbordes [drawing boards], 4 leaden chargeors for making moulds, 4 wheeled trucks for carting heavy stones, a small hatchett, a handsaw, a shovel, a wheelbarrow, 2 buckets, 2 barrows for small stones and 4 iron wedges. In the crypt (*les cruddes* or *crowdes*) were 6 stone hammers, 10 barrows, 2 wheelbarrows, a large pulley with 4 ropes for hauling up stones and cement, and 3 baskets for the same. A separate list of carpenter's tools makes mention of pikes (picks), shovels, a measure for lime, scales with an iron beam and weights, iron gouges and ladles, and soldering irons.

In July 1400, Henry IV permitted stone to be brought from the quarry at Stapleton toll-free. Later in the year quantities of iron were wrought into bars for the windows of the choir. The smith, John Harpham, was paid 16s. for making window bars, and £4 2s. for mending some of the masons' tools; 328 lb. of iron were used by William Smyth for window bars, for the making of which he received 12s. 4d. The names of the quarrymen and the wages they earned, averaging 3½ marks a fortnight, are also recorded in this year. For clearing up loose stone in the quarry a John Sowerby was paid 58s. 8d. and various sums were expended on sleddyng (sledging) masonry from the quarry to York.

In 1402–3 John Burgh, glazier, was employed at £4 7s. 9d. per annum; Gilbert the plasterer was paid 11d. and Clyfton earned 2s. for daubing (pro doubyng). These entries, which probably relate to the interior of the choir, show that the roof was completed, and mention is made in the same Roll of pavyng. Further, a donation of 15s. was made to the Commons of the City of York for clearing waste and rubbish out of the cathedral. For some years large sums were spent on the quarrying of stone and on cartage; work on the outside of the choir-arm continued and the central tower was commenced c. 1410. In 1415 under the direction of the King's master-mason, William of Colchester, thirty-nine masons were at work on the central tower, their wages totalling £241 3s. 2d. for the year. In the Register of Archbishop Neville is a letter from the chapter requesting the dean to inform the King that William of Colchester had been attacked by certain of the York masons; nevertheless the royal master-mason continued in office at York until 1419–20.

The Roll of 1415 is the earliest extant that sheds light on the sources of the fabric fund. Oblations, penitence-money, legacies and bequests are listed in detail. At the tomb of Archbishop Scrope (p. 33), the offerings amounted to £73 8s., and the total sum received exceeded £615. Then follow the items of expenditure.

Not connected with the building operations is an item of no little interest in the Roll of 1418–19. 'Paid to Martell, carrier, for sending 1 image of wood, to the executors of the archbishop of Canterbury, 3s. 4d.' The archbishop referred to was Thomas Arundel, d. 1414, who had been translated to Canterbury from York in 1396. With the intention of erecting a monument to him in Canterbury cathedral, his executors had sent for a wooden copy of the effigy at York.

Work on the great central tower of the cathedral continued long after the departure of William of Colchester, who was succeeded in 1421 by William Long. The new master-mason was paid a fee of £10, and £81 5s. 2d. was expended on wages of quarrymen at Thevedale, Huddlestone and Bramham and on the transport of masonry to York. Amongst the incidental expenses (*variae expensae*) of 1422 is an entry: 'For 1 jar of green ginger bought and given to my lord archbishop [Bowet], 3s. 9d.' The arms of the archbishop were painted in the south aisle of the choir at a cost of 4d. At the same time brushes of pigs' bristles were purchased for 15d. for the use of the labourers who white-limed the *severyse* (bays) of the south aisle.

Ten years later, Thomas Pak was the master-mason at a fee of £10. The purchase of a new long rope for hauling stone *super campanile* indicates that the south-west tower had been commenced. The balance in hand (*sic remanent*) at the end of the year 1433 was £36 18s. 0½d. The following year only fourteen masons were at work on the tower. Another ten years passed and large quantities of timber, iron and lead were still being purchased; probably the timber was for the south-western tower and the lead for the roof of the choir. Until lead was available it was the practice to roof a new building with a temporary covering of tiles or shingles. The Roll of 1433 accounts for the purchase of fodders of lead from various sources at a total cost of £27 5s. 5½d.

Thenceforward both income and expenditure show a remarkable decrease, and the number of masons and other craftsmen drops to a dozen and in some years less. In 1442 ten masons were at work, their wages amounting to £56 3s. 2d., and £3 12s. 6d. was paid to labourers. The next year, in addition to John Bowde the master-mason, and thirteen other masons, there were two setters, eight carpenters and a number of labourers. The receipts had fallen to £290 4s. 3¼d., and the expenditure was £260 4s. 5½d. By 1447 the south-western tower was well-nigh completed; the wages of the master-mason, John Barton, and eight masons amounted to £62 17s. 5d., five carpenters were paid £23 4s. 9d., and six labourers cost the chapter £14 18s.

From time to time the owner of the Huddlestone quarries, Sir John Langton and his family, had granted quantities of stone for the work on the cathedral, and in 1450 the chapter showed their appreciation of his beneficence by sending him 'one pipe of red wine' and other gifts. The Fabric Roll of that year mentions the payment of 3s. 4d. to William Nuttyng for expenses incurred in riding to Lincoln to enlist the services of John Porter, cementarius. He was away four days not without success, but after a short stay at York, Porter returned to Lincoln. In 1456, however, Porter was back again as master-mason, an appointment he held for ten years. In the first year of his office six masons, six carpenters and a few labourers were employed; one of the masons, John Whittylsey, came from Leicester, the chapter paying his travelling expenses. The purchase of lead and iron figure largely in the Roll of 1456. From J. Winton, a monk of Fountains abbey, 100 pigs of lead were bought at 4½d. a pig. Evidently the south-western tower was ready for the bells in 1458, for the Roll of that year shows a charge for a new pulley and other fitments. The lease of a quarry at Huddlestone expired in 1465, but stone being still needed, the chapter renewed it for a term of nineteen years. A larger body of masons was engaged in 1470, no doubt for the building of the north-western tower. The master-mason, Robert Spillesby, accompanied by a servant, rode out in quest of 'marblers', a twenty-eight-days' jaunt that cost the chapter 37s. 4d., and in June he visited several places in search of craftsmen. For the year 1470 the expenditure reached £335 0s. 7½d., and the *sic remanent* at the end of the year amounted to £20 3s. 7d. Entries in the Roll of this year furnish evidence that the central tower was in the final stage of construction. Three men were sent to Cawood for cutting timber that had been bought for the bosses of the tower vault, the cost of their trip being 6s. Much timber was purchased and fifteen carpenters were employed. Forty lengths of ash were bought for 16d. to make handles for the carpenters' tools, and David Carver was paid 17s. 4d. for carving a number of wooden bosses. Other men were engaged in making iron bars for the windows of the lantern, amongst whom was George Redeshaw, who received 30s. 2d. for his labour. In this year a quantity of glass was procured for the windows; a dozen or more glass painters were employed, some for a period of twenty-three weeks and more, at an average weekly wage of 3s. They lived and had their workshops in Stonegate, York.

The Roll of 1472 gives details of the colours and materials needed for painting the vault of the lantern. They include: 2 lb. of Indian blue, 2 lb. vermilion, 2 lb. ochre, 6 lb. red lead, 7½ lb. white lead, 4 lb. mastic gum, oil, gold leaf and two stones for grinding the colours. The year's bill for painting materials adds up to £21 4s. 5d.

After directing the building operations in the cathedral for six years, Robert Spillesby died in 1472 and the chapter chose as his successor William Hyndeley of Norwich, a mason of such repute that the chapter paid for the removal of his family and goods to York and assisted him in a law suit. The advent of Hyndeley is

duly recorded in the Fabric Roll of 1473. A special task awaited
him at York, viz., the erection of the stone pulpitum at the entrance
to the choir. When work on the pulpitum began, the master had
two masons under him; six carpenters who were employed were
paid £11 16s. 4d., and three labourers, £4 16s. 4d.

By this time (1473) the western towers were finished save for
the windows and the chimes. In addition to iron for the window
bars, 21 fodders of lead at 73s. 4d. each and solder to the value of
22s. were bought; and William Plommer, John Midleton and
Robert Burton worked on the leading of the windows for varying
periods at 6d. a day. An apprentice named Robert Newton was
paid 4d. a day. The chiming bells in the south-western tower were
tested by certain of the vicars-choral, who composed a tune for
the chimes and were rewarded by the chapter with wine that cost
15d.

Six years later twelve masons were assisting Hyndeley on the
building of the pulpitum, one of whom, Jacob Dam, a carver,
received 39s. for thirteen weeks' work. At a cost of 14s. 7d., 175
crockets were carved to adorn the screen. Sundry expenses in the
Roll of 1479 include an entry of 2s. 4d. for a man-servant's journey to Nottingham, where artificers were greatly in demand for
the building of the royal castle. His mission was to secure the
exemption of Hyndeley's men from the royal round-up.

In 1485 the wages bill for the master-mason and eleven others,
engaged on the erection of the pulpitum came to £42 5s. 10d.
William Busshell, *entayler*, carved 240 crockets and 32 gargoyles,
the latter for the external parapets of the cathedral, for which he
received 50s. 8d. In 1504 the year before Hyndeley's death, twelve
masons were working with him and there were glaziers, sawyers
and labourers, whose wages amounted to £66 13s. 5d.

York cathedral was now completed, and the subsequent Rolls
are in the main records of expenses incurred for minor undertakings, reparations and equipment. A few items of interest
emerge. In 1510, 2 hides were bought for the smith's bellows for
8s.; in 1516 Ursino Mylner was paid 49s. 4d. for binding choir-
books and for painting the red chest, an alms box that stood by
the south-eastern pier at the crossing; in 1519, two paintings of
the B.V.M., one above the red chest and the other at the entrance
to the north choir aisle, were executed by two painters for £10;
in 1526 John Applyn, a painter, received £7 3s. 4d. for regilding
the covering of S. William's shrine, and William Drawswerde, a
firm of some note in York, was paid 21s. 8d. for 'carving-work' on
the shrine. John How of London installed the organ in the choir
for 20s.

The short-lived revival of the old faith in Mary's reign is indicated in the Fabric Roll of 1556, under the heading 'Painters'. 'To Wylliam Freer for paintinge of the hye altare, £30. To the saide Wylliam Freer for paintinge Oure Ladye; To Rycharde Thickpenny, for a weeks borde of the saide Wylliam Freer and two painters with him, 12s. For ... painters for another weeke's borde, 12s. To Wylliam Greateheade for makeing of Mary and John, £3. For makinge of a tabernacle, 26s. 8d.'

In the archives of Canterbury cathedral is a document that provides details of the cost of the five-light Decorated window inserted in the south wall of S. Anselm's chapel. Put into English it reads: 'Memorandum, that in the year 1336 was made a new window in Christ Church, Canterbury, viz., in the chapel of the Apostles SS. Peter and Paul upon which was expended the following sums:

Imprimis, for the workmanship only, or labour
of the masons   ..   ..   £21 17s. 9d.
Item, for taking down the wall where the window was placed   ..   ..   16s. 9d.
Item, for lime and gravel   ..   ..   ..   £1 0s. 0d.
Item, for 20 cwt. of iron bought for the said window   ..   ..   £4 4s. 0d.
Item, for the labour of the smiths   ..   ..   £3 5s. 4d.
Item, for Caen stone bought for the same ..   £5 0s. 0d.
Item, for glass, and the labour of the glaziers .   £6 13s. 4d.

Total £42 17s. 2d.

The sum of £8 13s. 4d. was given by certain friends for the window, and the remainder of the money was furnished by the prior [Richard Oxenden].'

17. The Reformation, The Puritan Revolution and Nineteenth Century Restoration

Cathedral Priories converted into Secular Establishments by Henry VIII · Spoils of the Monastic Suppression · The Destruction of Shrines · Fate of the Conventual Buildings · Provision for Housing the New Secular Chapters at Canterbury, Durham, Winchester and other Cathedrals · Treasures of the Secular Cathedrals at the Reformation · The Suppression of Chantries and Confiscation of Property · The Collegiate Foundations of Ripon and Southwell · The Purging Zeal of the Reformer · Appointment of Commissioners for Spoliation in 1551 · Old S. Paul's Cathedral · The Puritan Ascendancy and the Civil War · Abolition of Episcopacy in 1642 · Havoc wrought by Cromwell's Troopers in Cathedrals · Richard Culmer at Canterbury · Vandalism at Rochester, Worcester, Peterborough, Lichfield, etc. · Wren's New Cathedral of S. Paul · The Maltreatment of Salisbury, Lichfield, Hereford, and Durham Cathedrals by James Wyatt in the late Eighteenth Century · The Gothic Revival and Restoration Mania of the Nineteenth Century · Gilbert Scott · His Measures to save Central Towers · The Restoration of S. Albans by Scott and Grimthorpe · Nineteenth-Century Rebuildings at Canterbury, Bristol, Peterborough and Southwark

⟦ DESECRATION AND PILLAGE at the Reformation, further spoliation and destruction by the Puritans in the seventeenth century, and maltreatment by the restoration enthusiasts of the nineteenth century have reduced our ancient cathedrals to the bare skeletons they present today.

Under the Act of 1539 that legalized the suppression of the greater monasteries, the eight cathedral-priories then existing were surrendered to the Crown with all their possessions. The sees, however, were not suppressed, and after the monks had been dispossessed, chapters of prebendaries were installed. Two or three years afterwards, the monastic churches of Westminster, Gloucester, Peterborough, Chester, Bristol and Oxford were elevated to cathedral rank. Bath abbey, the cathedral-priory of the joint see of Bath and Wells, which was in the process of reconstruction at the Dissolution was offered to the city for the sum of 500 marks. The offer being declined, the church was sold after being stripped of the glass, roofing lead and bells. In 1560 the owner, Matthew Colthurst, presented the 'carcase of S. Peter's church' to the citizens for use as a parish church, but thanklessly they made little of the gift and the nave remained roofless for fifty years. A worse fate befell the Benedictine cathedral-priory of Coventry, in which a stool for the Bishop of Coventry and Lichfield had been installed as early as 1100.[1] After the suppression in 1539 the cathedral was dismantled and speedily became derelict and the masonry served as a quarry for buildings in Coventry.

The first solicitude of the King's Commissioners who were appointed to gather in the spoils of the monastic suppression was the innumerable treasures of gold and silver, the priceless plate, crosses, candlesticks, censers, reliquaries, rings, jewelled gloves and the tapestries, but above all the precious metals and gems with which the shrines of the saints were encrusted. The sacristies were robbed of their copes and vestments, of altar cloths embroidered in gold and silver, of brocades and stuffs from the East, which were scattered and sold and even shipped abroad where they found a ready market. In an Inventory made at Christ Church, Canterbury, at the Suppression no less than two hundred and sixty-two copes are enumerated, an enormous collection that can be accounted for, from the fact that every suffragan bishop was required at his consecration to present a 'decent cope' to the cathedral.

By no means the least valuable treasures that were lost to posterity were the libraries, the collections of written copies of unnumbered books and of illuminated manuscripts, comparatively few of which have been preserved.

In 1541 when the shrine of S. Thomas of Canterbury was destroyed and the remains of Becket cast to the winds, the jewels and precious metals that were ripped from the feretrum were packed in two chests, so large that it needed sixteen men to carry them away. The Return of the valuables that went into the King's coffers included 4,994 oz. of gold, 4,425 oz. of silver-gilt and 5,286 oz. of plain silver, and at a subsequent date 26 oz. of gold and 4,090 oz. of plain silver afforded further plunder. For the removal of the lesser spoils that were sent to London twenty-six carts are said to have been used.

In the cathedral establishments of the New Foundation the newly constituted chapters found themselves in possession of

---

[1] Ranking in size and character with other great monastic churches, it was a cruciform building with a tower at the crossing and twin western towers. To the east of the cathedral stood the bishop's palace.

cloisters and various monastic buildings for which they had little use, the property being granted them by letters patent. As a visible sign of the importance and dignity of the cathedral body, the gate-houses at the entrance to the precincts were in many instances retained, the upper chambers being used as lodgings for a porter or other servant. Famous are the fine gatehouses still standing at Canterbury, Ely, Bristol, and Peterborough.

Dwellings within the precincts were needed for the bishop, the dean and prebendaries and for the lesser dignitaries and menials; and the monastic chapter houses could be put to the same pur-poses as in the Old Foundation cathedrals. But the dorter (dormi-tory), the frater (refectory), the farmery (infirmary), kitchen and other offices, designed for the communal life of the monks, were buildings that could be and in many cases were dispensed with. Nor were the secular chapters always willing to saddle themselves with the expense of maintaining the fabric of the cloisters.

Of the fourteen cathedrals of Henry VIII's Foundation, Can-terbury, Chester, Durham, Gloucester, Norwich and Worcester have retained their cloisters to this day. At Bristol and Oxford the cloister walks remain in part, but elsewhere, e.g. at Winchester, Ely and Peterborough the cloisters and much else have disap-peared.

The acute housing shortage in the precincts at Canterbury resulted in the demolition of many buildings solely for the sake of the materials. Thus, the dorter, frater, kitchen and farmery, none of which could be converted into residences were taken down. The buildings on the north side of the Green Court comprising the monks' granary, the bakehouse, the brewery and the laundry, were used as dwellings; and on the east side of the Court on the site of the hospitium, the deanery was erected in 1570. In the south-west corner was the cellarer's hall and lodging, that was retained for the King's use. The ancient palace of the archbishop at the south-west of the cathedral was destroyed by fire shortly after the Suppression and remained in ruins until it was rebuilt by Archbishop Parker in 1558.

At Durham the conventual buildings are preserved as in no other cathedral of the New Foundation save Chester. The cloisters were drastically altered in the eighteenth and nineteenth centuries and the chapter house has been entirely rebuilt. The larger part of the eastern and southern cloistral buildings date from the Nor-man period and the monks' kitchen at the south-west is preserved in its entirety. A valuable survival is the two-storeyed building on the west side of the cloister, with the spacious dorter on the upper floor (Fig. 11).

The lofty wall of the Close at Winchester marks the extent of the monastic precincts, but the changes wrought at various times have obliterated almost all traces of the cloisters and conventual buildings. The Norman chapter house was used by the dean and prebendaries for a century or so but was demolished in 1637 for the sake of the roofing lead. The prior's lodging survives as the deanery and retains many of its mediaeval features.

The cloistral buildings at Worcester were apparently not deemed superfluous by the secular chapter for they remained fairly intact until the Commonwealth, when in 1660 the lead and timbers were torn from the roofs and realized £8,204.

In the Library of Corpus Christi College, Cambridge, is a document that sheds much light on the fate of the monastic buildings at Ely in 1541. It was drawn up by four Commissioners and gives in detail the assignments made to the dean and prebendaries for their several houses. Except for 'the Bishop's mansion house' the buildings were to be converted into residences as the respective tenants could best contrive. Five of the prebendaries were housed in extensions of the Norman farmery, the minor canons took over the almonry, the sacristy and 'the newe Hall'. 'Necessary reparacions and edificez [were] to be done wher most necessary,' and two of the prebendaries were empowered by the Commissioners and the chapter 'both to pluck down and sell, and reserve for necessary buyldyng' any superfluous structures. They were held 'acomptable before the same Comyssyoners or dene and chapter iiij times in the year'. Evidently they had no need for the chapter house which was plucked down in due course; it was ordered 'to be chonged' by the Commissioners. The demolitions then carried out and the subsequent destruction by the Commonwealth surveyors in 1649 account for the disappearance of many of the pre-Reformation buildings at Ely.

The letters patent of June 1541, incorporating the secular chapter at Rochester granted the dean and prebendaries the cathedral church with all its chapels, bell-towers and enclosures, but reserved to the King all the buildings within the precincts. In the Bodleian Library are the accounts for structural alterations effected by the Crown, that show that the work of building and repairing lodgings for the King and Queen was put in hand immediately after the priory was dissolved. The royal lodgings occupied the monks' dorter in the eastern cloistral range; in April 1542, carpenters and plumbers were at work repairing the roofs of the lodgings. From midsummer to Christmas 1542, the 'gret hall which was the frater' and an adjoining chamber in the south cloistral block were being reconditioned if not rebuilt for the King's use.

The monks' farmery also was converted into residential apartments, probably for the King's retinue and servants. But houses and lodgings had to be found for the dean and prebendaries, and to this end the King set up a Commission to ensure that 'unto every one of them, according to their degrees, such convenient and dwelling houses about the church be devided, sorted and assigned . . . as far as the buyldyngs and grounde of the saide scite of the late pryor doth extend.' In the main the area available for these houses lay to the north and east of the cathedral choir. The dean's lodging, an L-shaped mansion, stood at the east of the cathedral. Three years after the death of Henry VIII the King's House within the precincts was granted to Lord Cobham, who made the property over to the dean and chapter in 1558. By then the members of the chapter were comfortably settled in their lodgings and the royal mansion was demolished. Before the end of the sixteenth century, little rem ned of the ancient buildings and the precincts were in much the same condition as at present.

When the new see of Gloucester was created, the bishop was granted the abbot's house that lay some distance north of the cloisters, and the prior's lodging to the west of the cloisters was assigned to the dean. Other houses in the precincts became the residences of the prebendaries and officers. No wholesale demolitions were carried out though the hall and chapel of the farmery were pulled down. The great cloisters and the chapter house were spared and the farmery cloisters, an irregular quadrangle, remained intact until the Civil War. The frater on the north side of the cloisters was destroyed by fire in 1540.

Of the priory buildings at Norwich, the dormitory and infirmary were converted into dwellings for the prebendaries, and the prior's lodging served as the residence of the dean. Part of the dormitory was used as a dining hall. Except for the infirmary, which remained in part until early in the nineteenth century, most of the conventual buildings had disappeared by 1640. The detached bell-tower was demolished in 1626.

At Bristol the Gatehouse on College Green and the Norman chapter house survive, but the conventual buildings were mostly swept away by the secular chapter. By letters patent of 1542, the abbot's lodging was given to the bishop; the mediaeval frater was converted into a two-storeyed building to provide chambers for the prebendaries, and houses were built in the cloister garth.

The monastic apartments that remain *in situ* at Chester afford ample proof that Henry VIII's chapter were not bent on the destruction of newly acquired property that might or might not be needed. The four walks of the cloisters (restored in recent times), the chapter house, the frater, the calefactorium or warming house, and the cellarium on the west side of the cloisters are invaluable on the whole, indicating as they do the arrangement of the chief apartments of the Benedictine monks who gave place to the secular chapter in 1541 (Fig. 18).

The elevation of the abbey church of Peterborough was not marked by the destruction of the cloisters and the conventual buildings, which survived more or less intact until the Commonwealth, when they were taken down and the materials sold; the chapter house was demolished and the bishop's palace stripped of its roofing lead.

At Oxford the monastic buildings were cleared away soon after 1525, when the priory was appropriated by Cardinal Wolsey for the college he was intent on founding. Some of the masonry was used to make walks in the meadows by the river, and the greater part of the cloisters together with the western bays of the nave of the church were taken down to provide room for the college buildings. The chapter house and parts of the east and north cloister walks escaped destruction.

The secular cathedral establishments were spared the upheaval that befell the cathedral-priories, and their constitution remained more or less unimpaired, though some of the rich prebends were seized by the Crown and granted to lay lessees. The shrines met the same fate as those in the monastic cathedrals, and spoliation became the order of the day. In 1538 the greedy and unscrupulous Henry VIII issued Commissions under the Privy Seal to local 'Visitors' to undertake the destruction of shrines and to appropriate for the King's use all the gold, silver and precious stones with which the shrines were adorned. The Commission of 14 November 1539, signed by Thomas Cromwell, the Lord Privy Seal, for the spoliation and demolition of the shrine of S. Richard in Chichester cathedral is typical.

'Henry 8 to our trusty and well beloved servant, Sir William Goring, and [William] Erneley, Esq. For as much as we have been lately informed that in our City of Chichester and Cathedral Church of the same, there hath been used long and is used much superstition and certain kynd of idolatry aboute the shryne and bones of a certain bishop of the same, which they call S. Richard, and a certain resort thither of sundry our subjects, which being men of simplicitie, by the inculcation of certain of the clerge . . . doo seke at the said shryne and bones of the same that [which] God only hath authoritie and power to grant, We, wylyng such superstitious abuses and idolatries to be taken away, command you with all convenient diligence to repayre unto the said Cathe-

dral Church . . . and there to take down that shrine . . . with all
the sylver, gold, juells, and ornamentes to the same shryne be-
longyng, and also all other reliques and reliquaries, with all the
plate, gold, juells, ornamentes aforesaid, to be safely and surely
conveyed and brought into our Tower of London, there to be
bestowed as we shall further determine at your arrival. And also
that you shall see bothe the place where the shryne standeth to be
raysed and defaced even to the very ground, and all such other
images of the church of any notable superstition hath been used
to be taken and conveighed away' (*Lamb MS. 577 P.R.O.*). The
shrine of S. Richard was accordingly destroyed and the two Visitors received £40 from the Crown for 'disgarnishing of the shrine
at Chichester and bringing the same to the Tower of London'.

In the King's letters dated 1540 referring to Lincoln cathedral
mention is made of 'a certain shryne and divers fayned reliques in
the cathedral . . . with which all the symple people be moch de-
ceaved and broughte into greate supersticion and idolatrye . . .
and being mynded to bringe our loving subjects to the righte
knowledge of the truth', the relics, chalices, pyxes, plate, jewels of
the bishop's mitre and hundreds of copes were carted off to the
Tower of London. The immense booty seized by the King's Commissioners is detailed in a memorandum of 1541; of gold, 2,621 oz.,
of silver, 4,285 oz., besides a big haul of diamonds, sapphires,
rubies and other precious stones. Further, the see of Lincoln was
impoverished by the alienation of thirty-four manors.

In the first year of Edward VI's reign an Act of Parliament was
passed for the suppression of chantries 'whereby certain chantries,
colleges, free chapels and possessions of the same were given to
the King's majesty'. The Act of 1547 gave the Crown all the endowments, properties and rents that had furnished stipends for
the chantry priests, together with the funds of all gilds and frater-
nities. 'And also be it ordained and enacted by the authority of
this present Parliament, that Our Sovereign Lord the King, shall
have and enjoy such goods, chattels, jewels, plate, ornaments and
other moveables as be the common goods of every such college,
chantry, free chapel or stipendiary priest, belonging or annexed
to the furniture or services of the several foundations' (*I Edward VI,
c. 14*).

Commissioners were appointed to survey the churches throughout the land 'thereby to know what money was bestowed to the
founding or maintenance of any priest or priests, anniversary or
obit or other like thing, light or lamp, by them or any of them'.
After the passing of the Chantries Act, a great number of chapels
that had been specially built in churches great and small for the

recitation of soul-masses were dismantled, the altars broken up and the enclosing screens thrown down. More than one-third of the seventy chantry chapels now surviving were founded by bishops in their own cathedrals. Apparently not all the post-Reformation prelates were disposed to sweep away chapels that had been founded by distinguished predecessors whose memory was still revered.

Under the Chantries Act the collegiate churches, now the cathedrals of Ripon and Southwell, were suppressed. In 1557 the Court of Exchequer ruled that the college of Southwell was exempt from the Act; the chapter was therefore restored and lasted until 1840.

The confiscation of chantry properties and endowments was followed by injunctions and proclamations that spelt further spoliation. An Order in Council issued in 1548 ordered the removal of all images from churches, as being things corrupt, vain and superstitious. The iconoclastic fury of the Reformer vented itself on pulpita and reredoses in the cathedrals; the statues of Our Lord, the Virgin Mary and the Apostles that occupied niches were removed and broken up; glass windows portraying figures of the Saints were shattered and mural paintings obliterated and whitewashed. A veritable orgy of destruction broke out at Old S. Paul's. When the Great Rood was being taken down by the King's Visitors in November 1547, two of the men engaged in the sacrilegious deed were killed, 'which the Papist priests said was the will of God'. This seemed to be the signal for the destruction of Roods all over the country. At Lincoln in 1548 Bishop Holbeach gave up all the remaining treasures that Henry VIII's Commissioners had thought proper to leave behind, and assisted by the dean, he pulled down and defaced most of the beautiful tombs in the cathedral 'and broke all the figures of the Saints round about the building and pulled down those of Our Saviour, the Virgin and the Crucifix; so that at the end of the year 1548 there was scarcely a whole figure or tomb remaining'. The purging zeal of the Reformer was such that in 1550 bishops were ordered to have all stone altars removed; the mensae were thrown down and reredoses wrecked or mutilated.

Under the Presidency of the Duke of Northumberland in 1551 the Privy Council directed that Commissioners should undertake a search through all the shrines of England for all the goods, plate, jewels and ornaments belonging to any church, chapel, gild or fraternity. Cathedrals and other churches were accordingly robbed of their treasures, reliquaries, plate, statuary, altar pieces and paintings of incalculable value, that had been amassed through the centuries. But all this plunder 'rather stayed the stomach than satisfied the hunger of the King's Exchequer, for the allaying whereof Parliament conferred the bishopric of Durham on the Crown (1553). Bishop Tunstall was then in durance for recusancy, which gave the Crown a readier grip on his bishopric' (*Fuller*).[1] Two years later the properties were restored to the see by Queen Mary.

Amongst the treasures surrendered by the chapter of Hereford were a golden chalice weighing 22 lb. 9 oz., two basins weighing 102 oz., and a pastoral staff of silver-gilt 11 lb. 7 oz. in weight.

The five years of Mary's reign were all too short to effect a complete and permanent restoration of the altars, roods and other 'objects of superstition' that had been swept away by Edward VI, and after Mary's death spoliation broke out anew. William Whittingham, who held the deanery of Durham from 1563 to 1579 'defaced all such stones as had any pictures of brass or other imagery-work or chalices wrought upon them, and employed them to his own use, and did make a washing house of them' (*Athenae Oxoniensis*).

In the century following the Reformation, our mediaeval cathedrals were subjected to little or no structural changes, the exception being Old S. Paul's, that narrowly escaped destruction in 1561. In June of that year the timber spire of the central tower was struck by lightning and within a short time was enveloped in flames. The burning timbers set fire to the roofs of the cathedral which were entirely destroyed. As a temporary measure, the building was rendered weatherproof by covering the high vaults with light boarding, and by 1566 strong timber roofs had been put up at a cost of £6,000. But the restoration was far from thorough, and after a long period of neglect the cathedral fell into a derelict state. In James I's reign a royal Commission was appointed to determine what should be done; the actual work of restoration was begun in 1632 and continued until the outbreak of the Civil War. The task of repairing the fabric was entrusted to Inigo Jones, Surveyor of His Majesty's Works, the pioneer of English Renaissance architecture. According to Stuart taste, there was nothing incongruous in grafting features of Classic origin on to the mediaeval fabric of Old S. Paul's. To ennoble the chief entrance of the cathedral, Jones erected a Classic portico against the west front; standing on a stylobate of five steps was a colonnade of Corinthian columns, and above the entablature was a balustraded parapet with pedestals for ten statues in Roman costume, of which only two, viz., James I and Charles I, were ever made. To the virtuosi of

---

[1] Henry VIII had despoiled the see of Durham of many of its franchises and had granted Anne Boleyn £1,000 a year out of its revenues.

the day the portico left nothing to be desired. The portals of the west front were replaced by Renaissance doorways and the aisle roofs were masked by large scroll-brackets. The method employed by Jones in repairing the exterior of the nave was to cut away the decayed stonework and the crumbling Gothic features, re-face with new masonry and dress the whole in Classic attire, an incrustation that ruined the mediaeval aspect of the western arm of the great church. Broad pilasters were substituted for Gothic buttresses, the parapet was 'modernized' and adorned with stone balls, and windows were stripped of their tracery and framed in the Classic mode. The western walls of both transepts were treated in a similar manner and the end wall of the south transept was completely transmogrified. Mercifully the eastern arm of the cathedral was spared, for on the outbreak of war in 1642 the work of restoration had only reached the transepts and the scheme then fell to pieces.

During the Puritan ascendancy and the Civil War of the seventeenth century our cathedrals were subjected to another purifying onslaught and a second wave of fanatical destruction swept over them. The Long Parliament of 1641, furious in its antagonism against the Church, ordered a visitation of all churches for the purpose of further vandalism. As a result, images, stalls, tables turned altar-wise, crucifixes and pictures that had survived the Reformation were wantonly desecrated and mutilated. In 1642 the *Root and Branch Bill* provided for the abolition of bishoprics and chapters; episcopacy was extirpated and a form of Presbyterian government was established. The havoc and irreparable ruin inflicted upon our ancient cathedrals during the Great Rebellion makes sad reading.

In 1642 the nave of Canterbury was used as barracks for the Commonwealth troopers, who stripped the lead from the roofs of the cathedral and of the chapter house and cloisters; the hangings in the choir were torn down, the organ destroyed, and the High Altar with its tabernacled reredos 'richly overlaid with gold' was overthrown. The monuments were shamefully defaced and were rifled of their brasses and iron grates. In the following year a 'more orderly reformation' of the cathedral was undertaken by a fanatic priest, Richard Culmer, whose delight lay in the destruction of the window glass. From the top of a ladder he threw down the glass from the great window in the north transept that had been the gift of Edward IV. The battering of one of the panels depicting S. Thomas was described by Culmer as 'rattling down proud Becket's glassy bones'. This same destructive fanatic stripped the pulpitum of all the images of saints and apostles. 'Many idolls

L

of stone', he wrote, 'were demolished. . . . Thirteen representing Christ and his twelve apostles, standing over the west door of the choir were all hewed down . . . and twelve mitred saints sate aloft which were all cast down headlong' (*Cathedrall Newes from Canterbury*, 1644). Compared with Canterbury, Rochester cathedral suffered little. On their way from Canterbury the rebels visited Rochester the same year, where their activities were described by Mercurius Rusticus in 1646. 'Coming to Rochester they brought the same affections with them which they had expressed at Canterbury; in wisdom they thought it not safe to give them the same scope here as there; for the multitude though mad enough, yet were not so mad . . . to approve such heathenish practices; by this means the monuments of the dead, which elsewhere they brake up and violated, stand untouched. Escutcheons and arms of the nobility and gentry remained undefaced, the seats and stalls of the quire escaped breaking down; only those things which were branded by the leaders of the Faction, for Popery and Innovation, on these they took liberties to let loose their wild zeal; they broke down the rayl about the Lord's table or altar, call it which you please; they seized upon the velvet covering of the Holy Table, and in contempt of those Holy Mysteries, removed the Table into a lower place of the church.'

Worcester cathedral was the scene of wanton destruction in September 1642, when the ill-disciplined Parliamentary forces entered the building, tore down the High Altar and the furniture and fittings of the choir and ransacked the crypt of stores and provisions that had been sent there for the support of the Royalists. After the battle of Worcester, six thousand Royalist prisoners were 'penned up in the cathedral'.

Similar vandalism occurred at Peterborough, 'which Cromwell did most miserably deface' in 1643. The organs and choir stalls were wrecked, and a great brass chandelier in the choir was knocked to pieces; all the tombs in the cathedral including that of Katherine of Aragon, were hacked down. The reredos of the High Altar, a curious piece of stonework was broken up. 'A stately screen it was, well wrought, painted and gilt, which rose up as high almost as the roof of the church in a row of three lofty spires, with other lesser spires growing out of each of them. . . . This had now no imagery work upon it or anything that might justly give offence, and yet because it bore the name of the High Altar, was pulled all down with ropes, lay'd low and level with the ground.' Before the end of the seventeenth century the fabric of the cathedral had fallen into such disrepair that the Lady Chapel north of the choir had to be taken down and the materials sold for funds to effect urgent repairs.

Few cathedrals sustained such extensive damage in the Civil War as did Lichfield in 1643. Shattered by two thousand cannon-shot, it was thoroughly ransacked by the Roundhead troopers. The spire of the central tower collapsed and lead was torn from the roofs and melted to make shot. The glass was shattered, the bells broken up, monuments mutilated, the statuary of the west front defaced and the chapter records destroyed. During riotous proceedings in the cathedral, one of the soldiers broke open the tomb of Bishop Scrope and found in it a silver chalice and a crozier. The wholesale ransacking of the monuments that followed his 'find' accounts for the paucity of mediaeval tombs in Lichfield cathedral at the present day. Cromwell's troopers kept courts of guard in the transepts and every day they hunted a cat with hounds through the cathedral aisles. A calf wrapped in linen was carried to the font and was the subject of a mock baptism.

When Dr. Hackett succeeded to the see of Lichfield in 1661, he found the cathedral in a desolate and ruinous condition. The day after his arrival at Lichfield, with laudable zeal he set about restoration; with his own coach horses and with teams and labourers, he removed the rubbish, himself laying the first hand to the work. He also raised a sum exceeding £9,000 towards the task and obtained a grant of a hundred trees from Needwood Forest from Charles II. The restoration was sufficiently advanced for the re-consecration of the cathedral on Christmas Eve, 1669.

Norwich cathedral was subjected to hideous profanities. Organ pipes, vestments and books were carried in a sacrilegious procession and burned in the market place in 1643. Bishop Hall, a witness of the proceedings, wrote: 'What clattering of glasses! what beating down of walls! what tearing up of monuments! what pulling down of seats! what wresting out of irons and brass from the windows and graves! what defacing of arms! what demolishing of curious stonework! what tooting and piping upon the destroyed organ pipes! and what a hideous triumph on the market day before all the country, when all the organ pipes and vestments together with the leaden Cross which had been newly sawn down from the Green Yard pulpit, and the service books and the singing books . . . were carried to the fire in the public market place.'

When the city of Lincoln was taken by the Parliamentary forces in 1644 the cathedral was occupied as a barrack, and the soldiery smashed the stained glass, damaged the tombs and carried off the bronze effigy of Edward I's queen, Eleanor, in the retrochoir. The diarist, Evelyn, records in 1654 that the soldiers 'went in the cathedral with axes and hammers, and shut themselves in till they had rent and torn off some barge-loads of metal, not sparing even the monuments of the dead'.

The city of Winchester was the centre of much hard fighting in 1644. Waller's men invaded the cathedral on horseback, and tombs, images and glass met with the same fate as in other cathedrals. 'Of the brass torn from the violated monuments might have been built a house as strong as the brazen towers of old romances' (*Mercurius Rusticus*). The mortuary chests containing the bones of saints and kings of the Saxon period were desecrated and the contents thrown outside the cathedral. Later they were recovered and replaced in the six painted chests that now rest on top of the stone screens in the choir.

During the siege of Hereford in 1645 the cathedral suffered at the hands of the Roundheads. The decagonal chapter house was destroyed, the lead of the roof being used to cover the keep of the castle; the cathedral library was plundered of valuable manuscripts, the glass windows were smashed and no less than a hundred and seventy monumental brasses were wrenched from their settings. At the restoration of 1786 other brasses weighing two tons in all were sold to a local brazier.

The magnificent accessories of the choir of Exeter cathedral were deemed fitting objects for Puritan mutilation. The gorgeous reredos of the High Altar had been defaced in Edward VI's reign, and the statues that adorned the tabernacling of the sedilia and of the bishop's throne fell easy prey to Puritan axes and hammers. The painted glass was shattered and the carved stalls accorded ill with the form of worship that was observed, when the Independents used the choir and were separated from the Presbyterian congregation in the nave by a brick wall. To permit of the erection of galleries, the piers of the choir were ruthlessly hacked, mutilations were general and the cloisters were pulled down. From such degradation Exeter cathedral was redeemed by Bishop Seth Ward, 1662–7, who spent £25,000 on restoration and improvements.

Such of the monuments in Durham cathedral as had escaped the iconoclastic proclivities of Dean Whittingham *c.* 1570, were grievously damaged by the three thousand Scottish prisoners who were confined in the cathedral after the battle of Dunbar, 1646. Before they regained their liberty they made fires of the woodwork of the choir and wrecked the Neville tombs that stood in the south aisle of the nave, formerly the Neville chantry chapel.

Carlisle cathedral fared badly too. In 1645 the cloisters and the chapter house were destroyed, and five bays of the Norman nave were pulled down by the Parliamentarian forces to furnish material for strengthening the city walls and for building guard-houses and batteries.

At Old S. Paul's the nave was converted into a cavalry barrack, and the brawling and insulting behaviour of the soldiers proved so intolerable a nuisance to dwellers in the churchyard in 1651, that the troops billeted in the cathedral were forbidden to play ninepins there between 9 p.m. and 6 a.m. The restoration of the monarchy gave promise of a happier future for London's ancient cathedral, and in 1663 Charles II appointed a Commission to consider its restoration. Early in 1666 Dr. Christopher Wren laid before the Commission a report on the state of the fabric and suggested that the interior should be recased 'after the Roman manner', and that a rotunda in the Renaissance style should be raised at the crossing. On Sunday, 2 September 1666, the Great Fire of London broke out and the fate of Old S. Paul's was sealed for all time. By the end of that fateful week the vast church was a grim skeleton beyond repair. Shortly afterwards, the west end of the nave was fitted up for use as a temporary choir, but all hopes of saving the cathedral were futile, and in November 1673, letters patent under the Great Seal were issued, announcing the decision to clear the site and erect a new cathedral 'that may equal if not exceed the splendour of the former church and become the principal ornament of Our Royal City'.

S. Paul's Cathedral, 1675–1710

Wren was appointed Principal Architect for 'repairing the whole City, the cathedral, the City churches and other public buildings'. In that office he completed the pioneer work of Inigo Jones, and established a free Classic style of architecture, English in character and suited to the needs of his time.

The present cathedral on Ludgate Hill is the supreme monument of English Renaissance architecture, and of the versatile genius of its creator. It was the first cathedral built in this country since the Reformation, and unlike the mediaeval cathedrals it was designed for Protestant worship. After three other plans and designs had been rejected, the first stone of the new S. Paul's was laid on 21 June 1675, and for thirty-five years the building proceeded under the constant supervision of the architect. The cost, amounting to £736,752 was partly borne by a duty that was levied on all coal brought into London, Wren receiving the princely salary of £200 a year. He gathered about him a band of capable craftsmen, notably Joshua Marshall and Edward Strong, master masons; Francis Bird and Gabriel Cibber, sculptors; Grinling

Gibbons and Jonathan Maine, woodcarvers, besides a host of skilled artificers.

Built of Portland stone, S. Paul's cathedral is cruciform on plan (Fig. 24), 510 feet in length from east to west. Perfectly symmetrical, it consists of an aisled choir of three bays with an apse at the east, north and south transepts each one bay deep, a dome at the crossing carried by eight huge piers, an aisled nave of four bays with flanking chapels at the western end, and a Corinthian portico flanked by steeples forming the west front. As at Wells cathedral, the towers are placed outside the aisles of the nave. In the external angles of the transepts are square bastion-like projections containing staircases and vestries, that structurally add support to the

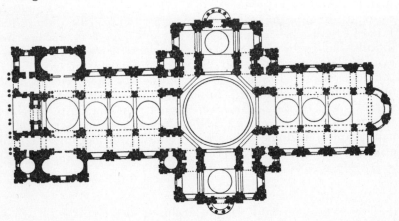

FIG 24. S. Paul's (Wren's)

dome. Extending beneath the whole of the cathedral is a crypt that has served as a mausoleum in which many famous Englishmen have been laid to rest since Wren was buried there in 1723.

Externally the elevation of the cathedral is designed in two storeys or 'orders', faced with coupled pilasters, the lower of the Corinthian order and the upper Composite (Pl. 101). The lower stage is the walling of the aisles, but the upper is an architectural sham, being nothing more than a curtain wall that hides the aisle roofs and the flying-buttresses, and the attic stage of the nave and choir. By raising the aisle walls to the height of the nave, an impression of grandeur and mass was imparted to the building as a whole. Necessarily the west front of the cathedral is designed in two storeys. The central part of the façade consists of a two-storeyed portico, composed of coupled and well-spaced columns, and is surmounted by a pediment in which is a sculptured representation of the Conversion of Saul, the work of Francis Bird. Ranging with the portico are two stages of the flanking towers, above which rise Classic steeples. Admittedly the west front of the cathedral gives no indication of the interior ordonnance. Attached to each transept is a semicircular portico consisting of six Corinthian columns.

The crowning glory of Wren's great church, indeed of the metropolis itself, is the dome. 'Every part of the vast building gathers up into the all-compelling unity of the central dome' (*Francis Bond*). It is seated on a drum, 20 feet above the cathedral roof, encircled by a peristyle of thirty-two columns, every fourth intercolumniation being filled with masonry that acts as a buttress to the dome. At the summit rises a stone lantern adorned with Corinthian columns and terminating in a gilt ball and cross, 365 feet above ground level. In the construction of the dome the ingenuity and the engineering skill of the master mind are displayed to the full. It is carried by eight piers, disposed in the same manner as those of the Octagon at Ely cathedral.[1] From the piers spring eight arches supporting the pendentives that carry the drum, at the base of which is a bold cornice with the Whispering Gallery above. The structure of the dome itself is triple. There is an inner dome built of brick, that is seen inside the cathedral; an outer dome of timber, covered with lead; and between the two is a brick cone, that carries the stone lantern and the timber framing of the outer dome (Pl. 100). The brick cone rests on the haunches of the inner dome like a huge candle-extinguisher. To counteract any tendency of being thrust outwards by the enormous weight of the superstructure, the inner wall of the drum was given an inward inclination and iron chainage was inserted at the base. The motive underlying the construction was to raise an external dome that would dominate the new London, and at the same time to build a lower dome that would be an integral part of the interior design. The means employed was fully justified by the result. It was Wren's intention to incrust the surface of the interior dome with mosaics, a form of decoration so costly that eventually the dome was painted with incidents from the life of S. Paul by Sir James Thornhill.

The arcades of the nave and choir are composed of huge piers and semicircular arches (Pl. 103). Each pier is faced with a Corinthian pilaster supporting an entablature with a boldly projecting cornice, and the arches are made to spring from smaller pilasters attached to the piers. Above the cornice is a low attic stage, and the clerestory wall is pierced with a segmental-arched window in each bay. From the clerestory level transverse arches demarcate

[1] The architect's uncle, Matthew Wren, was bishop of Ely from 1638 to 1667.

the bays of the nave and choir, which are roofed with flat domical vaults carried by pendentives. The aisles are comparatively low and are vaulted with similar saucer-shaped domes.

Despite the criticisms that have been levelled against Wren's masterpiece, chiefly concerning the two-storeyed exterior and the dome-construction, S. Paul's cathedral remains a noble and majestic monument, the work of a commanding personality, whose mastery of Renaissance architecture is manifest in the proportions, the unity of design and the details of this outstanding expression of his genius.

In the eighteenth century necessary repairs in our ancient cathedrals and many ill-advised alterations were carried out in an unsympathetic manner. Towers and turrets were strengthened at Peterborough, Rochester and Ripon; elsewhere, pavements were re-laid and incongruous screens, reredoses and woodwork installed, most of which have since been removed. A proposal to cut fluting in the Norman piers of Gloucester nave was happily rejected.

The irreparable damage wrought in the cathedrals by the band of enthusiastic 'restorers' in the nineteenth century was heralded by the depredations of the notorious James Wyatt, a man whom Pugin described as 'this pest of cathedral architecture'. Between 1787 and 1797 the cathedrals of Lichfield, Salisbury, Hereford, and Durham were committed to the mercies of 'this monster of architectural depravity'. At Lichfield in addition to the general 'restoration' of the doors, windows and pavement, the west front was plastered with Roman cement, two of the spires were partially rebuilt, the end wall of the south transept was strengthened by the erection of two huge buttresses, the stone vaulting of five bays of the nave was replaced by plaster, the Lady Chapel was thrown into the choir by the removal of the reredos and screen of the High Altar, and the choir arcades were walled up.

The damage inflicted on the fabric of Salisbury cathedral by reformer and Puritan was slight compared with the harm caused by Wyatt, who in 1789 was given a free hand in improving and beautifying the cathedral by a number of reckless alterations. The detached bell-tower at the north-west was demolished as also were the Norman porches brought from Old Sarum that were attached to the transept ends. The Perpendicular chantry chapels of the Hungerford and Beauchamp families on either side of the Lady Chapel were swept away on the plea that they were 'in such a state as to greatly exceed any ordinary or possible means of repair'. The masonry of these chapels was used to fashion the Perpendicular choir screen that replaced the thirteenth-century pulpitum.[1] To provide a pleasing vista in the choir, the High Altar was transplanted to the east end of the Lady Chapel. Tombs in all parts of the cathedral were uprooted and rearranged in orderly rows on the stone platforms between the piers of the nave, and in the process the effigies were shuffled and reset on tombs to which they never belonged.

From Salisbury to Hereford, where the collapse of the central tower in 1786 afforded Wyatt an opportunity to surpass his previous efforts. The falling tower had ruined the west front of the cathedral and seriously damaged a great part of the Norman nave. Wyatt shortened the nave by one bay and put up a new façade 'in a neat Gothic fashion', replaced in 1908 by the present west front of Oldrid Scott. In rebuilding the nave, Wyatt substituted a triforium and clerestory of nondescript design and crowned his efforts with an imitation high vault of wood. The spire of the central tower was taken down and the roofs of the nave and choir were lowered to give height to the tower.

In 1791 Wyatt embarked on an injudicious scheme to beautify the mighty Norman cathedral at Durham. A skin of masonry 3 inches deep was chiselled off the exterior so as to produce a uniform surface; the north porch of the nave, with its upper chambers for the monks who kept watch for sanctuary-men, was taken down and the eastern half of the chapter house (since rebuilt) was pulled down to add to the comfort of the dean and chapter. Pudsey's Galilee chapel at the west end of the nave narrowly escaped destruction, for Wyatt proposed making a carriage drive all round the cathedral, and he started ripping the lead from the roof when public opinion intervened.

It was inevitable that the so-called Gothic Revival of the nineteenth century, sponsored by such gifted Victorian architects as Augustus Pugin, Gilbert Scott and George E. Street, for the purpose of restoring the glories of mediaeval Gothic, should be followed by a Restoration-mania that swept the country for twenty-five years or more from the middle of the century. The central figure, the arch-restorer, was Scott who received commission upon commission from cathedral chapters to make new what was old and to purge our ancient cathedrals of everything that was not Gothic. Much mediaeval work that was in a state of decay was ruthlessly 'restored' to what it may or may not have been. 'The first step to restoration is to dash the old work to pieces,' wrote Ruskin. 'The second is usually to put up the cheapest and basest

---

[1] The arcading of the lower part of the old pulpitum, an exquisite piece of thirteenth-century Gothic was re-erected against the west wall on the north choir-transept.

L*

imitation which can escape detection; but in all cases, however careful, however laboured, an imitation still. . . . Do not let us talk of restoration. The thing is a lie from beginning to end.' In his remodelling of the west front of Ripon cathedral, Scott hacked out the mullions and tracery that had been inserted in the Lancet windows c. 1380 and reproduced the original Early English façade.

Scott did not lack a following of enthusiastic mediaevalists and ecclesiologists, with the result that many of our cathedrals and other churches were scraped, re-carved and re-fitted in accordance with the conception of mediaeval intention and craftsmanship. Much of Scott's work was in the nature of structural repairs and to his credit be it said, he corrected as far as possible the 'improvements' of Wyatt at Hereford, Lichfield and Salisbury. Of the utmost importance were the measures taken by Scott to stabilize the central towers of Salisbury, Ripon, Chichester, S. David's and S. Albans, some of them on the verge of collapse. The tower of Salisbury cathedral had been reinforced with cross-ties of iron by Sir Christopher Wren, and Scott ensured its security by adding diagonal ties.

The hazardous task of saving the central tower of S. David's cathedral must have taxed his ingenuity as never before. His Report to the Dean and chapter in 1862 leaves no doubt of the 'most severe dilapidations' of the entire building, and of the magnitude of the task confronting him. The operations were fraught with great peril, for careful investigation revealed that the two western piers at the crossing, each bearing a load of 1,150 tons, had broken up and the tower was held in position only by the walls of the nave and transepts acting as buttresses. To make matters worse, the west, north and south walls of the tower were in process of disintegration. The two faulty piers therefore had to be rebuilt from their foundations. The tower walls having been bound together by internal iron ties, and cased externally by a framework of timber girders, no less than 12,000 cub. ft. of timber shoring were put up to bear the weight of the tower during the reconstruction of the piers, stone by stone. Of such urgency were the dangerous operations that often they were continued through the night. Scott's Report of 1869 gives a full account of the work and of the restoration of the choir, nave and transepts that followed.

Another equally important restoration carried out by Scott was that of S. Albans which was in a sad state of decay. The long-disused nave was in an almost ruinous condition when Scott was entrusted with the task in 1862. His prime concern was to strengthen the foundations, but the need of reinforcing the fabric became apparent in July 1870, when the central tower threatened to collapse. It was at once shored up, but for several months the work of stabilizing the piers at the crossing caused grave anxiety. The same year, the retrochoir which served as a right of way, and the Lady Chapel that was used as a grammar school were recovered to the church. After Scott's death in 1878 the restoration was rashly entrusted to Lord Grimthorpe, who was guilty of reprehensible mutilations of the fabric and of architectural shams that deceive no one. The west front was completely transformed into the present façade of make-believe Gothic, and equally destructive were the Grimthorpian innovations in the nave and aisles. The wall of the south aisle was refaced externally with flint and brick and new Decorated windows were inserted. The three eastern bays were vaulted and buttresses were built that cut into the cloister arcading in a most unsightly manner. After reconstructing the fourteenth-century piers of the nave Grimthorpe shamefully declared: 'It took no small trouble to get the new stones worked as roughly as the old ones, so as to make the work homogeneous and bewilder antiquaries.' The transepts suffered too. The end wall of the south transept was rebuilt and beneath the five new Lancet windows Grimthorpe inserted the Norman doorway and arcading torn from the slype outside. Of the ornament round the doorway, he glibly remarked that he had gone to infinite trouble to get the carving so well done that 'people wrongly guess which are old and which are new stones'. An abiding memorial of the noble lord's achievements is the huge circular window in the north transept, whose only merit is in the adequate lighting of that part of the cathedral.

Worthy of mention are the rebuildings of the nineteenth century that took place at Canterbury, Bristol, Peterborough and Southwark cathedrals. In 1834, due to its 'tottering condition' but more probably to the crumbling masonry of the exterior, the north-western tower of Canterbury, a precious relic of Lanfranc's Norman cathedral, was pulled down and a new tower arose, designed by George Austin, to match the Perpendicular tower at the south-west.

In 1866 George Edmund Street was entrusted with the building of the nave of Bristol cathedral, that had been commenced but abandoned by Abbot Newland in the fifteenth century. The design is in harmony with that of the choir, the eccentric vaulting of the choir-aisles being reproduced in the aisles of the new nave. At Peterborough cathedral the central tower of the twelfth century was found to be in a state of movement in 1883, and reconstruction together with the supporting piers was put in hand. The work was undertaken by Loughborough Pearson, the architect of Truro cathedral; the stones of the tower were numbered and were mostly re-set in their former position.

In anticipation of the erection of Southwark to cathedral rank in 1904, the makeshift nave of 1838 was swept away in 1890 and a new one of perfectly correct Gothic was designed and erected by Sir Arthur Blomfield and completed in 1897.

The cathedral churches of this country have suffered little from ill-conceived restoration during the present century. Their guardians are now conscious of their duty to preserve rather than renovate. The words of Prof. W. R. Lethaby, Surveyor of the Fabric of Westminster abbey, 1906–28, have borne good fruit. 'The expert re-editing of old buildings, with all its pretensions to science, comes in practice to a muddling up of so much *copy* of old work, so much *conjecture*, and so much mere *caprice*, without leaving any record as to which is which. This actual obliteration of authentic remnants and evidence is what we call Restoration.'[1]

Surprisingly few English cathedrals of the first rank sustained any damage by enemy action in the two world wars, and in no case has the injury been irreparable. The most serious loss was the parish-church cathedral of Coventry, which was reduced to a ruin in a severe air-raid in 1940. Only the noble western tower and spire and the outer walls of the church were left standing.

Some twenty years ago a Central Council for the Care of Churches was set up by the Church Assembly, with Advisory Committees in every diocese; and in 1950 a special Committee came into being, with a distinguished list of authorities and consultants, whose prime concern is the preservation of the fabric and furniture of the cathedral churches of this land.

[1] *Westminster Abbey and the King's Craftsmen.* 1906.

18. The Architecture of
Modern Foundation Cathedrals

*The following pages comprise a survey of the parish-church cathedrals,
and of the larger and more ambitious cathedrals of Truro, Liverpool and
Guildford. They are dealt with in the order in which the Modern Sees
were founded. Being closely related to cathedral-architecture of the
Middle Ages, Ripon, S. Albans, Southwell and Southwark are more
appropriately included in chapters 12 to 15*

MANCHESTER (See founded 1848)

❡ THE CATHEDRAL CHURCH of S. Mary, Manchester, was originally founded as a collegiate church in 1421, on the site of a pre-
existing parish church of which little is known. In that year
Henry V granted a licence to Thomas de la Warre, the rector, to
refound the church as a college of secular priests, in honour of
S. Mary the Virgin, S. George and S. Denis. The college was to
consist of a master, six priest-fellows, four clerks and six lay-
choristers. It was virtually a chantry college, for it was ordained
that masses should be celebrated in the church every day for the
good estate of Henry V, the Bishop of Coventry and Lichfield,
and Thomas de la Warre, and for the souls of their progenitors. In
1422 the old church was taken down and the present building
commenced. Despite its comparatively modern aspect, the cathedral affords a good example of late Perpendicular Gothic, of parochial standard (Pl. 106). It is remarkable for its abnormal width,
due to the accumulation of chantry chapels that were built on either
side of the nave and choir. The eastern arm with a width of 112
feet exceeds that of any other English church except S. Michael's,
Coventry. Exclusive of the diminutive Lady Chapel at the east,
the length is 172 feet; there are no transepts; at the west rises a
tower that was rebuilt in 1868 (Fig. 25).

On his appointment, the first warden of the college set to work
rebuilding the choir and its aisles and the octagonal chapter house
at the south-east, and his successors continued the work of reconstruction for about a century. For some reason or other both

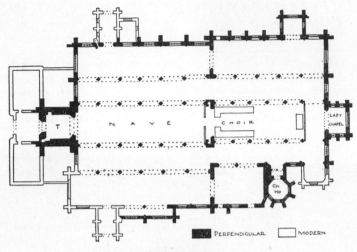

MANCHESTER

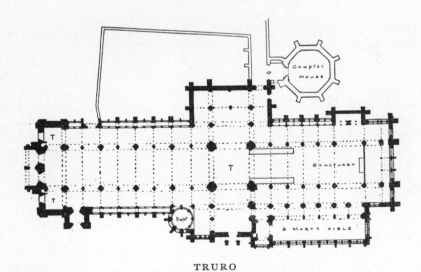

TRURO

FIG 25. Plans of Manchester and Truro

arcades of the choir were rebuilt later in the fifteenth century. It is about the same length as the nave, both being laid out in six bays. A curious irregularity occurs in the choir, the western end of which is 3 feet wider than the eastern. The nave and its aisles were completed by Ralph Langley, the fifth warden of the college, 1465–81, but the piers were entirely rebuilt in the nineteenth century. The bay design of the nave and choir lacks a triforium stage; the clerestory has large Perpendicular windows of five lights. The windows of the outer aisles are mostly of four lights, as also are those of the pyramidal-roofed chapter house at the south-eastern angle of the choir. In the panelled roof of the nave are carved bosses at the intersection of the main timbers, and the panelling of the more ornate roof of the choir is enriched with tracery.

The embattled parapet of the nave and choir, unbroken from east to west, is pierced with rectilinear panelling.

The oak rood-screen, now somewhat mutilated, was installed by James Stanley, warden from 1485 to 1509, during whose term of office the thirty choir stalls, splendid examples of Gothic woodwork, were erected, and were probably made by the craftsmen who fashioned the stalls at Beverley minster, the design being almost identical. They are surmounted by two-staged tabernacling and on the stall ends occur the arms of the de la Warre family. Of no less interest are the misericords, carved with animals, hunting scenes, men playing backgammon and other conceits.

During the forty years following the completion of the nave, a series of chantry chapels was grafted on to the aisles of nave and choir, though there is little evidence of their existence, for the altars have long since been removed and the parclose screens transferred from their former position. Flanking the north aisle of the choir was the large Derby chapel, built and endowed by the Stanleys, two of whom were successively wardens of the college. North of the nave was the chapel of S. James, founded *c.* 1507 by the Chetham family, and farther west the Holy Trinity chapel, built in 1498 by William Radcliffe of Ordsell. Flanking the south aisle of the choir was the Jesus chapel, erected in 1506 by Richard Beswicke at a cost of 400 marks. He is described as 'an especial benefactor of the church and built one side [arcade] of the choir'. The outer aisle on the south side of the nave originally consisted of two chapels, dedicated to S. Nicholas and S. George. In 1518 was remodelled the small Lady Chapel projecting only 18 feet beyond the choir; it was rebuilt in the eighteenth century, since when all the external stonework has been renewed.

From time to time the fabric of Manchester cathedral has been subjected to such drastic restorations that it is practically a modern structure.

TRURO CATHEDRAL (See founded in 1877)

Stamped with the individuality of the architect, John Loughborough Pearson, and an embodiment of the highest ideals of the Gothic revivalists of the nineteenth century, is the cathedral of Truro in Cornwall, the foundations of which were laid in 1880 (Pl. 102). Both in planning and design the cathedral is retrospective, the work of a cultured scholar and an able architect thoroughly acquainted with the principles and forms of mediaeval Gothic.

In its lay-out Pearson's cathedral is a reversion to the English plan of the thirteenth century, ill-suited though it was to the requirements of Victorian Protestantism. In size approximately equal to Ripon cathedral, Truro is a cruciform building, the eastern arm being an aisled rectangle with lofty but narrow choir transepts (Fig. 25). The choir is six bays in length with a squared ambulatory behind the High Altar; on the south is the sixteenth-century aisle of S. Mary's church that stood on the site and is now connected with the choir aisle by a lofty ambulatory. Beneath the choir is a vaulted crypt in the style of the late twelfth century, that serves as a singing school and vestries. The north transept, two bays deep, has eastern, western and return aisles, but owing to the restricted site, the south transept is of one bay and is aisled only at the west. At the east it abuts on S. Mary's aisle. To the west of the south transept is a circular baptistery (Fig. 25). At the crossing is a lofty tower and there are twin towers at the west, all of which are finished with stone spires. The nave, eight bays in length, has north and south aisles and between the towers is a vaulted narthex; there is a porch at the south-west and a larger one attached to the west front. The cloister walks and the octagonal chapter house on the north side of the cathedral are yet to be built (Fig. 25).

The eastern arm and the main transepts were erected during the lifetime of the architect, and the nave and towers were completed by his son, Mr. Frank Pearson.

In style the cathedral is an adaptation of Early English Gothic with traces of French influence, and the screens and canopies display details of the Decorated and Perpendicular phases. Internally, the design is three-storeyed. The main arcades spring from clustered piers with vaulting shafts, the triforium openings are plate-traceried, and recessed in the clerestory wall are two-light windows. In the east wall of the choir are two tiers of triple lancet lights with a traceried circle in the gable. The choir is covered with quadripartite vaulting and the nave has sexpartite vaults.

Above the High Altar rises an ornate reredos enriched with tiers of canopy work and sculpture, the central feature being the Crucifixion. On the south side of the choir stands the bishop's throne of wood surmounted by a tabernacled canopy, and the sanctuary is fenced on either side by stone screens. The choir transepts which are of the same height as the choir are lighted by tall lancet windows and have angle turrets. In the end walls of the main transepts are large rose windows with lancet lights below. Attached to the south transept at the east is a tall square turret with a pyramidal spire rising to a height of 140 feet; in the upper part of the turret are long two-light windows.

The central tower, 250 feet high, was built as a memorial of Queen Victoria's reign and rises two stages above the cathedral roof. In each face are triple lancets, and at the base of the octagonal spire are tall dormer lights and the angle pinnacles of the tower.

The nave of the cathedral is laid out in four coupled bays subdivided by intermediate piers, thus providing an arcade of eight arches on each side; the high vault which is more complex in its rib-structure than that of the choir, is supported by flying-buttresses. The aisles of the nave and the choir have quadripartite vaults and are lighted by lancet windows.

In their design the western towers that are about 200 feet in height, resemble the central tower. Flanking the central part of the west front are square turrets capped with pyramidal roofs; above the porch of the façade is a range of four lancets, surmounted by a large rose window.

LIVERPOOL CATHEDRAL (See founded 1880)

Admirable as Truro cathedral is as an archaeological exercise in the style of a bygone age, it is in no respect comparable with the monumental cathedral now in course of erection at Liverpool.

For nearly half a century after the formation of the see of Liverpool, the Renaissance church of S. Peter, built in 1699, served as the cathedral of the new diocese. In 1904 was commenced the new cathedral from the designs of Sir Giles Gilbert Scott, grandson of the Gothic revivalist of the last century. The site chosen for the cathedral was a hill, S. James's Mount, a commanding position away from the heart of the city, but dominating the Mersey. The exigencies of the site precluded the traditional orientation of the cathedral, and the main axis runs north-south, parallel to the Mersey.

More than half of this mighty church is now completed; in its finished state it will be the largest cathedral in Christendom save S. Peter's, Rome. But for the Lady Chapel, the plan (Fig. 26) is perfectly symmetrical, and was devised to meet the requirements of Protestant worship of the twentieth century. The eastern arm[1]

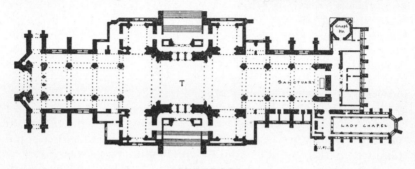

LIVERPOOL

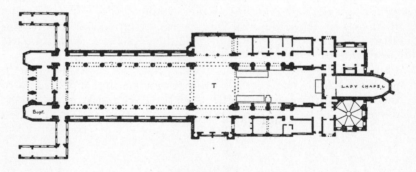

GUILDFORD

FIG 26. Plans of Liverpool and Guildford

consists of a choir of three bays of enormous span with narrow aisles, and is 138 feet in length. Beyond the reredos of the High Altar is a squared ambulatory, affording access to the Lady Chapel at the south, the low range of vestries at the east, and the octagonal chapter house on the north. West of the choir is a spacious central area, the full width of the building, 200 feet long and unobstructed by piers (Pl. 110). This is a new feature in cathedral planning, designed for the accommodation of vast congregations

---

[1] The terms eastern, western and so on are here used in the ritualistic sense.

and essentially a preaching space. Above this area rises the magnificent central tower, 308 feet in height and buttressed as it were by coupled transepts on the north and south with porches linking each pair and serving as the chief entrances to the great church. West of the central space and now in process of building is the aisled nave of three vast bays, to terminate at the west in a narthex. Excluding the buttresses the total length of Liverpool cathedral will reach 560 feet. The great central tower is designed in two stages, the upper being octagonal with similar turrets at the angles.

Most impressive externally is the massing of the several parts of the cathedral about the mighty tower, particularly the paired transepts at the base (frontispiece). Nor less effective is the quality of breadth ensured by the stern and purposeful restraint that rejected fussy and redundant ornament. In style the building is a solid version of Gothic; the huge walls impart a monumental effect to the exterior and interior. In Prof. C. H. Reilly's apt words: 'Here at Liverpool, Scott has veritably clothed the Gothic skeleton and covered the dead bones with substantial flesh.'

Inside the cathedral, the richly moulded piers of the choir are attached to the aisle-walls by solid cliffs of masonry, pierced in the lower part by pointed arches that span the aisles. The interior is lighted mainly by colossal windows in the north and south walls of the central area, in the east wall of the choir and in the transepts. Those of the central space are of three lights, 50 feet high, with simple circles in the head; in the transepts are lofty two-light windows of the same character, and the great east window is of four lights, with a massive central mullion and flowing tracery.

In the bay design the arcades are all-important; the arches are carried up to the springing of the four-celled vaulting, there is no triforium, but a blind top stage, lost in the gloom, is faced with a traceried parapet. The height of the choir vault is 116 feet and that of the central area 173 feet.

More in the nature of mediaeval Gothic than the main building is the Lady Chapel, the first part of the cathedral to be finished, consecrated in 1910. It is rectangular on plan with very shallow aisles, and is six bays in length, terminating at the east in a three-sided apse. At the west end is a narthex with a gallery above supported by a broad pointed arch. In the side walls are tall two-light windows of flowing tracery and three-light windows of similar design in the apse. The chapel is roofed with a lierne vault supported by immense buttresses that are the most prominent feature of the exterior. Above the windows externally are galleries with open balustrades, and at the south-west is a gabled porch, known

as the Children's Porch, remarkable for the two lofty lancet openings above the low entrance arch; in the gable is a sculptured
group representing the Good Shepherd.

Entered through a vestibule at the north end of the ambulatory
is the octagonal chapter house, lighted by two-light windows. The
little building is roofed with a concrete dome, surmounted by a
copper-covered cone.

NEWCASTLE CATHEDRAL (See founded in 1882)

For more than eight centuries before its elevation to a cathedral,
S. Nicholas, Newcastle upon Tyne, had been a parish church, the
appropriation of which had been granted to the Augustinian
priory of Carlisle by Henry I. Of the Norman church, that suffered extensive damage by fire in 1216 and again in 1248, all that
remains are fragments of masonry in the nave arcades of the
cathedral. The rebuilding of the chancel in the second half of
the thirteenth century fell upon the chapter of Carlisle, but the
reconstruction of the nave and transepts was the responsibility of
the parishioners and dates from the early part of the fourteenth
century. The work was retarded by the Black Death, and the
present nave was not commenced before 1359. The upper part of
the western tower and the lantern-steeple that crowns it were
added c. 1450.

S. Nicholas was one of the largest parish churches of the Middle
Ages, its size testifying to the prosperity of the merchant and craft
gilds of Newcastle and to the piety of the citizens, by whose benefactions the church was largely rebuilt. On plan the cathedral is
a cruciform structure, with an aisled choir, four bays in length;
north and south transepts, the northern having an eastern chapel
dedicated to S. George; a nave of four bays with aisles, and a
western tower, flanked on either side by lofty porches. Beneath the
north transept is a crypt now used as a chapel, but constructed in
the fourteenth century as a charnel house or bone-hole. It has a
barrel vault of stone supported by five stout ribs. The external
length of the church is 245 feet.

Curiously, the nave is of less width than the aisles, and the pavement slopes 16 inches from west to east. A not uncommon feature
of mediaeval planning occurs in the choir-arm, the axis of which
deviates from that of the nave and inclines to the south.

The church was subjected to such drastic restorations in the
nineteenth century as to change the character of the ancient
fabric. The fourteenth-century piers of the nave are octagonal, but

are devoid of capitals, and the clerestory stage and timber roof are modern. At the west end of the nave are two massive piers that carry the eastern wall of the tower, which is designed in three stages. The basement of the tower has a lierne vault bearing the inscription 'Orate pro anima Roberti de Rodes', the citizen who met the cost of erecting the lantern-steeple. The belfry stage has a pair of two-light Perpendicular windows in each face, and from the octagonal pinnacles at the angles of the parapet spring four flying-arches on which is poised the square lantern, pierced with rectilinear windows (Pl. 105). Above the lantern rises a slender octagonal spire, also supported by 'fliers'. During the Civil War, when Newcastle was besieged by the Scots, their General threatened to demolish the steeple, a calamity that was averted by the timely action of the mayor, who ordered Scottish prisoners to be confined in the belfry stage of the tower. As a result not a shot was fired against it.

The lantern-steeple is the special glory of the cathedral, and so enamoured was Sir Christopher Wren of the design that he reproduced it in a modified form at his London church of S. Dunstan-in-the-East.

Between 1783 and 1787 the interior of S. Nicholas church suffered at the hands of vandals who swept away the mediaeval screens, the pulpit and the stalls, and destroyed monuments and brasses. In 1834 the tower was found to be heeling over, and the lofty Perpendicular porches were then built as flanking buttresses, an undertaking that was followed by a recasing of the fabric in the Perpendicular mode. To this period belongs the great east window. Forty years later Scott strengthened the tower and rebuilt the lantern.

Since the founding of the see, no structural changes have been made in the building, but the re-furnishings, notably the rood-screen, the choir stalls and the reredos, designed by Mr. R. J. Johnson, and the installation of several altars have rendered the church more worthy of its cathedral dignity. Of special interest is the rearrangement of the choir-arm, an admirable adaptation in the mediaeval tradition. The High Altar is set up in the second bay from the east, and is backed by a lofty alabaster reredos with tiers of niched figures. Beyond is the ambulatory with altars beneath the three windows in the eastern wall.

WAKEFIELD CATHEDRAL (see founded in 1888)

The cathedral of All Saints, Wakefield, furnishes a splendid instance of a Norman parish church, that in the course of three or more centuries was completely transformed into a spacious Perpendicular structure. The original church, founded *c.* 1100, was an unaisled cruciform building with a central tower. A century later narrow aisles were added to the nave. The collapse of the tower in 1315 was followed by an entire remodelling of the church; the chancel was rebuilt, new nave arcades were erected that were nearly twice the height of the old, and the narrow aisles of the nave were replaced by aisles that absorbed the transepts. When the south arcade was put up, the lower halves of the old piers, alternately round and octagonal, were retained, but as they tilted eastwards, the new superimposed courses were built vertical, with the result that the piers are slightly crooked. About the year 1409 the tower at the west was erected at a distance beyond the western wall of the nave. Later in the fifteenth century, it was joined to the nave by extending the latter and its aisles some 12 feet westwards, and at the same time the clerestory and roof of the nave were raised. Finally, the chancel was remodelled, and north and south aisles were built, divided from the chancel by arcades of five bays.

By the end of the fifteenth century, all these changes had converted the church into a vast aisled rectangle, 138 feet in length, a plan that was much in favour for town churches of any size at that time. The rebuilding at various times is most evident from the assortment of cylindrical, octagonal and shafted piers in the arcades of the nave and choir. The south nave arcade is eight bays in length whereas the northern is only seven.

Externally the cathedral has the appearance of a large Perpendicular parish church; the aisles are lighted by expansive rectilinear windows and in the clerestory are square-headed windows. The nave, the chancel and the aisles have flat panelled roofs of timber. The plain western tower, that has angle buttresses attached to each face and a pair of two-light windows in the belfry stage, is noteworthy for the octagonal and crocketed spire of stone that rises to a height of 274 feet. At the angles of the parapet are crocketed pinnacles.

In 1898–1905 the cathedral was enlarged by an eastern extension designed by Loughborough Pearson. The chancel was lengthened by one bay, flanked by north and south transepts with eastern aisles. The extension provided a chapel, dedicated to S. Mark, in the retrochoir beyond the High Altar (Pl. 104). The clustered piers, the ribbed vaulting and the fenestration of the modern additions are executed in a Gothic style that is in perfect keeping with the mediaeval work.

BIRMINGHAM CATHEDRAL (see founded in 1905)

Since the diocese of Birmingham was formed in 1905, the parish church of S. Philip, a typical example of English Renaissance architecture of the early eighteenth century, has been the seat of the bishop. It was designed and built in 1711–19 by Thomas Archer, who is perhaps better known for the freakish design of S. John's church, Westminster. The cathedral-church of Birmingham, that is mentioned by a contemporary of Archer as being 'justly esteemed and a very beautiful structure' is a modified and smaller version of Wren's London church of S. Bride, Fleet Street. It is a rectangular building with galleried aisles, and is distinguished by a western steeple with a domical roof surmounted by a circular open lantern (Pl. 108).

Designed as a preaching house, the interior is a well-proportioned piece of Renaissance work. Dividing the galleried aisles from the nave are arcades of square fluted piers carrying round arches, above which is the entablature and coving of the flat ceiling. The chancel, a modern addition has free-standing Corinthian columns that stand forward from the nave arcades and support entablatures and the coffered ceiling. It is separated from the nave by a low ironwork screen that is attributed to the celebrated smith, Jean Tijou, who executed much of the ironwork in Wren's S. Paul's. Three windows in the east wall of the cathedral and another at the west are filled with glass designed by Burne Jones and made by William Morris.

SHEFFIELD CATHEDRAL (see founded, 1914)

The cathedral church of SS. Peter and Paul, Sheffield, which has undergone extensive alterations in the past twenty years, was formerly a parish church founded in the reign of Henry I. At the time of the Reformation it was a Perpendicular building, cruciform on plan, with a spired tower at the crossing. By the end of the eighteenth century, the church had fallen into deplorable decay and ruin, and immediate repairs were imperative. In 1805 the nave and aisles were rebuilt, but a thorough restoration of the church was deferred until *c.* 1880, when the building was transformed; the transepts were rebuilt, north and south porches added, and the nave was lengthened by 25 feet. The wooden galleries over the aisles of the nave were swept away, together with the pews that cluttered up the interior.

In 1919 a scheme was prepared for rendering the church worthy of its new dignity, but nothing was done until 1931, when entirely new plans were drawn up by Sir Charles Nicholson for the enlargement of the cathedral on a big scale. Much has already been accomplished; and when completed, Sheffield cathedral will cover an area approximately three times that of the mediaeval church. Instead of the normal orientation, the main axis will run north to south.

In the scheme of enlargement are incorporated the old chancel and its aisles, and the central tower, but otherwise all will be new (Fig. 27). The old nave and its aisles are to be taken down, and to the west of the old crossing will be erected what is virtually a complete church on a north-to-south axis. The northern half will comprise an aisled choir of four bays with a retrochoir beyond, and a long rectangular chapel, dedicated to the Holy Spirit as a further extension; the southern half will consist of a nave of six bays with aisles, terminating in a porch. In alignment with the central tower is to be a new tower at the west.

Considerable progress has been made in the northern extension of the cathedral, and most of the foundations of the remaining parts are already laid. The end wall of the mediaeval north transept has been taken down, and the transept extended northwards to make the Military Chapel of the York and Lancaster Regiment that is dedicated to S. George. The south transept will be treated in similar fashion, and carried southwards as S. Paul's Aisle. To the west of these transept-extensions will be the new choir of four bays and the nave of six bays, flanked by aisles on either side (Fig. 27). The aisles of the choir (or High Sanctuary) are continued northwards as a squared ambulatory leading to the Chapel of the Holy Spirit. On the site of the old vestry north of S. Catherine's chapel that flanks the ancient chancel stands the muniment room and the chamber reserved for the church burgesses. Running northwards beyond the muniment room is a long corridor, on each side of which are vestries and the sacristy. At the north-east is the rectangular chapter house, and the passage terminates at the north in a porch. Beneath the High Sanctuary is a three-aisled crypt dedicated to All Saints. From the octagonal columns that are void of capitals spring the ribs of the quadripartite vaulting.

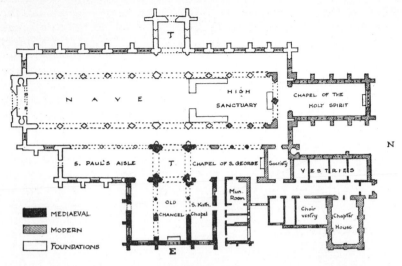

SHEFFIELD

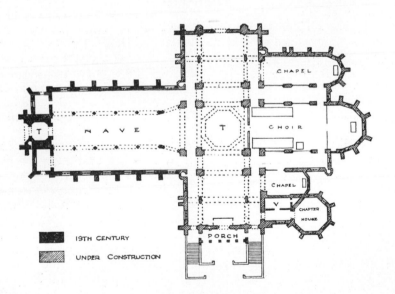

BLACKBURN

FIG 27. Plans of Sheffield and Blackburn

That part of the new building that had risen in the three years since its inception was consecrated in February 1939, and the foundations of the nave and its aisles were laid before the outbreak of war in September of the same year. Since the war, the Chapel of the Holy Spirit and the ambulatory have been finished, and there now remains the completion of the new choir-arm and the building of the nave.

In order to preserve a homogenity in style throughout the whole cathedral, the extensive additions are being erected in a Gothic that will harmonize with the Perpendicular Gothic of the ancient chancel.

When completed, the disposition of the several parts of Sheffield cathedral, dominated by the two towers, will exhibit a notable achievement in architectural composition.

BURY S. EDMUNDS CATHEDRAL (see founded, 1914)

In the pre-Reformation centuries, the church of S. James that is now the cathedral of Bury S. Edmunds was closely associated with the great Benedictine abbey, within the precincts of which it stood. The church was founded in 1125 by Abbot Anselm, to replace a parish church, dedicated to S. Denis, that was taken down by the convent to permit of an extension of the west front of the abbey-church. Although the new parish church was situated in the monastic precincts, its western wall in which was the main entrance, was built flush with the abbey wall, thus enabling parishioners to enter the church without trespassing on the monks' domain.

Immediately to the south of the church stands the magnificent gatehouse of the abbey, also built by Anselm, and a superb example of Norman architecture, now used as the bell tower of the cathedral. Of Anselm's Norman church only a few lumps of stone-work remain, for in the fourteenth and fifteenth centuries it was rebuilt in its entirety, the chancel being completed c. 1404.

With the exception of the nave roof and the chancel, which was rebuilt in 1711 and again in 1867, the cathedral church is Perpendicular Gothic throughout, dating mainly from the second half of the fifteenth century, though not completed until c. 1550. In 1502 the master-mason was John Wastell, a craftsman of high repute, who was responsible for the upper stages of the Angel Steeple at Canterbury (p. 274), and had worked at King's College chapel, Cambridge. Wastell remained at Bury S. Edmunds, supervising the building of the nave of S. James's church until his death in 1515. For another thirty-five years the work dragged on, not being finished until the reign of Edward VI, who made a gift of £200 towards the cost of the west end of the church.

On plan the cathedral consists of a nave of nine bays with aisles and a modern aisleless chancel designed by Gilbert Scott. There is no tower. The nave, which is 137 feet long, is a graceful example of Perpendicular Gothic, of simple character and almost devoid of ornament. The moulded arches carried by slender piers are of abnormal height, but the eighteen windows of two lights in each clerestory afford ample top-lighting to reveal the beauty of Gilbert Scott's hammerbeam roof, now coloured and gilded. The aisles are lighted by Perpendicular windows of three lights and in the west front are a central window of seven lights and lateral windows of five lights.

Twelve years ago plans were drawn up by Mr. S. E. Dykes Bower for enlarging the cathedral and improving the environment.[1] The Perpendicular nave will remain unchanged, but for a porch that is to be added at the north-west. The limitations of the site preclude any great lengthening of the cathedral, and the main additions will lie to the north-east. The existing chancel is to be replaced by an aisled choir of five bays and of greater height than the nave. It will be lighted by expansive four-centred windows, and the panelled roof will be coloured and gilded. The easternmost bays of both aisles of the nave are to be carried up to form shallow transepts, and at the crossing will rise a low lantern tower with a pyramidal roof and flèche, contrasting but not conflicting with the Norman bell tower.

To the north of the choir will be erected a two-storeyed block of buildings, comprising on the ground level vestries and offices; and above, a rectangular Lady Chapel adjoining the north choir-aisle, a square chapter house and vestries. From the north-west porch a cloister walk will be built against the north wall of the cathedral, and an eastern walk will afford access to the new eastern block. It is proposed to lay out the area south of the cathedral with stretches of lawn and with paved walks.

CHELMSFORD CATHEDRAL (see founded, 1914)

When the see of Chelmsford in Essex was created in 1914, the parish church of S. Mary the Virgin was elevated to cathedral status and is now dedicated to S. Mary the Virgin, S. Peter and S. Cedd.

[1] The Scheme of Enlargement is detailed in a beautiful brochure issued by the Cathedral Chapter and Council, 1953.

The cathedral is mainly of the fifteenth century and consists of an aisled choir of three bays, about 42 feet in length, with an un-aisled sanctuary at the east; a nave of four bays flanked by double aisles on the north, and a tower engaged by the aisles of the nave at the west (Pl. 113). To the north of the north choir aisle is a transept, beyond which is a modern square building, comprising a chapter room and a number of vestries. The eastern buttresses of the tower project into the nave in alignment with the arcades, and attached to the south aisle is a two-storeyed porch.

The cathedral occupies the site of a Norman church, fragments of which are incorporated in the walls of the tower. In 1424 the church appears to have been entirely rebuilt; an inscription formerly lettered in flint recorded that 'the townshepe of Chelmesford . . . hath been liberal willers and procurers of helpers to this werke'.

The choir, the nave and the north and south aisles dated from the early half of the fifteenth century, and the south porch was added c. 1460; by the end of the century the parishioners had built the western tower. To-day, all that remains of the Perpendicular church of pre-Reformation days are the choir, the tower and the porch. The ancient fabric was built mainly of flint rubble, with blocks of freestone.

The nave is a reconstruction that followed the collapse of the fifteenth-century nave in 1800, that occurred during excavations that undermined the foundations of the south arcade.

The north arcade of the choir is marked by a peculiarity in the westernmost bay, the broad round arch of which is subdivided into two pointed sub-arches that spring from a slender column, the spandrel being pierced with rectilinear panelling. The adjacent arch on the east is modern. The Perpendicular windows in the clerestory were inserted in 1878. The chancel arch was rebuilt in the last quarter of the fifteenth century. The porch furnishes a typical instance of East Anglian flushwork, of split flints in combination with narrow lengths of stone and the upper part is of sixteenth-century brickwork. The windows and entrance arch are modern restorations.

The tower of the cathedral, built of flint with stone dressings, is 90 feet high and is divided into three stages, with Perpendicular windows of three lights in each face. The arched doorway beneath the west window is square-framed, the drip-mould is ogee-arched and in the spandrels are foiled circles charged with heraldic shields of the Bourchier and de Vere families. The slender timber spire, originally covered with lead, was erected in 1749.

After the calamity of 1800 a new nave was built with moulded piers, pointed arches and three-light clerestory windows of little merit. It was roofed with a plastered ceiling of a complicated rib-design; the ceilings of the aisles were treated the same but have long since been replaced by timber roofs.

In 1873 the church was enlarged on the north side by the addition of the outer aisle of the nave and the north transept.

A few years after the church attained cathedral status, plans were drawn up by Sir Charles Nicholson for the enlargement of the building, a project that was to embody as much as possible of the mediaeval church. Much modified, the scheme has in part been carried out, by the addition of the sanctuary at the east end of the choir in 1926, and of the vestries, chapter room, and muniment chamber adjoining the north transept. In space and in the interior effect the choir has gained much by the addition of the sanctuary; the five-light window in the east wall is so correct that it might have been transplanted from a mediaeval church elsewhere.

COVENTRY CATHEDRAL (see founded, 1918)

Before its destruction by German bombs in November 1940, the church of S. Michael, Coventry, raised to cathedral status in 1918, was a worthy symbol of the newly constituted bishopric. It was one of the largest and most noble parish churches of the Perpendicular period, in superficial area second only to S. Nicholas church, Yarmouth.

The plan of S. Michael's testified to the prosperity of the industries and of the trade gilds of mediaeval Coventry; the assimilation of the gild chapels about the aisles of the nave and chancel imparted an interior width of 120 feet to the church, i.e. 14 feet greater than that of York cathedral (Fig. 28).

The main body of the church was built by the townspeople of Coventry in a period of about eighty years from 1373; the western tower was erected at the cost of William and Adam Botoner, mayors of Coventry, who contributed £100 a year from 1373 to 1394. The chancel and the five-sided apse at the east, surrounded by a series of low vestries are contemporaneous with the tower. The nave and the inner aisles were built between 1432 and 1450, as was also the spire of the tower. Early in the sixteenth century, outer aisles were grafted on to the aisles to provide chapels for the various craft gilds associated with the cloth trade and other industries of the place. On the north were the gild chapels of the Drapers, the Girdlers and the Smiths; on the south were the chapels of the Mercers, the Dyers and the Cappers. In these chapels, which were enclosed by timber screens, the members of the respective gilds assembled for corporate worship, and for the celebration of soul-masses on behalf of their deceased brethren.

Architecturally, S. Michael's was parochial Perpendicular at its best. The moulded piers of the spacious nave carried four-centred arches; in each bay of the clerestory were two four-light windows, the mullions of which were carried down to fill the spandrels of the arcades. The almost flat timber roof rested on camber beams; the aisles were lighted by windows of seven lights and in each wall of the apse was a lofty four-light window.

Fortunately, the tower and spire, whose design is unrivalled in parish church architecture survived the devastation of 1940. It is compounded of three features; the square tower of five stages and 140 feet in height, the octagonal lantern, and the slender spire of stone. The fenestration of the tower is of increasing richness from the base to the parapet, and all the windows have ogee-arched drip-moulds. The lantern is supported by flying-buttresses that spring from the angle-pinnacles of the tower, and the spire, panelled in the lower part, is banded and pierced with windows at intervals. The total height of tower and spire is 295 feet.

The interior of Coventry cathedral was gutted by showers of incendiary bombs dropped by German planes on the fateful night in November 1940. The timber roofs fell an easy prey to the flames and their collapse wrecked the arcades of nave and choir and the screens and pews, so that only the outer walls of the church and the western tower were left standing. The broken masonry and debris have long since been removed and the interior is now laid out with lawns and gravelled paths, and with hallowing places. The shell of the church is to remain as a permanent memorial and will serve as an open-air vestibule of the new cathedral.

In 1951 designs for a new cathedral by Mr. Basil Spence were accepted by the Reconstruction Committee and the Cathedral Council, and though the building exists only on paper at the moment, work has commenced on clearing the site for the foundations.

The new cathedral shows a complete break with mediaeval tradition as regards both plan and design; there is no looking back. The plan (Fig. 28) was devised to meet the needs of Christian observances of the present century, and the style is conceived in terms of contemporary architecture, the character of which is largely dictated by modern materials and methods of construction (Pl. 107). Except for the internal ordannance of nave and aisles, with the High Altar at the ritual east, there is nothing of tradition

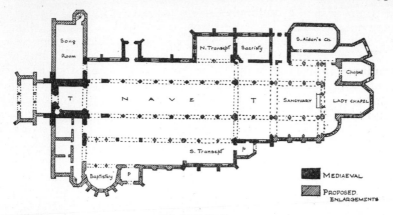

BRADFORD

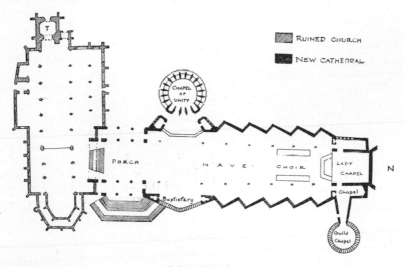

COVENTRY

FIG 28. Plans of Bradford and Coventry

in the planning, and in form, the walls, piers, windows and vaulting owe nothing to cathedral building of the past.

The cathedral will occupy a site at the north-east of the ancient
church, and the axis runs north-south, so that the High Altar will
stand at the northern end. A colossal arch opening into the porch
provides a connecting link between the old and the new churches.
Projecting from the east side at the southern end is the baptistery,

with an immense mullioned and transomed window, and on the west side is a circular 'Chapel of Unity' with a conical roof. To the east of the sanctuary is a smaller circular Gild Chapel.

The nave, 270 feet long, is divided from the aisles by seven slender columns that support the concrete vaulting; the aisle walls are not straight but are planned in zig-zag fashion, and the fenestration is so contrived that light will be directed towards the High Altar. In each angle of the zig-zag, one wall is a mullioned and transomed window from base to summit, and the other is a solid cliff of masonry. On a summer's day this system of fenestration will produce varying effects of lighting between sunrise and sunset.

BRADFORD CATHEDRAL (see founded, 1918)

In 1935 a scheme was initiated and plans were drawn up by Sir Edward Maufe for transforming and enlarging the old parish church of S. Peter, Bradford, to make it more suited to the functions of a cathedral. The church, the third to be built on the site, is a Perpendicular structure dating from 1358; a century passed before it was completed, except for the tower at the west that was added to the church in 1493–1508.

S. Peter's was planned with an aisled nave of nine bays, a short chancel of two bays with aisles, a porch at the north-west and a large western tower. At the restoration of 1899, north and south transepts were added to the mediaeval church.

The scheme of enlargement embraces an eastern extension, the erection of a dignified western porch on a raised terrace and of wings flanking the tower (Pl. 109), and the addition of a baptistery and porch at the south-west. The eastern extension is to comprise an aisled presbytery of three bays, the east wall of which will be opened up with three tall arches, affording glimpses into the ambulatory and the Lady Chapel beyond. Flanking the Lady Chapel on the north is to be a chapel dedicated to the Holy Spirit, and off the north choir-aisle will be another chapel dedicated to S. Aidan, with the chapter house above. A low tower is to rise above the old chancel. The wings attached to the tower are also of two storeys; the northern, completed in 1955, consists of the Song School with robing rooms beneath; the southern block will provide vestries for the bishop, the provost, canons, clergy and vergers. In line with the south transept is to be erected an outer aisle of the nave, with a polygonal baptistery and a porch adjoining it at the south-west. (Fig. 28).

As regards the architectural character of the new buildings, the architect, Sir Edward Maufe, in his Report states that 'the composition has been carefully considered in relation to the old work. ... It is thought that there should be no mere copying of mediaeval forms, but that we should build anew on tradition.'

LEICESTER CATHEDRAL (see revived in 1926)

Since its promotion to cathedral rank in 1927, the church of S. Martin, Leicester, has not been subjected to enlargements such as those at Sheffield and Bradford; like S. Nicholas, Newcastle, the cathedral of Leicester has merely been improved and furnished to adapt it to its new purpose.

The irregular plan of S. Martin's cathedral is due to the rebuildings and the addition of aisles and gild chapels from the twelfth century onwards. The gild of Corpus Christi, a religious fraternity founded in 1343, was closely associated with the civil administration of the town and was served by four priests; the brethren assembled for corporate worship in a chapel in S. Martin's church.

The Norman church, of which only small portions of masonry remain, was an unaisled cruciform building, with a tower at the crossing. In the thirteenth century wide aisles were added to the nave, and early in the following century, the aisles were rebuilt and an outer aisle with a lofty arcade was erected on the south, thereby absorbing the transept. The eastern end of the outer aisle, enclosed by screens, was made the chapel of Our Lady. In the Perpendicular period the chancel was remodelled with flanking aisles, and a clerestory was added to the nave, which also was lengthened by the building of a western bay. In the south-west corner was formerly a gild chapel of S. George, that has been restored and refitted as a Memorial Chapel of the men of the Leicestershire Regiment who fell in the First World War. The Perpendicular chancel arch is remarkable for the bold mouldings of its five orders, and the north-west porch of the nave is roofed with a fan-vault of oak.

In the nineteenth century the hand of the restorer was heavy at S. Martin's. The Norman tower at the crossing was taken down in 1861 because it was unsafe, and a lofty central tower with a broach spire of stone was erected; the clerestory and the roof of the nave were renewed, and the north aisle and porch were restored by Street and Loughborough Pearson. Practically everything east of the crossing is modern, for the chancel was restored out of all mediaeval recognition and the lateral chapels rebuilt. The exterior of the church has been largely refaced. In 1897 was

M

built the south-west porch in the Perpendicular style from the designs of Bodley; it has an upper chamber and above the entrance is a range of seven niched figures.

To render the cathedral worthy of its new dignity, the sanctuary has been panelled and extended westwards, stalls for the canons have been set up, and timber screens erected at the entrance to the choir and to the chapels of S. Dunstan and S. Katherine on each side, both of which have been refurnished. At the western end of the nave a gallery has been built to accommodate the choir, with the organ close by, an arrangement that was necessitated by the limited area of the eastern arm. The interior of the cathedral has been further embellished by the recent repainting of the roof in mediaeval colouring.

PORTSMOUTH CATHEDRAL (see founded in 1927)

On the creation of the see of Portsmouth, the throne of the bishop was installed in the parish church of S. Thomas of Canterbury, that for three and a half centuries prior to the Reformation had been served by Augustinian canons. Within a few years of the canonization of Becket in 1173, the cult of the new saint was popularized throughout the land, and in 1180 to do honour to the martyred archbishop, John de Gisors granted land to the Augustinian priory of Portsea on which to found a chapel dedicated to S. Thomas. Eight years later Bishop Richard Toclive of Winchester confirmed to the canons the church 'which they had begun to build'. Considerable portions of that church are embodied in Portsmouth cathedral. In its complete form it was a cruciform building, consisting of an aisled choir of two double bays, unaisled transepts, a tower at the crossing, and a nave with aisles. The choir-arm and the transepts have fortunately survived but the nave and the central tower sustained such damage during the Civil War, that they had to be taken down. In 1683–93 a new nave with a tower at the west was erected. To raise the necessary funds, amounting to £9,000, Charles II issued a licence for collections to be made in churches throughout England.

A few years after the church was made a cathedral, a long western extension was planned from the designs of the late Sir Charles Nicholson, a project that has occasioned an internal rearrangement. The late twelfth-century choir now serves as the sanctuary; the old nave is the ritual choir; the western tower, pierced with arches, is the central tower, to the north and south of which new transepts have been built, together with the eastern bays of a modern nave that ultimately will extend farther westwards.

Of unique interest is the Early English choir-arm of the cathedral, the north and south arcades of which consist of two double bays, the main piers being octagonal. The semicircular arches that spring from the piers each enclose two pointed sub-arches carried by intermediate Purbeck shafts. Above the piers are triple vaulting shafts that indicate a high vault, although the present wooden vault was put up in 1844. There is no triforium stage but in the clerestory are lancet windows with Purbeck shafts. Level with the clerestory are three wide lancet lights in the eastern wall. The choir aisles retain their original quadripartite vaults and are lighted with lancets. Beneath the lofty modern arch opening into the presbytery are the clustered piers that formerly carried the eastern arch of the crossing. Both transepts are 25 feet wide, but owing to the restricted site, the south transept is less deep than the northern; they were originally vaulted, but are now roofed with flat ceilings. In a trefoiled niche on the east wall of the north transept is a painting of the Last Judgment dating c. 1250 and restored by Prof. E. W. Tristram in 1939. To the south of the choir is the Navy Aisle, entered through an arch that was pierced in the wall of the transept. It was erected in 1938, the cost being met by donations from officers and men of the Royal Navy and Royal Marines.

The seventeenth-century nave, now the ritual choir, has Tuscan columns carrying round arches, and is roofed with a coved ceiling of plaster. Galleries that were built over the aisles in 1683 were removed thirty years ago. The plain tower at the west is surmounted by a large wooden-domed cupola with a lantern above.

GUILDFORD CATHEDRAL (see founded, 1927)

In July 1936, was laid the foundation stone of the cathedral-church of the Holy Spirit at Stag Hill, Guildford, the fourth Anglican cathedral to be built since the Reformation. Less than two years later the foundations of the whole building were completed.

The cathedral, which was designed by Sir Edward Maufe, is planned on cruciform lines, and architecturally is a modern derivative of Gothic tradition, simple and austere but none the less impressive. In the architect's own words: 'The idea has been to produce a design definitely of our own time and yet in the line of the great mediaeval cathedrals, and to build on tradition; to rely on proportion of mass, volume, and lines rather than on elaboration and ornament.' The cathedral is being built on a great 'raft' of reinforced concrete, bedded into the blue clay of the site. It will be 365 feet from east to west with a great tower as the central and dominating feature. On plan (Fig. 26) the cathedral consists of an aisled choir-arm, with a Lady Chapel as an eastern extension, shallow transepts without aisles, a wide nave of seven bays flanked by narrow aisles, and a narthex with north and south porches at the west. An innovation is the addition of a forecourt or garth on each side of the western end of the cathedral, the garth being enclosed by an arcaded wing or covered way leading to the porch (Pl. 114). The tower at the crossing will rise to a height of 175 feet. The Lady Chapel, which has a five-sided apse, is raised on a crypt chapel that has been in use for Divine worship for eight years, and beneath the presbytery and its aisles is an undercroft that houses the heating and lighting installations and provides a number of storerooms. Flanking the narrow aisles of the choir and sanctuary on the north are vestries and a library, and on the south the Children's Chapel and the chapter house; and beyond the sanctuary is a squared ambulatory that gives access to the Lady Chapel, the sacristy, and a squared chapel at the south-east.

In the twenty years since the foundation stone was laid much of Guildford cathedral has been built. The choir, the crossing and the lower courses of the tower, the transepts, the crypt of the Lady Chapel and the service sections attached to the choir-arm are now in existence, and the building of the nave was begun in 1955. When completed the cathedral will present an exterior of graceful simplicity, and the grouping of its various rectangular parts, culminating in the central tower will afford an example of architectural massing, expressive of strength and stability, and comparable with that of Salisbury cathedral (Pl. 115).

BLACKBURN CATHEDRAL (see founded, 1927)

Within a few years of the elevation of the parish church of S. Mary the Virgin, Blackburn, to cathedral rank, a project was set afoot for enlarging the building by the addition of an eastern extension that will treble the superficial area of the cathedral. The church of S. Mary, built 1820–6, was an early product of the Gothic Revival, from the designs of John Palmer. Decorated in style, it consists of a nave of five bays with north and south aisles, and a western tower, all of which are to be incorporated in the 'New Cathedral' of Blackburn.

Twenty years ago, the architect, the late Mr. W. A. Forsyth, prepared plans and designs for the proposed extension, which when completed will have converted the church of S. Mary into a cruciform cathedral, measuring about 275 feet from east to west (Fig. 27).

To a great extent the lay-out of the extension is in the mediaeval tradition, and embraces an aisled choir, terminating at the east in a polygonal apse; north and south transepts of considerable projection, with eastern and western aisles; an octagonal tower at the crossing, crowned with an octagonal lantern; a large chapel with a four-sided apse to the east of the north transept, and a smaller chapel east of the south transept. Entered from the south transept will also be an octagonal chapter house. Between the angle buttresses of the end wall of the transept, which has now been erected, is an arcaded porch with five open arches, the central one being occupied by an open-air pulpit (Pl. 111).

As the ground falls rapidly towards the east, the whole of the extension including the transepts is reared on an undercroft, that will be utilized as a hall, a refectory, vestries and rooms for conferences and meetings. In its complete form, Blackburn cathedral will be a noble building, in which new and old are combined in a perfect harmony of design.

DERBY CATHEDRAL (see founded in 1927)

For more than four centuries before the Reformation, the church that stood on the site of the cathedral of All Saints, Derby, was a collegiate establishment, served by a dean and seven priests. When the college was suppressed under the Chantries Act of 1547, All Saints church was made over to the parishioners. It was a Gothic building, with a choir for the members of the collegium, a nave and aisles and a western tower. All that now remains of the mediaeval church is the Perpendicular tower, erected in Henry VIII's reign.

Early in the eighteenth century the fabric was in so derelict a condition, that the high-handed vicar employed a gang of labourers to demolish the whole church save the tower, a feat that was accomplished in a single night in 1723. In accordance with eighteenth-century taste, the new church was built in the Renaissance style, from the designs of James Gibbs, the most distinguished of Wren's successors, and the architect of the famous Radcliffe Library, Oxford. The juxtaposition of a Gothic tower and a Renaissance church was an incongruity that mattered little at the time.

The western tower, typically Perpendicular in style and 178 feet high is, composed of three stages lighted by large windows, and the angle buttresses are carried up as pinnacles that rise 36 feet above the battlemented parapet.

The design of the church follows in the Renaissance tradition of Wren, and may be compared with S. Martin-in-the-Fields, Trafalgar Square, also the work of Gibbs and commenced in 1722. The cathedral is six bays in length, the aisles being divided from the nave by Tuscan columns that support chunks of entablature from which spring semicircular arches (Pl. 112). The two eastern bays forming the chancel are shut off from the nave by an iron screen wrought by Robert Bakewell of Derby. The nave is roofed with a barrel ceiling. A proposed extension at the east will lengthen the cathedral by three bays and a shallow apse.

THE CHOIR-ARM OF GLASGOW CATHEDRAL

By REASON OF the masterly lay-out and unique arrangement, the thirteenth-century choir-arm of Glasgow cathedral, the most important Gothic church in Scotland, may well be included in the development of cathedral planning.

In the year 1235 an entire reconstruction of the eastern arm of the cathedral was commenced, the work being completed by 1260. Owing to the rapid fall of the ground to the east, the whole of the new building, from the transepts to the eastern wall of the retrochoir was erected in two storeys, an upper and a lower church. To give height to the lower church the pavement of the choir above was elevated some three feet above the level of the nave. On plan the choir is an aisled rectangle, five bays long, beyond which is a square and doubled-aisled retrochoir, similar to the choir-arm of Southwark cathedral. Both in the upper and lower churches the easternmost aisle of the retrochoir was divided by screens into four chapels, and the aisle to the west was an ambulatory (Fig. 5). The retrochoir is of the same height as the aisles of the choir, and above it rises the gable wall of the sanctuary which is pierced by two arches behind the High Altar. The lower church, in which stood the shrine of S. Mungo is the special glory of Glasgow cathedral, differing from the choir above in the additional intermediate piers of the north and south arcades.

CHANTRY CHAPELS

THE FOLLOWING is a list of chantry chapels now remaining in our cathedral churches.

BRISTOL

Thomas, Lord Berkeley, 1348 — Projecting from the choir at the south-east.

Newton family, 1340–50 — East of the south transept.

CANTERBURY

Edward the Black Prince, 1363 — The Norman crypt beneath the south choir-transept.

Henry IV, c. 1430 — Between buttresses of the north ambulatory of the Saint's chapel.

Archbishop William Warham, 1507 — Between the north transept and the chapter house.

CARLISLE

John de Capella, c. 1490 — In the angle of the choir and the south transept.

DURHAM

Bishop Thomas Hatfield, c. 1362 — In the south choir-arcade.

ELY

Bishop John Alcock, c. 1490 — The easternmost bay of the north choir-aisle.

Bishop Nicholas West, c. 1533 — The easternmost bay of the south choir-aisle.

EXETER

Bishop John Grandisson, c. 1360 — A recess in the west front.

Bishop Hugh Oldham, c. 1516 — Between buttresses on the south side of the retrochoir.

Sir John Speke, c. 1518 — Between buttresses on the north side of the retrochoir.

William Sylke, Precentor, c. 1506 — In the north-east corner of the north transept.

GLOUCESTER

Abbot Thomas Seabroke, *c.* 1455   In the first bay of the south
                                    nave arcade from the east.
Abbot John Browne, 1514   Between the two southern piers
                                    at the crossing.

HEREFORD

Bishop John Stanbury, *c.* 1470   Projecting from the north
                                    choir-aisle.
Bishop Edmund Audley, *c.* 1500   Projecting from the south side
                                    of the Lady Chapel.

LINCOLN

The Works Chapel, *c.* 1342   The northern bay of the east
                                    aisle of the south transept.
Bishop Richard Fleming, 1425   Between buttresses of the north
                                    choir-aisle.
Bishop John Russell, *c.* 1490   Between buttresses of the south
                                    choir-aisle.
Bishop John Longland, *c.* 1530   Between buttresses of the south
                                    choir-aisle.

NORWICH

Bishop James Goldwell, *c.* 1490   In the south arcade of the
                                    choir.
Bishop Richard Nyx, *c.* 1530   Two bays of the south aisle of
                                    the nave.

S. ALBANS

Humphrey, Duke of Gloucester,   On the south side of the Saint's
                                    chapel.
Abbot Wallingford, *c.* 1480   Adjoining the High Altar on
                                    the south.
Abbot Thomas Ramryge, *c.* 1500   Flanking the High Altar on the
                                    north.

S. DAVID'S, PEMBROKE

Bishop Henry de Gower, *c.* 1340   In the southern half of the
                                    rood-screen.
Bishop Edward Vaughan, *c.* 1520   Formerly a small open court
                                    east of the sanctuary.

M*

SALISBURY

Walter, Lord Hungerford, 1429	Originally in the nave but removed to the south choir-arcade in 1789.
Bishop Edmund Audley, c. 1520	On the north side of the sanctuary.

WELLS

Bishop Nicholas Bubwith, 1420	In the north nave arcade.
Dr. Hugh Sugar, 1485	In the south nave arcade.
Bishop Thomas Beckington, 1452	In the south choir-arcade.

WINCHESTER

Bishop Adam de Orleton, c. 1345	Flanking the Lady Chapel on the north.
Bishop William Edingdon, c. 1366	In the south nave arcade.
Bishop William of Wykeham, c. 1400	In the south nave arcade.
Cardinal Beaufort, c. 1430	On the south side of the retro-choir.
Bishop William Waynflete, c. 1480	On the north side of the retro-choir.
Bishop Richard Fox, c. 1518	On the south side of the Saint's chapel.
Bishop Stephen Gardiner, c. 1550	On the north side of the Saint's chapel.
Bishop Thomas Langton, c. 1498	Flanking the Lady Chapel on the south.
Prior Thomas Silkstede, c. 1520	In the east aisle of the south transept.

WORCESTER

Prince Arthur, son of Henry VII, 1504	Adjoining the High Altar on the south.

YORK

Archbishop William la Zouche, 1350	Projecting from the south side of the choir.

MEDIAEVAL TOMBS

THE FOLLOWING are the most notable tombs in our cathedrals. Those marked (E) bear an effigy.

BRISTOL

Maurice, Ninth Lord Berkeley d. 1368 (E), and his mother, Lady Margaret d. 1337 (E)
Beneath an arch in the south wall of the Elder Lady Chapel.

Abbot Walter Newbury d. 1473 (E)
In a stellate recess in the north wall of the Lady Chapel.

Abbot William Hunt d. 1481 (E)
In a stellate recess in the north wall of the Lady Chapel.

Abbot John Newland d. 1515 (E)
In a stellate recess in the south wall of the Lady Chapel.

CANTERBURY

Archbishop John Peckham d. 1292 (E)
Against the end wall of the north transept.

Archbishop Simon Meopham d. 1333
In the screen of S. Anselm's chapel.

Edward the Black Prince d. 1376 (E)
On the south side of the Saint's chapel.

Archbishop Simon Sudbury d. 1381 (E)
On the south side of the choir.

Henry IV d. 1413 (E) and Joan of Navarre d. 1437 (E)
On the north side of the Saint's chapel.

Archbishop Henry Chicheley d. 1443 (E)
In the north arcade of the choir.

Cardinal Thomas Bourchier d. 1486 (E)
In the north arcade of the choir.

Archbishop William Warham d. 1532 (E)
Against the end wall of the north transept.

CHICHESTER

Bishop Robert Sherborne d. 1536 (E)
In the south aisle of the choir.

DURHAM

Bishop Thomas Hatfield d. 1381 (E)
Beneath the episcopal throne on the south side of the choir.

ELY

Bishop Hugh de Northwold d. 1254 (E)	On the north side of the sanctuary.
Bishop William of Louth d. 1298	In the south arcade of the choir.
Bishop Richard Redman d. 1505 (E)	On the north side of the choir.

EXETER

Bishop Henry Marshall d. 1206 (E)	On the north side of the choir.
Bishop Walter Bronscombe d. 1280 (E)	At the south-west end of the Lady Chapel.
Bishop Walter de Stapledon d. 1326 (E)	On the north side of the sanctuary.
Bishop Edmund Stafford d. 1419 (E)	At the north-west end of the Lady Chapel.

GLOUCESTER

Robert, Duke of Normandy (E)	In the centre of the choir.
Edward II, c. 1332 (E)	On the north side of the sanctuary.
King Osric d. 729: tomb of the sixteenth century (E)	On the north side of the sanctuary.

HEREFORD

Bishop Peter Aquablanca d. 1268 (E)	Between the north choir-aisle and the eastern aisle of the north transept.
William Lord Graunson d. 1335 (E)	On the north side of the Lady Chapel.
Bishop Thomas Charlton d. 1369 (E)	Against the end wall of the north transept.

LINCOLN

Bishop Henry Burghersh d. 1340 (E)	At the east end of the Angel Choir.
Nicholas, Third Baron Cantelupe d. 1355 (E)	Beneath the easternmost arch of the south arcade of the Angel Choir.
Sir Bartholomew Burghersh d. 1355 (E)	At the east end of the north choir-aisle.
Katherine Swynford d. 1403	On the south side of the sanctuary.

Bishop Richard Fleming d. 1431 (E)	On the north side of the Angel Choir.
Bishop John Russell d. 1495	On the south side of the Angel Choir.
Bishop John Longland d. 1547	On the south side of the Angel Choir.

NORWICH

Bishop James Goldwell d. 1499 (E)	On the south side of the choir.

OXFORD

Prior Alexander de Sutton d. 1316 (E)	On the north side of the Lady Chapel.
Lady Elizabeth Montacute d. 1359 (E)	On the south side of S. Katherine's chapel.

RIPON

Sir Thomas Markenfield (E) and wife, temp. Richard II	In the eastern aisle of the north transept.
Sir Thomas Markenfield (E) and wife (E) 1497	Against the end wall of the north transept.

ROCHESTER

Bishop Walter de Merton d. 1277 (E)	Against the end wall of the north choir transept.
Bishop Hamo de Hythe d. 1352	In the north choir aisle.
Bishop John of Sheppey d. 1360 (E)	On the north side of the choir.

S. DAVID'S

Bishop Henry Gower d. 1347 (E)	In the southern compartment of the pulpitum.
An unknown priest (E)	Beneath the easternmost window in the south aisle of the nave.
Edmund Tudor, Earl of Richmond, father of Henry VII d. 1456	In the centre of the presbytery.
Bishop John Morgan d. 1564 (E)	In the south arcade of the nave.

SALISBURY

William Longespée, First Earl of Salisbury d. 1226 (E)	In the easternmost bay of the south nave arcade.

Bishop Giles de Bridport d. 1262 (E)   In the south aisle of the choir.

Bishop Roger Mortival d. 1330   On the north side of the choir.

Bishop Richard Mitford d. 1407 (E)   At the junction of the south transept and the choir-aisle.

Bishop John Blyth d. 1499 (E)   Against the north wall of the north transept.

SOUTHWARK

John Gower d. 1408 (E)   In the north aisle of the nave.

WELLS

Bishop William Bytton d. 1265   In the south-east of the retro-choir.

Bishop William de Marchia (E)   In the end wall of the south transept.

Joan, Viscountess Lisle d. 1463   Adjoining Bishop Marchia's tomb.

Bishop Thomas Beckington d. 1465 (E)   On the south side of the presbytery.

Thomas Boleyn, precentor d. 1471 (E)   In the eastern aisle of the south transept.

Bishop Thomas Cornish d. 1513   In the north-eastern angle of the north transept.

WINCHESTER

Bishop William Edingdon d. 1366 (E)   In his chapel at the south-eastern end of the nave.

Bishop William of Wykeham d. 1404 (E)   In his chapel at the south-western end of the nave.

Cardinal Henry Beaufort d. 1447 (E)   In his chapel in the retrochoir.

Bishop William Waynflete d. 1486 (E)   In his chapel in the retrochoir.

WORCESTER

King John d. 1216 (E)   In the centre of the choir.

Bishop Godfrey de Giffard d. 1301 (E)   Within the screen on the south side of Prince Arthur's chapel.

Prince Arthur, son of Henry VII d. 1502   In his chantry chapel on the south side of the sanctuary.

York

Archbishop Walter de Grey d. 1255 (E)	In the eastern aisle of the south transept.
Archbishop William Greenfield d. 1316	In the eastern aisle of the north transept.
William of Hatfield, son of Edward III d. 1344 (E)	In the north aisle of the choir.
Archbishop Henry Bowet d. 1423	Between the retrochoir and the south aisle.
Archbishop Thomas Savage d. 1507 (E)	On the north side of the presbytery.

APPENDIX D

THE PHASES OF MEDIAEVAL ARCHITECTURE

THE ARCHITECTURE of this country from the seventh century to the Reformation is divided into four periods or phases of development: Saxon, Norman, Transitional and Gothic. Saxon architecture came to an end at the Conquest or soon afterwards, and the Norman period lasted from *c.* 1070 to *c.* 1145, and was followed by Transitional work, in which the change was effected from the round-arched style to the pointed Gothic. By about 1190 the pointed arch was in general use in all parts of the land, and this led to the development of the Gothic style that prevailed for three and a half centuries or more.

The name Gothic was first used as a term of contempt by the Renaissance enthusiasts of the seventeenth century who regarded everything non-Classical as barbarous. In the nineteenth century Rickman, Parker and Sharpe each in turn subdivided Gothic into phases, and the descriptive names Lancet, Geometrical, Decorated, and Perpendicular have been generally adopted ever since.

The most convenient subdivision is based on the treatment of the windows in each century. Thirteenth-century Gothic is known as Early English and embraces fifty years of so-called Lancet work (1200–50), and half a century of Geometrical. The name Lancet is given to the long narrow windows with acutely pointed heads, and Geometrical to the forms of tracery which fill the upper parts of the windows of the period. Fourteenth-century Gothic is known as Decorated or Curvilinear, the window tracery assuming curvilinear or flowing forms; and the Gothic of the fifteenth century is termed Perpendicular or Rectilinear and is characterized by the emphasis of the vertical line. Window tracery of this period becomes stiff and rigid. The final phase, that of the sixteenth century, often spoken of as Tudor Gothic, is a late version of Perpendicular. The second half of each century should be regarded as a transitional period, during which new forms were being evolved that became characteristic of the Gothic of the next century. It must be remembered that Gothic architecture was one of continuous development; at any one time progress might be rapid in some places but slow elsewhere. Any hard-and-fast delimitation into periods therefore can never be wholly satisfactory.

SUMMARY OF THE CATHEDRAL FOUNDATIONS

	Founda-tion	Pre-Reformation status	Internal length of cathedral in feet
Birmingham	Modern	———	
Blackburn	Modern	Parish church	248
Bradford	Modern	Parish church	
Bristol	New	Augustinian abbey	293
Bury S. Edmunds	Modern	Parish church	240
Canterbury	New	Benedictine cathedral priory	518
Carlisle	New	Augustinian cathedral priory	211
Chelmsford	Modern	Parish church	157
Chester	New	Benedictine abbey	350
Chichester	Old	Secular canons	408
Coventry	Modern	Parish church	380
Derby	Modern	Collegiate church	
Durham	New	Benedictine cathedral priory	469
Ely	New	Benedictine cathedral priory	517
Exeter	Old	Secular canons	383
Gloucester	New	Benedictine abbey	408
Guildford	Modern	———	365
Hereford	Old	Secular canons	325
Leicester	Modern	Parish church	
Lichfield	Old	Secular canons	370
Lincoln	Old	Secular canons	481
Liverpool	Modern	———	460
London	Old	Secular canons	500
Manchester	Modern	Collegiate church	215
Newcastle	Modern	Parish church	243
Norwich	New	Benedictine cathedral priory	458
Oxford	New	Augustinian priory	155
Peterborough	New	Benedictine abbey	439
Portsmouth	Modern	Parish church	
Ripon	Modern	Collegiate church	270
Rochester	New	Benedictine cathedral priory	313
S. Albans	Modern	Benedictine abbey	520
Salisbury	Old	Secular canons	450

	Founda-tion	Pre-Reformation status	Internal length of cathedral in feet
Sheffield	Modern	Parish church	260
Southwark	Modern	Augustinian priory	248
Southwell	Modern	Collegiate church	306
Truro	Modern	———	275
Wakefield	Modern	Parish church	
Wells	Old	Secular canons	371
Winchester	New	Benedictine cathedral priory	526
Worcester	New	Benedictine cathedral priory	399
York	Old	Secular canons	486

A SHORT BIBLIOGRAPHY

H. Batsford and C. Fry. *The Cathedrals of England.* 1934.

Bell's Cathedral Series. Illustrated Monographs each dealing with a single Cathedral. 1897–1904.

H. E. Bishop and E. K. Prideaux. *The Building of the Cathedral Church of S. Peter in Exeter.* 1922.

F. Bond. *The Cathedrals of England and Wales.* 1912.

F. Bond. *An Introduction to English Church Architecture.* 1913.

F. Bond. *Stalls and Tabernacle Work.* 1910.

M. S. Briggs. *Goths and Vandals.* 1952.

J. Britton. *The Cathedral Antiquities.* 6 Vols. 1836.

T. F. Bumpus. *The Cathedrals of England and Wales.* 1905.

C. J. P. Cave. *Roof Bosses in Mediaeval Churches.* 1948.

A. W. Clapham. *English Romanesque Architecture before the Conquest.* 1930.

A. W. Clapham. *English Romanesque Architecture after the Conquest.* 1934.

H. Cole. *King Henry VIII's Scheme of Bishoprics.* 1838.

G. H. Cook. *Mediaeval Chantries and Chantry Chapels.* 1947.

J. C. Cox. *The Sanctuaries and Sanctuary Seekers of Mediaeval England.* 1911.

K. Edwards. *The English Secular Cathedrals in the Middle Ages.* 1949.

H. Felton and J. Harvey. *The English Cathedrals.* 1950.

W. J. Loftie. *The Cathedral Churches of England and Wales.* 1892.

E. S. Prior. *The Cathedral Builders in England.* 1905.

J. Raine, ed. *Fabric Rolls of York Minster.* Surtees Society. 1859.

A. H. Thompson. *The Cathedral Churches of England.* 1928.

A. H. Thompson. *The English Clergy and their Organization in the later Middle Ages.* 1947.

M. E. C. Walcott. *Cathedralia: a Constitutional History of the Cathedrals of the Western Church.* 1865.

J. C. Wall. *Shrines of British Saints.* 1905.

A. Vallance. *Greater English Church Screens.* 1947.

Index

References to illustrations are printed in heavy type